SHAKESPEARE

AMONG

THE

MODERNS

SHAKESPEARE AMONG THE MODERNS

Richard Halpern

Cornell University Press

ITHACA AND LONDON

INDEXED IN ___MLA_____

First published 1997 by Cornell University Press
First printing, Cornell Paperbacks, 1997

Library of Congress Cataloging-in-Publication Data

Halpern, Richard.
    Shakespeare among the moderns / Richard Halpern.
       p. cm.
    Includes bibliographical references and index.
    ISBN 0-8014-3342-8 (cloth : alk. paper)
    1. Shakespeare, William, 1564–1616—Criticism and interpretation—History—20th century. 2. Criticism—Great Britain—History—20th century. 3. Criticism—United States—History—20th century.
4. Modernism (Literature)—Great Britain. 5. Modernism (Literature)—United States. I. Title.
PR2969.H35 1997
822.3'3—dc21
                                      96-52892

Printed in the United States of America

TCF This book is printed on Lyons Falls Turin Book, a paper that is totally chlorine-free and acid-free.

Cloth printing   10 9 8 7 6 5 4 3 2 1
Paperback printing 10 9 8 7 6 5 4 3 2 1

Contents

Acknowledgments

The research and writing of this book were greatly aided by financial support from various sources. I thank the National Endowment for the Humanities, which awarded me a Fellowship for University Professors; Dean Charles Middleton of the University of Colorado at Boulder, who provided a Dean's Fellowship; and the Graduate Committee on Arts and Humanities at the University of Colorado at Boulder, which furnished a travel grant to the Folger Library.

A slightly abridged version of Chapter 1 appeared in the journal *Representations* 45 (Winter 1994).

Parts of this book were presented as lectures or seminars at Yale University, The Johns Hopkins University, Harvard University's Center for Literary and Cultural Studies, and Wright State University. All those audiences prodded and probed, and thereby toughened my arguments; I thank them for it.

Like all books, this one has benefited from the readings, comments, and discussions provided by friends and colleagues. If my list of names is unusually short, this is because the named individuals were unusually generous. Janet Adelman, Margaret Ferguson, Sidney Goldfarb, Thomas Greene, John Guillory, Christopher Kendrick, Julia Reinhard Lupton, Jeffrey Nunokawa, and David Simpson all read chapters, commented incisively, and provided moral support. Lynn Enterline read through more of this manuscript than any friend should reasonably be asked to do. She did so uncomplainingly and with great insight. Finally, Rhonda Garelick saw this, like my first book, through every stage of its development. She read, commented upon, and corrected almost every draft of every chapter. I have happily stolen some of her phrases and ideas and, far more happily, enjoyed the privilege of her companionship over the years.

R. H.

SHAKESPEARE

AMONG

THE

MODERNS

Introduction:
On Historical Allegory

Once upon a time, modernists roamed the earth. They were large, lumbering creatures compared with the smaller, quicker species that predominate today. The fiercest and most awesome of the modernists, T. S. Eliot, exerted a far-reaching influence on the whole field of literary studies, and not least on the field of Renaissance criticism. Eliot's offspring, from G. Wilson Knight and L. C. Knights to Northrop Frye and Cleanth Brooks, shaped the twentieth century's understanding of Shakespeare from the 1920s through the 1960s. Then the climate began to change. Cool winds of theory blew in from France. Political upheavals altered the landscape. The modernists, unsuited to this new climate, eventually succumbed. In the postmodern era nothing remains but their gigantic bones, on which we occasionally cast a wondering but scornful glance as we go about other tasks.

With a few simplifications and exaggerations, this is the working narrative of the recent past with which Shakespeare criticism operates today. It is a story which is not so much told as acted out. Progressive critics of various stripes either maintain a massive silence with respect to the modernist line of criticism or regard it as a quaint and vaguely unhealthy phenomenon that, fortunately, has seen its day. More conservative writers look back wistfully on a time when critics of formidable learning and readable prose styles illuminated Shakespeare instead of unceremoniously knocking him about. What these two camps share is an assumption that a cultural rupture has taken place—that modernism once was, but (for better or worse) is no more.

This book sets out to investigate the ways in which canonical modern-

ism—principally Anglo-American modernism—set the tone for the twentieth century's reception of Shakespeare. By "reception" I mean
primarily literary-critical reception, but as the following chapters will
make clear, I also intend to look at performance and adaptation on both
screen and stage. Modernism influenced Shakespearean performance as
powerfully and persistently as it did Shakespeare criticism, and the two
develop in a meaningful if uneven tandem. One of my aims is to question
the assumption that modernism ever ended, at least with the abruptness
and finality attributed to it. Our "postmodern condition" represents a
mutation, rather then a cessation, of the modernist paradigm. This rather
broad claim is modified by the fact that I will be pressing it with respect
to a significant but culturally limited area: our ways of interpreting and
performing Shakespeare's plays. In this respect my argument is addressed
primarily to the community of academic Shakespeare critics. But since
Shakespeare has become an icon of considerable power, our construction
of him probably says something about the larger culture. Such, at least,
is the gamble on which I stake my book.

The principal assumptions governing this work are as follows. High
modernism not only dominated the cultural and critical reception of
Shakespeare during the first half of our century, but continues to exert
a powerful influence that is often unacknowledged or disavowed. The
persistence of modernist themes and interpretations can be traced to
three sources. First is the prestige of modernism as a literary movement
and its success in securing an institutional base in universities. Second is
the intrinsic intellectual power of the modernist reading of Shakespeare—a power which, I believe, cannot be reduced entirely to issues of
cultural hegemony. Indeed, the political labels that have become attached to this reading often mislead or oversimplify, although the conservative and sometimes outright reactionary currents of modernism can
hardly be denied. Third is the fact that the modernist reading responded
to a novel set of social, cultural, economic, and political developments
which have evolved, but not disappeared, since the modernist "period"
proper. The modernists' reading of Shakespeare has not vanished, because the world that gave birth to it has not.

One of the most distinctive and widespread characteristics of the modernist reading of Shakespeare is the presence of what I shall call historical
allegory. T. S. Eliot develops this concept in a general way in his essay
"Tradition and the Individual Talent," where he calls it the "historical
sense" and declares it indispensable for the literary critic. The historical
sense, he states, "involves a perception, not only of the pastness of the
past, but of its presence. . . . [It is] a sense of the timeless as well as of

the temporal and of the timeless and of the temporal together." [1] The presence of the past results, for Eliot, from the fact that the works of the tradition form an atemporal, ideal order among themselves. If from one perspective they are products of a specific historical era, from another they participate in a timeless structure that is eternally present. It is in this sense that Eliot's "historical sense" may be called allegorical.

Eliot's allegorical mode of reading allowed the past to be reconfigured in conformity with current needs and preoccupations; and nowhere did Eliot employ polemical allegory more vigorously and consistently than in his criticism of early modern writers. When he expresses the hope that his *Elizabethan Essays* will have "revolutionary influence on the future of drama," he reveals that he has constructed an image of Elizabethan drama largely in response to what he sees as a crisis in contemporary theater. His discussion of the historical past is thus largely governed by his grasp of the immediate cultural situation.[2] F. R. Leavis underscored the importance of this approach when he opined that "the intelligence and insight that made Eliot so decisive in critical comment on the 17th century are inseparable from his greatness as a twentieth-century poet."[3] L. C. Knights generalized Eliot's specific virtues by arguing that the essential qualification for *any* Shakespeare critic "is a lively interest in the present and the immediate future of poetry, an ability to make first-hand judgments here, coupled, I would add, with an understanding of the extra-literary implications of poetry—its relations to 'the general situation'—*at present.*"[4] Modernism constructs a Shakespeare lodged firmly in the twentieth century—what Jan Kott calls *Shakespeare Our Contemporary.*[5]

Of course, every era will, to some degree, refashion Shakespeare in its own image.[6] Literary tradition is constantly being reworked under the pressure of shifting ideological and cultural forces, an ongoing and largely unconscious process which may be called anachronism. What distinguishes the modernist practice of historical allegory is that this process

1. *Selected Prose of T. S. Eliot,* ed. Frank Kermode (London: Faber & Faber, 1975), p. 38.

2. T. S. Eliot, *Elizabethan Essays* (New York: Haskell House, 1964), p. 8.

3. F. R. Leavis, *English Literature in Our Time & The University: The Clark Lectures, 1967* (London: Chatto & Windus, 1969), p. 71.

4. L. C. Knights, *Explorations: Essays in Criticism Mainly on the Literature of the Seventeenth Century* (New York: New York University Press, 1964), p. 96.

5. Jan Kott, *Shakespeare Our Contemporary,* trans. Boleslaw Taborski (Garden City, N.Y.: Doubleday, 1964).

6. Gary Taylor, *Reinventing Shakespeare: A Cultural History, from the Restoration to the Present* (New York: Oxford University Press, 1989).

now becomes, to an unprecedented degree, both conscious and systematic. Historical allegory is anachronism raised to the level of policy. Of course, the emergence of historical allegory does not mean that the more ordinary, unconscious processes of anachronistic reading have ceased; nor do periods prior to the modernist one lack all sense of self-conscious or ironic anachronism. Shakespeare's own works contain instances of both spontaneous and highly self-conscious anachronism.[7] Modernist historical allegory differs only in its programmatic character and in its reaction to the thoroughgoing historicism of nineteenth-century thought.

A concrete illustration of historical allegory occurs in one of Eliot's remarks on Ben Jonson: "To see him as a contemporary does not so much require the power of putting ourselves into seventeenth-century London as it requires the power of setting Jonson in our London."[8] Making "Jonson our contemporary" requires a complex, dialectical movement. Like anachronism, it involves a direct mapping of the past onto the present. Unlike anachronism, however, this mapping takes place against an awareness of historical difference. While anachronism naively collapses two different historical periods by absorbing one into the other, historical allegory willfully violates distinctions without obliterating them. Eliot is clearly aware of the cultural and temporal gap that separates seventeenth- from twentieth-century London, and his allegorical mapping of the two retains this historical sense. Making Jonson our contemporary involves no simple choice between anachronism and historicism. As Eliot says, it "does not *so much* require the power of putting ourselves into seventeenth-century London as it requires the power of setting Jonson in our London" (my emphasis). The difference here is only one of degree: both processes are required, and the latter always retains some trace of the former. Historical allegory emerges in the shadow of historicism—or rather, *as* its shadow.

Knights wrote of Eliot: "He is well aware of the remoteness of the Elizabethan period, but at the same time he sees his subjects as an *immediate* part of our experience."[9] Knights's is about as clear a formulation

---

7. On self-conscious anachronism in Shakespeare, see Phyllis Rackin, *Stages of History: Shakespeare's English Chronicles* (Ithaca: Cornell University Press, 1990), pp. 47–48, 86–145. On self-conscious anachronism in the medieval Mystery Cycles, see Robert Weimann, *Shakespeare and the Popular Tradition in the Theater: Studies in the Social Dimension of Dramatic Form and Function*, ed. Robert Schwartz (Baltimore: Johns Hopkins University Press, 1978), pp. 80–84.

8. Eliot, *Elizabethan Essays*, p. 67.

9. Knights, *Explorations*, p. 99.

as one could want of what I mean by historical allegory. This double articulation clearly has nothing in common with the notion of "timeless" or "universal" literary classics, since immediacy is always generated from and against historical difference. It should not be thought, moreover, that only one half of this dialectic was new to the modernist period—for to recognize the "remoteness" of the Renaissance was fully as novel as the idea of violating it. Here a brief look at stage history may be helpful. The nineteenth century had seen the rise of antiquarian or (as they were called) "archeological" productions of Shakespeare which attempted historically accurate representations of the plays' various *mises-en-scène*.[10] This new historical consciousness arose in part as a reaction to mid-eighteenth-century productions in which the heroines, in particular, dressed à la mode. Such anachronisms in staging were employed not in an historically self-conscious attempt to make "Shakespeare our contemporary" but rather to signify all-important differences of social station among characters.[11] The pictorial representationalism of Victorian productions certainly established an unprecedented degree of historical consciousness in the staging of Shakespeare, but this consciousness focused on the fictional worlds represented in the plays rather than on Shakespeare's era or stagecraft. In fact, Shakespeare's plays were treated as historically transparent windows onto still older locales which attracted all the archeological interest. Charles Kean's 1853 production of *Macbeth*, for example, tried to render medieval Scotland with the greatest possible accuracy but at the same time employed the Locke-Davenant version of the text.[12] In this instance, Shakespeare's plays or stagecraft merited none of the antiquarian rigor expended on eleventh-century Scotland.

10. See Nancy J. Doran Hazleton, *Historical Consciousness in Nineteenth-Century Shakespearean Staging* (Ann Arbor: UMI Research Press, 1987); Richard Foukes, "Charles Kean's *King Richard II*: A Pre-Raphaelite Drama," in *Shakespeare and the Victorian Stage*, ed. Richard Foukes (Cambridge: Cambridge University Press, 1986), pp. 39–55; Marion Jones, "Stage Costume: Historical Verisimilitude and Stage Convention," in *Shakespeare and the Victorian Stage*, ed. Foukes, pp. 56–73.

11. Hazleton, *Historical Consciousness*, pp. 14–15. Post-Restoration productions, of course, put Shakespeare's plays to topical, political uses whose immediacy anticipates modernism in certain respects. Likewise, the eighteenth-century tendency to "improve," "refine," or "correct" Shakespeare betrays an allegorizing impulse. But while post-Restoration dramaturgy could revise history, it did not self-consciously violate *historicity*—that is, the generalized, deeply felt sense of historical and cultural distance that arose (and attached itself to the early modern period) only after the advent of Romantic historiography. On Shakespeare in the post-Restoration era, with particular focus on historical and political issues, see Michael Dobson, *The Making of the National Poet: Shakespeare, Adaptation, and Authorship, 1660–1769* (Oxford: Clarendon, 1992).

12. Hazleton, *Historical Consciousness*, pp. 83–86.

In the Edwardian period such traditionalist stagings were challenged from several directions.[13] One was the Elizabethan Revival spearheaded by William Poel, which attempted to recreate the original staging of Shakespeare's plays.[14] Poel did his best to simulate the Elizabethan playhouse from within the confines of the proscenium stage. As Cary Mazer notes, however, "Poel claimed that his advocacy of the Elizabethan stage stemmed, not from any desire for historical authenticity, but from the desire to stage Shakespeare as 'naturally and appealingly . . . as in a modern drama,' for which he found the platform stage indispensable."[15] Although Poel brought Shakespeare's stage into historical view, a sense of the era's remoteness emerges not with the Elizabethan Revivalists but with the criticisms of their work lodged by Harley Granville-Barker, whose celebrated Shakespeare productions of 1912–1914 were landmarks of the "New Stagecraft." Granville-Barker objected to Poel's approach because he felt that modern audiences could not spontaneously adapt themselves to Elizabethan stage practices.[16] What he called "our newly cultivated historical sense" invested (or burdened) him with a powerful awareness that bridging the distance between the modern and early modern periods required considerable labor.[17] Hence his own productions abandoned archaeological reconstruction for highly stylized, impressionistic stagings of the plays. Granville-Barker's productions were in turn followed by the vogue for modern dress productions which began in the mid-1920s.[18]

Each of the three successors to traditionalist stagecraft—the Elizabethan Revival, the New Stagecraft, and modern-dress productions—incorporates at least one of the conflicting impulses that constitute historical allegory. But it is really the constellation of these styles, rather than any one alone, that inaugurates an allegorical mode of representation. Modern dress productions place Shakespeare in twentieth-century London (or wherever), but they do so in reaction to the unprecedented

13. See Cary M. Mazer, *Shakespeare Refashioned: Elizabethan Plays on Edwardian Stages* (Ann Arbor: UMI Research Press, 1981).

14. Robert Speaight, *William Poel and the Elizabethan Revival* (London: Heinemann, 1954).

15. Mazer, *Shakespeare Refashioned*, p. 56.

16. See ibid., pp. 124–25.

17. Harley Granville-Barker, *More Prefaces to Shakespeare*, ed. Edward M. Moore (Princeton: Princeton University Press, 1974), p. 58, quoted in Mazer, *Shakespeare Refashioned*, p. 52.

18. On the first modern-dress productions, see J. L. Styan, *The Shakespeare Revolution: Criticism and Performance in the Twentieth Century* (Cambridge: Cambridge University Press, 1977), pp. 139–59. Early silent films included "modernized" versions and adaptations of Shakespeare's plays that preceded the first modern-dress productions on stage. See Robert Hamilton Ball, *Shakespeare on Silent Film: A Strange Eventful History* (London: George Allen & Unwin, 1968), pp. 132–34, 226–28.

historicism represented by Victorian "archaeology" and the Elizabethan Revival. Modern-dress productions of Shakespeare are never unselfconscious or fully at ease with their own contemporaneity; they always thrive on the pleasurable naughtiness of having violated cultural distance. "Hamlet in plus fours" shocked audiences of the 1920s partly because he so conspicuously displaced Hamlet in doublet and hose.

As I have expounded them thus far, the versions of historical allegory embodied in both Eliot's criticism and modernist stagecraft might seem to represent an essentially optimistic, redemptive cultural project. Making Shakespeare our contemporary, or placing Jonson in twentieth-century London, would appear to be ways of making the past directly present and accessible, and thus of annihilating the shadow of historical distance. This would be, at the deepest level, a project of resurrection or reanimation which would banish absence and loss themselves. Eliot's allegorical project, however, was considerably more complex than this. His views on producing Elizabethan plays, for instance, rejected both the modernizing and the revivalist approaches.[19] Eliot's perspective on Elizabethan drama bears some resemblance to Walter Benjamin's reading of baroque *Trauerspiel* in *The Origin of German Tragic Drama*, a book that casts a somber, prismatic light on modernism's historical allegory.

Benjamin's study opens by exploring the relations between baroque *Trauerspiel* and the current movement of Expressionist drama. Benjamin sees the emergence of Expressionism as the impetus for a renewed interest in *Trauerspiel*, and hence as a necessary precondition for his own investigations.[20] *The Origin of German Tragic Drama* thus contemporizes its subject matter as does Eliot's historical allegory. Yet the legitimate field of historical analogy, claims Benjamin, is threatened by a tendency for the present age simply to dissolve the past in the bath of its own preoccupations: "Just as a man lying sick with fever transforms all the words which he hears into the extravagant images of delirium, so it is that the spirit of the present age seizes on the manifestations of past or distant spiritual worlds, in order to take possession of them and unfeelingly incorporate them into its own self-absorbed fantasizing" (p. 53). Hence, while Benjamin identifies specific aesthetic parallels between baroque *Trauerspiel* and modern Expressionist drama, and moreover connects both movements with "periods of so-called decadence" (p. 55), he also carefully specifies limits and exceptions to these parallels. Analogies be-

19. Eliot, *Elizabethan Essays*, pp. 12–13.
20. Walter Benjamin, *The Origin of German Tragic Drama*, trans. John Osborne (London: New Left Books, 1977), pp. 53–54.

tween past and present must be grounded in historical sense if they are not to degenerate into self-absorbed fantasizing. Historical allegory must hobble its own analogizing impulse by granting the material it studies some unassimilable residue or opacity with respect to the present.

The most influential aspect of Benjamin's book has clearly been its exploration of baroque allegory in opposition to romantic ideologies of the symbol. Since this topic has already received extensive commentary, I will offer only the briefest remarks on how baroque allegory implies an associated vision of history which is in turn adopted by Benjamin for his own method of inquiry. As is well known, Benjamin contrasts the allegory as fragment or ruin with the symbol as "the image of organic totality" (p. 176). This structural difference entails contrasting images of time: "Whereas in the symbol destruction is idealized and the transfigured face of nature is fleetingly revealed in the light of redemption, in allegory the observer is confronted with the *facies hippocratica* of history as a petrified, primordial landscape" (p. 166). The synchronic totality of symbolic meaning implies a diachronic totality of history in which even loss, destruction, and suffering are woven into a redemptive story. Allegory freezes and fragments this redemptive flow of history, transforming temporal relations into the spatial ones of landscape. As a fragment, allegory does not "pass over" into the whole; it obstinately resists any totalizing movement. Benjamin's concept of "natural history" remaps time onto a nature conceived as the plane of pure spatial extension, where petrified events serve only as objects of melancholy contemplation.

This spatialization of time pertains not only to the content of *Trauerspiel* but to its form as well. "The acts [of *Trauerspiel*] do not follow rapidly from each other, but they are built up in the manner of terraces. The structure of the drama is such that there are several broad layers whose chronological perspective is identical" (p. 192). Like the historical content it depicts, *Trauerspiel* replaces linear development with an architectural or geological structure which petrifies event into distinct but simultaneous "layers" of significance and perspective. But *Trauerspiel*'s allegorical temporality is, in turn, an allegory for temporality as such; for the "tectonic structure" (p. 194) of *Trauerspiel* also governs the relation between *Trauerspiel* and twentieth-century Expressionism. Benjamin's investigations of the baroque construct a temporality in which present and past are not bound by the linear, developmental movement of (salvational) history but rather establish echoic relations across the chasm of a frozen, spatialized time. Benjamin's practice of *rettende Kritik*, of which *The Origin of German Tragic Drama* provides an early example, is predicated upon the fact that history itself "saves" nothing but rather consigns the past to oblivion.[21]

Benjamin's historical allegory is tied to Eliot's not only by its articulation of the contemporary and the historical but also by its melancholic construction of the past. Baroque and Expressionist art both arise in "periods of so-called decadence" (p. 55), and it is this shared spirit of decline that animates Benjamin's project of allegorical mapping. For Eliot, "even the philosophical basis, the general attitude toward life of the Elizabethans, is one of anarchism, of dissolution, of decay."[22] "It seemed as if, at that time, the world was filled with broken fragments of systems, and that a man like Donne merely picked up, like a magpie, various shining fragments of ideas as they struck his eye, and stuck them about here and there in his verse."[23] For Eliot, as for Benjamin, early modern culture is marked by the predominance of the fragment or the ruin. Works of art do not participate in a progressive movement of history but rather attest to an incipient "dissociation of sensibilities" with which the modern poet is saddled.

Modernist historical allegory does not light on just any period with equal interest; the late sixteenth and early seventeenth centuries offer it a privileged image of cultural decline. Benjamin's focus on baroque rather than Renaissance drama, and Eliot's tendency to avoid the very word "Renaissance," attest to a shared resistance to typological implications of rebirth.[24] Modernism's historical allegory is not a salvific project but a juxtaposition of losses; only in the early modern period does it find a sufficiently dark reflection of its own catastrophes.

More recent critics have also been inclined to avoid the term "Renaissance," and I believe that this habit has something to do with a persistence of modernist sensibilities. The currently preferred term, "early modern," effects a complete reversal of temporal perspective which resembles that of historical allegory. "Renaissance" denotes a repetition of past (classical) glories while "early modern" reconfigures the same period into an anticipation of the present—an anticipation, but not an

21. On Benjamin and *rettende Kritik*, see Jürgen Habermas, "Walter Benjamin: Consciousness-Raising or Rescuing Critique," in *On Walter Benjamin: Critical Essays and Recollections*, ed. Gary Smith (Cambridge: MIT Press, 1988), pp. 90–128. On *rettende Kritik* and *The Origin of German Tragic Drama*, see Richard Wolin, *Walter Benjamin: An Aesthetic of Redemption* (New York: Columbia University Press, 1982), p. 76.

22. Eliot, *Elizabethan Essays*, p. 18.

23. Ibid., p. 52.

24. See chap. 1 of Julia Reinhard Lupton, *Afterlives of the Saints: Hagiography, Typology, and Renaissance Literature* (Palo Alto: Stanford University Press, 1996).

identity, as the cautionary term "early" suggests. "Early modern" en-codes just that dissonant conjunction of allegorical contemporaneity and historical difference which occurs in the writings of Eliot and Benjamin, which is not to say that every critic who wields the term inherits their finely nuanced sense of method. Indeed, it has become increasingly as-sociated with a kind of positivist historicism which rejects all contexts or meanings other than the original ones as "ahistorical" or "anachronis-tic." I myself prefer to view modernism's allegorical readings of Renais-sance texts as a productive resource rather than an embarrassing encumbrance. My own readings of four Shakespeare plays in the follow-ing chapters take modernist allegories as their points of departure. All assume that such allegories reveal aspects of the plays that would tend to be overlooked by a purely historicist approach.

This book is constructed not as a systematic survey of modernist Shake-speare criticism or production but as a series of allegorical mappings, each tied to a significant facet of modernist culture and society. The five chapters do not develop linearly, one from the other. They are, rather, like spines or spokes radiating outward in different directions from a single hub; and while there are filaments of connection running through them, what unites them more essentially is their rootedness in a common center. Chapter 1 addresses imperialism and the cult of the primitive; Chapter 2 turns to mass culture; Chapter 3, on Northrop Frye, focuses on the university; Chapter 4 examines modernist anti-Semitism; and Chapter 5 offers the machine as emblem for both industrial society and for a distinctively modern construction of literary tradition. Each chapter isolates a well-known aspect of modernist culture and the ways in which it allegorically reforms or revises Shakespeare. There are, to be sure, various lines of continuity running among these apparently varied topics. The anthropological focus of Chapter 1, for instance, reappears in the later discussion of Northrop Frye's "myth criticism," while its remarks on racial ideology are echoed in the discussion of anti-Semitism in Chap-ter 4. Chapter 2's examination of mass culture both looks backward to Chapter 1 (in the modernist construction of the crowd as "primitive") and begins a consideration of the public sphere which continues in Chap-ter 3. These and other subsidiary threads of connection will, I hope, become apparent to the reader. Often, but not always, I will point them out.

The fundamental connections among the chapters, however, are of a different order. Each of my five topics not only affords us a view onto modernism but served modernism itself as a vehicle for allegorizing Shakespeare. Each chapter thus examines, from varying perspectives, the nature of historical allegory—that is to say, the relation between history and allegory, which itself shifts from case to case. While allegory might seem to be the recurrent, containing form for a series of discrete topical contents, it becomes, in fact, oddly entangled with these contents. Allegories of anti-Semitism, examined in Chapter 4, are complicated by the fact that allegory itself is coded as "Jewish" both in post-Hegelian theory and in *The Merchant of Venice*. In Chapter 5, meanwhile, the machine not only serves as allegorical vehicle but comes to figure the mechanical, "hollowed out" character of allegory itself. Each of my chapters not only offers an instance of modernist allegorizing, then, but attempts to make, either explicitly or implicitly, a statement about allegory and history.

Besides allegory, what ties my chapters together is a recurrent (though not quite continuous) focus on capitalism, particularly on what Marxists have identified as its imperialist or monopoly phase, as a foundational dynamic of modernist culture. This approach to modernism has a long and (in my view) distinguished lineage, from Lukács to Jameson. I recognize that in embracing it I am myself adopting a recognizably "modernist" approach to modernism, with both the strengths and weaknesses that this focus entails. I have, when appropriate, supplied postmodern trimmings; but in the end, I interpret modernism largely in traditional Marxist terms. Each of my chapters thus includes an economic focus. Chapter 1 argues that economic imperialism is the basis for modernism's cult of the primitive; Chapter 2 explores Habermas's view of mass culture as resulting from the collapse of capitalism's founding separation of the economic and the political; Chapter 3 situates Northrop Frye within the "long boom" of the postwar era and relates his critical method to what the Marxist theorists Oscar Negt and Alexander Kluge call the "media public sphere"; Chapter 4 explores the economic bases of anti-Semitism through Marx's writings on the commodity and Rudolph Hilferding's concept of "finance capital"; finally, Chapter 5 examines the machine as vehicle of capitalist modernization and the economy itself as site of a mechanical, involuntary "compulsion to repeat."

This book, then, has a double focus: on allegory and on the economic. Yet these two strands are not, themselves, as unrelated as they may at first appear to be. In the "Baudelaire" section of his long, uncompleted *Passagen-Werk*, Walter Benjamin provocatively linked literary allegory with commodity-culture: "The specific devaluation of the thingly world that lies in the commodity is the foundation of Baudelaire's allegorical intention."[25] The "devaluation [*Entwertung*] of the thingly world" is not, of

25. Walter Benjamin, *Gesammelte Schriften*, ed. Rolf Tiedemann and Hermann Schwep-

course, specific to Baudelairean allegory; Benjamin had discovered the same effect in baroque *Trauerspiel.* Allegory devalues its objects by subjecting them to a signifying intention. No longer meaningful "in themselves," they can only point to a spiritual meaning which does not inhabit their material realm. But this evacuation of significance is also part of the meaning of allegory, which demotes the actual world to an empty material remainder—a skull, for instance.

The commodity, Benjamin argues, similarly devalues the thing. As Marx describes it (and we shall pursue this notion at greater length in Chapter 4), the commodity has a double nature, even a double body, for it has at once a use-value (*Gebrauchswert*) and a value (*Wert*) (loosely, "exchange-value"). The use-value of a commodity is its "thingly" existence, those physical properties which enable it to fulfill a need or a desire. The value of a commodity is the amount of labor expended to produce it; this is the commodity's invisible, "spiritual" being. Now while commodities are, at one level, exchanged in order to procure different use-values, it is also true that under conditions of capitalist production, use-value becomes (as Marx puts it) a mere "bearer" [*Träger*] of value. The very fact that presumably incommensurable use-values can be exchanged at all implies a moment in which their concrete, thingly natures are temporarily extinguished in the face of their equality as values. Thus the commodity is, in essence, practical allegory—allegory in the sphere of social practice. The commodity devalues its own thingly existence, as does allegory, in order to signify an invisible realm of values.

Even more striking, perhaps, than this homology itself is the use which Benjamin makes of it:

> The relation between the commodity and allegory: "value" surpasses "signification" as natural incinerating-mirror of historical appearance. Its own appearance is more difficult to dissipate. It is, moreover, more recent. The fetish-character of the commodity was still relatively underdeveloped in the baroque age. The commodity had not yet engraved its stigma—the proletarianization of the producers—as profoundly in the process of production. It is for this reason that allegorical perception was the creator of style in the seventeenth century, that which it no longer is in the nineteenth century. As an allegorist,

penhäser, 7 vols. (Frankfurt am Main: Suhrkamp, 1972–1989), 1:1151. Translation quoted from Timothy Bahti, *Allegories of History: Literary Historiography after Hegel* (Baltimore: Johns Hopkins University Press, 1992), p. 210.

Baudelaire became isolated. He attempted to reconcile the experience of the commodity with allegorical experience. This undertaking was doomed to failure, and thereby showed that the recklessness of his approach was surpassed by the recklessness of the reality. Whence, in his work, a strain which seems sadistic or pathological only because it just misses reality—but only by a hair.[26]

Having drawn a parallel between allegory and the commodity, Benjamin might have posed the latter as the economic "base," or foundation, of the former. An historical impediment stands in the way, however: the fact that baroque allegory precedes the thoroughgoing commodification of culture. The commodity thus cannot offer an historical-materialist "explanation" of allegory. Instead, it occupies the inverse position: it is not what underlies allegory but what exceeds it, surpasses it.[27] The commodity renders allegory obsolete by perfecting and globalizing the latter's logic of representation. Under mature capitalism, allegory is no longer simply a literary technique but is rather the phenomenology of the entire social-material world. As a result, Baudelaire's allegorical poetic becomes a somewhat antiquated mechanism which always lags behind the social reality it attempts to depict. The *Passagen-Werk* thus reinterprets and refigures the historical allegory at work in *The Origin of German Tragic Drama*. Benjamin retroactively converts baroque allegory into a prefiguration of the commodity, which mock-typologically fulfills, overgoes, and cancels it. The baroque can now be mapped onto the present not because both are periods of "decline" but because of a more rigorous homology between the economic and the aesthetic.

Benjamin's meditations on Baudelaire raise broader questions about modernism's historical allegory and commodity culture. For in mapping past onto present, historical allegory equates two different historical periods in much the same way that commodity exchange equates incommensurable use-values. Historical allegory may thus ultimately contribute to an erosion or devaluation (*Entwertung*) of historical difference. The final term of this process would be the historical pastiche or "historicism" which, according to Fredric Jameson, marks postmodern culture: "the random cannibalization of all the styles of the past, the play of random stylistic allusion, and in general what Henri Lefebvre has called

26. Walter Benjamin, *Das Passagen-Werk*, ed. Rolf Tiedmann, 2 vols. (Frankfurt am Main: Suhrkamp, 1983), 1:438-39; my translation. Thanks to Janet Lungstrum and Marcus Bullock for textual advice regarding Benjamin's *Passagen-Werk*.
27. Compare Bahti, *Allegories of History*, pp. 206–12.

the primacy of the 'neo.' "[28] Although one may prepare the way for the other, modernism's historical allegory is not yet such a postmodern pastiche, for its allegorical mappings generally continue to be haunted by a sense of incompatibility and dissonance. Allegorical collapse still takes place against a backdrop of historical distance; it has not yet subsumed the latter into an amnesiac play of styles.

This is not to deny the strongly dehistoricizing impulse in late or academic modernism, as represented by both the New Critics and Northrop Frye. In the case of Frye, I shall argue, the purging of history is of a piece with his attempts to refit literature for consumption in the context of a commodified culture. The fragility of early modernism's historical allegory, or rather, of its historical component, points in the direction of a postmodern loss of temporal depth. Yet the following chapters will argue that, on the whole, modernism's allegorical readings of Shakespeare do not erode historical meaning but rather enrich it. By unleashing a conflicted, dialectical interplay between past and present, they construct a Shakespeare who is at once "our contemporary" and our bracing Other.

28. Fredric Jameson, *Postmodernism; Or, the Cultural Logic of Late Capitalism* (Durham: Duke University Press, 1993), p. 18.

Shakespeare In The Tropics:
From High Modernism To
New Historicism

One of the odder moments in the annals of bardolatry is surely supplied by Lautréamont: "Chaque fois que j'ai lu Shakspeare, il m'a semblé que je déchiquète la cervelle d'un jaguar" ("Every time I read Shakespeare, it seemed to me that I was hacking a jaguar's brains to bits").[1] If these lines have a cryptic appeal, it has little to do with their ability to generate any flash of sympathetic recognition. Whatever pleasures or intensities we may experience when reading Shakespeare, we probably don't feel quite like *that*; most of us simply can't squeeze from Shakespeare's brain, or from a jaguar's, the perverse ecstasy felt by Lautréamont. But the alienating strategies of this passage touch on more than the experience of reading, for the presence of the jaguar effects a radical series of geographical and cultural displacements. Shakespeare, the flower of European culture, finds himself transplanted to a tropical locale; indeed, the very notion of culture itself, as defined in Western traditions, gives way to a pointedly "savage" or "primitive" act in the hacking of the jaguar's brains.

Despite its dreamlike intensity and condensation, Lautréamont's linking of Shakespeare and the primitive is not entirely anomalous. Antonin Artaud, for one, would also admire the violently "primitive" qualities of English Renaissance drama and compare it with non-Western forms of performance such as Balinese dance theater. On the other side of the channel, Lytton Strachey, attending a student performance of *Henry IV*,

---

1. Lautréamont, *Poésies II* (1870), p. 1; rpt. in *Oeuvres complètes de Lautréamont* ([Paris]: La Table Ronde, 1970).

Part I at Cambridge just after World War I, found that the amateur and "unself-conscious" performance had "the charm of primitive art."[2] One of the things that distinguishes the modernist reception of Shakespeare from the late-Victorian one, in fact, is the frequency with which it deploys the discourse of primitivism.

Within the Anglo-American tradition, T. S. Eliot established the basic protocols for twentieth-century Shakespeare criticism—most centrally, perhaps, in his use of anthropological methods and themes. In his influential essay "The Beating of a Drum," Eliot insists on the importance of anthropology for literary critics, traces drama back to its origins in ancient ritual, and observes that the Fool in *King Lear* "has more than a suggestion of the shaman or medicine man." In a well-known passage, he writes:

> Primitive man . . . acted in a certain way and then found a reason for it. An unoccupied person, finding a drum, may be seized with a desire to beat it; but unless he is an imbecile he will be unable to continue beating it . . . without finding a reason for so doing. The reason may be the long continued drought. The next generation or the next civilization will find a more plausible reason for beating a drum. Shakespeare and Racine—or rather the developments which led up to them—each found his own reason. The reasons may be divided into tragedy and comedy. We still have similar reasons, but we have lost the drum.[3]

In this one brief passage lie the seeds of a critical method which bloomed into the work of such major Shakespeare critics as C. L. Barber, Northrop Frye, René Girard, and Robert Weimann. The twentieth century's reading of Shakespeare has often been, as I will argue in this chapter, fundamentally mediated by a primitivist discourse whose disciplinary language is anthropology—even when, as in the case of the New Criticism, this influence is not direct or immediately apparent. Conversely, Shakespeare has attracted more critical attention of an anthropological type than has any other major author in the English canon. The most recent instances of this, in the work of the New Historicists, have generally been portrayed as lying on the other side of the line that separates modernist from postmodernist theory. But, as I hope to show, certain

2. Lytton Strachey, "Shakespeare at Cambridge" (1919), in *Literary Essays* (New York: Harcourt, Brace, 1949), p. 22.

3. T. S. Eliot, "The Beating of a Drum," *Nation and Athenaeum,* 6 October 1923, pp. 11–12.

continuities tie even the most recent forms of Shakespeare criticism to the fundamental problematic laid down by Eliot and other high-modernist writers. If modernism set the terms for our century's reading of Shakespeare, it did so partly by displacing him from his given niche in English culture. Today, whether viewing Akira Kurosawa's adaptations or Ariane Mnoutchkine's productions of Shakespearean drama, or reading an essay by Clifford Geertz on the Balinese cockfight or by Stephen Greenblatt on colonial encounters with the New World, we are likely to confront a Shakespeare moved somehow outside the boundaries of Europe. This fact is not a mere curiosity or sidelight; it is central to our century's reception of Shakespeare and of the English Renaissance more generally. It is also, I will argue, germane to the development of modern literary criticism as a discipline.

Touring Shakespeare's Brain

Modernism succeeded in inventing a "primitive" Shakespeare. But the practice of reading him through an anthropological lens actually began with the Victorians, who were less concerned with situating Shakespeare in a non-Western context than with establishing his racial pedigree within the European family. What began as a relatively minor tradition within Victorian scholarship came to exert a disproportionate and belated influence on the modernists, whose reading of Shakespeare both built upon and critiqued it. The Victorians "anthropologized" Shakespeare in a manner whose politics and method were portentous.

A somewhat eccentric but, as we shall see, symptomatic essay on Shakespeare appeared in 1864 in the *Anthropological Review and Journal.* "Ethnology and Phrenology as an Aid to the Biographer,"[4] written by the well-known anthropologist J. W. Jackson, argues that ethnological and phrenological studies into the backgrounds of renowned writers can provide a scientific grounding to literary biography by revealing the ultimate—that is, racial—causes of great cultural achievement. To bolster his claims, Jackson "reads" the head of the Bard himself, as rendered in the bust at Stratford and "authentic" portraits, to discover Shakespeare's ethnic background and cranial capacity. Racially, we learn, Shakespeare is something of a mongrel: "Born in the central county of England, which nevertheless borders on Wales, the bard of Avon was doubtless by

4. J. W. Jackson, "Ethnology and Phrenology as an Aid to the Biographer," *Anthropological Review and Journal* 2 (1864): 126–40.

descent of that well mingled and thoroughly amalgamated Celto-Teutonic race, familiarly known as the Anglo-Saxon, but in reality consisting of elements from nearly every Caucasian stock in Europe, with possibly a remote tinge even from the Mongolic."[5] Of particular interest to Jackson is the predominant Celto-Teutonic strain, whose amalgamation has balanced the virtues of its component races. In language which strangely recalls Henry Tudor's uniting of the Houses of York and Lancaster, Jackson describes Shakespeare as "sage and bard in one majestic nature, the well refined result of the union of these two great types, which by their ethnic marriage have produced this glorious heir, possessed of Celtic intelligence without its overstrained excitability, and of Teutonic calm and self-possession without their accompanying materiality and phlegm."[6] The issue of Shakespeare's racial makeup, and particularly the question of Teutonic versus Celtic provenance, turns out to be of wider interest to Victorian culture. Here, Shakespeare's pre-eminence throughout the continent seems to result in part from his participation in the many European strains legible in the shape of his head. Shakespeare's presumed cultural "universality" is implicitly grounded in racial variety.

In Jackson's ethno-phrenological method, Shakespeare's head is at once the *source* of literary genius and, at the same time, a material *signifier* of "racial" genius—that is, of the strengths and weaknesses of different races for which Shakespeare now serves merely as a point of confluence, not a point of origin. But Shakespeare's head is more than just the pot in which this racial stew simmers; it imposes an allegorical structure on its constituent parts:

> A refining element from the higher nature would ever pervade both [the affections] and the passions, lighting up and transfiguring these inferior elements as with the supernal glory of a purer and nobler sphere. For let us never forget that, while the entire organization of Shakespeare demonstrates that he was an universal and truly representative man, it at the same time clearly shows the entire predominance of the higher over the lower elements in his being, which was, indeed, cast in an essentially spiritual, and, if we may so express ourselves, transcendental mould.[7]

Shakespeare's head, like the "wooden O" of the Globe Theater, comes to represent the world itself. More precisely, it represents the world as

5. Ibid., pp. 131–32.
6. Ibid., pp. 132–33.
7. Ibid., p. 134.

fantasized by British imperialism, with the higher and lighter races at once ruling over, and bringing enlightenment to, the lower and darker ones. While Shakespeare himself is primarily of European stock, Jackson adds that strange, hypothetical tincture of the Mongolian, and at the end of his essay credits the Bard with "Brahminical perception," thus invoking India, one of Britain's prime imperial holdings. Shakespeare's "universal" quality, his presumed ability to embody a world culture, has become implicitly tied to the empire on which the sun never sets.

While Jackson's essay is quite marginal, its main concerns were handled by some of the giants of Victorian culture. Thomas Carlyle's *On Heroes, Hero-Worship, and the Heroic in History* (1840), which sports a portrait of Shakespeare as its frontispiece, places the Bard in an explicitly racial and imperial context. Carlyle's Shakespeare, unlike Jackson's, is no racial crossbreed; he is, rather, of pure Germanic blood, "a rallying-sign and bond of brotherhood for all Saxondom."[8] Like Jackson's, however, Carlyle's Shakespeare becomes the focus for a discussion of imperialism:

> Consider now, if they asked us, Will you give-up your Indian Empire or your Shakspeare, you English; never have had any Indian Empire, or never have had any Shakspeare? Really it were a grave question. Official persons would answer doubtless in official language; but we, for our part too, should not we be forced to answer: Indian Empire, or no Indian Empire; we cannot do without Shakspeare! Indian Empire will go, at any rate, some day; but this Shakspeare does not go, he lasts for ever with us; we cannot give-up our Shakspeare![9]

True, Shakespeare is here depicted as a spiritual inheritance weighed *against* the material benefits of Empire; but the very symmetry suggests that Shakespeare is somehow also the mirror of Empire, its other self. In any case, the English can have their cake and eat it too, for loving Shakespeare not only requires no sacrifice of Empire; it is a means of *securing* Empire. Noting that colonial conquest is dispersing the English into a "Saxondom covering great places of the Globe," Carlyle muses about what can hold the English together, once distance, local custom, and economic competition begin to drive them apart. The answer? Shakespeare, of course. "From Paramatta, from New York, wheresoever, under what sort of Parish-Constable soever, English men and women are, they will say to one another: 'Yes, this Shakspeare is ours; we produced him,

8. Thomas Carlyle, *On Heroes, Hero-Worship, and the Heroic in History* (London: Chapman & Hall, 1897; rpt. New York: AMS Press, 1980), p. 248.

9. Ibid., p. 113.

we speak and think by him; we are of one blood and kind with him.' ''[10] While Shakespeare is, for Jackson, merely an allegorical embodiment of Empire, he is for Carlyle the ideological glue of Empire; and while for Jackson he plays his imperial role through racial inclusiveness, for Carlyle he plays it through racial particularity. Shakespeare welds the English world-kingdom together by being purely and distinctively Saxon.

If Carlyle's speculations seem merely fanciful today, they nevertheless assumed concrete existence in the form of the British Empire Shakespeare Society, whose 1907 report bore the ominous motto: "Using no other weapon but his name." With branches throughout the United Kingdom as well as in Demerara (British Guiana), Johannesberg, and later in India, the Society had as its principal object "To promote greater familiarity with Shakespeare's works among all classes throughout the British Empire."[11] An essay by the late secretary of the Shakespeare Association of India, published in *Empire Review* in 1925, reports that "at the time of [the Association's] inception the two communities of India, the native Indian and the foreign Briton, were being driven apart by the wedge of heated agitation; and the formation of a Shakespeare society provided a means of bridging the sundered communities by their common love for Shakespeare."[12]

Matthew Arnold's "On the Study of Celtic Literature" (1867) was written partly to refute such "Teutomaniacs" (Arnold's term) as Carlyle, Charles Kingsley, and, to a lesser extent, Ralph Waldo Emerson.[13] Arnold's book, contrasting the poetical nature of the Celts with the mate-

10. Ibid., p. 114.

11. The British Empire Shakespeare Society Offical Report, 1907 (Folger Shakespeare Library, Sh. misc. 1566), p. 4.

12. R. J. Minney, "Shakespeare in India," *Empire Review*, no. 292 (May 1925), pp. 534–35 (Folger Library, Sh. misc. 1761). Minney claims (with what degree of exaggeration one cannot be sure) that because most Indians learned English by reading Shakespeare's plays, Shakespearean English formed the idiom of the administrative and public spheres: "Until recently few Indians spoke anything else [but Shakespearean English], and few newspapers printed in English employed other than this form of language as their medium of expression. Leading articles were merely a jumble of phrases torn out of the plays of Shakespeare. Shakespeare coloured headlines and reports of the police court. In the law courts questions of inheritance were decided not according to law so much as according to Shakespeare, and Indian judges sent their fellow countrymen to death with consoling quotations from the plays of Shakespeare" (p. 533). For more on Shakespeare and English literature generally as means of colonial rule in India, see Ania Loomba, *Gender, Race, Renaissance Drama* (Manchester: Manchester University Press, 1989), pp. 10–37, and Gauri Viswanathan, *Masks of Conquest: Literary Study and British Rule in India* (New York: Columbia University Press, 1989).

13. Frederic E. Faverty, *Matthew Arnold the Ethnologist* (Evanston, Ill.: Northwestern University Press, 1951), p. 14.

rialistic and philistine qualities of the "creeping Saxon," insisted that the poetic gifts of a Shakespeare simply could not have grown from Germanic stock alone. "Shakespeare's greatness is thus in his blending an openness and flexibility of spirit, not English, with the English basis."[14] Arnold's insistence on the Celtic strain in Shakespeare's genius was an attempt to formulate a more liberal racial politics than Carlyle's, one which might soften the antipathy the English felt toward their Irish subjects by positing a great Indo-European unity in which both races shared.[15] Yet Arnold also argued that the poetical nature of the Celtic race rendered them "ineffectual in politics"; hence he consistently opposed Gladstone's Home Rule proposal. The Irish, he argued, should remain "a nation poetically only, not politically."[16]

Ethnological and racialist debates over Shakespeare formed only a minor tributary of Victorian criticism, though engaged in by some prestigious names. While these competing racial theories were equally chimerical, all harnessed Shakespeare's literary reputation to the politics of imperialism. Indeed, imperialism refigured the very terms of Shakespeare's literary fame. Early panegyrics, including those by Ben Jonson and John Milton, tended to emphasize the limitless temporal expanse of Shakespeare's fame: he is "a monument without a tomb," "not of an age but for all time," "dear son of memory, great heir of fame," and so on. By the age of empire, however, Shakespeare's greatness was measured not (or not only) by how long he lasted, but by how much geocultural territory he could embrace.[17] Carlyle's insistence that Shakespeare was a "World-Poet" assumes a unified global culture in which the bard reigns supreme—a culture rendered possible only under the influence of the British empire. Moreover, ethnology provides what seems to be a scientific basis for Shakespeare's international popularity either by presenting him as a mixture of European races or by situating him within the broad racial confines of the Indo-European family.

In the modernist period, anthropology would assume a much more central role in Shakespeare criticism—largely, but by no means exclusively, through the influence of T. S. Eliot. Concurrently, the emphasis

14. Matthew Arnold, "On the Study of Celtic Literature," in *Matthew Arnold: Essays in Criticism* (Ann Arbor: University of Michigan Press, 1962), p. 358.

15. Ibid., pp. 300–302.

16. Faverty, *Matthew Arnold*, pp. 140–42.

17. Ben Jonson, however, initiates this imperial movement in "To the Memory of . . . William Shakespeare": "Triumph, my Britain, thou hast one to show/ To whom all scenes of Europe homage owe" (41–42). *Ben Jonson: Poems*, ed. Ian Donaldson (New York: Oxford University Press, 1975), p. 309.

would shift from racial to cultural or ritualist explanations, and from a mainly European arena to a genuinely global one. Shakespeare criticism of the early twentieth century was often influenced by the same array of anthropological sources that fertilized high modernism in general: the Cambridge Hellenists, especially J. M. Cornford and Gilbert Murray, and comparative mythologists such as J. G. Frazer. Though Eliot himself rarely deployed anthropological concepts openly in his Shakespeare criticism, the famous concept of the "objective correlative" in his *Hamlet* essay, for instance, is influenced by contemporary theories of the fetish;[18] and in "The Beating of a Drum" he connects Shakespearean drama with Cornford's and Murray's theories on the ritual origins of ancient drama.[19] Eliot's profound influence on twentieth-century Shakespeare criticism, however, derived not only from his own Shakespeare criticism but also from his intellectual patronage of other writers and critics.

Perhaps the clearest and most immediate instance of Eliot's influence is Wyndham Lewis's *The Lion and the Fox: The Role of the Hero in the Plays of Shakespeare*.[20] First published in 1927, and then periodically over the next forty years, Lewis's brilliantly perverse reading of Shakespeare, largely ignored today, is in many ways the most representative high-modernist work of Shakespeare criticism. Section 3 in Chapter 3 of the book, devoted to the question of kingship in Shakespearean tragedy, argues that "the function of the king is curiously bound up with the idea of sacrifice" and insists that "overwhelming evidence to this effect is provided by Sir James Frazer in his wonderful series of books, *The Golden Bough*."[21] Lewis illustrates the nature of the "divinity that doth hedge a king," and its relation to sacrifice primarily by means of African parallels, drawing on such works as Robert H. Lowie's *Primitive Society*, A. B. Ellis's *The Eno-Speaking Peoples of the Slave Coast*, and Archibald Dalzel's *History of Dahomey*.[22]

Lewis employs ethnographical materials as a typically provocative act

18. See Marc Manganaro, *Myth, Rhetoric, and the Voice of Authority: A Critique of Frazer, Eliot, Frye, and Campbell* (New Haven: Yale University Press, 1992), p. 77. In *The Savage and the City in the Work of T. S. Eliot* (Oxford: Clarendon, 1987), pp. 72–73, Robert Crawford traces the objective correlative back, in part, to James Wood's *Practice and Science of Religion* (1906).

19. Eliot, "Beating of a Drum," p. 11.

20. Eliot had encouraged some of the intellectual interests that inform *The Lion and the Fox* by asking Lewis to review books on anthropology for *The Criterion* in 1925. Eliot himself then published a generally favorable review of the book in a special issue on Lewis in *Twentieth-Century Verse*, no. 6–7 (November/December 1937) and drew attention to it in his own *Elizabethan Essays*.

21. Wyndham Lewis, *The Lion and the Fox: The Role of the Hero in the Plays of Shakespeare* (New York: Barnes & Noble, 1966), p. 135.

22. Ibid., pp. 130–33, 142–43.

of "outlaw criticism,"[23] comparing King Lear with the Dakomi kings of Africa, for instance, partly in order to shock the Shakespeare scholars of his day. Yet his approach was typical of the comparative method in anthropology, whose purpose, as Eliot put it in his 1913 *Essay on the Interpretation of Primitive Ritual*, was "to make manifest the similarities and identities underlying the customs of races very remote in every way from each other."[24] Moreover, as Lewis argues, European societies have all destroyed *their* kings and nobles in their relentless obsession with cultural levelling. African tribal societies thus offer the only contemporary instances of Shakespearean values. While Lewis demonstrates a certain contempt for these cultures, he implies that they enjoy a limited superiority to the massifying societies of modern Europe in that they can better endure the institution of kingship. The Dahomey people are, in a sense, better equipped to experience the truths of Shakespearean tragedy than are Lewis's own countrymen.

The Lion and the Fox has a vexed and contradictory stance on race. Lewis employs contemporary anthropological studies to demolish Arnold's arguments about the Celts, the Saxons, and Shakespeare, and ridicules all such racialist theories.[25] On the other hand, he argues that "a great creative period . . . must have this chaotic spot in its centre: the incalculable factor of racial intermixture."[26] On yet another hand (one needs more than two when discussing Lewis), he deplores the impending end of "anglo-saxon, and generally of west european, ascendancy" whose day began with Shakespeare, and he admires the physiques of the Italian people as "superb types of Aryan heavyweights."[27]

Within the volatile ideological brew of *The Lion and the Fox*, however, Lewis's anthropology marks a sharp break with the practice of the Victorians. In particular, his use of African materials precludes any racialist or even diffusionist sense of tradition or kinship; comparing Shakespearean monarchs to the thonga kings inhibits any sense of Saxon, or Celtic, or Indo-European unity. Biology cedes to culture as discussions of blood-

23. See Sue Ellen Campbell, *The Enemy Opposite: The Outlaw Criticism of Wyndham Lewis* (Athens: Ohio University Press, 1988).

24. Quoted in Crawford, *Savage and the City*, p. 105.

25. Lewis, *The Lion and the Fox*, pp. 302–6, 312–18.

26. Lewis, *The Lion and the Fox*, p. 298. Eliot also insists on the racially mixed nature of English culture: "What I think we have, in English poetry, is a kind of amalgam of systems of divers sources . . . : an amalgam like the amalgam of races, and indeed partly due to racial origins. The rhythms of Anglo-Saxon, Celtic, Norman French, of Middle English and Scots, have all made their mark upon English poetry, together with the rhythms of Latin, and, at various periods, of French, Italian and Spanish." *Selected Prose*, p. 109.

27. Ibid., pp. 49, 47.

lines or cranial contour give way to comparisons of ritual or cultural habits among unquestionably separate races. Lewis intentionally disrupts any sense on the part of the English that they "own" Shakespeare as a distinctively national patrimony. "And then," he remarks, "there is the disquieting statement so often made that *Shakespeare is universal. Universal* bears an uncomfortable affinity to *international.* How can you be a typical Englishman and at the same time be 'universal'? they ask themselves doubtfully."[28] In *The Lion and the Fox* one can trace the seeds of its author's later infatuation with chauvinism and fascism, but his use of anthropology tends to work in the opposite direction.[29] Lewis's "international" Shakespeare mirrors the early modernists' own sense of cosmopolitanism and disrupts the Victorians' desire to hold some kind of racial or national "property" in Shakespeare. What it does not and cannot break with, however, is the culture of imperialism. By moving Shakespeare beyond Western bounds, Lewis and Eliot instigated a series of interpretive difficulties that would plague literary criticism for the rest of the century.

Antinomies of the Primitive

If anthropology transforms the modernist reading of Shakespeare, it is still unclear what motivates a specifically anthropological mode of critical scrutiny. Why is Shakespeare displaced from an English, or even European, context, where he would seem naturally to belong, and discussed in relation to the non-Western cultures studied by ethnologists? To answer this question, we must broaden our focus from the modernist reading of Shakespeare to the modernist understanding of the English Renaissance as a period, and from modernism's interest in anthropology to the larger question of modernism's encounter with the "primitive."

Modernism's sustained attention to Renaissance drama was largely polemical, for the ritualistic, stylized, and sometimes grotesque qualities of Renaissance plays made them useful weapons in the battle against late nineteenth-century traditions of dramatic and psychological realism; yet these were the very same qualities that modernist playwrights sought in non-Western forms of drama. Thus Antonin Artaud, for instance, could

28. Ibid., p. 17.

29. It is difficult to situate anthropology in any easy or univocal relation to the modernist infatuation with right-wing politics. Eliot's turn to a conservative Christianity entailed a diminution of his earlier anthropological interests. Lewis, however, found the theories of the diffusionist school fully compatible with his own (briefly held) Nazi theories of race. See Lewis, *Hitler* (London: Chatto & Windus, 1931), pp. 132–35.

enlist both *Arden of Feversham* and the Balinese dance theater as models for his theater of cruelty.[30] Bertolt Brecht, who first employed the term *Verfremdungseffekt* in his essay "Alienation Effects in Chinese Acting,"[31] likewise enlisted both English Renaissance and non-Western dramas in his search for a theory and practice of non-empathetic performance. (In the *Messingkauf Dialogues* Brecht remarks that later ages, unable to endure the immense suffering of Shakespeare's great tragedies, would describe them as "drama for cannibals.")[32] William Archer, the influential opponent of modernism and defender of dramatic realism, attacked Renaissance plays on the same grounds that constituted their appeal for Artaud and Brecht. "The great mass of Elizabethan . . . plays have nothing to say to modern audiences," he insists, "because they exemplify primitive and transitional types of art." Archer views non-Western and Renaissance dramas as bound by their shared failure to evolve a consistent form of dramatic and psychological realism, which he associates in turn with social, technological, and moral progress. Thus he compares the "juxtaposition of exaggerative and realistic art" in Shakespeare's plays to that found in Japanese Noh theater—to the detriment of both.[33] Wyndham Lewis dubs Shakespeare a "new barbaric great-poet" and attributes the artistic power of Renaissance drama to the fact that "the English were . . . very near to a savage condition, very fresh to life," though he agrees with Archer (and Brecht) that this savage quality renders Elizabethan plays inaccessible to modern audiences.[34]

The modernist reception of Renaissance theater placed it surprisingly often within a discourse of primitivism which assimilated contemporary, though non-Western, cultures to historically archaic ones—uniting them, as anthropology also did, under evolutionist assumptions.[35] Renaissance

---

30. Antonin Artaud, *The Theater and Its Double*, trans. Mary Caroline Richards (New York: Grove Weidenfeld, 1958).

31. *Brecht on Theatre: The Development of an Aesthetic*, trans. John Willett (New York: Hill & Wang, 1964), p. 99.

32. Quoted from Margot Heinemann, "How Brecht Read Shakespeare," in *Political Shakespeare: New Essays in Cultural Materialism*, ed. Jonathan Dollimore and Alan Sinfield (Ithaca: Cornell University Press, 1985), p. 205.

33. William Archer, *The Old Drama and the New: An Essay in Re-valuation* (Boston: Small, Maynard, 1923), pp. 19, 15. See also Jonas A. Barish, "The New Theater and the Old: Revisions and Rejuvenations," in *Reinterpretations of Elizabethan Drama: Selected Papers from the English Institute*, ed. Norman Rabkin (New York: Columbia University Press, 1969), pp. 2–31.

34. Lewis, *Lion and Fox*, pp. 59–61.

35. Levin Schücking's *Character Problems in Shakspere's Plays* (London: Harrap, 1922) and Elmer Edgar Stoll's *Shakespearean Studies, Historical and Comparative in Method* (New York: Macmillan, 1927) also insisted on the "primitive" conditions and conventions of the Elizabethan stage.

Englishmen were aligned with ancient Greeks and present-day Chinese, Japanese, and Balinese as the practitioners of a ritualistic, non-realist, and (except for the Greeks) non-empathetic drama.

Yet it is not quite accurate to say that the modernists simply equated the Renaissance with "primitive" cultures. Rather, they emphasized the *transitional* character of the period—its passage from a primitive state to the condition of modernity. Artaud, although an admirer of the Elizabethans generally, blamed Shakespeare for initiating the movement away from a ritualistic drama and toward a merely descriptive and psychologistic (i.e. modern) dramaturgy.[36] Artaud's views bear comparison with those of Wilhelm Wörringer and his English disciple T. E. Hulme, who contrasted the abstract and geometrical virtues of Byzantine, Egyptian, and Indian art with the vital, empathetic forms of representation inaugurated by humanism and the Renaissance.[37]

The most influential version of this transitional view—in the Anglo-American tradition, at least—was Eliot's theory of the "dissociation of sensibility." Spelled out in "The Metaphysical Poets" but mentioned as well in *Elizabethan Essays*, Eliot's postulate of a unified poetic sensibility which begins to disintegrate in the seventeenth century bears, I think, at least a distant kinship to the anthropologist Lucien Lévy-Bruhl's notion of a primitive, "pre-logical" thought which unifies emotional and ideational content.[38] Certainly the term became associated, through Leavis and the later Eliot, with the notion of an "organic community" in Elizabethan England which began to decompose under the pressures of modernization. For Eliot, moreover, the transition was not gradual and evolutionary but catastrophically rapid. In *Elizabethan Essays*, for instance, he describes the philosophy of the Elizabethan period as "one of anarchism, of dissolution, of decay."[39]

The modernist view of the Renaissance, then, was of an organic and agrarian society undergoing an accelerated transition to modernity; of a unified sensibility fragmenting into component parts; and of a ritualistic

---

36. Artaud, *Theater and its Double*, pp. 76–77.

37. Wilhelm Wörringer, *Abstraction and Empathy: A Contribution to the Psychology of Style*, trans. Michael Bullock (London: Routledge & Kegan Paul, [1953]); T. E. Hulme, *Speculations: Essays on Humanism and the Philosophy of Art* (London: Routledge & Kegan Paul, 1924).

38. See Lucien Lévy-Bruhl, *Les Fonctions mentales dans les sociétés inférieures*, trans. by Lilian A. Clare as *How Natives Think* (London: George Allen & Unwin, 1926), p. 36. On Lévy-Bruhl and Eliot, see Manganaro, *Myth*, pp. 91–94.

39. Eliot, *Elizabethan Essays*, p. 18. Again, on p. 42, he states that "it was a period of dissolution and chaos."

dramatic culture giving way to merely representational forms of art. Renaissance drama, moreover, was repeatedly associated with the cultural performances of both contemporary third-world and archaic or "primitive" cultures. Taken together, these elements strongly suggest a kind of historical allegory at work, organizing and lending coherence (if not historical veracity) to the modernist conception of the Renaissance. To put it bluntly, modernism constructed the English Renaissance as an allegory for the colonial encounter itself; the period's catastrophic experience of modernity and the disintegration of its organic and ritualized culture offered an historically displaced and geographically internalized image of the effects of contemporary imperialist penetration into indigenous third-world societies. If modernism tended to place Shakespeare in the contexts of "primitive" and non-Western cultures, it did so largely because the English Renaissance already, in some sense, refracted the West's encounter with its imperial subjects. In Artaud, in Brecht, in Eliot and Lewis—to name only some of the most illustrious modernists—Shakespeare serves as a shifter within a complex allegorical constellation, one uniting the various elements of an imperialist economy and culture.[40] The imperial framework of late Victorian criticism remains, but it has now taken on the structure of a symptom whose precipitating cause is not directly expressed.

If modernism subsumed Shakespeare within the discourse of primitivism, however, it did not do so in a merely topical or thematic way. More was at stake than a series of striking or polemical juxtapositions of Shakespeare and non-Western cultures—though these became increasingly frequent. The deepest methodological and epistemological assumptions of Shakespeare criticism also underwent a fundamental reorganization as a result of modernism's formative encounter with the "primitive."

Marianna Torgovnick has documented the central contradiction afflicting the modernist reception of non-Western art: an irreconcilable breach between the artifact's status as aesthetic object and its status as functional object—between, that is, a decontextualizing aesthetic *appro-*

40. In "Religion without Humanism," Eliot reveals—at least somewhat more explicitly—the connections between the "dissociation of sensibility" and the culture of imperialism: "I believe that at the present time the problem of the unification of the world and the problem of the unification of the individual, are in the end one and the same problem; and that the solution of the one is the solution of the other. . . . The problem of nationalism and the problem of dissociated personalities may turn out to be the same problem." Eliot, "Religion without Humanism," in *Humanism and America*, ed. Norman Foerster (New York: Farrar & Reinhart, 1930), p. 112; cited in Michael Levenson, *A Genealogy of Modernism: A Study of English Literary Doctrine 1908–1922* (Cambridge: Cambridge University Press, 1984), p. 197.

priation and a culturally contextualizing *interpretation* which tended to render the object alien to Western viewers. The former approach is embodied in the work of the art critic Roger Fry, whose *Vision and Design* (1920) concerned itself only with the formal or aesthetic properties of non-Western artifacts, ignoring the specificity of their provenance, use, or mode of production in order to concentrate on their significance for Western modernists such as Picasso. The latter approach is characteristic of ethnographical studies, which, by specifying the functional role of such objects within their original cultural context, tended to discourage formalist appropriation.[41]

This split, however, did not simply deploy itself along the disciplinary lines separating anthropology and art criticism. It also erupted within anthropology itself: specifically, in the clash between evolutionary comparatists such as J. G. Frazer and functionalists such as Bronislaw Malinowski. Whereas Frazer compares myths or rituals from different cultures and times, lifting them out of their original contexts to establish global patterns of correspondence and analogy, the Malinowskian monograph insists that cultural productions, rituals, and objects are meaningful only within the context of the culture that produced them.[42] Both Frazer and Malinowski exhibit a totalizing impulse, but their analyses assume in the one case a global and in the other a local totality. Moreover, Frazer's decontextualizing approach emphasizes continuities between non-Western, archaic, and present-day European cultures, thus encouraging modernist writers such as Eliot and Joyce in their literary appropriation of other cultures, much as Roger Fry's work legitimated primitivism in the visual arts. Malinowski's approach was less inviting to such uses.

Much has been made of the fact that Malinowski's *Argonauts of the Western Pacific* appeared in 1922, the year *The Waste Land* and *Ulysses* were published. It has been argued, in fact, that the movement from Frazer's vast and highly literary monument to the Malinowskian monograph marks the transition from a Victorian to a modernist anthropology.[43] I would maintain, rather, that modernist anthropology begins not when one mode displaces another but when the two coexist in fundamental

41. Marianna Torgovnick, *Gone Primitive: Savage Intellects, Modern Lives* (Chicago: University of Chicago Press, 1990), pp. 75–104.

42. See, e.g., Marilyn Strathern, "Out of Context: The Persuasive Fictions of Anthropology," in *Modernist Anthropology: From Fieldwork to Text*, ed. Marc Manganaro (Princeton: Princeton University Press, 1990), pp. 80–122.

43. See Marc Manganaro, "Textual Play, Power, and Cultural Critique: An Orientation to Modernist Anthropology," in Manganaro, ed., *Modernist Anthropology*, pp. 3–47. See also Strathern, "Out of Context."

incompatibility, and that this tension within modernist anthropology is only the institutional symptom—though also, to a large degree, both the instigator and conduit—of the antinomies of modernism's encounter with the primitive. As both an artistic and an intellectual movement, modernism was thrown into a state of epistemological disarray by its attempt to interpret and assimilate the products of non-Western cultures. In particular, it was burdened with the contradictory movements toward formalist or decontextualizing readings on the one hand, and toward localizing, functionalist explanations on the other. This particular interpretive dilemma would loom large in the history of twentieth-century literary criticism. There is always, of course, an inherent tension between formalist and historical, globalizing and localizing, or decontextualizing and contextualizing modes of explanation; but for works of art interpreted by Europeans and produced within the European tradition, this tension could often be suppressed or evaded because contextual and historical readings often reinforced a sense of shared heritage. The overt and unmistakable otherness of non-Western art, however, and the foreignness of the societies that produced them, meant that to contextualize and localize such works was necessarily to render them alien and unassimilable. Conversely, to appropriate them meant ignoring their original functions and context. Modernism's encounter with the primitive did not produce entirely new or unprecedented interpretive problems, but it foregrounded both the nature of the problems and their insolubility.

It is not surprising that such dilemmas returned to plague the Western tradition, because the encounter with the "primitive" raised questions about the universality of Western art and culture. As T. E. Hulme observed, "The change of sensibility which has enabled us to regard Egyptian, Polynesian, and Negro work, as *art* and not as archeology has . . . made us realise that what we took to be the necessary principles of aesthetic, constitute in reality only a psychology of Renaissance and Classical Art." This may, he holds, "be some indication that the *humanist tradition is breaking up.*"[44] The inevitable result of modernism's interest in non-Western art was a partial estrangement from Western canons of the aesthetic and a turning inward of the anthropological gaze.

That this gaze should come to rest on Shakespeare ought not to be surprising. As the supreme embodiment of a national, and indeed European, tradition, the figure of Shakespeare drew to itself the epistemological and cultural contradictions spawned by modernism's discourse of primitivism. The Renaissance itself, as a particularly privileged era in the

44. Hulme, *Speculations*, pp. 12, 55.

West's sense of cultural achievement and unity, felt the pressure of modernism's anthropological way of seeing.

A telling instance of this is Eliot's essay on "Four Elizabethan Dramatists," which he provided as a polemical introduction to his *Elizabethan Essays*. "Four Elizabethan Dramatists" offers an extended response to William Archer's attacks on Renaissance drama in *The Old Drama and the New*, and it employs Archer as a kind of fulcrum point in attempting to define a distinctively modernist approach to the Renaissance. Archer, as we have seen, assaulted Elizabethan drama for its "primitive" qualities, specifically for those ritualistic and conventional elements which, in his view, impeded the achievement of dramatic realism and verisimilitude. Archer regarded Elizabethan drama as akin to, and to be rejected along with, non-Western and archaic forms of ritualized performance.

In a sense, Archer already "anthropologizes" the question of Renaissance drama before Eliot even enters the debate. Eliot does not directly address Archer's non-Western illustrations, but his methodological response is telling. Archer, he claims, has gotten the problem exactly wrong: "The weakness of the Elizabethan drama is not its defect of realism, but its attempt at realism; not its conventions, but its lack of conventions." As an additional blow, he adds that this latter problem—the lack of conventions—saddles the Elizabethans with "the same weakness as that of modern drama."[45]

The roots of Eliot's position can be found in "The Beating of a Drum," where they appear in more clearly anthropological form. "The drama," he argues there, "was originally ritual, and ritual, consisting of a set of repeated movements, is essentially a dance." With this much, even Archer would agree. But Eliot then goes on: "It is the rhythm, so utterly absent from modern drama, either verse or prose, and which interpreters of Shakespeare do their best to suppress, which makes Massine and Charlie Chaplin the great actors that they are, and which makes the juggling of Rastelli more cathartic than a performance of 'A Doll's House.' "[46] Eliot, like Artaud, here associates Elizabethan drama with "primitive" ritual in a combined assault on dramatic realism. His defense of the vaguer "convention" in the later *Elizabethan Essays* clearly derives from this early ritualist position.

The flaw in Elizabethan drama, Eliot claims, cannot be that its conventions are bad, because there are no intrinsically "bad" dramatic conventions. Rather, the Elizabethans lack a "firm principle of what is to be

45. Eliot, *Elizabethan Essays*, pp. 12, 10.
46. Eliot, "Beating of a Drum," p. 12.

postulated as a convention and what is not." This can be seen, for instance, in their inconsistent handling of ghosts.[47] Eliot's relativist take on dramatic convention must be understood in light of Archer's Eurocentric contempt for the "primitive," and it seems clear that Eliot's more tolerant view derives in part from his anthropological reading. Eliot, in other words, treats Elizabethan convention with exactly the same detachment and suspended judgment that modern ethnographers were attempting to apply to foreign societies. Indeed, the "flaw" in Elizabethan drama derives (in his view) not from its ritualized conventions but from the fact that the Elizabethans no longer consistently observe or understand them. Like native subjects disoriented by Western contact, the Elizabethans, in their rapid transition to modernity, have begun to lose their grip on their own cultural forms and traditions.

Eliot's methodological approach in *Elizabethan Essays* appears to be a simple defense of formalism over realism: literary works, he insists, are to be judged solely according to their own internal principles of order, consistency, and decorum—not according to how accurately they portray their own societies or how we may feel about their conventions. Yet this literary formalism is penetrated through and through with colonial allegory, and its organizing principles derive from modernism's encounter with the "primitive." This side of Eliot's formalism comes closer to the surface in his treatment of the "objective correlative" in the *Hamlet* essay. *Hamlet*'s failure, as described therein, is precisely a problem of form. It is not that the emotions generated by the play are in themselves unacceptable; rather, it is that the play lacks an adequate form—the objective correlative—to *contain* them. Eliot's criticism of the play is entirely consistent with his methodology throughout the *Elizabethan Essays* in focusing on the adequacy and consistency of dramatic convention. Yet his description of the emotions produced by *Hamlet* is telling: "The intense feeling, ecstatic or terrible, without an object or exceeding its object, is something which every person of sensibility has known; it is doubtless a subject of study for pathologists. It often occurs in adolescence; the ordinary person puts these feelings to sleep, or trims down these feelings to fit the business world; the artist keeps them alive by his ability to intensify the world to his emotions."[48] Here the term "ecstatic," in particular, resonates with a ritualist or primitivist force, and Eliot's insistence that the role of the artist is to keep such feelings alive recalls his pronouncements that "poetry begins, I dare say, with a savage beating a drum in a jungle, and it

47. Eliot, *Elizabethan Essays*, pp. 16–17.
48. Ibid., p. 63.

retains that essential percussion and rhythm," or again: "The artist, I believe, is more *primitive*, as well as more civilized, than his contemporaries, his experience is deeper than civilization, and he only uses the phenomena of civilization in expressing it."[49] *Hamlet*'s failure, in one sense merely a formal problem, is more fundamentally that of having released "ecstatic" and primitive energies without a containing convention. Here literary judgment results from the turning inward of an anthropological and primitivist discourse.

Eliot's latently anthropological defense of Elizabethan drama effectively answers Archer's contempt for "primitive" dramatic forms, but it entails certain methodological difficulties whose full effects would soon be felt. Eliot does not deny Archer's claim that Elizabethan dramatic conventions are fundamentally different from modern ones; he simply claims that this fact should not form the basis for literary valuation. Eliot, that is to say, grants the historical alienation of Elizabethan culture, much as ethnographers accept the cultural difference between their own cultures and those they study. All that matters about conventions, he argues, is that they form a coherent and consistent totality, not that modern readers share in that totality. Eliot asks for something like a Coleridgean suspension of disbelief, only now that capacity is exercised not in the face of inherently improbable fictions but in the face of other periods or cultures.

The inevitable tendency of such an approach is to open (or widen) a rift between historical understanding and imaginative participation, or between contextualizing and decontextualizing approaches—precisely the dilemma afflicting the modernist experience of the "primitive." I would argue, in fact, that the methodological dilemmas generated by modernism's attempt to understand non-Western art redounded upon the historical study of Western culture as well. Earlier historical scholarship on Shakespeare and Elizabethan drama tended to be a confidently empirical brand of antiquarianism. Its governing assumption was that older texts contained obscure references and allusions which the historical scholar could explain. Adding local background was felt to facilitate a literary or imaginative appropriation of the text. Beginning with the modernist period, however, and largely under the influence of anthropological study, the notion—or the anxiety—began to emerge that perhaps the Elizabethan age was separated by an unbridgeable cultural and historical distance from our own, and that increased historical contex-

---

49. Eliot, *Selected Prose*, p. 95; review of Wyndham Lewis's novel *Tarr*, cited in Crawford, *Savage and the City*, p. 93.

tualization, far from enriching the imaginative consumption of older works, might actually alienate them from modern sensibilities. Wyndham Lewis, for instance, quite openly declared that modern audiences were incapable of appreciating Shakespearean tragedy, and he cited African tribal societies not so much to elucidate the Shakespearean text as to outline a domain of cultural experience which modern readers could perhaps grasp intellectually but could by no means participate in. In his important essay "Historical Scholarship and the Interpretation of Shakespeare," the critic L. C. Knights, an enthusiastic disciple of Eliot, warned that "the attempt to reconstruct the Elizabethan or Renaissance meanings of Shakespeare's plays is almost inevitably attended by the danger of obscuring their imaginative life."[50] Here, we might say, Eliot's anthropological chickens have come home to roost, for the study of Shakespeare is now plagued by the same difficulties attending the study of tribal art. By drawing Shakespeare into the field of the primitive, modernism burdened literary criticism with the contradictions inherent to the discourse of primitivism. Henceforth historical and literary, contextualizing and decontextualizing interpretations would be (to alter Theodor Adorno's famous phrase) "the two halves of a total interpretation—to which, however, they do not add up."

This critical dilemma was by no means limited to the study of Shakespeare, though I think there is good reason to regard Shakespeare as a privileged point of origin from which the antinomies of primitivism radiate. In any case, the methodological problems raised for modernism by anthropology and primitive art ought to be seen as both source and symptom of a more global process marked by the mutation of capitalism from its industrial to its monopoly or imperialist phase. Fredric Jameson has already outlined this transition and its relation to literary modernism:

> Colonialism means that a significant structural segment of the economic system as a whole is now located elsewhere, beyond the metropolis, outside of daily life and existential experience of the home country, in colonies over the water whose own life experience and life world—very different from that of the imperial power—remain unknown and unimaginable for the subjects of the imperial power, whatever social class they may belong to. Such spatial disjunction has as its immediate consequence the inability to grasp how the system functions as a whole. Unlike the classical stage of national or market capitalism,

50. L. C. Knights, *Further Explorations* (Stanford: Stanford University Press, 1965), p. 145. Knights's essay originally appeared in *Sewanee Review* 63, no. 2 (1955).

then, pieces of the puzzle are missing; it can never be fully reconstructed; no enlargement of personal experience (in the knowledge of other social classes, for example), no intensity of self-examination (in the form of whatever social guilt), no scientific deductions on the basis of the internal evidence of First World data, can ever be enough to include this radical otherness of colonial life, colonial suffering, and exploitation, let alone the structural connections between that and this, between absent space and the daily life of the metropolis. To put it in other words, this last—daily life and existential experience in the metropolis—which is necessarily the very content of the national literature itself, can now no longer be grasped immanently; it no longer has its meaning, its deeper reason, within itself.[51]

One literary effect of this structural mutation was to shatter the immanence of national experience on which nineteenth-century realism relied. The modernist concern with style is, as Jameson argues, a response to this representational crisis. Yet modernism also generates a less hermetic response to the same problem, which is the cult of primitivism itself—an attempt to grasp the "experience" of the colonized other directly, either through the aesthetic appreciation of artifacts or through the anthropological study of third-world cultures. The discourse of the primitive is modernism's effort to reappropriate those geocultural realms whose spatial absence has opened a void within the metropolitan culture.

Yet as we have seen, the antinomies of the primitive reproduce within modernist discourse the very gaps that Jameson describes above—principally, between the experiential and the interpretive or cognitive realms. The macrostructural contradictions of imperialism are regenerated, as if through fractal reduction, at the microlevel of primitivist art criticism and anthropology. Attempting to plug the hole in the metropolis's systemic self-understanding by importing cultural materials from the third world only replicates the original problem by reinscribing it in the very reception of the new material. That this dilemma should then spread to Western cultural productions—in this case, to Shakespeare—is no surprise, since the basic problem is really a structural dislocation *within* the metropolitan culture itself. More precisely, it is a problem which cannot be located in either term but only in their uneven and overdetermined relation. "Primitive" Shakespeare is an image of this cultural contradiction, a condensation or lamination of the periphery onto the center, a superposition of the excluded other onto the emblematic heart of the (for-

51. Fredric Jameson, "Modernism and Imperialism," in *Nationalism, Colonialism, and Literature*, intro. Seamus Deane (Minneapolis: University of Minnesota Press, 1990), pp. 50–51.

merly) domestic or national culture, which now cannot be grasped as such. At the very moment when capitalism evolves into a new and unrepresentable form, modernism has recourse to precapitalist culture—both that of the third world and that of Shakespeare, the latter now construed as a decisively pre-modern dramatist—in an impossible effort to recapture what imperialism has at once made central to the metropolis and, at the same time, placed irretrievably beyond reach.

Because it is symptomatic of a larger, structural contradiction, the conjoining of Shakespeare and primitivism is no mere fashion of high modernism, soon to be swept away. On the contrary, it installs itself as a remarkably persistent element of both Shakespearean performance and Shakespeare criticism. While this chapter focuses on the latter, I would like to discuss at least one major Shakespearean production, in part because it so fully embodied the modernist reading of Shakespeare, and thus illustrates how the influence of this reading spread beyond the walls of the academy, and in part because it initiated a tradition of presenting Shakespeare plays in third-world settings which is still very much alive, both on stage and on screen. The production I have in mind is Orson Welles's "Voodoo" *Macbeth*, done in conjunction with John Houseman in 1936 as part of the W.P.A.'s Negro Theatre Project in Harlem. Welles set his production of *Macbeth* in Haiti, circa 1820, with an all-black cast. Voodoo priestesses and drummers took the place of Shakespeare's witches against a stylized jungle backdrop (see Figure 1).[52] African dancer and choreographer Asadata Dafora was hired to create the dances and chants for the play.[53]

Welles's production, which by the end of its successful run in Harlem and on tour had drawn over a hundred thousand viewers,[54] probably owed more to Eugene O'Neill's *The Emperor Jones* than it did to modernist Shakespeare criticism. Yet his recourse to Haitian culture to embody the witchcraft of *Macbeth* recalls Wyndham Lewis's use of African kingship to illuminate Shakespeare's tragic kings. Of course Lewis's intention is merely to shock his white readers, while Welles aims to make Shakespeare available to a largely African-American audience. Yet even this project, despite its progressive intentions and general popularity, was fraught with

52. See *Orson Welles on Shakespeare: The W.P.A. and Mercury Theatre Transcripts*, ed. Richard France, Contributions in Drama and Theatre Studies no. 30 (Westport Conn.: Greenwood, 1990), pp. 12–15.

53. *The Dance Photography of Carl Van Vechten*, intro. Paul Padgette (New York: Schirmer, 1981), p. 7.

54. Edith J. R. Isaacs, *The Negro in the American Theatre* (New York: Theatre Arts, 1947), p. 110.

Figure 1. Orson Welles's 1936 production of *Macbeth.* From the Library of Congress Federal Theatre Project Collection at George Mason University, Fairfax, Virginia.

political tensions. Some members of the Harlem community were less than pleased that the production was managed by whites while others feared that it might be "another vast burlesque intended to ridicule the Negro in the eyes of the white world."[55] Langston Hughes complained:

> You also took my spirituals and gone.
> You put me in *Macbeth* and *Carmen Jones*
> And all kind of *Swing Mikados*
> And in everything but what's about me.[56]

For whites traveling uptown to see the production, Welles's savage representation of Haiti might well have blended with their own cultural preconceptions about Harlem itself. Attending a production of *Macbeth* was thereby transformed into the equivalent of an anthropological field trip. Welles himself was sometimes given to imperialist and orientalist fantasizing, having claimed to several biographers that he was first introduced to Shakespeare while "traveling to the High Atlas Mountains of Morocco with a satchel full of Elizabethan plays, which he studied while domiciled in the palace of an Arab sheik."[57] But the ambiguous relation between "Voodoo" *Macbeth* and imperialism is precisely the mark of its modernist status, tying it to the work of Eliot, Lewis, and others. The staging of Shakespeare in non-Western settings would become a staple device for both European and non-European directors, notable examples from film being Kurosawa's *Ran* and *Throne of Blood* and Ismail Merchant and James Ivory's *Shakespeare Wallah*.

Within Shakespeare criticism, as opposed to Shakespearean production, explicitly primitivist or anthropological approaches disappear in the decades after the 1930s. There are exceptions, of course, such as G. Wilson Knight's 1947 essay on "Shakespeare and the Incas: A Study of *Apu Ollantay*,"[58] but while the modernist legacy dominated in Shakespeare studies, the latter's interest in non-Western culture seemed for the most part to evaporate. What could not be banished, however, were the methodological contradictions derived from modernism's encounter with the primitive, which asserted themselves within the two dominant

55. John Houseman, *Run-Through* (New York: Simon & Schuster, 1972), p. 191. Quoted in *Orson Welles on Shakespeare*, p. 13.

56. "Note on Commercial Theater," *Selected Poems of Langston Hughes* (New York: Random House, 1990), p. 190.

57. *Orson Welles on Shakespeare*, p. 1.

58. Included in G. Wilson Knight, *Shakespeare and Religion: Essays of Forty Years* (New York: Barnes & Noble, 1967), pp. 139–80.

critical movements of the 1950s and 1960s: the New Criticism and myth criticism.

Eliot's influence on the "Fugitive Group" which formed the core of the New Critics has been well documented.[59] It is important to point out, however, that the protocols for the "New Critical" reading of Shakespeare probably owe less to the work of the Southern Agrarians than they do to the English critics G. Wilson Knight and L. C. Knights.[60] G. Wilson Knight was, in a sense, Eliot's own anointed in the field of Shakespeare criticism. Eliot personally carried Knight's early Shakespeare essays to Oxford University Press, where they were published as *The Wheel of Fire* (1930), and he based his poems *Marina* and *Coriolan* partly on Knight's readings of the romances and *Coriolanus*.[61] Knight, for his part, read Shakespeare's plays according to aesthetic and critical principles which, while not mainly derived from Eliot's, were in many ways consonant with them. Of principal interest here is Knight's insistence on formal immanence as the basis for reading Shakespeare's plays. Knight abjured "criticism," the evaluation and comparison of works, in favor of "interpretation," the analysis of each work as a unty in its own right. In claiming that "we should . . . regard each play as a visionary unit bound to obey none but its own laws," Knight adopts a more or less Eliotic stance, and in rejecting authorial intention, source study, character, and biography in favor of verbal and imagistic patterns in the plays, Knight adumbrates the methods of the New Critics.[62] Knight has been called (not quite accurately) "the earliest significant critic attempting to interpret Shakespeare's plays as modernist art-works."[63]

Knight's "immanent" approach to Shakespeare is developed further by L. C. Knights, most famously in "How Many Children Had Lady Macbeth? An Essay on the Theory and Practice of Shakespeare Criticism" (1933).[64] The essay and its mocking title have, correctly, been seen

59. See Louise Cowan, *The Fugitive Group: A Literary History* (Baton Rouge: Louisiana State University Press, 1959). See also Hugh Grady, *The Modernist Shakespeare: Critical Texts in a Material World* (Oxford: Clarendon Press, 1991), pp. 113–26.

60. On Knight and Knights, as well as the third major "symbolist" Shakespearean, Caroline Spurgeon, see S. Viswanathan, *The Shakespearean Play as Poem: A Critical Tradition in Perspective* (Cambridge: Cambridge University Press, 1980).

61. G. Wilson Knight, "T. S. Eliot: Some Literary Impressions," in *T. S. Eliot: The Man and His Work*, ed. Allen Tate (New York: Delacorte, 1966), pp. 246–47.

62. G. Wilson Knight, *The Wheel of Fire*, expanded ed. (London: Methuen, 1949), pp. 14, 1–9.

63. Grady, *Modernist Shakespeare*, p. 89. Pride of place here must go to Eliot and Lewis, of course; but Knight is the first significant *academic* critic to expound modernist canons of reading in Shakespeare criticism.

64. Reprinted in Knights, *Explorations*, pp. 15–54.

largely as a reaction to A. C. Bradley's late-Victorian brand of character criticism. This Knights decisively rejects in favor of attention to verbal patterns, insisting that a play is, in the end, nothing but language. Like the later New Critics, Knights values close reading over historical background, and places a high value on complexity and difficulty, which for him, as for the New Critics themselves, are tied to the defense of a high-modernist aesthetic. Thus Knights insists that "*Macbeth* has greater affinity with *The Waste Land* than with *The Doll's House*."[65] Finally, Knights's essay contains a surprisingly full exposition of what Cleanth Brooks would later come to call the "heresy of paraphrase," insisting that the only "full" presentation of a poem is to be found in the words of the poem themselves, and that all critical commentary is therefore, to some degree, distorting.[66]

While both Knight and Knights produce an explicitly modernist Shakespeare, neither invokes the tropes of primitivism. It is true that Knight's interest in spiritualism and Eastern religion pervades his criticism, as in his praise for the "Nirvanic mysticism of *Timon of Athens*;"[67] and Knights approvingly quotes Yeats on the Japanese Noh theater in discussing the formalism of Elizabethan plays.[68] But neither critic shows a sustained interest in anthropological models or in placing Shakespeare in non-Western contexts. Both move toward the purely formal, immanent analyses which would characterize New Critics such as Brooks. Yet while primitivist references disappear from the critical surface, the antinomies of primitivism install themselves all the more surely at the level of method—for the very turn toward formalism was motivated by the contradiction between contextualizing and decontextualizing, historicizing and aestheticizing approaches initiated by modernism's encounter with the primitive. Both Knight and Knights insist that historical criticism is at odds with formalist reading, and both complain about the increasing specialization of historical scholarship, which, they fear, will alienate Shakespeare from the general reader.

While this chapter will not yet address the New Historicism, it may be useful to anticipate one issue now, for the antinomies of modernist in-

65. Ibid., p. 33.
66. Ibid., p. 32.
67. Knight, *Shakespeare and Religion*, p. 5.
68. Knights, *Explorations*, p. 22. Knights invokes non-Western dramatic forms as part of an attack on naturalism very much like Eliot's or Artaud's. He insists as well that the "primitive traditions" of morality plays and the peculiarities of Elizabethan dramatic and stage conventions "determine that Elizabethan drama should be non-realistic, conditioned by conventions that helped to govern the total response obtained by means of the language of each play" (*Explorations*, pp. 19–20).

terpretation bear directly on the claims of the New Historicist project. Stephen Greenblatt writes that he coined the term "New Historicism" in order "to signal a turn away from the formal, decontextualized analysis that dominates new criticism" and toward "an interest . . . in the embeddedness of cultural objects in the contingencies of history."[69] What we may now ask, I think, is whether this move is an unambiguous sign of progress or whether it is merely another oscillation within the critical dilemma of modernism, condemned as it is to a seemingly endless alternation between contextualizing and decontextualizing approaches. And if the New Historicism is caught within this dilemma, is this the result of avoidable intellectual weaknesses, or is it, as I believe, the symptom of its untranscendable situation within the culture of late imperialism?

The New Criticism attempted to resolve this interpretive dilemma by opting wholeheartedly for a decontextualizing approach to literature. Shakespeare isn't placed in a primitivist social context or indeed in *any* concrete social context, even an English one. New Critics such as Knight and Knights treat Shakespeare somewhat as Roger Fry treated tribal art, and for similar reasons, fearing that historical context would impede aesthetic and imaginative appreciation.

Yet it is too easy to place the New Critics neatly to one side of the modernist divide. The New Criticism doesn't simply choose decontextualizing over contextualizing approaches; rather, it distributes them around the boundary of the text. For if literary works are detached from any totalizing social framework of the kind produced, for instance, in ethnographical studies, the works themselves come curiously to resemble such a totalizing context. Just as, according to functionalist anthropology, a given cultural practice, ritual, myth, or artifact can have meaning only within the context of the social totality of which it forms a part, so, for the New Critics, do the literary elements that constitute any given work receive their full significance only through the total context provided by the work itself. As Marc Manganaro has pointed out, the New Critical reading of a single work is in some respects literary criticism's formal equivalent of the Malinowskian monograph.[70] It is as if the anthropological model of society were evacuated as context in order to be introjected by the text.

As a result, the New Critical text comes to bear the methodological anxiety attending the study of primitive cultures. Cleanth Brooks's "her-

69. Stephen Greenblatt, *Learning to Curse: Essays in Early Modern Culture* (New York: Routledge, 1990), pp. 163–64.
70. Manganaro, *Myth*, p. 113.

esy of paraphrase," a concept that can be traced through Knights and Knight back to Eliot, posits a relationship between literary critic and text which is not very different from that between ethnographers and the societies they investigate. In both cases, the totalizing quality of the object under study resists translation into the terms of the analyst: both the text and tribal societies are necessarily falsified or distorted in the process of description, and in both cases analysis remains irreducibly external to its object. For Brooks, moreover, this exteriority is defined by the fundamental dichotomy between poetic language, on the one hand, and critical, scientific, or rationalist language on the other. It is not too great a leap, I think, to translate these two terms into precapitalist and capitalist forms of discourse. The encounter of criticism and poem is thus, in some allegorical sense, the encounter of capitalist modernity with precapitalism, or even of metropolitan culture with periphery. This allegory is energized by the Southern Agrarians' resistance to capitalist modernization—that is, by a struggle internal to the West—but it is also, as part of the legacy of modernism, necessarily a colonial allegory as well.[71] Thus the New Critical view of the literary text as somehow ahistorical and unchanging—fixed in the discursive timelessness of the poetic—resembles Western views of "primitive," or non-Western, cultures. I am not trying to argue here that the New Criticism is directly influenced by anthropology; I am simply trying to show that as part of the legacy of modernism, it inherits the antinomies of primitivist discourse, and that these silently pervade its critical method.

The New Criticism's main rival after World War II was myth criticism, which evolved directly from modernism's interests in ritual and comparative religion. The influence of this tradition on Shakespeare studies may be gauged by Alfred Harbage's despairing remarks about his students in 1952: "When our questioning youths speak of the *Wasteland* qualities of this play, the pagan ritualism in that, the incestuous motivation of a third . . . one wonders what they have been reading, or by whom they have been indoctrinated. In simple fairness to them, we must let them see in Shakespeare a little less of Frazer and Freud, and a little more of Erasmus."[72] This strain of modernism was at once crystallized and transfigured by Northrop Frye, whose important work I will discuss in Chapter 3. Here I will only advert to the way in which myth criticism and the New

71. On the anti-modernizing tendencies of the Southern Agrarians, see John Fekete, "The New Criticism: Ideological Evolution of the Right Opposition," *Telos* 20 (Summer 1974): 2-51, and Grady, *Modernist Shakespeare*, pp. 113–26.

72. Alfred Harbage, *Shakespeare and the Rival Traditions* (New York: Macmillan, 1952), pp. xiv–xv.

Criticism parceled out among themselves the legacy of modernism. If the New Criticism, in effect, internalized the protocols of a Malinowskian anthropology, then myth criticism more explicitly adopted the mantle of a Frazerian or comparatist method. If the New Criticism resolutely decontextualized literary texts, myth criticism just as resolutely ordered them within the global context of presumably universal and worldwide mythoi. The competition between myth-critical and New Critical methods, then, simply redrew the original fault lines running through modernism's aesthetic and critical theory. In their methodological conflicts they replayed the antinomies introduced by modernism's encounter with the primitive. Thus Cleanth Brooks's and Northrop Frye's renderings of Shakespeare can both lay claim to traditions laid down by Eliot. By this I mean not only an anthropological influence but, just as important, the latent status of this influence—for unlike Lewis, who fearlessly evoked studies of African societies in his Shakespeare criticism, Eliot tended not to draw attention to the anthropological problematic informing his essays on Elizabethan drama. As a result, the influence of this tradition on his work, and on that of his successors, tended to become at once more implicit and more purely methodological. In Lewis's book, the open presence of non-Western cultures has a polemically destabilizing force. The immediate inheritor of this topical or thematic primitivism, we may say, was Orson Welles. The inheritors of Eliot's more covert anthropology were the myth critics and the New Critics, who tended to confine themselves to European traditions, and whose participation in the culture of imperialism was manifested predominantly in the ghostly sphere of method.

Shakespeare as Native Informant

The topical and methodological strains of modernism's interest in the primitive did not remain divided, however; they merged and resurfaced in the New Historicism, for which this chapter attempts in part to provide an extended genealogy or pedigree. While the New Historicism is generally portrayed as a variety of postmodernism, I would argue that it also entails a recrudescence of high modernism. The "postmodernity" of the New Historicists results not from some absolute break with modernist practice but rather from its radical refiguring. I shall pursue this line of argument by focusing on the work of Stephen Greenblatt, which bears an interesting relation to the traditions of Eliotic criticism.

Greenblatt's book *Shakespearean Negotiations* opens with a striking meditation on the foundational motives for historical criticism:

> I began with the desire to speak with the dead.
>
> This desire is a familiar, if unvoiced, motive in literary studies, a motive organized, professionalized, buried beneath thick layers of bureaucratic decorum: literature professors are salaried, middle-class shamans. If I never believed that the dead could hear me, and if I knew that the dead could not speak, I was nonetheless certain that I could re-create a conversation with them. Even when I came to understand that in my most intense moments of straining to listen all I could hear was my own voice, even then I did not abandon my desire. It was true that I could hear only my own voice, but my own voice was the voice of the dead, for the dead had contrived to leave textual traces of themselves, and those traces make themselves heard in the voices of the living. Many of the traces have little resonance, though every one, even the most trivial or tedious, contains some fragment of lost life; others seem uncannily full of the will to be heard.[73]

In this memorable passage, which proclaims the capacity of the dead to speak through the living, one should not be surprised to hear echoes of critics past. Greenblatt's portrayal of the literature professor as a "salaried, middle-class shaman" strikes an Eliotic note in locating a "primitive" or ritualistic core beneath the superficies of civilization.[74] Moreover, Greenblatt's language of resurrecting the dead recalls crucial elements of Eliot's critical and poetic methods. In "Tradition and the Individual Talent," Eliot writes that "not only the best, but the most individual parts of [a poet's] work may be those in which the dead poets, his ancestors, assert their immortality most vigorously."[75] Robert Crawford writes compellingly of Eliot's "poetics of resuscitation," and observes: "Frequently what appears original, fresh speech in Eliot turns out to be the language of the dead, revivified for his own ends. The near past continually resuscitates the distant."[76] Greenblatt is in some sense a descendent of Eliot's Tiresias, who, in *The Waste Land,* reports back to the living after having "walked among the lowest of the dead."

73. Stephen Greenblatt, *Shakespearean Negotiations: The Circulation of Social Energy in Renaissance England* (Berkeley: University of California Press, 1988), p. 1.
74. In the introductory essay of *Learning to Curse,* Greenblatt employs similar language when he describes the New Criticism as performing "hierophantic service to the mystery cult" of the text (p. 1).
75. Eliot, *Selected Prose,* p. 38.
76. Crawford, *Savage and the City,* pp. 7, 8.

Writing about the birth of his interest in Renaissance culture, Greenblatt remarks that while a Fulbright Scholar at Cambridge, "I had been struck by what seemed to me the uncanny modernity of Sir Walter Ralegh's poetry (which at that time meant that certain passages reminded me of "The Wasteland")."[77] Of interest here is not so much the offhand reference to Eliot's work as a similarity in the two critics' protocols of reading, for what struck Eliot too about Renaissance culture was its essential *modernity*, which allowed him to read in that period's "anarchism, dissolution, and decay" a reflection of his own times.[78] Eliot's capacity to see the twentieth century in the sixteenth and seventeenth does not, moreover, contradict his "primitivist" reading of the Renaissance, for his anthropological outlook entails both a sense of the historical sedimentation of cultures and, at the same time, a sense of the persistence of the archaic. As a result (and this is something he shares with Greenblatt), his awareness of historical difference is always transected by the sense of an eternal present which renders the past directly contemporaneous.

I certainly do not want to suggest that Stephen Greenblatt is a cultural avatar of T. S. Eliot, or that he or the other New Historicists simply rehearse a modernist problematic. But I think it is useful to emphasize some of the continuities between these two cultural movements. When Greenblatt's essay "Invisible Bullets" illuminates the *Henriad* by narrating Thomas Harriot's encounter with Native Americans, this tactic—at least at the level of performance—has more than a little in common with Orson Welles's "Voodoo" *Macbeth* or Wyndham Lewis's citations of African tribal societies to explain Shakespearean tragedy. Greenblatt's frequent juxtapositions of Renaissance and non-Western cultures not only find a precedent in the practice of the high modernists but retain something of the same power to surprise. Greenblatt's art of "telling stories" self-consciously harks back to the practices of "primitive" or narrative societies, thus allowing him to occupy both sides of the line that presumably separates anthropological observer and primitive subject—a tactic not unrelated to Lewis's and Eliot's claims to be at once hypercivilized and savage.[79] As a result of shared ethnographical influence, Eliot and

77. Greenblatt, *Learning to Curse*, p. 2.
78. Eliot, *Elizabethan Essays*, p. 18.
79. It is worth remarking that both Eliot's and Greenblatt's interest in primitive and non-Western societies originated not in ethnography but in popular culture. Greenblatt reveals that "as a child, my favorite books were *The Arabian Knights* and Richard Halliburton's *Book of Marvels*." Greenblatt, *Marvelous Possessions: The Wonder of the New World* (Chicago: University of Chicago Press, 1991), p. 1. Eliot's childhood reading included the tales of Captain Mayne Reid, Rudyard Kipling, and R. L. Stevenson (Crawford, *Savage and the City*, pp. 14–18).

the Renaissance New Historicists display a fascination with, and valorization of, "local" cultures[80] and an interest in the theater as a collective institution.

Both the persistence and the transformation of colonial allegory appear in Stephen Greenblatt's essay "Invisible Bullets," on which I will focus as an exemplary, indeed defining instance of New Historical method. That essay, we recall, begins with Thomas Harriot's (probably unwitting) attempt to test the "Machiavellian hypothesis" about religious belief on the Algonquian Indians he encounters on a visit to the Virginia colony. Greenblatt then turns to Shakespeare's *Henriad*, wherein Harriot's recording of alien voices is reproduced by Prince Hal (and, at another level, by Shakespeare), with the difference that the process of testing and recording is now directed against internal "others," such as the lower classes and, later, the Irish, Welsh and Scots.

Greenblatt's essay strikingly reproduces a number of elements in modernism's allegory of colonialism, only now the latter is no longer a symptom but a fully self-conscious problematic. Like Eliot, Greenblatt narrates the transition to modernity as destructive and catastrophic. Yet the colonial encounter is no longer the repressed subtext of Europe's internal development but its *model*; as Donald Pease notes (with some exaggeration), "Greenblatt generalizes the applicability of . . . colonialist practices until colonialism becomes the internalized norm descriptive of all of Renaissance culture."[81] Greenblatt reads the *Henriad* as a staging of internal colonialism, with the lower classes playing the role of "alien tribe" (Greenblatt's term).[82] The progressively totalizing triumph of a centralized, royal power, for which Greenblatt's reading has become somewhat notorious, is itself figured along imperial lines, as the incremental assimilation of culturally "distinct realms, each with its own system of values"[83] into the national equivalent of a world-system.

---

80. Here Leah Marcus, even more than Greenblatt, comes to mind. In *Puzzling Shakespeare: Local Reading and Its Discontents* (Berkeley: University of California Press, 1988), she points out the danger that localization may become associated with "a kind of retrograde regionalism" (p. 36)—the stance embodied in Eliot's later writings, such as *After Strange Gods* (1934), *The Idea of a Christian Society* (1940), and *Notes toward the Definition of Culture* (1948).

81. Donald Pease, "Toward a Sociology of Literary Knowledge: Greenblatt, Colonialism, and the New Historicism," in *Consequences of Theory: Selected Papers from the English Institute, 1987–88*, ed. Jonathan Arac and Barbara Johnson (Baltimore: Johns Hopkins University Press, 1991), p. 137.

82. Greenblatt, *Shakespearean Negotiations*, p. 49.

83. Ibid., p. 47. Leah Marcus's reading of *Measure for Measure* in *Puzzling Shakespeare* likewise describes a kind of internalized juridical imperialism in which " 'unlocalized' canon law reached out to encompass and erase local difference" (p. 174).

The emergence of colonialism as an explicit issue transforms the modernist problematic in a number of ways, not the least of which is the disappearance (or at least the attenuation) of the discourse of primitivism. For modernism, the "primitive" was an aboriginal, timeless realm reproduced or represented through the apparently transparent medium of ethnography, and available for comparison with, or enrichment of, European culture. In Eliot's view, the ideal anthropologist was self-effacing, a recorder of "facts" who did not impose interpretive or theoretical structures on reports of non-Western cultures. What was of interest to Eliot was the recorded cultures "in themselves," not the process by which they were produced or the inevitable relations this entailed between metropole and periphery. For Greenblatt, by contrast, it is precisely the ethnographic moment that counts—that is to say, the scene of contact wherein a colonial representative both records and intervenes in an indigenous culture.

It may be too much to say, however, that the modernist discourse of the "primitive" simply disappears in New Historical criticism; for it subsists in defining the place of the cultural others, whether internal or external, who must endure a process of colonization. The very concept of modernity is meaningless without the presence of those who are the subjects or victims of modernization, and a good deal of the rhetorical poignancy of Greenblatt's work involves recording the disruption or destruction of pre-modern cultures.

Critical awareness of colonialism was, for the most part, forced onto Western intellectuals by the cultural, political, and military resistance of the colonized themselves. If we now cannot read *The Tempest* without seeing in it a drama of colonialism, we ultimately owe this insight to the work of O. Mannoni, Frantz Fanon, George Lamming, Roberto Fernández Retamar, Aimé Césaire, and others. Much of what we would call the "postmodernity" of New Historical criticism—its interest in the question of the other, its problematizing of the distinction between the subject and object of historical scrutiny, its elevation of local over global knowledge—results directly from the influence of the anticolonial struggles of the 1950s and 60s. In this limited field, at least, the shift from a modernist to a postmodern criticism can best be mapped not along Jamesonian lines, as the effect of an economic transition from imperialist or monopoly capital to "late" or multinational capital, but rather in terms of a political struggle within the broader confines of an imperial economy.

New Historicism cannot transcend the imperialist horizon of modernist criticism, but it occupies a different position within it. This new position, as I have been suggesting, enables a focus on concrete, as opposed to merely analogical, relations between metropole and periphery, with the result that attention to the cultural dynamics of ethnography supplements interest in its findings. Indeed, in the case of Greenblatt's "Invisible Bullets," it may be necessary to refine Donald Pease's contention that colonialism becomes the internalized norm of Renaissance culture and say instead that this norm is provided by ethnography itself. It is, after all, the "recording of alien voices"[84] that in Greenblatt's essay binds together the activities of Thomas Harriot as colonial explorer and Prince Hal as Machiavellian penetrator and assimilator of a lower-class milieu. Both internal and external colonization are predicated here on the production of ethnographic knowledge. As did the modernists, Greenblatt brings Shakespeare into relation with non-Western culture; only now, the emphasis does not fall on any direct comparison between the Algonquians and the English lower classes. Non-Western cultures illuminate the West not as storehouses of comparable myths and practices but because they are subjected to a shared form of ethnographic scrutiny. The other, one might say, is no longer a source of direct cultural content but a position within an epistemic regime. Indeed, the other makes an appearance only as the product of specific relations of the production of ethnographic knowledge.

"Invisible Bullets" is organized by ethnographic allegory, by which I mean the establishment of ethnography as a model both for the internal structure of Renaissance culture *and* for the New Historicist's analysis of that culture. Thomas Harriot's recording of alien voices is replicated not only within the *Henriad* by Prince Hal, but also by Shakespeare as author of the *Henriad*, and, at yet another level, by Greenblatt himself as recorder of the now "alien" voices of Renaissance culture. Modernist Shakespeare criticism had also made the Renaissance a subject of ethnographic inquiry, thereby producing certain methodological dilemmas. Greenblatt's work does not—indeed, cannot—resolve these dilemmas, but it does adopt a different view of them. Formalist and aesthetic appropriation, or an alienating historicism—the two modernist alternatives—are rejected in favor of a process of "negotiation" with the cultural past in which both its differences and its points of contact with the present are brought into play.[85] The very term "negotiation" sug-

84. Greenblatt, *Shakespearean Negotiations*, p. 48. Similar concerns emerge in Steven Mullaney's essay "Strange Things, Gross Terms, Curious Customs: The Rehearsal of Cultures in the Late Renaissance," *Representations* 3 (1983): 40–67. In fact, much of what I have said about "Invisible Bullets" applies to Mullaney's essay as well.

85. See, e.g., Greenblatt's remarks in *Shakespearean Negotiations*, p. 6.

gests a relationship of address or interchange—no longer the production of "objective" knowledge about the Renaissance as cultural other, but an ethnographic engagement with it as a kind of partner in dialogue, with whom various modes of relation may be worked out. Thus Thomas Harriot's "testing" of certain hypotheses through interchanges with an alien society provides a model for Greenblatt's own work as historical critic. In this sense the literary critic is less a salaried, middle-class shaman than a salaried, middle-class ethnographer (a much less paradoxical notion). The difficulty of speaking with the "dead" is not that *they* are dead but that their *culture* is; yet this historical estrangement allows negotiated encounters. The dead are not dead, they are merely other.

My discussion of Stephen Greenblatt's work has thus far focused on the question of the "Renaissance" as the cultural subject of ethnographic inquiry. It has not addressed the specific place of Shakespeare, or the texts of his plays, within this field. The issue is important, since one of the defining characteristics of New Historical criticism is a certain decentering of the text in relation to the critical project. "Invisible Bullets" includes a reading of some important elements of the *Henriad*, but its historical materials are not mere background to the plays. Rather, the essay cultivates an irresolution about the relation between text and context, so that the *Henriad* may be seen either as that which is illuminated by the discussion of Harriot or as just another window through which to view Renaissance culture. Since the essay posits Shakespeare's authorial activity as one of recording alien voices, it seems to place him in the role of ethnographer, along with Harriot, Prince Hal, and Greenblatt himself. Or rather, he hovers uncertainly between the positions of subject and object of ethnographic knowledge.

What is Shakespeare's place in the range of structured positions established by an ethnographic model? Neither clearly ethnographer nor clearly "native," he occupies some third position, at once conduit and datum of historical information. I would suggest that his role is that of the native informant who offers a kind of privileged access to his culture. Both translator and betrayer, the native informant mediates the process of negotiation necessary to the ethnographer's or colonist's work. Greenblatt's book *Marvelous Possessions* ends with a chapter titled "The Go-Between," which focuses on the role played by the translator and informant Doña Marina in Cortés's conquest of Mexico. The figure of the native guide appears as well in one of Greenblatt's earliest essays, "Learning to Curse: Aspects of Linguistic Colonialism in the Sixteenth

Century.''[86] That essay closes with a consideration of Caliban's well-known lines in *The Tempest*:

> I prithee let me bring thee where crabs grow;
> And I with my long nails will dig thee pig-nuts,
> Show thee a jay's nest, and instruct thee how
> To snare the nimble marmazet. I'll bring thee
> To clust'ring filberts, and sometimes I'll get thee
> Young scamels from the rock. (2.2.167–72)[87]

Caliban plays many roles in *The Tempest*, but here he clearly serves as native informant. As the lone instance of his kind, he has no tribe about which to report, so he tells his new masters Stephano and Trinculo about the "qualities of th'isle"; yet his structural role is the same. Greenblatt comments on these lines:

> The rich, irreducible concreteness of the verse compels us to acknowl-edge the independence and integrity of Caliban's construction of re-ality. We do not sentimentalize this construction—indeed the play insists that we judge it and that we prefer another—but we cannot make it vanish into silence. Caliban's world has what we may call *opacity*, and the perfect emblem of that opacity is the fact that we do not to this day know the meaning of the word "scamel."[88]

This passage, it seems to me, maps out with unusual clarity the transition from a New Critical stance to what would come to be known as a New Historical one. The residues of the New Criticism inhere in Greenblatt's insistence on the "rich, irreducible concreteness of the verse," and on the imaginative integrity of Caliban's linguistic world. Yet Greenblatt ren-ders manifest the ethnographical problematic that informed the New Criticism by identifying the linguistic concreteness of poetry with the cultural integrity of an alien, non-Western society (even if it is, in this case, a society of one).

Moreover, Caliban's mediating role is overdetermined. Within the fic-

---

86. Originally printed in *First Images of America: The Impact of the New World on the Old*, ed. Fredi Chiapelli (Berkeley: University of California Press, 1976), pp. 561–80. Reprinted in Greenblatt, *Learning to Curse*, pp. 16–39.

87. *The Riverside Shakespeare*, ed. G. Blakemore Evans (Boston: Houghton Mifflin, 1974). All subsequent citations of the plays are from this edition.

88. Greenblatt, *Learning to Curse*, p. 31.

tion of the play, Caliban serves Stephano and Trinculo as informant and guide to his mysterious isle. Yet in Greenblatt's commentary, Caliban also mediates between us, the twentieth-century readers of the play, and the strange richness of Renaissance culture. Greenblatt remarks at the very end of the essay: "But as we are now beginning fully to understand, reality for each society is constructed to a significant degree out of the *specific* qualities of its language and symbols."[89] Although he is still speaking in the context of the discovery of the New World, his comments also adumbrate a core assumption of the New Historical approach to the English Renaissance, which, though less alien than "primitive" cultures, has its own historico-cultural opacity. Greenblatt's essay thus operates an ethnographic allegory which maps Caliban's isle onto the Renaissance. We, modern readers, are the Stephanos and Trinculos whose travels through a half-known landscape are made easier by the negotiations of a native guide. And our "Caliban" is Shakespeare, the poet-as-native-informant. It is Shakespeare, after all, who actually provides us with the puzzling word "scamel," thus signifying the irreducible particularity and opacity not of Caliban's culture, but of the culture of the English Renaissance. We are the disoriented visitors to Shakespeare's isle, not Caliban's.

If this allegory has a distinctly modernist flavor, it nevertheless reverses the polarities of its precursors. In Eliot's criticism, methodological problems pointed to an embedded colonial content. In the New Historicism, by contrast, colonialism becomes largely an allegory of method; that is to say, narratives of colonial encounters come to signify both the interpretive dilemmas and the interpretive possibilities of Renaissance historicism. The colonialist as ethnographer, negotiating his way through miasmas of "epistemic murk,"[90] stands in for the work of the historical critic in his exploration of a culturally foreign (yet directly contemporary) terrain. This situation is at once the fulfillment and the ironic inversion of the modernist reading of Shakespeare. For Eliot, Lewis, and Welles, the juxtaposition of Shakespeare and "primitive" cultures served as a kind of alienation effect, estranging the experience of a dramatist who, for the Victorians, had come to seem all-too-comfortably a national possession. Their Shakespeare, like the jaguar, eyes us savagely through the dense foliage of time. Our Shakespeare, more ambiguously, is both guide and quarry, leading us through a cultural landscape which, as in a dream, seems both alien and our own.

89. Ibid., p. 32.
90. This suggestive term is Michael Taussig's in his *Colonialism, Shamanism, and the Wild Man: A Study in Terror and Healing* (Chicago: University of Chicago Press, 1987).

2

That Shakespeherian Mob:
Mass Culture and the
Literary Public Sphere

By Easter of 1931, nearly three million people were out of work in Britain, and the unemployment insurance fund was more than 100 million pounds in debt. In the October general elections, the Labour Party was soundly defeated by the National Coalition. Meanwhile, the Nazi Party had won 107 seats in the Reichstag compared to 77 for the Communists. Against this backdrop, T. S. Eliot was writing editorials for *The Criterion* attacking socialist economic policies and what he took to be the debilitating effects of mass culture. He was also composing "Triumphal March" and "Difficulties of a Statesman," initially intended as parts of a much longer (and unfinished) series of poems but eventually published as the only two parts of *Coriolan*.[1]

In employing one of Shakespeare's Roman plays to give form to his own poetic reflections on mass politics, Eliot joined the ranks of more left-leaning modernists such as Bertolt Brecht and Orson Welles. Brecht adapted Shakespeare's play for his *Coriolanus* and drew on *Julius Caesar* for his novel *Die Geschaft des Herrn Julius Caesar*. Welles produced *Coriolanus* unsuccessfully for the W.P.A. in 1936, but the next year scored a stunning success with his modern-dress version of *Julius Caesar*. Welles's production, which portrayed Caesar as a fascist dictator and explored the violent incoherence of the fascist mob, was an exercise in, as well as a meditation on, mass politics. Prior to the

---

1. For both fact and phrasing, this paragraph is indebted to Russell Kirk, *Eliot and His Age: T. S. Eliot's Moral Imagination in the Twentieth Century* (New York: Random House, 1971), pp. 181–90.

opening, Welles flooded New York with a quarter of a million hand-
bills announcing:

JULIUS CAESAR
!!DEATH OF A DICTATOR!!

The Communist Party supplied theater groups which helped sustain the
production, and probably also served as a financial backer.[2]

Reviewing Welles's production for *The New Republic* (29 December
1937), Heywood Broun remarked that "Shakespeare has written so timely
and provocative a piece that the critics were actually arguing whether he fa-
vored fascism or communism or was perhaps a Trotskyite."[3] Shakespeare
was, in fact, a favorite of both left and right in the age of mass politics. His
were the most frequently staged non-Russian plays during the early years of
the Soviet government, with the first Soviet minister of education, Anatoli
Lunacharsky, displaying particular fondness for *Coriolanus* and *Julius Caesar.*[4] Shakespeare was also, conversely, the most-produced playwright in
Nazi Germany during the war years.[5]

While Shakespeare's Roman plays provided Marxists like Brecht with
a model for class struggle, they allowed figures as ideologically diverse as
T. S. Eliot, Wyndham Lewis, and Orson Welles to ponder the crises of
liberal culture brought on by monopoly capitalism, economic failure,
mass politics, and mass culture.[6] Among Shakespeare's works the Roman
plays assume singular importance for modern political thought because
it is there, and there alone, that something like an urban, public space
emerges. It is there too that charismatic, dictatorial leaders, the milita-
rized milieu of the Roman state, and the turbulent presence of the Ro-

2. Welles, *Orson Welles on Shakespeare*, pp. 18, 103, 108–9.

3. Quoted ibid., p. 20.

4. Louis Marder, *His Exits and His Entrances: The Story of Shakespeare's Reputation* (London:
John Murray, 1963), p. 356.

5. Alwin Thaler, *Shakespeare and Democracy* (Knoxville: University of Tennessee Press,
1941), p. 25. Lest it be thought that fascist appropriations of Shakespeare were limited to
Germany, however, see Terence Hawkes's fascinating essay "Shakespeare and the General
Strike" in his *Meaning by Shakespeare* (New York: Routledge, 1992), pp. 42–60.

6. Heywood Broun described Brutus in Welles's production as exemplifying "the unhappy fate of the liberal in a world torn by strife between the extreme left and the extreme
right." *Orson Welles on Shakespeare*, p. 104. Welles himself describes Brutus as "the classical
picture of the eternal, impotent, ineffectual, fumbling liberal; the reformer who wants to
do something about things but doesn't know how to and gets it in the neck in the end. . . .
He's the bourgeois intellectual, who, under a modern dictatorship would be the first to be
put up against a wall and shot." Welles, *The Mercury, A Weekly Bulletin of Information Concerning
the Mercury Theatre* [n.d.], quoted in John Ripley, *Julius Caesar on Stage in England and America
1599–1973* (New York: Cambridge University Press, 1980), p. 223.

man plebs seemed to anticipate the more chaotic developments of early twentieth-century politics.

But if Shakespeare's plays offered high modernists a language for articulating their anxieties about mass culture, they also registered an historical diminution of the literary space in which modernist protest could be heard. The reduction of modernism's literary public was itself seen as the splitting of what had been a relatively unified literary sphere into mass culture on the one hand and high-modernist and avant-gardist cultures on the other. Within this context, Shakespeare's status as a broadly popular playwright allowed modernism to chart its own relative cultural isolation. In his pamphlet *Mass Civilization and Minority Culture* (1930), F. R. Leavis writes:

> "Shakespeare," I once heard Mr. Dover Wilson say, "was not a highbrow." True: there were no "highbrows" in Shakespeare's time. It was possible for Shakespeare to write plays that were at once popular drama and poetry that could be appreciated only by an educated minority. *Hamlet* appealed at a number of levels of response, from the highest downwards. The same is true of *Paradise Lost, Clarissa, Tom Jones, Don Juan, The Return of the Native.* The same is not true . . . of *The Waste Land, Hugh Selwyn Mauberley, Ulysses,* or *To the Lighthouse.* These works are read only by a very small specialized public and are beyond the reach of the vast majority of those who consider themselves educated.[7]

Shakespeare stands at the historical threshold of a unified cultural public sphere which, Leavis maintains, seriously begins to unravel only toward the end of the nineteenth century. Of course, not all modernists regarded Shakespearean popularity as the sign of their own marginalization. Orson Welles produced Shakespeare's works and those of other Elizabethan playwrights (including Thomas Dekker's *The Shoemaker's Holiday*) in his attempt to construct a progressive and popular theater. Brecht's Shakespeare served similar purposes. But for the more conservative, elitist, or esoteric strains of modernism, Shakespeare embodied a now-unattainable cultural reach. Thus his specter occupied both ends of high modernism's paralyzing engagement with mass culture. The Roman plays embodied fears of mob rule and mass politics, while the example of Shakespeare's popularity only highlighted the apparent disappearance

7. F. R. Leavis, *Mass Civilization and Minority Culture* (Cambridge: Minority Press, 1930; rpt. Arden Library, 1979), p. 25.

of a cultural public forum within which modernist protest might have some effect.

The historical preconditions for mass culture, as I define it here, are the development of a mature industrial capitalism and its attendant conditions such as urban concentration, an industrial working class, electoral democracy, a hegemonic (broadly liberal) middle-class culture, and the beginnings of means of mass communication, such as newspapers and cheap printed books. These preconditions, established in England and America during the nineteenth century, allow a kind of proto-discourse on mass culture to form even before the modernist period. The "crisis" of mass culture during the early twentieth century depended on such further developments as the invention of electronic media, especially radio, film, and (later) television; the increasing concentration of these and other means of cultural production in the hands of economic monopolies and the consequent development of a "culture industry"; the rise of advertising and propaganda; the spread of mass production (Fordism, Taylorism); the crisis of electoral democracy as debated by Walter Lippmann, John Dewey and others; and the challenges to liberal hegemony initiated first by working-class movements and the Bolshevik revolution of 1917 and then later, in the 1930s, by widespread economic failure and unemployment and by the rise of fascism. By "mass culture" I therefore mean a set of global conditions reorganizing the totality of cultural production and consumption in modern culture rather than a specific *class* culture. Mass culture is not the expression of some pre-existing social group known as "the masses"; it is, rather, the sum of the conditions that *produce* the historically unprecedented phenomenon of massification and that reorganize the relations of different class cultures as they had developed during the nineteenth century. I thus wish to distinguish the field of my investigation here from that which defines the long tradition of studies on Shakespeare and the "popular."[8]

As it is generally used, however, "mass culture" nevertheless connotes popular culture as produced within the global framework outlined above, and the term carries with it an ineradicably demotic charge. It is impossible simply to oppose the concepts of mass and popular culture, just as it is wrong to collapse their meanings together. In what follows, then, I shall focus at times on the emergence of a mass popular culture from older popular forms. High modernism adopts an array of attitudes toward this massified popular culture but for the most part sees itself as an elite

8. For a survey of this tradition as well as a recent example of it, see Annabel Patterson, *Shakespeare and the Popular Voice* (Cambridge, Mass.: Basil Blackwell, 1989).

alternative to it (and sometimes an antagonist of it), even as it sometimes quotes, cites, and draws inspiration from it. Modernist discourse about mass culture tends also to merge with an older thematic of the "mob," a term which originates in classical antiquity but becomes re-energized after the French revolution of the eighteenth and the working-class uprisings of the nineteenth century, engenders a whole (pseudo-) science of "crowd psychology" in the late nineteenth and early twentieth century, and is refigured yet again with the rise of fascism. In what follows I shall make little effort to distinguish between the "masses" and the "mob" because it seems to me that modernism itself made little effort to do so.

"A plague of undifferentiation"

In *The Lion and the Fox*, Wyndham Lewis sees the public's inability to appreciate Shakespeare's grandeur as the sign of an uncontrollable leveling drive in modern culture:

> To-day . . . in the universal organized revolt against authority it is not only the head of a state or the head of a family—the king (on account of political privilege), the man (on account of sex privilege), the employer (on account of his monopoly of wealth)—but, with an ingenious thoroughness, every form of even the most modest eminence, that is attacked. . . . The revolutionary waves, again, have long extended the scope of their action, and have found fresh "kings" or leaders in every province of life. It is in the course of this universal king-hunt, naturally, that the revolutionary crowd arrives, sooner or later, beneath the statue of William Shakespeare. The poet, a forefinger pressed upon his temple, gazes pensively at the assemblage, his short fat calves crossed; one toe pressing his pedestal, as one finger presses his temple. The revolutionary crowd exults. This is evidently a king of some sort! It is not a moment to be on a pedestal, as the monumental Shakespeare must already have had many occasions, of late, of observing.[9]

In its assault on Shakespeare, part of the larger "herd-war against the head," Lewis's mob embodies the primary threat felt by conservatives in the face of a massified, democratic culture: the collapse of social and cultural *distinction*, for which Shakespeare here serves as a supreme em-

9. Lewis, *Lion and Fox*, pp. 135–36.

bodiment. Lewis's refrain is taken up, some years later, by the Shakespeare scholar A. L. Rowse, who applies it to Elizabethan culture as a whole in his 1952 presidential address to the English Association: "The age valued ability—it did not hamper and discourage it at every turn, in the interests of a monotonous sameness not worth having. The Elizabethans appreciated quality, in the objects they made with their hands no less than in things of the mind—so not unnaturally their products in both kinds exemplify the sense of quality which the standardized products of a mass-civilization, a herd-society, can never do."[10] Rowse employs Shakespeare and Elizabethan society generally in a direct and unapologetic attack on the policies of the Labour government. Unlike Lewis, he does not conjure up revolutionary mobs sweeping down the streets, but the structure of his anxiety is even more characteristic of conservative modernism's reaction to mass culture. What Rowse fears is not class conflict, not a clashing of irreconcilable opposites, but rather an entropic dispersion and leaking away of difference, a gradual lapse into monotony and sameness—not a bang but a whimper. In this characteristically modernist nightmare, class warfare is almost an object of nostalgia, since it offers at least an articulation of contrasts, and not a disorienting slide into the mass.

The modernists, and to some extent the Victorians before them, saw the primary conflicts in modern culture less as a struggle between rich and poor than as a confrontation between the large and the small, or the individual and the mass. Carlyle wrote *Heroes and Hero-Worship*, he claimed, precisely because the modern age does not worship, or even tolerate, heroes.[11] Ford Madox Ford complained that the standardizing and leveling effects of democracy, mass education, and mass culture had led to the "passing of the great figure" which had so dominated Victorian culture: writers like Carlyle, Ruskin, Mill, Newman, Arnold, Tennyson, and George Eliot.[12] This outlook not only inspires Wyndham Lewis's fantasy of Shakespeare and the revolutionary crowd but informs his very conception of Shakespearean tragedy, in which he sees the overthrow of Shakespeare's "colossi" or tragic heroes by puny, insignificant opponents: "So Iago is the *small* destroyer, the eternal Charlie Chaplin figure of human myth, the gods on his side, their instrument in their struggle with the hero. . . . He is the ideal *little man* with the sling and the stone. Othello is the ideal human galleon, twenty storeys high, with his head in

10. A. L. Rowse, *A New Elizabethan Age?* (London: Oxford University Press, 1952), p. 7.
11. Carlyle, *Heroes and Hero-Worship*, p. 12.
12. Levenson, *Genealogy of Modernism*, pp. 50–51.

the clouds, that the little can vanquish." Tragedy is thus for Lewis "in its essence democratic and religious, the enemy of human energy and success, . . . the opponent of action."[13] In the fall of Shakespeare's tragic heroes, Lewis views the democratic resentment that will result in a mass culture. Conversely, the imaginary crowd that assaults Shakespeare's statue simply reenacts the structure of Shakespearean tragedy, which now returns to haunt its creator.

Lewis would no doubt have found a chilling corroboration of his fears in the title and cover illustration of one of the numerous prose summaries of Shakespeare's plays marketed in the late nineteenth and early twentieth centuries for a popular readership. *Shakespere Boiled Down*, published by the New Home Sewing Machine Company of Chicago (1890), was largely an advertising gimmick designed to associate the Bard's cultural prestige with a brand-name product. The pamphlet's cover featured a portrait of the Bard slowly simmering in an oversized pot (see Figure 2). But this commodified context had a reciprocal influence on the reception of Shakespeare's plays. Boiling Shakespeare's works down to their narrative bones reduces the sheer labor of reading entire plays, just as the New Home sewing machine presumably reduces the labor of making clothes. By eliminating the difficulties as well as the beauties of Shakespearean language, and by reducing the plays to easily memorizable plots, such prose summaries allowed a mass readership to assume at least the veneer of a high-cultural education.

The cover illustration to *Shakespere Boiled Down* thus literalizes the pamphlet's effects by converting the plays into objects of (alimentary) *consumption*, here allied with the mass marketing of sewing machines for the home. In addition, the image suggests a fundamental cultural ambivalence in which reading Shakespeare's works is viewed as being at once "good for you" (i.e., figuratively "nutritious," like a soup or stew), and a chore which one tries to make as effortless and painless as possible. This cultural ambivalence finds its expression in the "boiling down" of the great man—that is to say, reducing him in stature so as to fit more comfortably into a democratized and massified culture. (To his credit, it must be said that Shakespeare endures his culinary fate with wonderful impassiveness). Wyndham Lewis's anxieties about his age are here reflected back to him from a mass cultural image in which the lineaments of the colossus or great figure are slowly reduced to a shapeless concoction, the unindividuated fluid of the crowd.

While "Shakespere Boiled Down" gives off a decidedly home-cooked

---

13. Lewis, *Lion and Fox*, pp. 189, 170.

Figure 2. "Shakespeare Boiled Down" (New Home Sewing Machine Co., Chicago, 1890). By permission of the Folger Shakespeare Library.

aroma, it also recalls a more exotic dish: missionary stew, prepared in the cannibal's pot. This condensation of the foreign and the domestic may recall the "tropical" Shakespeare of Chapter 1. In fact, modernism had frequent recourse to the "primitive" in attempting to come to grips with mass culture. In *The Lion and the Fox*, Wyndham Lewis justifies his use of *The Golden Bough* by claiming that "the institutions of the primitive herd approximate to something that can be found, in however degenerate a form, in any herd at all."[14] African societies thus provide him with an imaginary lens onto both Shakespeare and mass culture. The primitive and the modern "herd" converge as well in the roughly contemporary discourse of crowd psychology. The most widely known of the crowd psychologists, the Frenchman Gustave Le Bon, writes that "by the mere fact that he forms part of an organized crowd, a man descends several rungs on the ladder of civilization. Isolated, he may be a cultivated in-dividual; in the crowd, he is a barbarian—that is, a creature acting by instinct. He possesses the spontaneity, the violence, the ferocity, and also the enthusiasm and heroism of primitive beings."[15]

It was de rigueur in the writings of crowd psychologists to make at least passing reference to Marc Antony's funeral oration in act 3, scene 2 of *Julius Caesar*.[16] Antony's speech was taken as a model for how to exploit the suggestibility of crowds, particularly by appealing to their imaginative and visual faculties. The writings of the crowd psychologists penetrated into Shakespeare criticism indirectly through their influence on the mod-ernists and directly through an essay published in the 1912 *Publications of the Modern Language Association*. "The Shakesperean Mob," by Frederick Tupper, Jr., tried to demonstrate how Shakespeare's Roman plays cor-roborated the view of the crowd described by Le Bon, Gabriel Tarde, Boris Sidis, and Edward Alsworth Ross.[17] Tupper traces the "disaggrega-tion of consciousness" undergone by the crowds in *Coriolanus* and *Julius Caesar*, their visual and tactile excitability, and the dominance of a "reflex consciousness" which causes "mob-energy" to pass like an electrical charge from one auditor to another.

A single essay in *PMLA*, of course, hardly constitutes a literary move-ment. Tupper was not the only writer in this period to apply the princi-

14. Ibid., p. 138.

15. Gustave Le Bon, *The Crowd: A Study of the Popular Mind* (1895; New York: Viking, 1960), p. 32.

16. See, for instance, ibid., pp. 69–70; Boris Sidis, *The Psychology of Suggestion* (New York: D. Appleton, 1911), p. 12; Edward Alsworth Ross, *Social Psychology* (New York: Macmillan, 1908), p. 21.

17. Frederick Tupper, Jr., "The Shakesperean Mob," *PMLA* 27 (1912): 486–523.

ples of crowd psychology to literary matters,[18] yet his portrait of the Shakespearean mob is interesting more for its resemblances to Wyndham Lewis's than for suggesting some wholesale influx of crowd psychology into Shakespeare criticism.[19] Still, his work is not quite the dead-end it may seem, and the intellectual matrix that gave rise to it survives even today—and nowhere more clearly, I believe, than in the work of the French critic René Girard. One of Girard's recent essays, both representative of his persistent concerns and unusually germane to my purposes, is "Collective Violence and Sacrifice in *Julius Caesar.*"[20] Here Girard has chosen a play which submits with exemplary ease to his interest in the figure of the scapegoat. Caesar, Girard shows, is chosen as sacrificial victim by Brutus not because of his difference from him but because of his resemblance to him. Brutus's envy then spreads through mimetic contagion to the other conspirators and finally to the crowd in the Roman Forum. For Girard, Caesar's murder is a scapegoating ritual, a purgative act of collective violence triggered by the collapse of social differences within the Roman Republic.

Girard's reading of *Julius Caesar* exhibits striking similarities both to the theories of the crowd psychologists and to modernist discourse on the masses. His notion of "mimetic suggestibility," for example,[21] strongly recalls the crowd psychologists on the suggestibility of the mob. His description of the crowd in the Forum likewise echoes the crowd psychologists on the subrational and "primitive" thought processes of the mob.[22] Importing an anthropological model of scapegoating and sacrificial ritual to explain the logic of the crowd only reinforces his ties to figures such as Le Bon and Lewis who see in the primitive an analogue to the modern mob mentality. Even more telling is Girard's insistence on the fact that rivalry always occurs between doubles, and that outbreaks of collective violence generally indicate a collapse of the social distinctions that serve to order and contain society. "When mimetic rivalry escalates beyond a certain point, the rivals engage in endless conflict which undifferentiates

18. See Henry Dwight Sedgwick, "The Mob Spirit in Literature," in his collection *The New American Type and Other Essays* (Boston: Houghton Mifflin, 1908), pp. 25–50.

19. John Palmer's *Political Characters of Shakespeare* (London: Macmillan, 1948), pp. 20–23 includes a discussion of oratory and the mob in *Julius Caesar* which clearly (though implicitly) employs the major premises of the crowd psychologists.

20. René Girard, "Collective Violence and Sacrifice in *Julius Caesar,*" *Salmagundi*, no. 88–89 (Fall 1990–Winter 1991): 399–419.

21. Ibid., p. 401.

22. Girard writes of the crowd in the Forum: "A mob never lacks 'subjective' and 'objective' reasons for tearing its victims to pieces. The more numerous the reasons, the more insignificant they really are." Ibid., p. 409.

them more and more; . . . What Shakespeare portrays [in *Julius Caesar*] is no conflict of differences, but a plague of undifferentiation."[23] In the "plague of undifferentiation" Girard imagines just that collapse of cultural distinctions of which modernists such as Eliot and Lewis had long complained.

Girard's theories of "mass" or collective social phenomena depend, of course, on a crucial figure whom I have not yet had occasion to mention: Friedrich Nietzsche, who inhabits a line running from Carlyle to Wyndham Lewis and beyond.[24] Just as Girard's preoccupation with envy clearly reworks the Nietzschean theme of *ressentiment* and the desire to drag the great man down to the level of the mass, so his emphasis on the theater as site of mimetic contagion recalls Nietzsche's contempt for the theater as a place of deindividualized, mass consciousness.[25]

These themes pervade all of Girard's Shakespeare criticism; what makes the essay on *Julius Caesar* of particular interest is the play's political context. For as Girard strongly suggests, a disastrous collapse of social distinction is somehow connected with the very form of the Roman republic, which he describes as "unraveling from top to bottom."[26] The chaotic permissiveness of Shakespeare's Rome, in which plebeians wander about as if on holiday, without the distinguishing signs of their craft, and engage in cheeky banter with the senatorial class, contributes to the "plague of undifferentiation" which overthrows the republic and ushers in Imperial rule.

Girard's political allegory here is almost painfully obvious. Republican Rome clearly stands in for liberal-democratic culture, which always threatens to invert itself, under pressure of massification, into one or another totalitarian form. It is certainly wrong to suggest, as Hayden White does, that Girard's social ideals would find their fulfillment in Nazi Germany.[27]

23. Ibid., pp. 400, 401.
24. For a brief, deft deconstruction of Girard's "feud" with Nietzsche, see Mihai Spariosu, "Mimesis and Contemporary French Theory," in Spariosu, ed., *Mimesis in Contemporary Theory: An Interdisciplinary Approach*, vol. 1, *The Literary and Philosophical Debate* (Philadelphia: John Benjamins, 1984), p. 107, n. 29. I am indebted to Louis Burkhardt for this reference.
25. "No one brings along the finest senses of his art to the theater, nor does the artist who works for the theater. There one is common people, audience, herd, female, pharisee, voting cattle, democrat, neighbor, fellow man; there even the most personal conscience is vanquished by the leveling magic of the great number; there stupidity has the effect of lasciviousness and contagion; the neighbor reigns, one becomes a mere neighbor." Friedrich Nietzsche, *The Gay Science*, trans. Walter Kaufmann (New York: Random House, 1974), p. 326.
26. Girard, "Collective Violence," p. 401.
27. Hayden White, "Ethnological 'Lie' and Mystical 'Truth,' " *Diacritics* 8, no. 1 (Spring 1978): 8.

Rather, it seems to me, his work should be understood as a kind of repetition compulsion prompted by the traumatic rise of European fascism in the 1930s. Girard's emphasis on the scapegoat reacts primarily to the Nazi thirst for new "others" to victimize—Communists, gypsies, homosexuals, Jews—and his interest in "mimetic contagion" recalls the terror of the fascist crowd. That this political context should surface so clearly in a discussion of *Julius Caesar* is hardly surprising, given the fact that fascism borrowed so much of its symbolism and heraldry (indeed, its very name) from ancient Roman culture. Girard, of course, reserves at least as much vituperative energy for the political Left as for the Right, and his anxious attachment to the preservative powers of social distinction is conservative, if not downright reactionary, in its force. He is to be grouped less with anti-fascist progressives like Orson Welles than with conservatives like Eliot, with whom he shares an apparent conviction regarding the "anarchic" and ultimately self-destructive nature of liberal culture, as well as nostalgia for an imagined *Gemeinschaft* held together by the force of religious ritual.

It is in response to the perceived threat of mass culture as a specifically *undifferentiating* force that the modernist conception of Shakespeare's popularity takes shape. In the passage from F. R. Leavis quoted earlier in this chapter, Shakespeare's plays appeal to a broad cultural audience yet maintain cultural and class distinctions within the unifying field they construct. The same principle, expressed even more strongly, appears in Eliot's "The Use of Poetry and the Use of Criticism":

> The most useful poetry, socially, would be one which could cut across all the present stratifications of public taste—stratifications which are perhaps a sign of social disintegration. The ideal medium for poetry, to my mind, and the most direct means of social 'usefulness' for poetry, is the theatre. In a play of Shakespeare you get several levels of significance. For the simplest auditors there is the plot, for the more thoughtful the character and conflict of character, for the more literary the words and phrasing, for the more musically sensitive the rhythm, and for auditors of greater sensitiveness and understanding a meaning which reveals itself gradually.[28]

For Eliot, as for Leavis, Shakespeare's broad popularity overcomes the "stratification of public taste" which now results in the cultural isolation

---

28. T. S. Eliot, *The Use of Poetry and the Use of Criticism* (Cambridge: Harvard University Press), p. 153.

of high modernism. Yet—and this is the point—Shakespeare unifies a public sphere without simply erasing boundaries of discrimination, as mass culture is held to do. Shakespearean popularity thus locates a dilemma in modernist thought: the very unification of the public sphere which the modernists desired also held the perceived threat of a chaotic blurring of difference. Shakespeare's overcoming of stratification and his appeal to a unified public has as its terrifying double mass culture's collapse of stratification and its creation of an undifferentiated public.[29] Shakespeare's cultural "work" in this context is to embody a cultural public space in which distinctions are not so impermeable as to lead to social disintegration—yet not so fragile as to give way altogether. (An analogous dream of unity-in-degree undergirds E. M. W. Tillyard's *The Elizabethan World Picture*, with its elegantly ranked yet harmoniously orchestrated hierarchies.)[30] If Shakespeare's Roman plays illustrated for the modernists the threat of mass culture, Shakespeare himself represented a longed-for reconciliation of forces which, unchecked, had seemed to produce at once unbridgeable division and terrifying anarchy.

Fantasies of the turbulent, demotic crowd may suggest—wrongly—that modernist anxiety about mass culture is merely a thinly veiled fear of the working classes. While it is certainly true that proletarian organization and agitation enters into the discourse of mass culture, modernist discomfort results rather from a blurring of class lines, and with it the fading of a clearly defined class enemy. As Stanley Aronowitz observes, "Plainly, the masses include the mass of the middle classes. Indeed, for de Tocqueville and Ortega on the right, as for Veblen on the left, the urban middle class is invariably the bearer of cultural degeneration."[31] To this list Aronowitz might also have added Matthew Arnold, for whom middle-class philistinism was the primary threat to his ideal of culture. Eliot, too, regarded the collapse of cultural standards as a result of the rule of "a class so democratised that whilst still a class it represents itself to be the whole nation."[32] Middle-class materialism, vulgarity, and utilitarianism

29. This distinction between a Shakespearean and a mass-cultural audience is at times precarious even for Eliot, who describes Elizabethan theater-goers as "an alert, curious, semi-barbarous public, fond of beer and bawdry, including much the same sort of people whom one encounters in the local outlying theatres to-day, craving cheap amusement to thrill their emotions, arouse their mirth and satisfy their curiosity." Eliot, *Use of Poetry*, p. 44.

30. E. M. W. Tillyard, *The Elizabethan World Picture* (London: Chatto & Windus, 1943).

31. Stanley Aronowitz, "Is a Democracy Possible? The Decline of the Public in the American Debate," in *The Phantom Public Sphere*, ed. Bruce Robbins (Minneapolis: University of Minnesota Press, 1993), p. 77.

32. Eliot, *Use of Poetry*, p. 13.

were, if anything, the primary class targets of both modernist and Arnoldian polemic. Mass culture was seen less as a popular or working-class invention than as the internal devolution and degeneration of liberal, middle-class culture.

An anti-philistine strain can be detected in Shakespeare criticism at least as early as 1853, when Walter Bagehot insisted on Shakespeare's "disbelief in the middle classes" and "contempt for the perspicacity of the *bourgeoisie*."[33] More interesting, perhaps, is the influence of middle-class tastes on the staging of Shakespeare's plays, and the reaction against it. The Victorian period saw the rise of spectacle in Shakespearean production. An 1875 *Antony and Cleopatra*, costing between four and five thousand pounds to produce, actually staged the sea fights and barge scene which are only described in Shakespeare's play. Earlier productions include a *King Lear* with violent storms and a *Coriolanus* with two hundred senators in togas. Beerbohm Tree (1853–1917) caught the spirit of the age when he declared that the public wanted Shakespeare staged "as munificently as the manager can afford."[34]

The use of spectacle in Shakespearean production raised warnings from such critics as A. C. Bradley and Sidney Lee. Lee deplored the "plethora of scenic spectacle and gorgeous costume, much of which the student regards as superfluous and inappropriate." Citing Hamlet, Lee expresses his contempt for modern "groundlings . . . capable of nothing but inexplicable dumb shows and noise": "They would be hugely delighted nowadays with a scene in which two real motor cars, with genuine chauffeurs and passengers, raced uproariously across the stage."[35]

The rise of spectacle in Shakespearean production clearly foreshadows certain elements of a mass-cultural aesthetic. The Victorian *Antony and Cleopatra* described above is a distant ancestor of Cecil B. De Mille's 1934 film and of the 1963 *Cleopatra* with Elizabeth Taylor. But who are the "groundlings" denounced by Sidney Lee? Precisely the bourgeois patrons who could afford the high ticket prices for such a performance. In their study of Shakespeare and mass culture at the turn of the century, Roberta E. Pearson and William Uricchio note that working-class audiences who attended inexpensive Shakespearean productions and one-man recitals did not seem to share this middle-class need for spectacle. When Shakespeare's plays began to be made into films (largely in an

33. Walter Bagehot, "Shakespeare the Man," rpt. in *Shakespearean Classics* (New York: University Society, 1903), pp. 36, 37.
34. Marder, *His Exits*, pp. 43, 70–77.
35. Sidney Lee, *Shakespeare and the Modern Stage* (New York: Scribner's, 1906), pp. 2, 23. See also A. C. Bradley, *Oxford Lectures on Poetry* (London: Macmillan, 1926), pp. 388–93.

effort to add cultural respectability to the early nickelodeons), the 1908 Vitagraph production of *Julius Caesar* "employed the spectacle of the higher-priced theatre rather than the stark presentations of, for example, the Ben Greet Company."[36] The mass-cultural taste for spectacle, then, seems to filter down into Shakespearean production from bourgeois theater and the culture industry instead of percolating up from working-class entertainment. In any case, Shakespearean production during the modernist period tended to abjure this Victorian taste for spectacle. The rising popularity of modern-dress versions in the 1920s continued a reaction against spectacle (and, more broadly, mass culture) which began with William Poel's "Elizabethan" productions of the plays.

Similar lessons about mass culture and social class emerge from Lawrence W. Levine's book *Highbrow/Lowbrow*. Levine's highly informative and entertaining chapter on Shakespeare effectively argues the following points: in nineteenth-century America Shakespeare's plays were a broadly popular form of entertainment; the audience at Shakespearean performances came from all strata of American society, constituting a kind of social microcosm; Shakespeare was therefore the index of a shared public culture; and the marked decrease in Shakespeare's popularity from the mid-nineteenth to the mid-twentieth century results from his appropriation by certain social groups who presented his works in an alienating fashion in both theaters and schools.

Levine's book seems to confirm, for the American case at least, the belief of modernists such as Leavis and Eliot that Shakespeare had both represented and helped to constitute something like a universal public sphere which crossed class divisions, and that this broad cultural realm had persisted until relatively recent times. What Levine's book disproves is the modernist assumption of hierarchized cultural taste and discrimination within the Shakespearean audience. This audience constituted something like a plebeian public sphere, meaning one that incorporated working class strata among others.

Levine emphasizes not only the broad class composition of the Shakespearean audience but also its reactive, critical, and sometimes disruptive character: "To envision nineteenth-century theater audiences correctly, one might do well to visit a contemporary sporting event in which the spectators not only are similarly heterogeneous but are also—in the manner of both the nineteenth century and the Elizabethan era—more than

36. Roberta E. Pearson and William Uricchio, "How Many Times Shall Caesar Bleed in Sport: Shakespeare and the Cultural Debate about Moving Pictures," *Screen* 31, no. 3 (Autumn 1990): 258–59.

an audience; they are participants who can enter into the action on the field, who feel a sense of immediacy and at times even of control, who articulate their opinions and feelings vocally and unmistakably." [37] (One cannot help thinking here of the crowd in *Julius Caesar*'s crown-offering ceremony, who applaud and hiss Caesar "as he pleased and displeased them.") Only when theatrical audiences became sharply segregated by class was this critical, dialogical interaction replaced by quiet, dignified spectatorship. In other words, it is the bourgeois theater which, by the late nineteenth century, begins to encourage the passive habits of "consumption" that also characterize mass culture.

Thus it is all the more ironic that Shakespeare has recently been enlisted in the crusades of conservative educational critics who wish to purge university curricula of multicultural and mass-cultural materials. As an undisputed "classic" of English literature, Shakespeare is ranged against the trashy and debased products of American pop culture. Yet historically, Shakespeare has often both depended upon and furthered the intercontamination of different cultural realms. The popularity of Shakespeare's plays throughout the eighteenth and nineteenth centuries depended on their almost always sharing the same theatrical bill with popular and farcical interludes, afterpieces, *divertissements*, and other forms of light entertainment.[38] Levine argues that while the presence of these supplementary forms does not mean that people didn't like Shakespeare's plays or appreciate their finer points, it is nevertheless true that when they were removed in the late nineteenth and early twentieth centuries to allow the production of "pure" Shakespeare, theatrical attendance declined considerably.[39] Shakespeare's continuing preeminence among English playwrights thus depended upon his sharing the stage with cultural "trash." Conversely, Shakespeare's plays—and particularly *Julius Caesar*—have helped sustain marginalized and derided cultural media by lending them an air of legitimacy. Shakespeare's works, for instance, were staged to help overcome a widespread anti-theatrical prejudice in eighteenth- and early nineteenth-century America, and were crucial in securing acceptance for the theater as a legitimate cultural institution. In the early days of cinema, too, fifteen-minute versions of

37. Levine, *Highbrow/Lowbrow: The Emergence of Cultural Hierarchy in America* (Cambridge: Harvard University Press, 1988), p. 26.

38. Ibid., pp. 21–23, 33–34; Esther Cloudman Dunn, *Shakespeare in America* (New York: Macmillan, 1939), pp. 66, 70, 142, 171; Marder, *His Exits*, pp. 61–62.

39. Levine, *Highbrow/Lowbrow*, pp. 33–34.

Shakespeare's plays were produced in abundance to counter charges that films were immoral and culturally degrading.[40] The first of these was the 1908 Vitagraph production of *Julius Caesar*, which itself caused a commotion. (Charges of immorality were raised when Caesar was shown in a "short skirt" and the Chicago police demanded cutting of the film's assassination scene.)[41] Subsequent films often staged the Bard's works in popularizing modern settings, as in *Taming Mrs. Shrew* (Rex 1912) and *A Galloping Romeo* (Selig 1913).[42] Orson Welles chose *Julius Caesar* to open the new Mercury Theatre in 1937. And when Classics Illustrated began publishing its comic-book versions of Shakespeare's plays in the 1950s, the first title released was again *Julius Caesar* (February 1950).[43] Each of these choices was probably influenced by local factors (the conspirators in the Classics Illustrated version, for instance, clearly resonated with the anti-Communist hysteria of the period, while the figure of the popular general recently returned from foreign victories found its real counterpart in Eisenhower or MacArthur), but other, more secular determinants were also involved. One, of course, was the perennial use of *Julius Caesar* as a high school text, which made it relatively familiar to a mass audience. Another was the play's own concern with the interplay between an elite patrician culture and a "mass" audience, which allowed such hybrid cultural forms to reflect on their own status. In depicting Antony's funeral oration on its cover, the Classics Illustrated version imaged its own "mission" of bringing literary masterpieces to the people (see Figure 3).

The subsequent history of *Julius Caesar* thus enacts the play's own thematic (to be analyzed in the following section) of interpenetrating cultural spaces. While modernism decries the splitting of a unified reading public into elite and mass spheres (yet jealously guards the boundaries between them), the role of Shakespeare in popular and early mass culture suggests a less anxious (if not entirely untroubled) and certainly less exclusive relation between "high" and "low" culture. Indeed, Shakespeare contributes to the modernists' dreaded "plague of undifferentiation" by helping to erode the boundaries between cultural publics.

40. Pearson and Uricchio, "How Many Times," pp. 246–49.
41. Ibid., pp. 246–48.
42. Ibid., p. 248.
43. *Julius Caesar, Classics Illustrated* no. 68 (February 1950) (Folger Library Sh. misc. 1705).

Figure 3. Classics Illustrated no. 68, *Julius Caesar.* Copyright © 1950 and 1978 by the Frawley Corporation. All rights reserved by First Classics, Inc., with permission of the Frawley Corporation. *Classics Illustrated* is a registered trademark of the Frawley Corporation.

Vicissitudes of the Public Sphere

My discussion turns on two terms which, to this point at least, I have refrained from either defining with any precision or relating to each other: "mass culture" and "public sphere." The latter term in particular has become associated with the name of Jürgen Habermas. His book *Strukturwandel der Öffentlichkeit* (1962), translated as *The Structural Transformation of the Public Sphere* (1989), addresses the crisis of "public opinion" in post-liberal capitalism. It also constructs a distinctive historical narrative about the decay of the public sphere and the rise of mass culture which has become the focus of considerable debate.[44] Habermas's views on mass culture are clearly influenced by Frankfurt School figures such as Theodor Adorno and Max Horkheimer, but in a general way they also echo the views of more conservative English modernists such as Eliot and Leavis. I want to treat Habermas as an exemplary modernist here, and to test his narrative of the rise and decline of public culture against the case of Shakespeare's *Julius Caesar*.

As the subtitle of Habermas's book suggests, the public sphere is a "category of *bourgeois* society." It arises from a set of transformations which move political and aesthetic discourse from the court society of a late feudal aristocracy to a more public space occupied by bourgeois strata. The bourgeois public sphere originates in institutions such as the English coffeehouse and the French salon, which originally serve as sites for the critical discussion of arts and letters, but (in the English case especially) soon include economic and political disputes. From its literary origins, the bourgeois public sphere develops into a set of institutions and organs (including newspapers and journals) in which the property-owning classes debate issues relating to their interests in the newly created sphere of civil society.

While giving birth to new organs of debate, the public sphere also—and this, for Habermas, is its most crucial aspect—introduces new principles of social and political legitimation. In place of monarchical or aristocratic power, the public sphere relies on the principles of reason, justice, and law. Its governing assumption is that the people, exercising

44. Jürgen Habermas, *The Structural Transformation of the Public Sphere: An Enquiry into a Category of Bourgeois Society*, trans. Thomas Burger (Cambridge: MIT Press, 1989). Responses to, and developments of, Habermas's approach include Oskar Negt and Alexander Kluge, *Public Sphere and Experience*, trans. Peter Labanyi, Jamie Daniel, and Assenka Oksiloff (Minneapolis: University of Minnesota Press, 1993); *Habermas and the Public Sphere*, ed. Craig Calhoun (Cambridge: MIT Press, 1992); *The Phantom Public Sphere*, ed. Bruce Robbins (Minneapolis: University of Minnesota Press, 1993); *Public Culture* 5, no. 2 (Winter 1993).

the powers of critical reason in public debate, can arrive at a consensus on matters that concern them.

For Habermas, this new realm of public reason both arises from and depends on the relative separation of civil society (economy) and state inaugurated by capitalism. The market delineates both a space of private interest separate from the public realm of the state, and a field in which noncoercive negotiation among (putative) equals enables persuasion and reason, rather than power, to operate. The bourgeois public sphere is originally a space for public discussion of private matters, but in the course of the eighteenth century it engages the form of the state itself, which it submits to the glare of publicity and tries to make accountable to the dictates of public reason.

Habermas fully recognizes that the concept of critical reason as developed in the public sphere is ideological, since its apparent abstraction and universality presuppose a relative homogeneity of interests among the property-owning classes comprising the original bourgeois public. But he insists that the principle of critical reason also contains a nonideological and utopian principle. This, however, is compromised by the very conditions of its historical birth, for the capitalist marketplace, far from guarding against intrusions of power and safeguarding a relative equality of participants, magnifies differences of wealth and power. As the capitalist economy generates social and economic problems that cannot be contained through the (ideally) self-regulating field of the market, the state assumes a regulatory capacity which soon erodes the distinction of public and private on which the public sphere was founded. Moreover, the old ideal of a reasoned consensus in public debate gives way to compromise among irreconcilable interest groups when the working classes begin to demand a say. Thus the ideal of the bourgeois public sphere begins to dissolve, a process which begins under liberal capitalism but is accelerated by the growth of monopoly capital and the welfare state.

Of particular interest here is the section in Habermas's book entitled "From a Culture-Debating to a Culture-Consuming Public,"[45] which addresses the problem of mass culture. The "culture-debating public" is, of course, the bourgeoisie of the coffeehouses and salons who wrest from a court-based aristocracy the right to dispute literary and aesthetic matters. The reception of literary works in the context of critical reason leads, moreover, to an almost inevitable conjunction of literary and political debate, so that literary culture contains a politically critical element. Bounds are set on this debate by the fact that a commodified

45. Habermas, *Transformation*, pp. 159–75.

culture limits access to participants of a certain economic level, but Habermas insists (rightly or wrongly) that at first it is only the access to culture, and not the nature of the cultural products themselves, which is commodified.

Mass culture, for Habermas, begins when commodification extends from the form to the content of cultural artifacts—that is to say, when they begin to be produced "consumption-ready." A mass-cultural public, he argues, passively consumes rather than critically debates its literature and art. Consumption is essentially a privatized, isolated process, even if conducted in groups, and does not give rise to a communicational matrix. The consumptionary mode, moreover, is fostered not only by culture but by the welfare state, which serves as a distributor of services to be consumed rather than of policies to be debated, and which employs bureaucratic procedures that reduce the scope for public discussion. Mass media such as television and film discourage viewer response in comparison with older bourgeois organs such as the newspaper, with its spaces for readers' opinion and debate.

For Habermas, the degeneration of the public sphere results from structural transformations in the capitalist economy and state which effect fundamental changes in public communication. These changes are described in a passage from C. Wright Mills's *The Power Elite*, on the difference between a "public" and a "mass," which Habermas quotes approvingly near the end of his book (I will cite Habermas's long quotation selectively): "In a *public*, as we may understand the term, (1) virtually as many people express opinions as receive them. (2) Public communications are so organized that there is a chance immediately and effectively to answer back any opinion expressed in public. . . . In a *mass*, (1) far fewer people express opinions than receive them; for the community of publics becomes an abstract collection of individuals who receive impressions from the mass media. (2) The communications that prevail are so organized that it is difficult or impossible for the individual to answer back immediately or with any effect."[46] Mass culture, in this view, results from the breakdown of a dialogical system, rendering individuals only the receivers rather than the senders of opinion and information.

It might be argued that Habermas's assessment of mass culture is excessively pessimistic, and that he overlooks the scope for criticism, dialogue, and debate even within the consumption of mass culture. He nevertheless makes a compelling argument that certain structural trans-

46. C. Wright Mills, *The Power Elite* (New York: Oxford University Press, 1956), quoted in Habermas, *Transformation*, p. 249.

formations tend at least to discourage critical debate and to encourage passive consumption in both the cultural and political realms. In any case, Habermas's narrative of the decline of the public sphere provides a suggestive context for tracing the critical history of Shakespeare's Roman plays, especially *Julius Caesar,* and so I shall make abundant (if sometimes critical) use of it in what follows.

Shakespeare's works played a small but real role in shaping the bourgeois public sphere by training public speakers in the eighteenth and nineteenth centuries. Rhetorical manuals such as Thomas Sheridan's *A Course of Lectures on Elocution* (1762), William Enfield's *The Speaker* (1782), and Hugh Blair's *Lectures on Rhetoric and Belles Lettres* (1783) employed Shakespearean passages to illustrate both beauties and faults of oratorical style and to train speakers in expressive recitation. By subsuming literature within oratory, these works "testified . . . to the reigning conception of literature as a public or civic discourse fit for socializing future citizens."[47] Brutus's and Marc Antony's orations in *Julius Caesar* naturally occupied positions of honor within this tradition, not only because they were exemplary instances of rhetorical technique but because the wielding of public discourse by the Roman senatorial class offered the speakers of the bourgeois public sphere a flattering and culturally legitimating image for their own activity.[48]

Shakespearean allusions were also a significant resource for the eighteenth-century art of political caricature, an important new form of public debate. Writes Jonathan Bate: "The development in eighteenth-century England of a recognizably 'modern' political system was accompanied by the growth of caricature as an influential medium in the shaping of public opinion, and in particular as a manifestation of the (comparative) freedom of the Press and the opposition's right to criticize governments and ministers." The mechanical techniques and pictorial nature of the political prints allowed them to reach and radicalize a wide popular audience, although, as Bate points out, the primary consumers of this art were "the metropolitan middle ranks, . . . many of them from

47. Gerald Graff, *Professing Literature: An Institutional History* (Chicago: University of Chicago Press, 1987), p. 42.

48. In an introduction to Bell's edition of *Julius Caesar* (1773), Francis Gentleman wrote of the play: "We wish . . . our senators, as a body, were to bespeak it annually; that each would get most of it by heart; that it should be occasionally performed at both universities, and at every public seminary, of any consequence; so would the author receive distinguished, well-earned honour; and the public reap, we doubt not, essential service." Quoted in Michael Dobson, "Accents Yet Unknown: Canonisation and the Claiming of *Julius Caesar,*" in *The Appropriation of Shakespeare: Post-Renaissance Reconstructions of the Works and the Myth,* ed. Jean I. Marsden (New York: St. Martin's Press, 1991), p. 11.

a dissenting background, highly attuned to both cultural and political events, who were so crucial to the debates of the 1790s.''[49] Political caricaturists made abundant use of Shakespeare's plays as sources of readily recognized cultural and political allusion, and here again the Roman plays played a prominent role. The earliest of the many engravings in the British Museum's collection that allude to Shakespeare is George Bickenham's satiric comparison of Horace Walpole to Julius Caesar, *The Stature of a Great Man or the English Colossus* (March 1740).[50]

The idea of republican government generated intense and often ambivalent responses throughout Europe, and these found a powerful theatrical mirror in *Julius Caesar*, which could lend itself to pro- or anti-monarchical interpretations.[51] In England, the "Whig" acting text of the play, which became the dominant version from the 1690s through all of the eighteenth century, took a pro-Brutus stance, while the Duke of Buckingham's adaptations, *The Tragedy of Julius Caesar, altered* and *The Tragedy of Marcus Brutus* (both 1722), were distinctly royalist.[52] On the Continent, meanwhile, the abbé Conti's *Il Cesare* (1726), Voltaire's *La Mort de César* (1731), and Herder's *Brutus* (1774) all reworked Shakespeare's play to suit new political circumstances. Voltaire's play grew from the author's translations of Brutus's and Antony's orations, and, like its Shakespearean original, encoded a complex response toward the idea of republican government. *La Mort de César* enjoyed its greatest success during the Revolutionary period; it was staged no fewer than forty-eight times between 1790 and 1796. But it was presented in a revised version constructed by a government censor who found the play insufficiently republican, while in its original form it was embraced by anti-Jacobin groups during the Directorate.[53] Whatever political turn Shakespeare's

49. Jonathan Bate, *Shakespearean Constitutions: Politics, Theatre, Criticism 1730–1830* (Oxford: Clarendon, 1989), pp. 70, 6, 18–19.

50. Ibid., p. 70.

51. See Dennis Fletcher, "Three Authors in Search of a Character: Julius Caesar as Seen by Buckingham, Conti, and Voltaire," in *Mélanges à la mémoire de Franco Simone*, 4 vols. (Geneva: Slatkine, 1980-83), 2:439–53. On the (infrequent) comparisons between Cromwell's execution of Charles I and Brutus's assassination of Caesar, see Annabel Patterson, *Censorship and Interpretation: The Conditions of Writing and Reading in Early Modern England* (Madison: University of Wisconsin Press, 1984), pp. 152–54. The advertisement for a June 1770 performance of *Julius Caesar* at Philadelphia's Southwark Theater promised to depict "the noble struggles for Liberty by that renowned patriot Marcus Brutus." See John Ripley, *Julius Caesar on Stage in England and America 1599–1973* (New York: Cambridge University Press, 1980), p. 100.

52. See Dobson, "Accents Yet Unknown," pp. 13–21.

53. Critical introduction to *La Mort de César* by D. J. Fletcher, in *The Complete Works of Voltaire*, vol. 8 (Oxford: Voltaire Foundation, 1988), pp. 7–9, 103–7.

play was given by its different adapters, however, *Julius Caesar* provided both an ideological image for the new bourgeois public sphere and a means of oratorical training for its participants.

The public functions of literary culture depended, of course, on institutional contexts and supports: the coffeehouses, salons and journals of the eighteenth century and the public lectures, literary societies, and other forums for public literary culture of the nineteenth. Shakespeare's popularity in America was spread in part by the Lyceum movement, just as in Britain his works were often the topic of lectures at the Mechanics' Institutes.[54] The very nature of such public institutional contexts often encouraged the interpenetration of literary and social judgment which, for Habermas, constitutes the "critical" function of the literary public sphere. In the early months of 1818, for example, competing public lecture series on Shakespeare were delivered by the conservative Samuel Taylor Coleridge (at the London Philosophical Society) and radical democrats John Thelwall and William Hazlitt (the latter at the Surrey Institution). Hazlitt's remarks on Shakespeare's *Coriolanus* in his *Characters of Shakespear's Plays* (1817) also sparked a highly politicized debate, conducted in pamphlets and the pages of the *Quarterly Review*, with the powerful Tory editor William Gifford.[55]

A vibrant tradition of oratorical education persisted into the second half of the nineteenth century, when it still served as the basis for literary study in American colleges.[56] Declamation competitions and debating societies provided valuable training for a class which "would one day enter law, politics, or the ministry, callings in which oratorical powers were essential."[57] One of the reasons for Shakespeare's popularity in nineteenth-century America was therefore the predominance of oratory in American political and cultural life.[58] Conversely, the "declaiming" style of the great nineteenth-century Shakespearean actors, which suppressed

54. Marder, *His Exits*, pp. 31, 297; Richard D. Altick, *The English Common Reader: A Social History of the Reading Public, 1800–1900* (Chicago: University of Chicago Press, 1957), p. 203.

55. Bate, *Shakespearean Constitutions*, pp. 164–76.

56. See Gerald Graff, *Professing Literature*, pp. 19–51.

57. Walter P. Rogers, quoted ibid., pp. 42–43. Esther Cloudman Dunn writes: "How definitely this American training in rhetoric was a preparation for a later career in pulpit or legislature or courtroom (or theatre, too, though this fact would not have been admitted) is shown by the absence of elocution in a volume constructed exclusively for 'young ladies.' Ebenezer Bailey, Principal of the Young Ladies' High School in Boston, in the 1820's compiled *The Young Ladies' Class Book*. It is full of passages from Shakespeare. But there are no instructions for elocution, nor use of these passages for declamation." Dunn, *Shakespeare in America*, p. 235.

58. See Levine, *Highbrow/Lowbrow*, pp. 36–37; Dunn, *Shakespeare in America*, pp. 190–95, 224–35.

subtlety of psychological portrayal in favor of pure elocutionary force, derived from the oratorical practices of the public sphere.[59] But this public literary sphere soon came under pressure from the capitalist economy which had once helped to found it. Oratorical training assumed a public that was relatively uniform with respect to social class *and* a bourgeoisie interested in the public good, both of which were threatened by the development of industrial capitalism. By the 1860s, oratorical culture was already in decline, and training in rhetoric was becoming irrelevant to the future professional careers of students who were more interested in profitable business activity than in public address.[60]

Even after its decay, oratorical culture survived as "public speaking" in American high school education, and with it the almost universal experience of being made to read *Julius Caesar*, whose preeminence in the secondary school curriculum is a topic too little remarked on.[61] The play's depictions of classical oratory and politics clearly fit it for a system in which "civics" was, until not too long ago, still a taught subject. The play's Roman setting, moreover, made it suitable for the kind of pseudoclassical philological training embodied in G. L. Craik's notorious *The English of Shakespeare; Illustrated in a Philological Commentary on his Julius Caesar*, whose American edition by W. J. Rolfe was endlessly recirculated in high schools during the second half of the nineteenth and the early twentieth centuries. Finally, the play's plot, in which rebellion against imperial rule is suitably defeated and punished, no doubt supplied a welcome lesson in the politics of the authoritarian classroom.[62]

Just as *Julius Caesar* had enjoyed a relatively privileged role among Shakespeare's works during the rise of the bourgeois public sphere, so it now came to mark the perceived decline of a critical, debating public and its replacement by ignorant masses easily swayed by propaganda and

59. See Dunn, *Shakespeare in America*, p. 148.

60. Graff, *Professing Literature*, pp. 21, 46–51.

61. *Julius Caesar* was apparently the first of Shakespeare's plays to be part of secondary school education, beginning with a performance at the Westminster School in 1728. See Dobson, *Making of the National Poet*, p. 3.

62. One early twentieth-century manual for teaching Shakespeare in the high schools opines that "Shakespeare is always loyal to the institutions of the Family and the State," and gives the following interpretation of the principles organizing his work: "First, the Shakespearean Drama is ethical. It portrays a world of conflict—principles in conflict. . . . Second, the Shakespearean Drama finally brings all conflicting elements into harmony: . . . the discordant element must be destroyed; if the individual does not repent he must die, as in Tragedy; the element of mediation may enter, the individual repents, and harmony is restored without the necessity of death and the play becomes a Comedy." Mary E. Ferris-Gettemy, *Outline Studies in the Shakespearean Drama* (Galesburg, Ill.: Mail Printing Company, 1904), pp. 52, 67.

advertising. Writing in 1940, G. Wilson Knight warned that "the people can, as Shakespeare suggests in *Julius Caesar*, be easily manipulated by a master-mind, and in our day of mass propaganda the dangers are great."[63] Brents Stirling, writing in 1949, similarly found *Julius Caesar* to be "not a pretty example of how to manipulate the electorate."[64] Such responses, along with Orson Welles's production of the play, are certainly prompted by the rise of fascism and, later, the Cold War. But it would be misleading to see them as concerned only with external threats, since techniques of social engineering and public relations had also come to dominate the industrialized democracies. Writers from Walter Lippman to John Dewey to Edward Berneys had been debating the degeneration of electoral democracy from the 1920s on.[65]

Julius Caesar illustrated not only the new powers of mass propaganda, but those of advertising as well. A pamphlet published around 1930, entitled *Shakespeare as a Salesman and Advertising Man*, may not be critically distinguished but is interesting as a cultural symptom. The pamphlet (recording the text of a lecture delivered by one H. E. Roesch, Des Moines manager for the Remington Typewriter Company, before the local Ad-men's Club), promises that "the same psychological principles used by Antony in his oration over the body of Caesar will, if employed in the selling of goods, bring as great a measure of success, and effectively win the day." (Shakespeare himself also garners praise as a "practical advertising man" with "*Copy* of *great drawing power*.")[66] Shakespeare's image was used to sell everything from Cadillacs to corned beef, and quotations from his works adorned handbooks teaching business executives the techniques of public speaking.[67]

Roesch's pamphlet is noteworthy largely for its depoliticizing of *Julius Caesar*. Roesch transforms the Forum scene from a public struggle over forms of government into a purely "private" economic contest between salesman and consumer. Marc Antony's rhetorical skills now serve to maximize profits, not to overthrow states. I shall argue later that this

63. Knight, *Shakespeare and Religion*, p. 99.

64. Brents Stirling, *The Populace in Shakespeare* (New York: Columbia University Press, 1949), p. 31.

65. See Robbins, ed., *The Phantom Public Sphere*.

66. H. E. Roesch, *Shakespeare as a Salesman and Advertising Man* (Des Moines: Successful Farming, n.d.), pp. 4–5. Folger Shakespeare Library Sh. misc. 1834.

67. "Shakespeare as a Salesman for Cadillac Cars" (c. 1934: Folger Shakespeare Library, Sh. misc. 548); Levine, *Highbrow/Lowbrow*, p. 54; William G. Hoffman, *Public Speaking for Business Men* (New York: McGraw Hill, 1923); Charles W. Mears, *Public Speaking for Executives* (New York and London: Harper and Brothers, 1931).

appropriation of Shakespeare's play is not quite as ludicrous as it may first appear. In any case, it should not be opposed to the more political responses cited just above. For as Habermas argues, both the "plebisci-tory-acclamatory form of regimented public sphere characterizing dicta-torships in highly regimented public societies"[68] *and* the practices of public-opinion management at work in post-liberal culture assume a re-configuration and attenuation of the political realm in line with practices of economic consumption.

Shakespeare cannot prophesy the bourgeois public sphere of the eigh-teenth century any more than he can the mass culture of the twentieth; but if two (very different) later periods have adopted *Julius Caesar* to meditate on their own cultural situations, this does not necessarily mean that the play is infinitely plastic in its meanings or the prey of an arbitrary interpretive will-to-power. Rather, *Julius Caesar* stages the contest between patrician and plebeian cultures in a way that encourages later appropri-ations as a banner for, respectively, "culture-debating" and "culture-consuming" publics.

Like many of Shakespeare's plays, *Julius Caesar* reflects on the status of the popular theater and its relation to the audience. But this aspect of the play occupies a privileged place if we accept the belief that *Julius Caesar* was the first of Shakespeare's works performed in the new Globe Theatre, and was written partly with this occasion in mind. (Self-consciously or not, Orson Welles used his adaptation of *Julius Caesar* to inaugurate the Mercury Theatre.)[69] Caesar's murder, which even the con-spirators imagine in future theatrical reenactment, seems an appropri-ately tragic ritual for sanctifying a new theatrical space, and the play's crowd scenes (especially the crown-offering ceremony and the funeral orations) are appropriate to founding a site for popular entertainment. I want to argue that, in addition, *Julius Caesar* can be read as a reflection on the theater's dual status as prototype for both the bourgeois public sphere *and* mass culture. Such a reading will, in the eyes of a more "re-sponsible" historicism, seem as flagrantly anachronistic as Welles's fascist setting or other modernist appropriations. Recent treatments of the Ro-man plays by historicists ("new" or otherwise) have tended to focus on strictly contemporary topics such as popular-festive elements or the influ-ence of the 1607 Midlands uprising on *Coriolanus*.[70] This emphasis on a

68. Habermas, *Structural Transformation*, p. xviii.

69. Welles, *Orson Welles on Shakespeare*, p. 103.

70. See, for example, Michael D. Bristol, "Lenten Butchery: Legitimation Crisis in *Cor-iolanus*," in Jean E. Howard and Marian F. O'Conner, *Shakespeare Reproduced: The Text in*

now-recognizable constellation of the popular/carnivalesque/insurrectional is perfectly valid in its own right, but in helping to ground the plays in an historical context it tends also to bind them to a merely reflective status. What such an approach misses is precisely the noncongruence of the Roman plays with their historical context: of an urban milieu with an (essentially agrarian) carnivalesque, of the Roman republic with Elizabethan monarchy, and so forth. The historical meanings which later periods were able to derive from *Julius Caesar* are ultimately based on the play's complexly non-synchronous relation with its historical moment. It is because of this that modernist allegorizations, which focus on the issue of mass culture, may uncover facets of the play which would otherwise be missed.[71]

The action of *Julius Caesar* is structured by double divisions of social space which are at once decisive and troubled. The first of these, on which all classical political theory relied, separates private and public, or domestic and political, spheres. This boundary and its transgression organize the gender politics of the play. The second division parcels out public space between the Senate and the Forum and structures the play's class politics by defining patrician and plebeian spheres.[72] The Senate, dominated by the patrician class, is the space of politics; in it the play foreshadows a "bourgeois public sphere." Its chief representative is Brutus, whose patriotically-minded murder of a tyrant makes him the darling of anti-monarchical, republican thinkers of the Enlightenment. The Forum, dominated by the plebs, is an economic rather than a political space, or rather both at once: it is simultaneously marketplace, court, and oratorical platform. Here Marc Antony triumphs, and it is on Antony's oration that the theoreticians of crowd psychology, advertising, and propaganda focus. The Forum thus offers a prototype for a mass-cultural space.

History and Ideology (New York: Methuen, 1987); Patterson, *Shakespeare and the Popular Voice*, pp. 120–53; Richard Wilson, " 'Is this a Holiday?': Shakespeare's Roman Carnival," *ELH* 54, no. 1 (Spring 1987): 31–44.

71. This allegorizing tendency was not limited to readers of Shakespeare's play but can also be found in the work of classical historians. For instance: "The same glaring contrast which meets us in Europe and America to-day was present in the Roman world of Caesar's time. On one side stood the wealthy few, who lavished their millions in tasteless luxury, and on the other side were the helpless and destitute many. The sources of the evil lay beyond the reach of reform. . . ." H. L. Havell, *Republican Rome* (New York: Frederick A. Stokes, 1914), p. 527.

72. For a highly intelligent reading of *Julius Caesar* which employs a similar division of social space, see Timothy Hampton, *Writing from History: The Rhetoric of Examplarity in Renaissance Literature* (Ithaca: Cornell University Press, 1990), pp. 205–36.

The political struggle of *Julius Caesar* is largely a contest between the material, rhetorical, theatrical, and even interpretive practices of its two public spaces.[73] The conspirators murder Caesar at the Senate-house, and try to situate their act within the political, patrician ideologies that dominate there.[74] Antony triumphs when the scene shifts to the plebeian milieu of the Forum. Both spaces, moreover, embody different characteristics of the early modern theater, and leave it poised between two distinct (but, it in a sense, simultaneous) historical trajectories.

Yet *Julius Caesar* maintains neither the integrity nor the symmetry of its initial contrast between Senate and Forum. Indeed, the ''engine of history'' in the play seems to be an imbalance between the two, causing the former to collapse in on itself and be swallowed up by the latter. Brutus's conspiracy fails largely because of his idealist belief in the autonomy and integrity of the senatorial space, while Antony relies on his mastery of the Forum to topple his opponents. *Julius Caesar* thus foreshadows not only the two terms of Habermas's theory, but something like the same narrative relation between them, as the ''critical'' space of the patricians seems to degrade into the ''consuming'' space of the plebeians.

This, at least, is how the play is interpreted from the perspective of the ''bourgeois public sphere'' and those modernist critics of mass culture

73. By defining political struggle in this way I run the danger of overlooking issues of gender, since I have already argued that the play assigns women to the private realm, and I now exclude that realm from ''political struggle.'' Of course, the classical *polis* is defined by just such an exclusion, yet *Julius Caesar* continually transgresses and undermines this boundary. Here I am using the term ''political'' in a traditionally Marxist way to denote the sphere of the state apparatus, and I mean only that women in *Julius Caesar* do not explicitly contend for rule of the state. For a useful discussion of gender in the play and how it is excluded from certain conceptions of the political, see Darryl J. Gless, ''*Julius Caesar*, Allan Bloom, and the Value of Pedagogical Pluralism,'' in *Shakespeare Left and Right*, ed. Ivo Kamps (New York: Routledge, 1991), pp. 185–203. For an informative discussion of gender and the constitution of ''the'' public sphere, see Nancy Fraser, ''Rethinking the Public Sphere: A Contribution to the Critique of Actually Existing Democracy,'' in Robbins, *Phantom Public Sphere*, pp. 1–32.

74. Of course I am speaking loosely when I say that Caesar is murdered at the ''Senate-house,'' but in doing so I only reflect the play's own inconsistent and confused grasp of Roman topography. At 2.4.1, Portia sends Lucius to ''the Senate-house'' to report on how Caesar answers his suitors. The place of this scene is also referred to as the ''Capitol'' (e.g., 2.4.11). Yet just after the murder, the conspirators describe Caesar's body as lying along ''Pompey's basis'' (3.1.115). The play thus conflates three distinct places. The *Curia* or Senate-house is located not on the Capitol but on the outer reaches of the area known as the ''Forum,'' which includes the Forum proper—an open square of 200 by 300 feet— within it. On the day of Caesar's assassination, however, the Senate meets not in the *Curia* but in a portico attached to Pompey's Theater, located on the Campus Martius (again, not on the Capitol). Strictly speaking, the Senate is not a fixed topographical space in the sense that the Forum is, since its location could differ according to occasion. On Roman topography see, e.g., Michael Grant, *The Roman Forum* (New York: Macmillan, 1970).

who follow in its wake. Both evince an anxiety over the turbulent strength (yet apparent manipulability) of the plebeians. The eighteenth century's method of processing this anxiety was excision. Both Voltaire and Buckingham omit the scene in which the enraged crowd murders Cinna the poet, while in Conti's version of the crown-offering ceremony, the reactions described are those of the future conspirators, not of the plebs. These cuts are designed not to meliorate Shakespeare's depiction of the mob but rather to eliminate potentially inflammatory scenes. Hence Voltaire also omits any direct representation of Caesar's murder and of the conspirators washing their hands in his blood, since these violate both neoclassical convention and political prudence.[75] (Voltaire also, interestingly, excludes Portia and Calphurnia from his play.)[76] Even at the birth of bourgeois society these plays betray nervousness about the instability of public space, in which the critical yet "responsible" voice of bourgeois reason threatens to spill over into mob violence.

The unifying principle behind Voltaire's revisions—and here I am taking him as representative of Enlightenment tradition—is purgation, an attempt to flush the play clean of its embarrassing corporeality: Caesar's dying body, the conspirators' hands sticky with his blood, the bodily excess of both the plebeian and the female. In this, Voltaire enacts the logic of the bourgeois public sphere, which can likewise sustain its rational, critical spirit only at the price of a continual purging which both delimits and identifies its "public." Voltaire's purgative compulsion also symbolically repeats the actions of Shakespeare's Brutus, who thus foreshadows bourgeois reason most powerfully through his idealism, in both the good and bad senses of the word.

Brutus's idealism, with all its ambiguity, is summed up in Antony's final comment that he alone of all the conspirators acted "in a general honest thought/ And common good to all" (5.5.71–72). Political virtue, in this view, consists in suppression of personal motive and in unswerving devotion to the commonwealth. Yet Brutus's "commonwealth" is merely a political abstraction, the disembodied dream of a unified Rome that is in fact riven by class division and conspiratorial intrigue. Only members of the patrician, senatorial class find this political generality compelling. Brutus's failure in the Forum results largely from the fact that he ad-

75. Many of these same cuts were made in English productions of Shakespeare's play. See Ripley, *Julius Caesar on Stage*, pp. 26, 30, 37, 52, 55.

76. See Fletcher, "Three Authors," pp. 444, 448; for more on Buckingham's dramatic and stylistic revisions, see G. C. Branam, *Eighteenth Century Adaptations of Shakespearean Tragedy* (Berkeley: University of California Press, 1956).

dresses the "people," an abstract, political concept, while Antony addresses the plebs, a concrete, material class.

The disembodied nature of Brutus's "people," their status as patrician mirage and senatorial idealization, is made clear by Cassius's plot to ensnare Brutus in the conspiracy. This he does by leaving written notes, claiming to be from Roman citizens, urging Brutus to free them from Caesar's tyranny. Cassius's stratagem, which is not found in Plutarch, produces (to borrow Walter Lippmann's title) a "phantom public," compelling to Brutus precisely because of its status as textual trace or captivating absence. Brutus's virtue cannot be summoned by the people (as there is no such thing), but only by the disembodied *concept* of "the people." The conspirators likewise envision the restaging of Caesar's assassination before a grateful but future—and therefore strictly imaginary—public.

Brutus's political idealism finds further expression in his advice on how to carry out the murder:

> Let's be sacrificers, but not butchers, Caius.
> We all stand up against the spirit of Caesar,
> And in the spirit of men there is no blood;
> O that we then could come by Caesar's spirit,
> And not dismember Caesar! But, alas,
> Caesar must bleed for it! (2.1.166–71)

Brutus's intended victim is not Caesar (a personal rival) but the spirit of Caesarism, the principle of tyranny which, unfortunately, resides in Caesar's body. Political idealism receives its ironic reward when Caesar's spirit or ghost returns to plague Brutus, while Antony makes brilliant use of Caesar's material remains in the Forum.[77] When Brutus claims "We shall

---

77. Following the trail of Brutus's miscalculations can lead us to the nature of Caesar's power. There is, of course, more than a kernel of truth to Brutus's intuition that his real antagonist is not Caesar the man but the "spirit" of Caesarism. This is to say that Caesar's charisma arises less from personal characteristics than from his structural position; indeed, his "personality" (or rather, impersonality) is little more than an expression of his role. To be "Caesar" is, from a psychoanalytic perspective, nothing more than to be the embodiment of paternal law. Brutus's error is his belief that this law can be broken by murdering the father, but he and the other conspirators only end up playing the role of the "primal horde" in Freud's *Totem and Taboo*. The dead Caesar is even more powerful than the living one, not only as guilt-dealing ghost but also as the "will" which symbolizes the Lacanian Law-of-the-Father. A psychoanalytic reading (as exemplified by Marjorie Garber, "A Rome of One's Own," in her *Shakespeare's Ghost Writers: Literature as Uncanny Causality* [New York:

be call'd purgers, not murderers" (2.1.180), he describes the assassination as a medicinal bloodletting performed on the abstract body of the
commonwealth, the "body politic" which is constituted by the purgative
categories of senatorial discourse. Brutus's disembodying spirit passes
over into Voltaire and other Enlightenment redactors of Shakespeare's
play, who preserve the integrity of critical reason by purging the body,
and who at the same time preserve the integrity of a bourgeois, male
public by purging both women and the plebs.

In the modernist period, as we have seen, focus shifts from Brutus and
his senatorial virtue to Antony and his rhetorical victory in the Forum.
(Welles actually occupies an ambiguous position here, to which I can't
give the attention it deserves.) Whether as master-demagogue or super-
salesman, Antony embodies the techniques of mass persuasion that so
fascinate modernist sensibilities. I want to look now at Antony's victory
through the lens of crowd psychology, which we may take as representing
a (reactionary) theory of the plebeian public sphere.

If Enlightenment produced a disembodied public to support its belief
in universal reason, crowd psychology, by contrast, emphasizes the materiality of the mob. According to Frederick Tupper (who exactly follows
Gustave Le Bon here),[78] Antony wins the crowd "with the impression of
the idea on the mob-mind through sensorial excitability. Antony fires the
multitude not by working upon its reason, its critical spirit, but by presenting a succession of vivid images,—grouped around Caesar's corpse,
his wounds, his garments, his will—that inflame the imagination and

---

Methuen, 1987], pp. 52–73) will focus on Caesar's paternal and hence disembodied status.

But along with the ghostly Caesar, the Caesar of will or law, there abides another and no
less powerful Caesar who is purely corporeal. This Caesar first appears in Cassius's narrative
of the swimming match in act 1, scene 2. There Cassius scornfully recalls Caesar's challeng-
ing him to cross a raging river but then crying "Help me, Cassius, or I sink!" halfway across.
"And this man / Is now become a god," complains Cassius (1.2.111, 115–16). This theme
of the sinking or falling Caesar is continued in the episode of "falling sickness" which ends
the crown-offering ceremony, also related in act 1, scene 2. Caesar's final "fall" or assassination is thus not so much a unique event as an expression of bodily habit; he is by nature
a sinking object, a dead weight, a plummet, a corpse. His self-conscious stoicism, his insistence that he is "unmoved" by prayers or flattery, is fully of a piece with this inertial
corporeality. Hence the murder doesn't reduce his political potency in the least; on the
contrary, Caesar's wounded corpse moves the crowd more powerfully than he ever could
in life. Cassius's fatal miscalculation is thus in interpreting Caesar's sinking as a sign of
weakness whereas it is in fact a sign of his peculiar strength. Indeed, it may not be too
outlandish to argue that Caesar is in some sense *already dead* when the play begins, and that
the assassination merely enables him to become his "true self"—or rather selves, that is to
say, ghost *and* corpse. Caesar may not be the first (and he is certainly not the last) ruler to
discover that his political posture improves when it is rigidly horizontal.

78. Le Bon, *The Crowd*, pp. 69–70.

arouse emotion and sensation.''[79] The subrational nature of the mob is grounded in a sensorial materiality which works not through the effect of ideas on the spirit but through the impression of images on the senses and imagination. The crowd cannot be won through reason but only with "the realization of the accepted idea through motor excitability": "Mark how the mob-energy is increased by the reflection of suggestion from man to man, each influencing and influenced, thus gaining force until it drives the multitude into a frenzy of excitement, a fury of activity. The limitation of voluntary movements, the thronging and pressing around Caesar's body, which Antony encourages, exalt suggestibility and facilitate the circulation of the feelings."[80] The crowd's receptivity to persuasion is increased through the very physical pressure its members exert on one another; when a certain threshold is reached, the crowd becomes super-conductive, passing its impressions (*not* ideas) along like an electrical current. Now the crowd has truly become a "mass," a pure *res extensa* in contrast to the *res cogitans* of bourgeois spirit. Its mechanical motions mimic thought; but because it is only receptive, it cannot exert any coun-terpressure as critical reason can. As "mass" the crowd merely endures the patterns of actions imposed on it by the informing mind of its master.

This physical analogy has its limits, however. For in the natural sci-ences, mass possesses an inertia which tends to resist setting into mo-tion—but the "mass" of the crowd lacks even this inertial resistance to outside force. Its materiality is thus, in a paradoxical sense, virtually mass-less, like that of leaves or feathers. Tupper describes the plebeians in *Julius Caesar* as "swayed hither and thither by every gust of rhetoric," and he does no more than paraphrase Jack Cade in 2 *Henry VI*, who asks, "Was ever feather so lightly blown to and fro as this multitude?" (4.8.55–56). Crowd psychology produces a weightless materiality, a materiality of sensorial impression which flows like electrical charges instead of lurch-ing and colliding like particles. For Habermas, too, the "consumption" of mass culture is defined precisely by its lack of resistance or counter-pressure. If the spirit of Enlightenment reason is afflicted with the ma-teriality of the body, then, the "masses" of both crowd psychology and Habermasian theory are also afflicted with spirit.

For the moment, however, I want to emphasize the materiality of the plebeian public sphere, no matter how subtle, airy, or elusive it may be. For it is this materiality that in *Julius Caesar* first opposes, and then col-lapses, Brutus's idealized realm of public reason. The materializing pro-

79. Tupper, "Shakespearean Mob," p. 507.
80. Ibid., pp. 507, 508.

cess begins with the portents that precede Caesar's murder. In Calphurnia's recounting to Caesar, lionesses whelped in the streets and ranks of warriors, fighting in the clouds, "drizzled blood upon the Capitol" (2.2.21). Public space, that is to say, begins to thicken; it becomes clogged with the bodily materiality of the excluded women and plebs, and with assorted spooks and denizens of religious superstition. Once sprinkled with blood, the Capitol can no longer serve as the pristine, crystalline medium of senatorial reason, of unproblematically patriotic motives, or of an abstract "people." It begins to take on "mass." *Julius Caesar* may here be said to invert the final action of Aeschylus' *Oresteia*. At the end of the *Eumenides*, Athena founds a civic (and masculine) system of justice to replace the murky, matriarchal vengeance of the Furies. Born of a man, Athena establishes a rational space by suppressing the female body. In *Julius Caesar*, this process reverses itself as public space suffers a return of the repressed. Yet the bloody cesarean at the play's center enables not only female but plebeian materiality to emerge into the political day. If the theatrical space of Renaissance drama serves as a prototype of the bourgeois public sphere, it also shows how easily the space of critical reason can become encumbered by its repressed other.

Something similar occurs in the problem of plebeian bad breath, a topic of continual patrician complaint in both *Julius Caesar* and *Coriolanus*. Writes Brents Stirling: "As the facts are assembled, it is uncomfortably apparent that when Shakespeare's commoners gather, something occurs which with slight whimsicality could be called a collective halitosis of democracy in action. Anyone who has read in sequence the Cade scenes, *Julius Caesar*, and *Coriolanus* may have been uneasy at the motif of proletarian stench which occurs in all three plays, and in *Coriolanus*, becomes a minor obsession." Stirling notes, moreover, that this is a peculiarly Shakespearean theme, found neither in his sources nor in the works of other contemporary playwrights.[81] Remarks about bad breath arise consistently in connection with plebeian attempts to speak out on public issues, and in public spaces such as the Forum. Occupying an intermediate state between the discursive and the corporeal, plebeian breath compromises the purity and transparency of public space, befouling the pristine atmosphere of senatorial judgment. It should be noted, however, that this corporeality is once again airy and diffuse, just like the spirits and apparitions that appear over the Capitol. Dense and repellent only in comparison with patrician breath, that of the plebs nevertheless reminds us that the law does not emerge from

81. Stirling, *Populace in Shakespeare*, pp. 66, 72.

some disembodied ether of reason but is encumbered with the particularity of material and personal interests.[82] Plebeian breath, moreover, occupies and dominates a space associated not only with public debate but with theater and theatrical crowds.[83]

But while plebeian materiality comes to fill all political spaces in *Julius Caesar*, the play neither imagines nor desires a plebeian victory over the senatorial class. To note the triumph of the material over the spiritual (and even this is an oversimplification) is not to proclaim plebeian power, although the influence of Bakhtinian theory may tempt us to do this. *Julius Caesar* is not a "festive" or "carnivalesque" play, and the anarchy that grants the plebeians a momentary rule seems merely to turn them into tools of one conspiratorial faction. What the discourse of crowd psychology reminds us is that the materiality of the crowd may be a means of theorizing its subjection as well as a means of theorizing its utopian, subversive force.

In fact, the historical significance of Mikhail Bakhtin's theory of the carnivalesque may reside largely in the ways it both took up and transformed the categories of crowd psychology. Bakhtin's festive crowd is a collective entity, just like the "mob-mind" of the crowd psychologists; it is also an essentially corporeal, material existence, as are the crowds of Gustave Le Bon and Gabriel Tarde. But for Bakhtin, the materiality of the crowd's body has "weight"; it resists and remains opaque to the blandishments of hegemonic culture. Moreover, he undoes in advance the Habermasian opposition between criticism and consumption by describing a popular mode of consumption which is itself critical. That is to say, Bakhtin scrambles the (essentially Platonic) oppositions between spirit and body, reason and passion, criticism and subjection which underlie Enlightenment theory. It is Bakhtin's emphasis on an active, critical mode of consumption that makes him valuable to theorists of mass culture who wish to avoid the pitfalls of Frankfurt School theories of passivity and manipulation.

Bakhtin's categories, however, apply to *Julius Caesar* only within a very limited range. The cobbler in act 1, scene 1 displays both a festive rebelliousness and a carnivalesque use of punning, playful language in his banter with the tribune. Yet he and his cohorts slink off after being rebuked for their fickleness, in what seems almost a symbolic defeat and banishing of the carnivalesque itself. This local defeat is magnified and

82. When in 2 *Henry VI* a follower of Jack Cade wishes "only that the laws of England may come out of your mouth," one bystander remarks to another: "Nay, John, it will be stinking law, for his breath stinks with eating toasted cheese" (4.7.6–7, 11–12).
83. See *Julius Caesar* 1.2.242–48.

repeated, moreover, across the performance history of the play. Early modern stagings of *Julius Caesar* had to make do with a few paltry players to suggest the Roman mob, and these seem to have employed the techniques of carnivalesque humor. An eighteenth-century edition of the play complains that in the Forum scene, in response to Antony's famous "Friends, Romans, countrymen, lend me your ears!" (3.2.73), "We have seen some very comical comedians put up their hands to their ears, as if *Antony* meant to be taken in a literal sense—wretched buffoonery."[84] By mocking and literalizing Antony's "lend me your ears," early modern players resist the siren song of oratory. To lend one's ears is not only to listen or attend, but in some deeper sense to hand one's hearing and consciousness over to another, to allow oneself to be enchanted by the power of rhetoric. Debasing Antony's first rhetorical trope, the audience indicates that it prefers to *keep* its own ears, and that it chooses dialogical mockery over passive receptiveness. With their plebeian ridicule of authority, their linguistic playfulness, and their use of the body to debase elevated ideals, the comedians stage an exemplary if compact display of the Bakhtinian carnivalesque. Yet as written, act 2, scene 3 of *Julius Caesar* does not sustain this improvised gesture of comic resistance. On the contrary, the seeming manipulability of Shakespeare's crowd has made the play attractive rather to theorists of mass propaganda, as we have already seen. Moreover, such "buffoonery" will probably strike not only a neoclassical but a modern sensibility as inappropriate to the tone of the scene. There is little in Shakespeare's text that attributes a comic or carnivalesque quality to the crowd in the Forum. Here, somehow, Shakespeare's conception of the Roman plebs seems to contradict the techniques of the early modern stage for representing lower-class characters.

In the nineteenth century, beginning with John Philip Kemble's 1812 version of the play, productions tended to represent rather than merely suggest the Roman mob by bringing a crowd of actors onto the stage (thirty in Kemble's production). Successful crowd scenes now had to be carefully arranged; the most widely admired productions were those in which the mob didn't merely mill about but was ordered into "living scenery" or, later, more dynamic flows and movements.[85] Such stagings renounced carnivalesque anarchy for disciplinary techniques of theatrical crowd control. In his *Miscellanies* (1835), John Finley commends the orderly arrangement of the mob in Kemble's production but offers an in-

---

84. Francis Gentleman's preface to *Julius Caesar* in *Bell's Shakespeare* (1773), quoted in Ripley, *Julius Caesar on Stage*, p. 37.
85. See Ripley, *Julius Caesar on Stage*, pp. 35, 56, 77–87, 148, 154–71.

teresting criticism about the costume in another of Kemble's "Roman" productions, Addison's *Cato*: "The Roman characters were all dressed differently, but it was the peculiarity of the Roman people, that no nation ever observed such a uniformity of dress. . . . the Roman people were a nation in regimental."[86] Finlay's conception of a disciplined, uniform society suggests an army or an industrial proletariat more than it does an early modern carnival. If motley is the dress of the Shakespearean fool, its variegated colors suggesting the anarchy of the popular-festive, the uniformity of the Roman plebs seems instead to anticipate something like the modern "masses."

Later productions of *Julius Caesar* did not necessarily falsify the play by de-carnivalizing the plebs. The text of *Julius Caesar* simply does not, for the most part, employ the bodily excess or the linguistic playfulness of "classically" carnivalesque figures such as Falstaff in depicting the plebs; hence it responds only fitfully to analysis using Bakhtinian categories.[87] Finlay's remarks about Roman "uniformity," I think, pinpoint something about the cultural *differences* between Roman and early modern societies that can illuminate the significance of the "Roman play" as a genre, and locate possible incompatibilities between such plays and the resources of early modern theater. I am arguing, therefore, that historically later stagings of the play are not merely anachronistic, but that by violating the norms of early modern theater they get at certain aspects of *Julius Caesar* which rub against the grain of its historical moment—specifically, a conception of the plebs which cannot entirely be contained within popular-festive culture.

Politically unsavory though it may be, crowd psychology apparently succeeds in describing important aspects of the behavior of Shakespeare's plebs. For instance, it makes a seemingly unassailable point in emphasizing Antony's use of visual props—the bloody mantle, Caesar's corpse, the will—in winning the crowd. The crowd psychologists score again in pointing to the seeming fickleness of the mob as evidence of its manipulability. When Brutus speaks, the crowd is for Brutus; when Antony speaks, the crowd is for Antony. The same fickleness is evoked at the very beginning of the play when the plebs go on holiday to celebrate Caesar's victory, even though they had formerly cheered Pompey. This fickleness makes

86. John Finlay, *Miscellanies* (Dublin, 1835), p. 254.

87. The same may be said for Robert Weimann's distinction between *locus* and *platea*, which can partly but not fully explain the differences between Senate and Forum in *Julius Caesar*. See Weimann, *Shakespeare and the Popular Tradition in the Theater: Studies in the Social Dimension of Dramatic Form and Function*, ed. Robert Schwartz (Baltimore: Johns Hopkins University Press, 1978), esp. pp. 73–85.

the crowd appear manipulable, but unstably so—incapable of independent action, yet so passive and mindless that every new demagogue immediately erases the memory of his predecessor. Their fickleness is a sign of that apparent weightlessness which makes the crowd seem like leaves or feathers.

Here the crowd psychologists do manage to describe aspects of the plebs' behavior that Bakhtinian theory would have difficulty explaining. Yet I believe that the fickleness, and hence the manipulability, of the crowd in *Julius Caesar* has been exaggerated—or rather, results from the application of patrician concepts and values to the actions of the plebs. The value of crowd psychology resides in dislodging Bakhtinian certainties rather than in achieving a coherent reading of the play. At the very opening of *Julius Caesar,* the tribune rebukes the plebs for their disloyalty to Pompey in now applauding Caesar. But what does disloyalty mean here? The plebs had formerly cheered Pompey because of the tributes and captives he brought to Rome; he was, for them, a source of national pride, material prosperity, and spectacular entertainment. Now Pompey is dead, and Caesar serves the same function. Both generals used their popularity in pursuit of personal ambition. What loyalty is owed, then, to Pompey? Why should the plebs displease their new provider by attaching themselves to a dead predecessor whose benefits to them were equally self-interested? Caesar's autocratic ambitions, moreover, pose a threat not to the plebs but to the patricians, who are the political ruling class.[88] The plebs, then, display not "fickleness" but a kind of materialism of the present, which renders past actions merely abstract by comparison. The difference between patricians and plebs here is that the former are attached to ethical abstractions (loyalty to the dead) which, moreover, merely rationalize their current class interests, while the plebs have a less mediated and indirect, more materially visible attachment to their own class interest. The plebs, in other words, *are* unswervingly loyal—to themselves, which is their only reasonable motivation.

The same principle is at work in the funeral scene.[89] Brutus appeals to patriotism and the "common good"—real but relatively abstract princi-

88. "The interventions of the people in affairs led on to monarchy. To the urban proletariate this was no disadvantage. It was the aristocracy who suffered from loss of liberty." P.A. Brunt, "The Roman Mob," *Past and Present* 35 (December 1960): 27.

89. Some of what follows relies on Richard A. Burt, " 'A Dangerous Rome': Shakespeare's *Julius Caesar* and the Discursive Determinations of Cultural Politics," in *Contending Kingdoms: Historical, Psychological, and Feminist Approaches to the Literature of Sixteenth-Century England and France*, ed. Marie-Rose Logan and Peter L. Rudnytsky (Detroit: Wayne State University Press, 1991), pp. 109–27.

ples, especially since Caesar's threat was really to the current political form of patrician rule. Brutus cannot, moreover, point to acts that Caesar has committed but only to his ambition and to the possibility of future tyranny. Antony appeals not to political reason but primarily to the economic benefits Caesar has brought—and still brings—to the plebs.[90] The crucial effectiveness of the will lies in the fact that even when dead, Caesar continues to enrich the plebeians, and is thus still a suitable object for their loyalty. Antony prevails by invoking the materiality of the present, and it is in this context that his use of visual props should be judged.[91] While the plebs respond to Brutus's appeal to patriotism and the common good, they react more powerfully and consistently to material motives and material evidence. The "manipulability" of the plebs is thus limited by a canny if largely implicit sense of their own class interests: although they suddenly change their minds, they are never seen to choose against themselves.

The fact is, then, that Shakespeare's plebs answer fully neither to Bakhtin's notion of a critical, "festive" people nor to crowd psychology's fantasy of mindless, easily-managed mobs. The plebs seem "manipulable," but only within limits that they themselves ultimately define. A subtler and more accommodating explanatory model than either of the two examined here comes from Habermas. I have been treating Habermas as an extension of Enlightenment traditions, and this is true up to a point. Yet for him, mass culture does not arise when unlettered mobs overrun bourgeois public space. Rather, the latter is undone by structural transformations in the conditions that gave rise to it—transformations which do not, moreover, negate these conditions but further elaborate and develop them.

90. Aristotle points out that each rhetorical mode has its characteristic time: for judicial the past, for deliberative the future, and for epideictic (as in Antony's speech) the present. "In epideictic the present is the most important; for all speakers praise or blame in regard to existing qualities, but they also make use of other things, both reminding [the audience] of the past and projecting the course of the future." Aristotle, *On Rhetoric*, trans. George A. Kennedy (New York: Oxford University Press, 1991) 1358b.4–5.

91. The very word "props" should remind us that the materiality I have been describing as plebeian is also theatrical. Shakespeare's depiction of the Roman mob is surely influenced by his experience of dramatic audiences, who are also "fickle" in the sense that their approval must be earned anew with every performance. Drama is caught in the eternal present of repetition, in which a play's (or playwright's) effective existence depends on continual reenactment and representation—that is, on the materiality of the present. Theatrical audiences, like the plebs, react to immediate pleasures, not to memories of past benefits. Yet one would hardly think to excoriate them for "disloyalty" if, having enjoyed a play by one author, they then cheer a play by some other author. Audiences, like the plebs, are beholden only to themselves, not to the providers of their entertainment. But this is a sign of their reason, not their unreason.

Like the other thinkers discussed here, Habermas operates a "two-sphere" model of society. These spheres, however, do not correspond to "bourgeois" and "plebeian" cultures. They are, rather, the private realm of civil society and the public realm of the state brought into being by capitalism's progressive disembedding of the economic from the political. It is this structural separation that both gives birth to and is in turn mediated by the bourgeois public sphere. Although the members of this public understand themselves as private individuals debating the public good, they are also private economic interests demanding control over the public conditions on which the reproduction of capital depends. The bourgeois public sphere is, in effect, the medium through which civil society (economy) directs the state. Thus it at once inaugurates "politics" as a discourse and, at the same time, subjects political interests to private ones. It speaks a political tongue but perceives politics largely from the perspective of business, and in a sense tries to reduce the political *to* business.

The demise of a "culture-debating public," as Habermas narrates it, is not the denial but the fulfillment of this dream. While capitalism in its laissez-faire stage insists on its autonomy from the liberal state, and thus grants the political a relative autonomy, capitalism in its monopoly phase engages the state directly on behalf of its own managerial ends. Public debate gives way to "a consensus created by sophisticated opinion-molding services under the aegis of a sham public interest." This reintegration of the economic and the political effects "a refeudalization of the public sphere" in which the "showy pomp" of manufactured publicity replaces critical debate. Moreover, it means that "the state has to 'address' its citizens like consumers,"[92] thereby producing a "culture-consuming" public—one whose cultural and political life has been refashioned in conformity with economic demand.

Habermas thus takes an Enlightenment narrative and subjects it to a structural or dialectical irony. Now it is not the masses, as "others," who undermine the bourgeois public sphere, but rather the contradictory self-development of the very structural conditions that produced bourgeois public discourse in the first place. This process results not in the swallowing of "high" culture by "low" (at least, not directly), but in the subsumption of the political by the economic, and thus of a critical discourse by advertising and public relations, on the one hand, and "consumption" on the other. The political dwindles to an empty simulacrum of its former self as its structural autonomy is progressively compromised.

92. Habermas, *Structural Transformation*, p. 195.

We are now in a better position to grasp the ways in which *Julius Caesar* offers a purchase for later allegorizations. While the play seems at one level to portray the capture of "high" culture by "low," it may be more correct to say that it portrays the capture of the political by the economic. As we have seen, Brutus moves in a world of political abstractions; he battles on behalf of the Roman republic, of the "common good," of Senatorial rule. Antony, conversely, wins the crowd by bypassing the public discourse of politics and appealing to his listeners' "private" interest in economic gain. The foundation of Antony's triumph is laid at the play's very opening, in the following exchange between patrician and plebe:

> *Flavius* But wherefore art not in thy shop to-day?
> Why dost thou lead these men about the streets?
>
> *Cobbler* Truly, sir, to wear out their shoes, to get myself into more work.
> But indeed, sir, we make holiday to see Caesar, and to rejoice in his
> triumph. (1.1.27–31)

The tribune Flavius suspects some political meaning to this shoemaker's holiday, but the cobbler replies with a joke about his business interests. Plebeian consciousness, in other words, is more at home in the "civil society" of economic concerns than it is in vying for control of the Roman state. Even the cobbler's second, more serious answer depicts the gathering as mere entertainment or holiday rather than as a political demonstration. Flavius and the cobbler do not so much argue as talk past each other. The former sees every movement of the plebs as political, while the latter cares for the state and its leaders only insofar as they contribute to his prosperity or amusement.

This brief exchange foreshadows the later scene in the Forum, where the plebeians respond more powerfully to the image of Caesar as economic provider than they do to the image of Caesar as political tyrant. The man who "did the general coffers fill" (3.2.91) and whose will leaves "to every individual man seventy-five drachmas" (3.2.243) proves more compelling than the fate of the Roman republic. Shakespeare's plebs are in some sense "beyond politics." Indeed, they are already to Antony what they will be for H. E. Roesch: *consumers* of both rhetorical address and economic benefits. For the plebs, Caesar is precisely as he appears in his dream: a life-giving fountain, which, however, spouts cash as well as blood. Caesarism is thus the foreshadowing of the modern welfare state. It is a source of benefits to be consumed rather than policies to be de-

bated. And if this perhaps fanciful equation suppresses important historical differences, it at least reveals those elements in *Julius Caesar* which
prove receptive to modernist allegorization.

The nature of the "public sphere" in *Julius Caesar* receives its densest,
most compact expression in the shout uttered by the plebs at the opening
of the Forum scene: "We would be satisfied! Let us be satisfied!" (3.2.1)
Brutus understands the plebs as demanding explanations for Caesar's
death. In this interpretation (which is by no means simply incorrect),
theirs is the cry of a critically reasoning public. But Antony understands
that the demand to be "satisfied" may also be fulfilled through bribes
or even entertainment. (Perhaps the plebs is asking for a show!) If the
crowd is, from one perspective, a critical and engaged citizenry, it is from
another a more detached, cynically self-interested group of consumers.
The double-construction of the crowd's demand not only expresses an
ambiguity at the very heart of Shakespearean representation (at once
critical and merely spectacular) but also anticipates the cynical fate of
public reason which will form the subject of the following section.

The Irony of Irony

Nowhere else do Shakespeare, high modernism, and mass culture lock
together in so sticky an embrace as in these famous lines from *The Waste
Land*:

> But
> O O O O that Shakespeherian Rag—
> It's so elegant
> So intelligent[93]

Here (one is interminably reminded, and will be reminded once more)
Eliot paraphrases lines from a popular song of 1912:

> That Shakespearian rag,
> Most intelligent, very elegant,
> That old classical drag,
> Has the proper stuff, the line "Lay on MacDuff."[94]

93. All quotations of Eliot's poetry are from T. S. Eliot, *Collected Poems, 1909–1962* (New
York: Harcourt Brace Jovanovich, 1963).
94. See B. R. McElderry, Jr., "Eliot's 'Shakespeherian Rag,'" *American Quarterly* 9 (1957):
185–86.

Quoting this pop tune in the context of *The Waste Land* is a quintessentially "modern" gesture. Eliot not only causes mass or popular culture to obtrude abruptly on his poem's largely high-cultural register but also evokes the technology of mechanical reproduction (one is surely meant to hear these lines in the tinny voice of the gramophone). Eliot himself was an enthusiastic adept of the foxtrot and other new dances,[95] so it cannot simply be assumed that he disapproves of popular songs as such. Yet a certain uneasiness hangs about this moment, and the very jauntiness of the "Rag" seems to deepen rather than alleviate the ponderous melancholy of *The Waste Land*.

Of course, Eliot doesn't cite just any moment in mass culture here; he cites mass culture when it in turn cites high culture. Like Narcissus gazing into the pool, Eliot stares down at the "Shakespearean Rag" and finds a curious mass-cultural mirror of his own poetic. For *The Waste Land* itself also cites decontextualized snatches of Shakespeare's plays—Shakespearean "rags"—in its effort to shore up fragments against cultural ruin. The pop song parodies Eliot's own attempts at conservation, for instead of surrounding its high-cultural allusions with a nimbus of elegiacal reverence, it takes a wryly appreciative yet hardly respectful attitude toward the works of (as the song puts it) "Bill Shakespeare."

The particular lines that Eliot paraphrases, however, engage not in citation but in evaluation, an act that occupies the heart of Eliot's own work as cultural critic. Evaluation both establishes and adjusts the "ideal order" which literary works sustain among themselves; it underlies Eliot's attempts both to conserve and to revise the literary canon,[96] and with it culture as such. It is here, in the work of evaluation, that the "Shakespearean Rag" seems to fall short in a way which is at once comic and disturbing. By associating the adjectives "elegant" and "intelligent" with things Shakespearean, the song engages in an unoriginal (and partly disingenuous) bow to Shakespeare which counts nevertheless as a crude form of literary criticism. But the chosen terms confusingly merge the characteristics of literary greatness with those of fashionable society. "Elegant" sounds more appropriate when applied to a tuxedo than to Shakespeare; or rather, the word evokes a world in which dropping Shakespearean tags creates precisely the same effect of elegance as that produced by the wearing of the tuxedo. And "intelligent" is a rather tepid description of Shakespeare's talents. To a critic such as Eliot, such

95. See Hawkes, *Meaning by Shakespeare*, pp. 90–93.
96. For a brilliant discussion of Eliot's theories of canon formation and their relevance to mass culture, see John Guillory, *Cultural Capital: The Problem of Literary Canon Formation* (Chicago: University of Chicago Press, 1993), pp. 134–75.

evaluative terms would sound ludicrously inappropriate. The vocabulary with which mass culture comes to praise Shakespeare actually buries him, just as the syncopation of the lines mangles Shakespeare's name in its relentless rhythmic drive. And yet this isn't quite right either, for strictly speaking the words "elegant" and "intelligent" don't modify "Shakespeare" but rather the "Shakespearian rag"—that is, the song itself. What is described as intelligent and elegant isn't Shakespeare's oeuvre but rather a ragtime tune that can quote such a "high-tone" author. Shakespeare is thus transformed into a detachable signifier of literary and social distinction—a kind of brand name that promises "quality." It is the hook by which the song hopes (correctly, in the event) to propel itself into profitability.

The best gloss on Eliot's citational strategy here may be found in a complaint by F. R. Leavis: "Not only does the modern dissipate himself upon so much more reading of all kinds: the task of acquiring discrimination is much more difficult. A reader who grew up with Wordsworth moved among a limited set of signals (so to speak): the variety was not so overwhelming. So he was able to acquire discrimination as he went along. But the modern is exposed to a concourse of signals so bewildering in their variety and number that, unless he is especially gifted or especially favoured, he can hardly begin to discriminate."[97] The traditional, critical function of the cultural public sphere is undone by the noise or clutter which (according to Leavis) now fills it. Eliot quotes the "Shakespearean Rag" partly in order to help reproduce just that "bewildering" variety of signals which constitutes modernity and which, for Leavis, impairs the powers of literary discrimination. Moreover, the song's own evaluative vocabulary seems badly degraded and confused, so that it not only causes but embodies a lack of discrimination. Because the Shakespearian Rag stumbles in its attempts to deploy an evaluative and hence critical language, it is both a product of mass culture and one that demonstrates the supposedly debilitating effect of that culture on its listeners. In its seeming failure to discriminate, the song represents an aesthetic equivalent to the crisis of undifferentiation which René Girard locates in the social structure of a mass society.

This undiscriminating or uncritical absorption of cultural products is what Habermas means by "consumption." The "Shakespearian Rag" is not only a commodity itself but one that predigests Shakespeare into an insipid, commodified form. By consuming—that is, obliterating—Shakespeare, moreover, the song threatens both the cultural traditions and the

97. Leavis, *Mass Civilization*, pp. 18–19.

exquisite discrimination on which Eliot's own difficult and erudite poem relies. The tune of that "Shakepearian Rag" echoes across the vast stretches of a mass-cultural "wasteland" in which *The Waste Land* itself cannot be properly read or appreciated.

Now we can begin to gauge the point to Eliot's citation of a specifically *Shakespearian* rag. For one thing, the mixing of high and low is itself characteristically Shakespearean: allotting a voice to pop culture in his high-modernist poem may be seen as Eliot's equivalent of, say, the inclusion of the gravediggers' scene in *Hamlet*. Eliot views Shakespeare's cultural range as an important source of his universal appeal, sustaining the mystery of an audience which is at once unified and stratified. Yet as we have seen, Eliot and Leavis both deem that audience defunct. In its place comes the mass-cultural audience which simply collapses all distinctions and discriminations. Mass culture has disturbed the structured system of high and low that sustained Shakespearean dramaturgy. And in fact, Eliot's deployment of mass culture in his poem doesn't imitate a Shakespearean dialectic so much as point to its undoing. For the voice of the "Shakespeherian Rag" isn't like that of Shakespeare's clowns; at least as paraphrased by Eliot, it seems not to mock high culture so much as to suffocate it in a deep but uncomprehending embrace. It points to an implosion of the cultural system, not to a flexing of its constitutive tensions.

As a defensive response, Eliot engages in ironic counter-quotation. Modernist irony encases mass-cultural materials in a layer of critical consciousness and thereby allows them to be safely imported into the high-modernist text without violating its sense of cultural discrimination. Here its effect and purpose is to posit the pop song as less self-aware and subtle than Eliot's poem. Of course, the real "Shakespearian Rag" adopts a witty and implicitly critical take on high culture, but Eliot's brief paraphrase conveys none of the original song's satirical edge. "The Shakespearian Rag" *does* in fact give vent to a plebeian humor like that of Shakespeare's clowns, but Eliot simply won't admit this countervoice into *The Waste Land*. His irony works only in one direction, and thereby makes mass culture into the debased thing he seems to protest. Irony's sole task here is to distinguish modernism's "critical" citation of mass culture from mass culture's own (presumed) acts of uncritical consumption. Irony points to a self-conscious judgment of cultural messages as opposed to the putatively helpless and passive reception experienced by the targets of advertising, propaganda, and hit songs. It is modernism's protective amulet in the cultural wasteland—and it will be draped not only around Eliot's neck but, increasingly, around Shakespeare's as well.

Eliot's modernist techniques of irony receive theoretical elaboration in the first essay of Northrop Frye's *Anatomy of Criticism*. In announcing that "we are now in an ironic phase of literature,"[98] Frye declares an allegiance with high modernism that colors his treatment of literary irony. Frye regards the ironic mode as a descent from the low mimetic, and he raises the topic of irony in a discussion of low-mimetic comedy. For Frye, the governing *mythos* of comedy is the unification of society through the expulsion of a *pharmakos* or scapegoat figure. This plot can be amusing when the chosen victim is a ridiculous braggart, a boring pedant, a tyrannical father, or any of the other stock figures of comic drama. Yet Frye also recognizes a danger inherent in the comic *mythos*: "We pass the boundary of art when this [scapegoat] symbol becomes existential, as it does in the black man of a lynching, the Jew of a pogrom, the old woman of a witch hunt, or anyone picked up at random by a mob, like Cinna the poet in *Julius Caesar*."[99] Frye argues that in literature's playful enactment of scapegoating, "mob emotions are boiled in an open pot, so to speak," and are thus dissipated harmlessly. Still, he worries about forms of popular fiction such as the detective novel with its obsessive hunting down of "suspects."[100] Frye's anxieties about scapegoats and mob violence, along with the seemingly inevitable reference to *Julius Caesar*, reveals a set of concerns similar to those of René Girard. Frye's nervousness, moreover, tends to settle on popular genres in which the boundary between fiction and reality is supposedly less carefully delineated than it is in high literary forms. Melodrama, in particular, walks a dangerous line:

In melodrama two themes are important: the triumph of moral virtue over villainy, and the consequent idealizing of the moral views assumed to be held by the audience. In the melodrama of the brutal thriller we come as close as it is normally possible for art to come to the pure self-righteousness of the lynching mob.

We should have to say, then, that all forms of melodrama, the detective story in particular, were advance propaganda for the police state, in so far as that represents the regularizing of mob violence, if it were possible to take them seriously. But it seems not to be possible.[101]

98. Northrop Frye, *Anatomy of Criticism: Four Essays* (Princeton: Princeton University Press, 1957), p. 46.
99. Ibid., p. 45.
100. Ibid., p. 46.
101. Ibid., p. 47.

Irony is what separates the literary reader from the violent mob. The self-righteous passions of the mob-mind are directly melodramatic, but the ironic reader is immune to melodramatic ideas because "it seems not to be possible" to take them seriously—even though Frye lists several contexts in which it *is* possible: lynching, pogroms, and so forth. Irony has taken on a more daunting role for Frye, guarding not only against cultural cretinism but also against mob rule and the police state. Totalitarian societies arise where listeners take propaganda seriously, while liberal democracy depends on the critical distance offered by literary irony (if not in the work, then in the reader).

Yet things are not quite so simple as that:

> Cultivated people go to a melodrama to hiss the villain with an air of condescension: they are making a point of the fact that they cannot take his villainy seriously. We have here a type of irony which exactly corresponds to that of two other major arts of the ironic age, advertising and propaganda. These arts pretend to address themselves seriously to a subliminal audience of cretins, an audience that may not even exist, but which is assumed to be simple-minded enough to accept at their face value the statements made about the purity of a soap or a government's motives. The rest of us, realizing that irony never says precisely what it means, take these arts ironically, or, at least, regard them as a kind of ironic game.[102]

Here Frye's argument becomes much more diabolical, and much more interesting. Mass culture has, it turns out, two audiences. The cretinous one, which accepts its messages with credulity, is a "dummy" audience in both senses of the word: stupid, but also an empty slot, like the dummy hand in bridge. This audience "may not even exist," for it is the creation of the ironist (including the modernist), who defines his or her position against it. The second audience ("the rest of us") is the *real* audience addressed by advertising and propaganda, those "major arts of the ironic age." Mass culture, in other words, assumes that its messages will be received ironically; its irony is built in, accounted for in advance. While seeming to provide critical distance, irony actually facilitates the reception of mass cultural messages by flattering the addressee, who clandestinely enjoys feelings of superiority to an imaginary audience of cretins. Frye's position here is intriguingly close to that of Adorno and Hork-

102. Ibid.

heimer: "The triumph of advertising in the culture industry is that consumers feel compelled to buy and use its products even though they see through them."[103] "*Because* they see through them," Frye might add. This is the irony of irony, which modernism discovered in its late phase: instead of resisting mass-cultural consumption, irony has become the very medium of consumption. Its apparent capacity to sustain a patrician, critical realm of culture is thus undercut by its ubiquitous role in the plebeian sphere. Once again, the Forum swallows the Senate.

I want to claim that these two examples from Eliot and Frye have a larger, emblematic significance and that the status of irony as modernism's master trope is thoroughly imbued with the problem of mass culture. For modernist critics, the ability to perceive an ironic discrepancy between manifest and latent meaning becomes virtually identified with interpretation as such; and it is what distinguishes (or attempts to distinguish) criticism from the mere consumption of literature. As Frye insists, "the theorist of literature and the consumer of literature are not the same at all, even when they co-exist in the same man."[104] This distinction is directly relevant to Shakespeare since, as Gary Taylor points out, irony is frequently used to underwrite the "two-audience" theory of Renaissance theater, demarcating an intellectual elite from the groundlings.[105] Discussions of irony are not always accompanied by references to mass and high cultures, of course, but it can be argued that this context is almost always present, including when (as in the New Criticism's frequent recourse to irony as interpretive trope) it is not explicitly invoked. Irony is the figure through which mass culture imprints itself on modernist criticism, even when the masses themselves don't put in an appearance. It will thus enable us to shift our historical view past the turbulent 1930s, and our literary view past the urban, massified context of the Roman plays.

When it was first published in 1959, C. L. Barber's *Shakespeare's Festive Comedy* represented a groundbreaking study of Shakespeare's early comedies in the context of popular festivity and entertainment.[106] Nowadays Barber's book looks somewhat quaint and idealizing when compared with

103. Max Horkheimer and Theodor W. Adorno, *Dialectic of Enlightenment*, trans. John Cummings (New York: Herder & Herder, 1972), p. 167.

104. Frye, *Anatomy of Criticism*, p. 20.

105. Taylor, *Reinventing Shakespeare*, pp. 247–48.

106. C. L. Barber, *Shakespeare's Festive Comedy: A Study of Dramatic Form and Its Relation to Social Custom* (Princeton: Princeton University Press, 1959). The judgment of Barber's book as "groundbreaking" is Annabel Patterson's, *Shakespeare*, p. 59.

the work of Marxist critics such as Mikhail Bakhtin and Robert Weimann. While he is not unaware of the class tensions expressed in popular festivity, Barber tends to emphasize its conservative functions: "Festivities were occasions for communicating across class lines and realizing the common humanity of every level. And the institution of the holidays and entertainments was a function of community life where people knew their places and knew the human qualities of each in his place."[107] Barber's approach reflects the largely quiescent state of American political culture in the 1950s, and it is pointless to criticize him for this. I believe that, in any case, the politics of Barber's book reside not in his treatment of contrasting class cultures but in a more vague and diffuse engagement with modern mass culture as mediated through the book's treatment of Shakespearean irony.

Before turning to this, however, I want to remark briefly on Barber's general approach to festivity, which emphasizes the "release" of pent-up energies enabled by holiday sports: "A saturnalian attitude, assumed by a clear-cut gesture toward liberty, brings mirth, an accession of wanton vitality. In the terms of Freud's analysis of wit, the energy normally occupied in maintaining inhibition is freed for celebration."[108] Barber's focus on festive release, I believe, ought to be seen in the context of what might be called a "crisis of leisure" in postwar culture. Adorno and Horkheimer had already argued in *Dialectic of Enlightenment* (1944) that the products of the culture industry turn leisure time into a prolongation of the industrial work day rather than an escape from it. Herbert Marcuse further developed this theme in *Eros and Civilization* (1955) when he claimed that leisure in capitalist societies offers only a "repressive desublimation" of the psychic energies otherwise devoted to surplus labor. Barber's interest in festive release suggests a nostalgic, utopian response to the same contemporary crisis of leisure that Frankfurt School critics engaged in a more direct and oppositional fashion. Barber construes the Renaissance as a twilight of festivity in which the release offered by popular culture is threatened by the rising work ethic of puritanism, and in which a diminution in "awe of man for master" dissipates the fun of festive inversion and abuse.[109] Like the Frankfurt School theorists, then, he describes a leisure imperiled by work. Barber allegorizes the Renaissance not through the medium of social class but through psychic econ-

107. Barber, *Shakespeare's Festive Comedy*, p. 111.
108. Ibid., p. 7.
109. Ibid., pp. 16, 25–26.

omy; the fate of Renaissance festivity provides him with a window onto the dwindling opportunities for both political and libidinal release in the repressive consumer culture of the 1950s.

Barber's treatment of irony in *Shakespeare's Festive Comedy* is crucial both to his historical reconstruction of Renaissance drama and to his allegorical reflections on mass culture. By the 1590s, he argues, unselfconscious festivity was possible only in the countryside; in the city the need to defend festivity against puritan and middle-class opposition made it more self-aware. Shakespeare, coming to London from a small market town, "was perfectly situated to express both a countryman's participation in holiday and a city man's consciousness of it."[110]

The self-consciousness of festivity in Renaissance theater secures Barber's argument that festive patterns lead "through release to clarification"—that is, to an enhanced cognitive grasp of social and natural relationships.[111] Barber, like Frye, very much resists the modernist temptation toward a "ritualist" and therefore primitivist interpretation of Renaissance drama. He sees in this drama not a *form* of agrarian ritual but a self-conscious *citation* of it—not a naïve or primitive reenactment but an ironic contextualization. In actual festivity, he writes,

> No one need decide . . . whether the identifications involved in the ceremony are magically valid or merely expressive. But in the drama, perspective and control depend on presenting, along with the ritual gestures, an expression of a social situation out of which they grow. So the drama must control magic by re-understanding it as imagination: dramatic irony must constantly dog the wish that the mock king be real, that the self be all the world or set all the world at naught. When, through a failure of irony, the dramatist presents ritual as magically valid, the result is sentimental, since drama lacks the kind of control which in ritual comes from the auditors' being participants. Sentimental "drama," that which succeeds in being neither comedy nor tragedy, can be regarded from this vantage as theater used as a substitute for ritual, without the commitment to participation and discipline proper to ritual nor the commitment to the fullest understanding proper to comedy or tragedy.[112]

Renaissance drama is caught between a wish for collective identification and release, and an ironic distancing from it. Without the latter, argues

110. Ibid., p. 17.
111. Ibid., pp. 6–10.
112. Ibid., pp. 220–21.

Barber, drama collapses into the pseudo-ritual of the "sentimental," a category which he treats rather as Frye does melodrama.

Barber's insistence on the ironic citation of popular forms recalls Eliot's poetic technique in *The Waste Land*, even as his invective against drama *as* ritual torpedoes the dramatic practice of modernists such as Eliot and Artaud. Moreover, his attachment to irony aligns him in certain ways with the New Critics, as does his allegorical contest between agrarian and modernizing cultures. Since his most searching investigation of Shakespearean irony focuses on *1 and 2 Henry IV*, it invites comparison with Cleanth Brooks and Robert Heilman's treatment of the same plays in *Understanding Drama*.

In both readings, the question of irony turns on the figure of Falstaff, who questions the plays' official values of honor, chivalry, and kingship. Falstaff embodies the spirit of criticism, though in a uniquely congenial and inoffensive way. The fundamental problem of reading *1 and 2 Henry IV*, both for Barber and for Brooks and Heilman, is how to handle the competing claims of opposed value systems. Barber, of course, has an explanatory structure ready to hand: the saturnalian inversions of popular festival, which temporarily subvert rule so as ultimately to reinforce it. Yet the reason why the *Henry* plays so fascinate Barber is the inability of the holiday spirit to account adequately for Falstaff's role:

> But Falstaff proves extremely difficult to bring to book—more difficult than an ordinary mummery king—because his burlesque and mockery are developed to a point where the mood of a moment crystallizes as a settled attitude of scepticism. As we have observed before, in a static, monolithic society, a Lord of Misrule can be put back in his place after the revel with relative ease. The festive burlesque of solemn sanctities does not seriously threaten social values in a monolithic culture, because the license depends utterly upon what it mocks: liberty is unable to envisage any alternative to the accepted order except the standing of it on its head. But Shakespeare's culture was not monolithic: though its moralists assumed a single order, scepticism was beginning to have ground to stand on and look about—especially in and around London. So a Lord of Misrule figure, brought up, so to speak, from the country to the city, or from the traditional past into the changing present, could become on the Bankside the mouthpiece not merely for the dependent holiday scepticism which is endemic in a traditional society, but also for a dangerously self-sufficient everyday scepticism. When such a figure is set in an environment of sober-blooded great men behaving as op-

portunistically as he, the effect is to raise radical questions about social sanctities.[113]

Falstaff's essential modernity consists in a diffuse skepticism toward ruling values which can no longer be localized or limited either temporally, in the traditional holiday calendar, or personally, in the character of Falstaff. And the difference between Parts 1 and 2 of *Henry IV* resides primarily, for Barber, in the ways they handle the threat of a generalized skepticism.

I introduced Falstaff in the context of irony and then quoted Barber on Falstaff's skepticism, but it might be objected that irony and skepticism are not the same thing. Barber, in fact, tends to restrict the term "irony" rather as the New Critics do, to the effects of literary structure; hence a play may portray Falstaff "ironically," but Falstaff's own ironic stance is described as skepticism. Barber locates literary irony in structural parallels between the tavern and court scenes, and shows how Falstaff's role in *1 Henry IV* reflects ironically on the rhetorical claims of absolutist monarchy; but he also argues that *1 Henry IV* casts an ironic light on Falstaff, and thus controls the threat of his skepticism by making it an object of laughter. Irony and skepticism are thus, in some sense, opposed here. Barber then goes on to claim that in Part 2 of *Henry IV*, irony no longer suffices to control the corrosive effects of skepticism, and so the play resorts to a magical scapegoating ritual in order to cleanse itself. For Barber, the banishment of Falstaff is just such a ritual, and it represents a double artistic failure: first, because skepticism has become generally diffused and cannot be expunged in one symbolic figure, and second, because in treating this ritual magically instead of ironically, the play narrows rather than widens its intellectual grasp and thus regresses to a more primitive form. Skepticism has in effect overpowered irony, calling for cruder methods of control.

Falstaff's skepticism is distinguished from holiday skepticism by its unlocalized quality; yet this resistance to temporal or positional limits takes on an ethical and political element as well. Holiday skepticism follows a bipolar logic: it represents the revolt of low against high, release against repression, body against spirit, freedom against law, and so forth. Its role as *counterprinciple* to hegemonic values is precisely what makes carnival important to both Barber and Bakhtin. But in transcending its holiday context, Falstaffian irony loses its ethical and political bearings as well. Because Falstaff's raillery is opportunistic rather than principled, he be-

113. Ibid., pp. 213–14.

comes not the mocking inversion of ruling-class values but their mirror: "In a play concerned with ruthless political maneuver, much of it conducted by impersonal state functionaries, Falstaff turns up as a functionary too, with his own version of maneuver and impersonality."[114] Skepticism thus loses any critical or oppositional power; a better term for it might be cynicism, although Falstaff lacks the bitterness often associated with the cynic. The spirit of skepticism causes apparent opposites to collapse into each other; it produces not bipolar struggle but just that "plague of undifferentiation" discussed in this chapter's first section.

In line with this, it becomes increasingly difficult to distinguish irony from skepticism in Barber's work. Like the New Critics, Barber values irony for providing an "extension of awareness."[115] By allowing the reader to hold competing claims or perspectives in tension without declaring allegiance to any one, irony sustains mature literary judgment. But Falstaffian skepticism does much the same thing by seeing through all ideals and truth-claims and therefore falling prey to none. If irony proves unable to contain skepticism in 2 Henry IV, this may be because it is skepticism's other face.

Brooks and Heilman's reading of Henry IV, like Barber's, both celebrates Shakespearean irony and reveals the strains which irony has begun to show: "It will be evident that Shakespeare's final attitude toward his characters (and toward the human predicament, generally) is one of a very complex irony, though it is an irony which will be either missed altogether, or easily misinterpreted as an indifferent relativism—that is, a mere balancing of two realms of conduct and a refusal to make any judgment between them."[116] So complex is Shakespearean irony that it entails not only the possibility but the likelihood of misreading, and it is difficult to say whether this results from the play itself or from incompetence in its readers. (The reader who misses irony altogether may invoke the specter of Frye's imaginary, cretinous addressee.) In either case, irony once again faces a collapse of differences—differences both from non-irony and from an "indifferent relativism" which itself suggests impaired powers of judgment and distinction. On one side lies incomprehension; on the other, moral apathy.

The perils of irony once more cluster about Falstaff, although here he is portrayed as childlike and innocent, unlike Barber's opportunistic schemer: "Like the child, [Falstaff] is fundamentally a moral anarchist.

114. Ibid., p. 216.
115. Ibid., p. 217.
116. Cleanth Brooks and Robert B. Heilman, *Understanding Drama* (New York: Henry Holt, 1945), p. 386.

But Falstaff is—again like the child—not a missionary anarchist. He does not for a moment intend to convert others to his views; he is not the moralist, certainly, nor the inverted moralist, the cynic."[117] Again, two complementary heresies emerge: moral or political commitment results from turning the critical powers of irony into principled action and persuasion, while cynicism results from failing to do so. The hypothesis of a childlike Falstaff, which is largely unconvincing on its own merits, seems designed to guard the play from both of these options. The reader, meanwhile, is advised to adopt a pointedly *mature* irony: "Is it not possible that Shakespeare is not asking us to choose at all [between Falstaff and Hal], but rather to contemplate, with understanding and some irony, a world very much like the world that we know, . . . the adult world, where except when crises evoke extraordinary devotion and resolution, compromises and scheming are a regular, and perhaps inevitable, part of human experience[?]".[118] The insupportable burden of irony produces a world-weary tone, as the authors ask us, first, to refrain from choosing alternatives (a state perilously near to "relativism,") and, second, to stare unblinkingly at the sordidness of life without either opposing it or donning the alienating armor of cynicism. Falstaff's impossible childishness answers to the reader's impossible maturity.

The dangers of Falstaffian irony are clearly heightened for Brooks and Heilman by the historical moment of their essay. *Understanding Drama* was published in 1945, near the end of World War II—a time when Falstaff's defense of cowardice and mockery of chivalric honor would be especially touchy subjects. While never directly mentioned, the war colors the whole essay. A section entitled "Falstaff and the World of History" begins: "The student may possibly object to so heavy an emphasis upon the battlefield scenes: . . . Besides bringing all the characters together, . . . the battle scenes subordinate Falstaff, for all his delightfulness, to something larger . . . and this subordination itself is a unifying process."[119] Battle offers "crises [that] evoke extraordinary devotion and resolution," thus providing a respite from the scheming and compromise of everyday life. The spirits of cynicism and pacifism, which Falstaff calls from the "vasty deep," must be, if not suppressed exactly, at least "subordinated to something larger" during wartime. But this pervasive sense of emer-

117. Ibid., p. 380. This view derives from Bradley, who, after listing the serious subjects Falstaff mocks, remarks, "These are the wonderful achievements which he performs, not with the sourness of the cynic, but with the gaiety of a boy" (*Oxford Lectures*, p. 263).

118. Brooks and Heilman, *Understanding Drama*, p. 384.

119. Ibid., pp. 382–83.

gency had subsided somewhat by the time Barber wrote in the mid- and late-1950s.

In both essays, modernist irony is plagued by a mutant strain called either skepticism or cynicism. I prefer the latter term, which also provides the focus for Peter Sloterdijk's *Critique of Cynical Reason*. Sloterdijk defines cynicism as *"enlightened false consciousness*. It is that modernized, unhappy consciousness, on which enlightenment has labored both successfully and in vain. It has learned its lessons in enlightenment, but it has not, and probably was not able to, put them into practice. Well-off and miserable at the same time, this consciousness no longer feels affected by any critique of ideology; its falseness is already reflexively buffered."[120] Cynicism is, for Sloterdijk, both the culmination and the revenge of Enlightenment critique. It fulfills the mandates of critical reason by relentlessly exposing the idealisms and mystifications of power, yet feels powerless to act on its insights—with the result that enlightenment becomes a source of nagging dissatisfaction rather than liberation.

Sloterdijk argues that modern cynicism began in courtly society and in the urban bourgeoisie. Yet today,

> the cynic appears as a mass figure: an average social character in the upper echelons of the elevated superstructure. It is a mass figure not only because advanced industrial civilization produces the bitter loner as a mass phenomenon. Rather, the cities themselves have become diffuse clumps whose power to create generally accepted *public characters* has been lost. The pressure toward individualization has lessened in the modern urban and media climate. Thus modern cynics . . . are no longer outsiders. But less than ever do they appear as a tangibly developed type. Modern mass cynics lose their individual sting and refrain from the risk of letting themselves be put on display. They have long since ceased to expose themselves as eccentrics to the attention and mockery of others. The person with the clear, "evil gaze" has disappeared into the crowd; anonymity now becomes the domain for cynical deviation. Modern cynics are integrated, asocial characters. . . . They do not see their clear, evil gaze as a personal defect or an amoral quirk that needs to be privately justified. Instinctively, they no longer understand their way of existing as something that has to do with being evil, but as participation in a collective, realistically attuned way of seeing things. It is the universally widespread way in which enlightened people

120. Peter Sloterdijk, *Critique of Cynical Reason*, trans. Michael Eldred (Minneapolis: University of Minnesota Press, 1987), p. 5.

see to it that they are not taken for suckers. . . . It is the stance of people who realize that the times of naïveté are gone.[121]

Cynical reason takes the same demystifying gaze which enlightenment focused on naïve ideologies and turns it back on itself. The causes of disappointment with enlightenment are many, but in the above-quoted passage Sloterdijk points to a degeneration of public culture caused by the rise of a massified urban society. Here he seems to approach the views of Habermas, with whom his work has significant, though largely unstated, affiliations. Enlightenment, one might argue, is the project of a bourgeoisie equipped not only with critical reason but with the means to put it into effect—with the opportunity to debate in newspapers, parliament, and other public institutions. Cynicism is the fate of critical reason when it is deprived of a public, dialogical space; that is, when the structures of a mass society prevent individuals from responding in an immediate and effective way to the messages they receive.[122] Then critical reason confronts its own impotence and sinks into either apathy or opportunism, the "hardheaded" realism of the mass cynic who has no illusions about the world and no illusions about bettering it. Sloterdijk's mass cynic reveals the contemporary inspiration behind C. L. Barber's interest in a diffuse "everyday skepticism," without moral or critical bearings, and behind Brooks and Heilman's fears of cynical, indifferent relativism.

Cynical reason "sublates," in a mock-Hegelian way, Habermas's distinction between a culture-debating and a culture-consuming public. It produces a public of consumers who see through the false claims of advertising but continue to buy and use its products—who aren't fooled by the sham rhetoric of politicians but vote anyway or retreat into a grumbling but submissive apathy. Habermas and the other modernists miss the point when they see the culture industry as demanding an uncritical consumption of its products. Mass culture is neither more nor less critical than high culture; it does not eliminate but simply neutralizes criticism, while the system learns to subsist and reproduce itself on the basis of its cynical by-products. Criticism and consumption, those bipolar opposites, thus succumb to a plague of undifferentiation.

121. Ibid., pp. 4–5.
122. I do not wish to suggest, however, that Sloterdijk views cynicism as a mere blocking of enlightenment. For one thing, he argues that cynicism is entwined with enlightenment from the beginning; for another, he expresses certain reservations about philosophies of praxis, which contradict any conception of cynicism as reason that is "blocked" in the sense of lacking outlets for practical effect.

The Critique of Cynical Reason allows us to construe a political allegory enfolded within the studiously apolitical categories employed by Brooks, Heilman, and Barber. Their two essays on *Henry IV* negotiate an indirect contest between high-modernist and mass cultures by means of a collapsing antithesis between irony and cynicism, which Shakespeare is asked (impossibly) to uphold. Modernist irony can't be an antidote to cynicism because it is only a subspecies of it, conditioned by the same structural constraints. It is condemned to mediate a foundering opposition between criticism and consumption, resistance and collaboration.

In elaborating the relations between irony and cynicism I have thus far tended to disregard or marginalize the claims of skepticism, the third term in this triad. The most distinguished of the current advocates for a skeptical reading of Shakespeare is Stanley Cavell, whose essays on this topic have been collected into the volume *Disowning Knowledge in Six Plays of Shakespeare* (1987). While Cavell openly acknowledges having profited from the writings of C. L. Barber, *Disowning Knowledge* distances itself from Barber's work in a number of ways, both gestural and methodological.[123] Barber examines holiday skepticism in the context of festive comedies, while Cavell focuses on Shakespearean tragedy, and thus tends to associate skepticism with the "higher" of the dramatic modes. (He investigates comedy only in the context of popular film, a mass-cultural form). Tragedy, in Cavell's book, not only serves as a privileged point of origin for philosophical skepticism but invests it (and, crucially, the response to its challenge) with the grandeur of tragic heroism—a fact that becomes especially clear in the introductory chapter on *Antony and Cleopatra*. Cavell's version of skepticism is thus, in a sense, generically insulated from the kind of cynical debasement seen in Barber. Yet Cavell's

123. The most interesting gesture occurs early in the preface to the volume. There Cavell recalls a telephone call he received from Barber in the spring of 1971, asking him to join Barber in a proposed seminar on the relations between Shakespeare's works and those of any other major author. Writes Cavell: "I [was] moved as much by the tone of the invitation and by the idea of it as by the fact that they came from a scholar I had not then met but whose book *Shakespeare's Festive Comedy* I had, with so many others, profited from. But I went on to decline the invitation, arguing that preparation for such an undertaking would require from me, at a guess, about ten years" (Stanley Cavell, *Disowning Knowledge in Six Plays of Shakespeare* [Cambridge: Cambridge University Press, 1987], p. viii).

This little story is peculiar in more than one way. While it expresses both warmth and respect toward Barber, it nevertheless ends in a snub—which Cavell now makes public. Moreover, the point of recounting this episode at all is rather obscure. It seems to be the first of the repeated (and utterly disingenuous) gestures of intellectual modesty that Cavell makes in this book, along with repeated (and equally disingenuous) insistence that he is, after all, only an *amateur* Shakespearean. Yet the effect of the story is rather different. Given the fact that his stature is unquestionably greater than Barber's, Cavell's claimed modesty argues implicitly for Barber's intellectual hubris.

extraordinary essay on *King Lear* displays a narrative structure which is, in some respects, intriguingly similar to that of Barber's essay on *Henry IV.*

Part Two of the *King Lear* essay is devoted largely to general reflections on tragedy and modern life. Modernity, Cavell argues, has inverted the traditional relation between tragic theater and the world. Theater used to be a privileged place in which we could witness human suffering without actually being obliged to intervene in it; we could be, as Cavell puts it, ethically "present" to tragic characters without actually being in their presence. Now, however, passive indifference to suffering has become the norm, and so theatrical spectatorship is no longer a special case but depressingly ubiquitous:

> Since we are ineluctably actors in what is happening, nothing can be present to us to which we are not present. Of course we can still know, more than ever, what is going on. But then we always could, more or less. What we do not now know is what there is to acknowledge, what it is I am to make present, what I am to make myself present to. I know there is inexplicable pain and death everywhere, and now if I ask myself why I do nothing the answer must be, I choose not to. That is, doing nothing is no longer something which has a place insured by ceremony; it is the thing I am doing. And it requires the same energy, the same expense of cunning and avoidance, that tragic activity used to have to itself. Tragedy, could it now be written, would not show us that we *are* helpless—it never did, and we are not. It would show us, what it always did, *why* we (as audience) are helpless. Classically, the reason was that pain and death were in our presence when we were not in theirs. Now the reason is that we absent ourselves from them.[124]

The *Lear* essay clearly bears the marks of its historical moment (1967); the death and suffering to which Cavell refers is exemplified primarily, as he makes clear, in the Vietnam War, to which as citizen and intellectual he feels opposed—yet in regard to which he finds himself choosing the course of paralysis or inaction.

For Barber, as we have seen, modernity arises when "holiday skepticism" crosses its traditional, ritualized limits and inhabits the everyday world. For Cavell, something very similar occurs with tragic passivity. Doing nothing seems to have a skeptical basis; there is, to be sure, a problem of knowledge here ("What we do not now know is what there is to ac-

124. Ibid., pp. 116–17.

knowledge, what it is I am to make present, what I am to make myself present to.'') Yet this failure of knowledge occurs not because the world has fallen away from us but because "we," Lear-like, have chosen to avoid the world and its claims upon us. Skepticism may not be identical with cynicism but is dogged by it, just as irony is in Barber's work. Cavell's use of "we," moreover, which both indicts him as an individual and absolves him as mere participant in a generalized abdication, betrays the logic of Sloterdijk's "mass cynic."

Sloterdijk treats irony as a product of modernity, not postmodernity, yet cynicism may be as close as we can come to an official ideology (or anti-ideology) of the postmodern age. The valiant, failed efforts of Brooks, Heilman, and Barber to distinguish irony from cynicism suggest a residual sense of shame, a self-deception whose motives are nonetheless somewhat noble. But in the postmodern era, cynicism parades about openly; if not more widespread, it is at least more comfortable with itself, and therefore all the more cynical.

The filial relationship between modernist irony and postmodern cynicism provides yet another view onto the New Historicism. While I have already discussed Stephen Greenblatt's essay on the *Henriad* in my first chapter, we may grasp another aspect of Greenblatt's work by juxtaposing it with our two modernist essays on the same plays. Or rather, is isn't Greenblatt's work in particular that interests me here; Steven Mullaney's essay "Strange Things, Gross Terms, Curious Customs: The Rehearsal of Cultures in the Late Renaissance," strikingly similar to Greenblatt's in its analysis of Tudor power, suggests that both are to some degree products of a 1980s *Zeitgeist*.[125] Both essays evoke a dialectic of subversion and containment; both acknowledge the oppositional role of popular culture in the Henry plays, yet narrate a process by which the plays' ruling classes neutralize and appropriate this threat; both show that by learning to mimic the lower classes, Prince Hal reinforces his own hegemonic rule; and both take this process as emblematic of larger cultural processes at work in early modern culture.

Unlike their New Critical predecessors, Mullaney and Greenblatt place the *Henriad* in an explicitly political context of class struggle and colonialism. Yet the narrative structures of their essays are remarkably similar to that of Brooks and Heilman. For the latter, it is dramatic irony that subordinates Falstaffian irony and thus neutralizes its threat, while for the former it is the institutional powers of monarchy. In both cases an

125. Greenblatt's essay originally appeared in *Glyph* 8 (1981): 40–60. Mullaney's essay appeared in *Representations* 3 (Summer 1983): 40–67.

oppositional voice is safely contained, though the New Historicists seem to view this with some regret while the New Critics view it with relief.

In *Learning to Curse*, Stephen Greenblatt rejects the notion that historicism requires a suspension of judgment and insists that it involves instead a direct engagement with the past. He traces this attitude, moreover, to the influence of the Vietnam War on intellectuals of his generation.[126] Greenblatt's defense of the historian's right to judge, and thus to "take sides," can be seen as directed not only against the detached objectivity of the "old" historicism but also against the suspension of judgment demanded by New Critical protocols of ironic reading. Of course, Greenblatt's harshest critics have generally been to the left of him politically, and they have criticized his work more often for being too *little* engaged than for violating canons of historical objectivity. Greenblatt is surely right to name the Vietnam War as one factor encouraging the rise of engaged or politicized strategies of reading, yet he may overlook the consequences of its aftermath, as described by Sloterdijk, in forming the political outlook of the New Historicism:

> Besides "commitment," and entwined with it, we find in our memory another recent sediment—the experience of the student movement, scarcely settled, with its ups and downs of courage and depression. This most recent sediment in the history of political vitality forms an additional veil over the old feeling that something ought to be done about this world. The dissolution of the student movement must interest us because it represents a complex metamorphosis of hope into realism, of revolt into a clever melancholy, from a grand political denial into a thousand-faceted, small, subpolitical affirmation, from a radicalism in politics into a middle course of intelligent survival."[127]

The master plot of the New Historicism repeatedly re-enacts this pattern of commitment followed by disappointment, of utopia ceding to accommodation—in short, of subversion followed by containment. What one detects in the typical New Historicist essay is an impulse toward political engagement or advocacy which then generates as its counter-impulse a determination not to be tricked into a naïve or utopian position. To quote Sloterdijk again: "Today, the word 'committed' is said with a mixture of acknowledgment and indulgence, as if it were a fragile sediment from a younger psychological layer that has to be handled with the ut-

---

126. Greenblatt, *Learning to Curse*, pp. 166–67.
127. Sloterdijk, *Critique of Cynical Reason*, p. 89.

most care. It is almost as if our sympathy goes less to those for whom another commits himself or herself than to the commitment itself in its rarity and fragile naïveté."[128] In their deadlock between commitment and cynicism, the New Historicists indulge *both* of the alternatives which modernist irony sought to avoid.

Greenblatt directly confronts this deadlock in the anecdote that introduces his essay "Towards a Poetics of Culture." "In the 1970s," he writes,

> I used to teach courses with names like "Marxist Aesthetics" on the Berkeley campus. This came to an inglorious end when I was giving such a course—it must have been the mid-1970s—and I remember a student getting very angry with me. Now it's true that I tended to like those Marxist figures who were troubled in relation to Marxism—Walter Benjamin, the early rather than the later Lukács, and so forth— and I remember someone finally got up and screamed out in class "You're either a Bolshevik or a Menshevik—make up your fucking mind," and then slammed the door. It was a little unsettling, but I thought about it afterwards and realized that I wasn't sure whether I was a Menshevik, but I certainly wasn't a Bolshevik. After that I started to teach courses with names like "Cultural Poetics." It's true that I'm still more uneasy with a politics and a literary perspective that is untouched by Marxist thought, but that doesn't lead me to endorse propositions or embrace a particular philosophy, politics or rhetoric, *faute de mieux.*[129]

While appealingly confessional, this story is also more than a little self-justifying, not only in its contrast between the thoughtful, nuanced Greenblatt and the rudely fanatical student but also in its subtly figured insistence that political commitment slammed the door on Greenblatt, rather than the reverse. What is most interesting about this tale, however, is that it echoes an endnote at the close of "Invisible Bullets" on *Shakespeare's* politics:

> Perhaps we should imagine Shakespeare writing at a moment when none of the alternatives for a resounding political commitment seemed satisfactory; when the pressure to declare himself unequivocally an adherent of one or another faction seemed narrow, ethically coarse, po-

128. Ibid., p. 88.
129. Greenblatt, *Learning to Curse*, p. 147.

litically stupid; when the most attractive political solution seemed to be to keep options open and the situation fluid.[130]

Greenblatt's anecdote retroactively uncovers the historical allegory at work in this construction of Shakespeare, whose politics reassuringly echo those of his twentieth-century critic.

I do not, however, want to "localize" Greenblatt's and Mullaney's essays with respect to the aftermath of the Vietnam War any more than I want to localize Brooks and Heilman's with respect to World War II. The significance of the antiwar movement, for my purposes, is simply that it offers a late, condensed reprise of the history of enlightenment; for the movement was, from one perspective, nothing less than an attempt to reconstitute the public sphere: that is, an effort on the part of an informed public to exercise its critical reason on an issue of general importance, and to break the monopoly of information and opinion held by government and the mass media. This critical public sphere was also shot through with the carnivalesque, epitomized in some of the events of May, 1968. Increasingly, however, communication not only traveled through alternative outlets but came to be filtered through the mass media as well, with all the opportunities for distortion and co-optation this entailed. Enormous rallies and, eventually, civil unrest struck conservatives not as principled resistance but as the anarchic rule of the "mob." In short, the student movement provoked an intense re-efflorescence of the mutually antagonistic categories I have been describing in this chapter.

In tracing the recuperation of non-hegemonic voices and cultures in early modern England, the New Historicism also allegorizes the fate of the public sphere in the late twentieth century. I say "also" here to avoid premature judgment that one task necessarily dominates the other. There is surely an analogy between the technologies of power described in Greenblatt's and Mullaney's essays, and those which, in our time, help the mass media to process, subsume, and largely neutralize critical or oppositional discourses. It is less clear whether the cynical narrative of what (by analogy to high modernism) we might designate as a "high" New Historicism simply imposes current concerns on an earlier age, or whether the present dilemma of the public sphere enables us to perceive a real but previously unnoticed phenomenon. It is not possible simply to dismiss the notion of a "cynical" or skeptical Shakespeare, any more than it is possible to dismiss the wariness, the anxious glances over the shoul-

130. Greenblatt, *Shakespearean Negotiations*, p. 175 n. 65.

der, that seize New Historicists whenever they are faced with utopian or subversive opportunities.

The answer to cynicism is surely not a return to naïveté. Perhaps, however, we may discover a certain cynicism toward cynicism, just as late modernists discovered the irony of irony. Perhaps, that is, we may learn that "hard-headed realism" can itself become a source of illusions, and that we can be suckered by our own determination *not* to be taken in. The ur-plot of New Historicism, in which what begins as a critical impulse ends in a parable of cynical reason, surely reflects the experience of an objective impasse in the evolution of the public sphere. But we should not let this experience harden into a reflex, lest we misconstrue some late twist in the work of that master ironist known as history.

3

Modernist in the Middle:
The Centrality of Northrop Frye

It is no accident that Northrop Frye occupies the third and middle chapter in this study of Shakespeare and modernism, for Frye's career dominated Anglo-American literary criticism in the middle decades of this century.[1] Like the Tower of Babel he was so fond of referring to, Frye achieved an eminence in the field of literary studies that remains unequaled by any successor. And like that biblical tower, Frye's elaborately constructed system now lies in ruins. Frye's eclipse, however, occurred not despite but because of the fact that his work represents a powerful culmination of modernist criticism. Frye successfully, if temporarily, prolonged modernist critical practice in the universities at a time when modernism as a literary movement had petered out. Moreover, as Frank Lentricchia observes, the date of *Anatomy of Criticism*'s publication (1957) also allowed it to look forward to postmodern responses to the poetic traditions on which it draws.[2] Frye's centrality to my own argument depends in part on the fact that his career spanned those decades during which modernism established an absolute hegemony over Shakespeare criticism (via Frye's work and that of his main competitors, the New Crit-

1. In the proceedings of the 1965 English Institute, devoted to assessing Frye's work, Murray Krieger writes: "Whatever the attitude toward Northrop Frye's prodigious scheme, one cannot doubt that, in what approaches a decade since the publication of his masterwork, he has had an influence—indeed an absolute hold—on a generation of developing critics greater and more extensive than that of any one theorist in recent critical history." Murray Krieger, ed. *Northrop Frye in Modern Criticism* (New York: Columbia University Press, 1966), p. 1.

2. Frank Lentricchia, *After the New Criticism* (Chicago: University of Chicago Press, 1980), p. 26.

ics), before it began to cede its place to postmodern currents. Yet Frye's work does not offer a gateway to the postmodern; if he occupies an important transitional moment, he does so by representing the impasse reached by late or academic modernism.

Frye's stature as a Shakespeare critic exemplifies this impasse. Of Frye's several books on Shakespeare, the first and most important was *A Natural Perspective: The Development of Shakespearean Comedy and Romance* (1965). While T. S. Eliot and G. Wilson Knight had both expressed interest in Shakespearean romance, Frye's book was part of a thoroughgoing effort to rehabilitate literary romance which exceeded and in most respects contradicted the canons of Eliotic modernism. The privileged position occupied by romance as a genre in Frye's criticism is surely one of its windows on the postmodern—and yet in Shakespeare criticism, at least, this aspect of Frye's work seems also to have come to little. Recent criticism has paid some attention to Shakespeare's romances—particularly *The Tempest*—but it has done so primarily in a topical way, ignoring precisely the status of these plays as *romances*. While Frye's revisionary aims largely succeeded with respect to romantic poetry, they ultimately had limited influence on the course of Shakespeare criticism. My intention in what follows is neither to argue for the revival or resurrection of Frye's system (this being a miracle best left to Frye's favorite genre, the romance) nor to "critique" it (a pointless exercise, at this juncture) but to situate Frye at his vanishing point, which is also his point of greatest significance. In tracing the larger outlines of his literary system, I want to emphasize the privileged role played in it by romance as a literary mode, with the ultimate aim of assessing Frye's reading of Shakespearean romance. The specifically Shakespearean dimensions of Frye's work will be addressed primarily in the last section of this chapter. The first two sections attempt to position Frye with respect to his modernist precursors and postmodern successors, and by so doing to provide a general context for Frye's reading of Shakespearean romance.

Totality and Autonomy:
Literature's Peaceable Kingdom

Anatomy of Criticism embraces the twin goals of totality and autonomy. On the one hand, it envisions a "synoptic view" of literature whose professed purpose is not to replace but to organize and coordinate the existing plurality of methods into a unified system; on the other, it attempts to supply literary criticism with its own distinctive object and method of study. The "Polemical Introduction" to the *Anatomy* elaborates both of these aims while also specifying Frye's tense and complex relationship with Eliotic modernism: "It is clear that criticism cannot be a systematic study unless there is a quality in literature which enables it to be so. We have to adopt the hypothesis, then, that just as there is an order of nature behind the natural sciences, so literature is not a piled aggregate of 'works,' but an order of words."[3] Literature, that is to say, must form a total and autonomous structure if literary criticism is to have its own systematic object of study and not decline into mere bricolage. Frye traces the origins of this notion of total order back to T. S. Eliot: "Mr. Eliot's essay *The Function of Criticism* begins by laying down the principle that the existing monuments of literature form an ideal order among themselves, and are not simply collections of the writings of individuals. This is criticism, and very fundamental criticism. Much of this book attempts to annotate it."[4] While Frye's debts to Eliot are visible throughout the *Anatomy*, and nowhere more clearly than here, his deferential tone is misleading, for he does not "annotate" Eliot's notion of the ideal order but in fact radically revises it. To Eliot, the order of literature is not only a set of shared traditions but also a hierarchy of values which allots each work its major or minor status. Frye, however, vigorously repudiates evaluation as a task for the literary critic, and declares, in distinctly un-Eliotic fashion, that criticism "should show a steady advance toward undiscriminating catholicity."[5] By expelling considerations of value from the literary *order*, Frye turns it into a *structure*, which is not at all the same thing, since individual works are accorded a place but no longer a ranking. He thereby expels from the Eliotic tradition all those questions of judgment and public taste which loomed so large in the work of F. R. Leavis. Frye knows, of course, that critics will always prefer some works to others, and he frequently indulges in comparisons of value; but he insists that judgment, as a mere matter of opinion, has no place in a progressive or scientific criticism, and he rejects the notion that his own system can lay a more systematic or objective basis for literary rankings.

Frye so drastically revises and expands Eliot's ideal order that one may reasonably wonder whether Eliot's work really plays the foundational role Frye claims. In many respects, Frye's syncretic literary "universe" seems more Joycean than Eliotic in its dimensions. James Joyce's work domi-

3. Northrop Frye, *Anatomy of Criticism: Four Essays* (Princeton: Princeton University Press, 1957), p. 17.
4. Ibid., p. 18.
5. Ibid., p. 25.

nates the *Anatomy*, from its emphasis on mythic parallels to its Viconian cycles of literary history, its inclusion of mass or popular culture, its encyclopedic exuberance of form. The Joycean totality, embodied in the figure of HCE or Here Comes Everybody, probably contributes more to Frye's conception of literature than does Eliot's more restrained and conservative "order."

Shortly after endorsing Eliot's vision of literature, in fact, Frye constructs an elaborate and highly suggestive metaphor which impugns Eliot's critical authority. Criticism, Frye states, must dismiss

> all the literary chit-chat which makes the reputations of poets boom and crash in an imaginary stock exchange. That wealthy investor Mr. Eliot, after dumping Milton on the market, is now buying him again; Donne has probably reached his peak and will begin to taper off; Tennyson may be in for a slight flutter but the Shelley stocks are still bearish. This sort of thing cannot be part of any systematic study, for a systematic study can only progress: whatever dithers or vacillates or reacts is merely leisure-class gossip.[6]

This rather less respectful image of Eliot's ideal order is more than a casual swipe, for it invokes the "double discourse of value" which, as John Guillory has shown, ties aesthetics to political economy.[7] Frye's image of a literary stock market not only satirizes the seeming capriciousness of canonical revision but implicitly engages the relation between aesthetic value and exchange-value, one that is crucial to Frye's conception of literature as totality. The problem of the commodity, as addressed by classical political economy, was its split between use- and exchange-value. As use-values, commodities perform distinctive and presumably incommensurable functions, which since Aristotle's time has raised the question of how they can be traded for one another or assigned relative values and ratios of exchange.[8] Exchange-value is a principle of universal commensurability which permits a total *system* of commodity exchange to arise despite the particularity or incommensurability of individual commodities considered as use-values. Literary aesthetics faces a similar problem in defining the mystical substance of aesthetic value which allows works of art to be compared with one another and organized into an "ideal order."

6. Ibid., p. 18.
7. Guillory, *Cultural Capital*, pp. 269–340.
8. On Aristotle and value, see Karl Marx, *Capital: A Critique of Political Economy*, trans. Ben Fowkes, 3 vols. (New York: Vintage, 1977), 1:151–52.

Frye does not solve the value problem; instead, he simply jettisons the entire concept of literary value. But in doing so he once again foregrounds the commensurability issue. If not aesthetic value, what is the mysterious substance (or, as Frye puts it, "quality") that unites works of different genres, styles, and periods into an organized and autonomous body called "literature"? In Frye's case, the answer is narrative. Literary works participate in the "order of words" because their embedded narratives or plots resonate with, and find a place in, the overarching narrative or mythic cycle which Frye maps in the *Anatomy*. Myths, Frye argues, are "narrative pregeneric elements of literature,"[9] and his other major categories of mode, symbol, and genre are also primarily narrative in conception.

Substituting narrative structure for literary value as the plinth on which the "ideal order" of literature stands shifts the focus of critical attention toward narrative forms of literature. While the New Criticism tended to concentrate on lyric poetry, Frye's method embraced forms such as romance, which lacks both the verbal density and the ironic structure on which New Critical analysis relied. A focus on narrative also drew attention to popular or mass-cultural works which the New Criticism, with its allegiance to a high-modernist aesthetic, tended to deride.

While Frye's mode of constituting a literary totality contains its own mystifications, it has at least one advantage over the discourse of literary or aesthetic value. As with the commodity, the aesthetic value of a work of art seems somehow to emanate from, or to be immanent to, the work itself, instead of arising from a practice of universal commensuration or exchange. In Frye's system, however, the individual work must always refer to the totality or macro-narrative of literature; literary meaning is always relational and intertextual, and cannot pose as self-contained or self-originating. Yet for all that, Frye does not entirely overcome the illusion of immanence produced by the value form. If the individual work must always refer to the totality in which it participates, it does so by means of an apparently inherent or embedded narrative which Frye as critic claims merely to uncover. But narratives do not just rest in works like rifts of ore; rather, Frye's method involves an occulted *practice* which "pre-prepares" literary works for analysis by construing them as plots or stories. In the case of Shakespeare, Frye never really discusses the plays as theatrical productions or performances. Rather, Shakespeare's works are reduced to their extracted narratives. Frye's approach differs from that of Eliot, whose *Elizabethan Essays* focus as much on style as on struc-

9. Frye, *Anatomy of Criticism*, p. 162.

ture, and from that of the New Critics, who focus more on irony, imagery, and verbal texture—but follows the example of Freud, who also construes both Shakespearean and Sophoclean drama largely from the perspective of their embedded plots. Frye's literary totality, like the system of commodity exchange, thus relies on an unacknowledged labor of narrative abstraction to render concrete works (literary "use-values") commensurable.

Frye rejects the labor of critical evaluation not because he hopes to rescue literature from the logic of the commodity but because such evaluation, based solely on opinion, has no place in a progressive and scientific enterprise. His imaginary stock exchange satirizes not so much the fact of literary value as its apparent volatility. What bother Frye are the boom and bust cycles of reputation which seem to depend more on the caprice of authoritative individuals such as Eliot than on objective and impersonal factors. Criticism cannot "progress" in a stable fashion if its objects are exposed to unexpected dips and surges in prestige. Such violent shifts cast doubt on the ontological and methodological solidity of criticism's subject matter, and hence on criticism as a discipline. Frye's system cannot dispense with literary value, therefore, but must attempt to stabilize it and thus replace a boom-and-bust cycle with regulated growth based on an ever-expanding canon. His approach may be described with only some facetiousness as a kind of literary Keynesianism. Eliot's radical experiments in canon revision occurred during the fiscal instabilities of the first half of this century, while Frye's adherence to stable growth accords better with the "long boom" of the 1950s and 1960s, which produced steady increases in university enrollments and funding as well.[10] Frye's attacks on literary judgment partly reflect his attempt to wrest criticism from the hands of influential poet-critics such as Eliot, Allen Tate, and John Crowe Ransom, and install it in the institutional context of the American university, where, he hoped, it could assume a more progressive and scientific form.

The totalizing aspects of Frye's system are largely directed "inward": they aim to constitute the literary field as a unified and self-organizing object of study. But the mythic, narrative structures of the *Anatomy* also point outward toward the larger, social world, and thereby negotiate the boundaries of literary autonomy. In his essay on "*Ulysses*, Order, and

10. See Laurence R. Veysey, "Stability and Experiment in the American University Curriculum," in *Content and Context: Essays on College Education*, Carnegie Commission on Higher Education Report (New York: McGraw-Hill, 1973), p. 15; cited in Graff, *Professing Literature*, p. 155. On the long postwar boom, see Ernest Mandel, *Long Waves of Capitalist Development: A Marxist Interpretation*, rev. ed. (New York: Verso, 1995), pp. 49–75, 99–100, 103.

Myth," Eliot writes that myth "is simply a way of controlling, of ordering, of giving a shape and a significance to the immense panorama of futility and anarchy which is contemporary history."[11] Myth is modernism's primary resource for imposing imaginative unity on the shattered and fragmented experience of modern life; indeed, it posits modernity as the broken remnants of a lost totality which it attempts to reconstruct. In particular, modernist myth hopes to compensate for the unifying power of religious belief, and thus plays a role comparable to that of art itself for thinkers such as Friedrich Schiller and Matthew Arnold. Or rather, myth occupies an intermediate position between religion and art; it enacts a movement from belief or dogma to the aesthetic, a movement which will prove crucial to Frye's construction of Shakespearean romance.

The importance of myth in Frye's system derives largely from its quasi-religious status. Because it occupies the boundary between belief and imagination, myth both defines a literary totality and specifies its relation to a larger social context. Societies, argues Frye, organize myths into larger, coherent bodies known as mythologies, and they do so for reasons of belief or social concern rather as acts of imagination. Yet what *enables* myths to cohere is an immanent principle of narrative structure. While the realm of belief treats this structural principle or formal cause as mere instrument, the latter can nevertheless detach itself and become its own end or final cause. Thus, as Frye points out, not only sacred texts but secular ones, such as folktales, can become organized into larger narrative cycles. Myths secure the religious or cultural coherence of a society but at the same time give rise to a relatively autonomous, literary totality.

Because it both arises and detaches itself from religious belief, myth provides Frye with a distinctive and ingenious solution to the problem of literature and dogma—a problem which dominates literary criticism from Arnold to Eliot and the New Critics. Writes Chris Baldick: "The general project of Arnold and his followers can be described as an attempt to replace the current dogmatic and explicit forms of ideological expression with the implicit and intuitive properties of literary 'sensibility.' "[12] John Guillory construes this crucial transformation as a replacement of dogma by doxa, that is, of statements of belief with a set of habits or dispositions so ingrained and formative that they may be said to an-

11. Eliot, *Selected Prose*, p. 177.
12. Chris Baldick, *The Social Mission of English Criticism, 1848–1942* (Oxford: Oxford University Press, 1983), p. 228; quoted in Guillory, *Cultural Capital*, p. 136.

tedate belief, and are therefore incapable of being either affirmed or denied:

> Literature itself can be installed as a sensibility that performs the social function of doxa . . . without ever requiring the "imperfect" supplement of orthodoxy, without specifying directly what these beliefs are. . . . The success of this replacement even depended on how thoroughly literature could be made to resist translation into doctrine, a translation Cleanth Brooks called, in a revealing shibboleth of the New Criticism, the "heresy of paraphrase."[13]

Frye's approach to the problem of literature and dogma both draws on and revises the Arnoldian tradition. Frye insists that literature must not be reducible to dogma, but he tends also to avoid recourse to literary sensibility as a solution, since this leads back to the domain of judgment, and hence to evaluation.

In Frye's view, literature frees itself of dogma not by excluding belief but by including all possible beliefs into a total system which then transcends any particular conviction or ideology. "Precisely because its variety is infinite, literature suggests an encyclopedic range of concern greater than any formulation of concern in religious or political myth can express."[14] It is not the individual literary work that can transcend dogma; only literature as a whole can do this, when grasped by a critical mind that is able "to conceive of literature as a totality, as an imaginative body and not simply as an aggregate":

> Once again, literature in its totality is not a super-myth of concern, truer because more comprehensive than all existing ones combined. Literature is not to be believed in: there is no "religion of poetry": the whole point about literature is that it has no direct connection with belief. That is why it has such a vast importance in indicating the horizons beyond all formulations of belief, in pointing to an infinite total concern that can never be expressed, but only indicated in the variety of the arts themselves.[15]

13. Guillory, *Cultural Capital*, p. 138.
14. Frye, *The Critical Path: An Essay on the Social Context of Literary Criticism* (Bloomington: Indiana University Press, 1971), p. 103.
15. Ibid., p. 128.

Literature is to belief as *langue* is to *parole*; it is less an encyclopedic collection of all possible beliefs than the systemic condition of their possibility. It constitutes what one might call, at the risk of neologism, a "metadoxy."

While literature, so construed, denies allegiance to political or religious creeds, Frye's position nevertheless entails a politics, as he recognizes. Frye endorses Arnold's view of culture as expressed in *Culture and Anarchy* (1869), a view which, he says, "was conservative because it was aware of and accepted its tradition, and because it was a source of social authority. It was liberal because it was held, not through faith or dogma, but through reason and imagination, incorporating a sense of beauty and the virtues of the liberal attitude, including tolerance and suspended judgment."[16] Yet as Arnold recognized, while the modernizing process could loosen the hold of traditional authority or dogma, it could not supply a ready substitute for what was lost in religious experience. For Frye as well, literature must not only liberate from dogma but offer something in place of the satisfactions of faith. Literature as totality must not only produce a liberating metadoxy but must also recreate, through the power of literary imagination, something *like* the experience of the divine. Hence the literary totality is, for Frye, not merely a structure but also a visionary body—not only an organizing principle but also a sublime object:

> In the anagogic phase, literature imitates the total dream of man, . . .
> When we pass into anagogy, nature becomes, not the container, but
> the thing contained, and the archetypal universal symbols, the city, the
> garden, the quest, the marriage, are no longer the desirable forms that
> man constructs inside nature, but are themselves the forms of nature.
> Nature is now inside the mind of an infinite man who builds his cities
> out of the Milky Way. This is not reality, but it is the conceivable or
> imaginative limit of desire, which is infinite, eternal, and hence apoc-
> alyptic.[17]

What began as an Eliotic "ideal order" has now taken on Blakean lineaments, and the result may be described as either romantic modernism or visionary liberalism. Just as modernist city planning uproots local particularities but then helps to forge, under the pressure of its abstractions,

16. Ibid., 72.
17. Frye, *Anatomy of Criticism*, p. 119.

a new urban sublime, so does Frye's modernizing criticism produce a totality which is at once systematic and apocalyptic.[18]

We may now begin to describe the place of Shakespeare, and (more broadly) of romance, in Frye's literary system. "Shakespeare," writes Frye in *A Natural Perspective*, "had no opinions, no values, no philosophy, no principles of anything except dramatic structure."[19] Giving a structuralist turn to the romantic view of Shakespeare as the poet of universal empathy, Frye makes him into a perfect embodiment of his own critical principles. Shakespeare is, par excellence, the poet whose universalizing imagination transcends dogma, investing itself only in the overarching structures of imagination and dramatic art. At the same time, however, "Shakespeare's impartiality is a totally involved and committed impartiality: it expresses itself in bringing everything equally to life."[20] The totalizing aspects of Shakespeare's art effect not only a negative movement of detachment from all merely partial viewpoints, but a universalizing and encyclopedic reinvestment of the whole, now grasped not through the powers of belief and commitment but through those of imagination and art. Frye allegorizes Shakespeare, then, not in relation to some social or historical referent but as an embodiment of literature as such. It is true that Shakespeare finally lacks anagogic intensity, at least compared with visionary poets such as Milton or Blake, but Frye compensates for this fact by emphasizing the formative power of romance in Shakespeare's plays.

Romance enjoys a singularly privileged place in Frye's system of modes and genres, despite that system's inherently equalizing tendencies. This position as *primus inter pares* results from the fact that romance embodies, more than all other forms, the double movements of totality and autonomy which, for Frye, constitute the essence of literature. In *The Secular Scripture*, his most extended study of romance, he argues that romantic

18. Here I am drawing on the comparison between Frye and Georges-Eugène Haussmann with which Angus Fletcher opens his brilliant essay, "Utopian History and the *Anatomy of Criticism.*" Just as Baron Haussmann's boulevards allowed easy movement through the tangled thicket of Parisian neighborhoods, argues Fletcher, so does the *Anatomy* lend order and coherence to a disorganized maze of critical methods. "Theoretical networks like the *Anatomy* . . . openly resist the uncontrolled evolution of historically changing cityscape, on which they impose a simpler, reductive, more efficient system of intercommunication. They replace narrow alleys and byways with cold impersonal 'cannon-shot' boulevards. Many a fine and private place must go to make way for the new metropolis" (Fletcher, "Utopian History," in Krieger, *Northrop Frye*, p. 32).

19. Northrop Frye, *A Natural Perspective: The Development of Shakespearean Comedy and Romance* (New York: Columbia University Press, 1965), p. 39.

20. Ibid., p. 44.

narratives undergo a totalizing organization like that of sacred myths.[21] But while the latter form themselves into systems under extraliterary pressure, specifically the need of social institutions for a coherent dogma or belief-system, romances and folktales are under no such pressure. They would thus seem to be autopoietic or self-organizing, their coherent universe the symptom of a purely immanent law of the imagination. Like myths, romances also form cycles, but they do so autonomously and therefore manifest more purely the nature of literature.

As a secular and "merely" popular form, romance frees itself of dogma by falling below it; it is not so much a metadoxy as a sub-doxy. Yet as the title "secular scripture" suggests, it does not lack all relation to the sacred—for it requires, more than any other genre, a simulation of belief. In a discussion of Shakespearean romance and romantic comedy, Frye writes:

> A doctor once remarked to me that he was unable to enjoy a performance of *Twelfth Night* because it was a biological impossibility that boy and girl twins could resemble each other so closely. Shakespeare's answer, apparently, would be for drama what Sir Thomas Browne's is for religion: "Methinks there be not impossibilities enough for an active faith." In fact this is more or less what Paulina does say in *The Winter's Tale*, when one of the most prodigiously unlikely scenes even in Shakespeare reaches its climax: "It is required you do awake your faith." We may compare the assumed name of Imogen, Fidele. Of course the faith spoken of is what we should call imaginative faith, but this imaginative faith is something much more positive than any mere suspension of disbelief, however willing.[22]

The improbabilities of romantic fictions, signs of their frivolous and popular status, can suddenly flower into high mystery. In its special demands on "imaginative faith," romance confirms literature's Arnoldian status as successor to religion. And Shakespearean romance, by combining a skeptical transcendence of dogma with hieratic solemnity and a strict insistence on imaginative faith, perfectly embodies Frye's conception of literature.

Frye's engagement with the Arnoldian problem of "literature and dogma" is no mere intellectual exercise; for throughout Frye's work runs a palpable fear of social control over the arts, a fear directed primarily

21. Northrop Frye, *The Secular Scripture: A Study of the Structure of Romance* (Cambridge: Harvard University Press, 1976), p. 15.
22. Frye, *Natural Perspective*, pp. 18–19.

at Marxism and Christianity. "To defend the autonomy of culture," he therefore insists, "seems to me the social task of the 'intellectual' in the modern world: if so, to defend its subordination to a total synthesis of any kind, religious or political, would be the authentic form of the *trahison des clercs*."[23] Here totality—or more precisely, a totalitarianism that would integrate literature from without—is posed as the antithesis of literary autonomy. Frye's answer to this perceived threat is not to abandon totalizing thought, in the manner of various poststructuralist and postmodern reactions, but rather to withdraw it into the confines of the literary system. For the more literature constitutes an exhaustively complete set of internal relationships, the less purchase it offers to any attempts at external synthesis. "The anagogic view of criticism thus leads to the conception of literature as existing in its own universe, no longer a commentary on life or reality, but containing life and reality in a system of verbal relationships."[24] While this sounds like aestheticism, it has for Frye a social content because the literary totality is essentially defensive, ranging itself against the threat of social totality.

This fear of external synthesis prompts Frye to elevate romance, which supposedly refers only to its own conventions, over realism, which refers to an outer social world. It similarly nourishes Frye's suspicions toward all forms of historicizing criticism.[25] Consequently, the historical dimension of Eliot's "historical allegory" tends to wither away in his work, much as it did with the New Critics. It is not so much annihilated as sublated: Frye's allegorical practice fortifies itself not against the specificities of historical difference but rather against history as such, whose pressure is constantly felt in the defensive totality and autonomy of his system. Likewise, Frye fends off the synthesizing implications of anthropology. Ritual, Frye insists, is a magical attempt to control the outer world; but myth and drama, although born from ritual, detach themselves from it. Ritual is the content, not the origin, of drama, and hence criticism need not situate dramatic or other literary forms in an historical or social context; thus Frye appropriates certain elements of anthropology while managing to expunge the entire thematics of the "primitive" discussed in Chapter 1 of this book. Commenting on the difference between romantic and realistic narrative, he remarks: "The

23. Frye, *Anatomy of Criticism*, p. 127.
24. Ibid., p. 122.
25. Frye, *Critical Path*, 24. Frye's formulation is a subtle one which bears some resemblance to a theory of literary autopoiesis. See Richard Halpern, "The Lyric in the Field of Information: Autopoiesis and History in Donne's *Songs and Sonnets*," *Yale Journal of Criticism* 6, no. 1 (1993): 185–215.

romantic tendency is antirepresentational, and so is parallel to the development of abstract or primitive movements in painting. Critics of painting have learned to examine such pictures on their own terms; critics of fiction have to learn to look at romances, with all their nonrepresentational plots and characters, equally on their own terms."[26] Frye construes "primitive" art in the manner of Wilhelm Wörringer and T. E. Hulme: as the abstraction of form from representational content. His concept of the primitive does not, in anthropological fashion, lead him toward a nexus of social practice, but merely reinforces the formalism of a modernist aesthetic.[27]

Frye's distinctive and slightly anxious vision of a literary totality is partly a product of the Cold War era. But it also responds to a mutation within literary modernism triggered by its increasing confinement to an academic setting. Frye's conception of criticism as a scientific, progressive, and autonomous discipline embraces the bureaucratic structures of the modern university.[28] At the same time, however, Frye expresses a consistent and explicit admiration, throughout his critical career, for the Arnoldian ideal of the public man of letters. As Robert Denham points out in a collection of Frye's radio interviews collected by the Canadian Broadcasting Corporation, "Ten of Frye's books were originally lectures, and the large majority of the essays in his nine collections began as public addresses."[29] Above and beyond Frye's predilection for public speaking was his goal, present in his published work as well, of accessibility to a general, literate public.

Frye's criticism is thus informed by a split allegiance to the university and the public sphere. While he betrays a nostalgia for the older style of the public critic, for instance, he abjures the public critic's traditional

26. Frye, *Secular Scripture*, p. 38.

27. Compare *Secular Scripture*, p. 181. There Frye discusses "the sense of formal design in . . . the cultural products in a museum, which may range from Benin bronzes to Viking ships, from Chinese pottery to Peruvian textiles. We know that all the cruelty and folly of which man is capable was all around these artifacts when they were produced, and that some of that cruelty and folly may be reflected from the art itself. Nevertheless there is something in the energy of design and the purity of outline that lifts them clear of all this. Whatever the culture was, its designed products belong in the state of innocence, as remote from the evils of that culture as Marina was from the brothel in *Pericles*."

28. Hugh Grady argues in *Modernist Shakespeare* that the replacement of a generalized literary public sphere with the restricted, bureaucratic setting of the university is the fundamental fact underlying the rise of modernist Shakespeare criticism. Grady pays little attention to Northrop Frye, but he has interesting things to say about G. Wilson Knight's spatializing conception of the Shakespearean text—an approach which clearly influenced Frye.

29. Robert Denham, *A World in a Grain of Sand: Twenty-Two Interviews with Northrop Frye* (New York: Peter Lang, 1991), p. 1.

role as arbiter of cultural taste.[30] In the *Anatomy* he assigns to critical theory the role of mediator between the specializing university scholar and the public critic or man of letters.[31] Just as myth faces both "inward" toward its immanent structural patterns and "outward" toward larger social concerns of dogma and belief, so does Frye's criticism face inward toward the structure of literature as an object of academic study and outward toward broader issues of public culture and the social order. To say this, of course, is not to claim that Frye can actually synthesize these two realms; rather, that they persist in a state of insoluble but therefore generative contradiction.

Frye attempts to square the circle by making defense of literary and academic autonomy the sole public task of the critic. The university serves a public function, Frye believes, not by endorsing a specific ideology or set of values but by remaining a uniquely value-free institution which subjects different beliefs to tests of truth.[32] The intellectual's task is thus not to endorse social doctrine but to maintain the *Wertfreiheit* or objective neutrality of the university as the sole social space in which doctrines can be subjected to a special kind of testing and understanding. The university, it now appears, is not only the institutional equivalent but the indispensable social base for the "metadoxy" which Frye locates in literary mythology. Only in the university is the whole gamut of possible belief systems at once preserved and suspended. In effect, Frye's critical system simply projects onto its subject matter the liberal university's double claim to encyclopedic inclusiveness and intellectual autonomy.

Thus does Frye attempt to distinguish withdrawal from retreat; a true Blakean visionary, he sees a world in the university's grain of sand. Like the cynical strategies outlined in the third section of Chapter 2, this tactic justifies the refusal of social partisanship or engagement on the part of the literary intellectual. And like those cynical strategies, this one too reacts to a perceived crisis in the literary public sphere. But here, the response is to reconstitute that sphere in an imaginary form. Frye's critical system, with its syncretic mythologies, incorporates a (presumably) total range of social belief at the same time that it withdraws into an academic setting. Myth criticism thus reproduces as literary content the lost coherence of social form. It enables a criticism confined to the school to generate a fictitious substitute for a unified cultural public sphere.

It also enables us to read Frye's allegorization of Shakespeare in a more

30. Frye, *Critical Path*, p. 74.
31. Frye, *Anatomy of Criticism*, p. 11.
32. Frye, *Critical Path*, p. 135.

material, institutional key; for the same qualities that make Shakespeare's works—and particularly Shakespearean romance—into an allegory of the literary as such, also make them into an allegory of the university. Shakespeare's "involved and committed impartiality," in other words, his encyclopedic metadoxy, reflects the curricular structure of the university as the institutional base of Frye's literary theory. Like the university, Shakespeare's dramatic world is at once withdrawn from society and society's compendious distillation.

In a characteristic moment of self-irony, Frye writes: "I have even compared the literary universe to Blake's Beulah, where no dispute can come, where everything is equally an element of a liberal education, where Bunyan and Rochester are met together and Jane Austen and the Marquis de Sade have kissed each other."[33] In conjoining Blake's visionary realm with the literary curriculum of the liberal academy, Frye not only reveals the institutional underpinning of his system; he also points, unwittingly, to that system's undoing. In an age of multiculturalism, curricular wars, and canon debates, it is almost impossible to remember a time when liberal education was regarded as a realm "where no dispute can come." Frye's literary system depended on a unity (or at least harmony) of cultural materials which was imaginable only during the relative calm of the Anglo-American academy during the 1950s and early 1960s, prior to the student, civil rights, and feminist movements which would not only challenge the autonomy of literary studies but fracture the dream of a unified cultural totality—literature's peaceable kingdom. Frye's particular attraction to Shakespearean romance may thus stem in part from the tone of reconciliation that pervades this genre, making it into the image of his own, essentially irenic, vision.

Containing the Popular

To say that Frye's critical system was undone by social changes it could not foretell or accommodate may contribute to a false impression that it was essentially conservative. To the contrary: Frye's method was progressive in a number of ways and was, by some, even regarded in its day as potentially subversive. If Frye's system proved too inflexible to adapt to evolving cultural circumstances, its most interesting failures occurred not when it actively resisted change but when its most progressive elements ran up against insuperable limits. This is clearest, perhaps, in Frye's treat-

33. Frye, in Krieger, ed., *Northrop Frye*, p. 143.

ment of popular culture and its relation to literary study—an area in which romance once again plays a crucial role.

One of the aspects of Frye's criticism which most unnerved some contemporaries was his refusal to evaluate. Not only did Frye's critical method provide no means of distinguishing "good" works from "bad," but it failed to discriminate between high and low culture. Frye's structural method found room not only for the classics of the canon but for "the detective story, the thriller, the Western, the adventure story, the science fiction, the kind of love story that depends on the formula that one critic has called the clinch-tease."[34]

Simply to note Frye's predilection for popular forms tells us little, of course, without some sense of how he constructs the category of the popular. In *A Natural Perspective*, he writes:

> By popular we usually mean what is temporarily fashionable, for reasons that can be derived from the social conditions of any given time. But there is a more permanent sense in which a work may be popular, not as a best-seller, but in the sense of providing a key to imaginative experience for the untrained. The popular in this sense is the continuing primitive, the creative design that makes its impact independently of special education.[35]

This "usual" meaning of "popular" is unsatisfying to Frye for two reasons. First, a temporary or ephemeral burst of popularity signals that instability of literary values which Frye fended off with the weapon of the imaginary stock exchange. Second, the immediate fashionability of the popular depends on "social conditions of any given time"—that is to say, extraliterary determinations. An acceptable version of the popular will have to be stable or enduring in value and subject to immanent, literary criteria. Frye's solution to this problem is to define popular literature as a form in which timeless literary archetypes appear with unusual force or clarity:

> We have associated archetypes and myths particularly with primitive and popular literature. In fact we could almost define popular literature, admittedly in a rather circular way, as literature which affords an unobstructed view of archetypes. We can find this quality on every level of literature: in fairy tales and folk tales, in Shakespeare (in most of

34. Frye, *Natural Perspective*, p. 3.
35. Ibid., p. 53.

the comedies), in the Bible (which would still be a popular book if it were not a sacred one), in Bunyan, in Richardson, in Dickens, in Poe, and of course in a vast amount of ephemeral rubbish as well.[36]

Frye redefines the popular in such a way as virtually to eliminate the question of social origins. Popularity is now determined by a clarity of narrative or mythic form which enables literary works to be read and appreciated without formal training.

Frye's specific inflection of the popular has complex and somewhat contradictory implications. The notion of the popular is spread so broadly that it threatens to lose its class character altogether; yet at the same time, it both lends academic respectability to genuinely popular culture and attempts to stem the slide of older popular works toward the graveyard of moribund and elite classics. In the case of Shakespeare's once-popular plays, the challenges produced by historical distance are in large part linguistic. This kind of difficulty tends to be accentuated by the New Criticism because of its focus on verbal texture and poetic language. By construing Shakespeare's plays as plots, however, Frye tends to mitigate the effects of historical distance. If these plays still cannot be consumed *as* popular culture, they can at least be consumed in relation to it.

Frye's defense of popular culture centers, as is hardly surprising, on romance. Indeed, romance is usually what he means when he speaks of popular culture: "The bulk of popular literature consists of what I have been calling sentimental romance."[37] *The Secular Scripture* is, essentially, an *apologia* for romance, a mode which needs defending partly for its popular status and partly (although for Frye, this is a point closely related to the first) because it lacks the irony and verbal complexity so prized by the New Critics. In compensation for these deficiencies, Frye claims, romances have a kind of primitive vitality resulting from the clarity of their archetypal content and the persistence of their basic plot elements.[38] In short, romances are popular because they are formulaic and conventional. Their conventionality may itself seem another flaw rather than a compensating virtue, and it places romance in perilous proximity to the "ephemeral rubbish" of mass culture. But the point is that the persistence of these plots offers even transitory works a point of contact with

36. Frye, *Anatomy of Criticism*, p. 116.
37. Frye, *Secular Scripture*, p. 23.
38. "Archetypal criticism seems to find its center of gravity in the mode of romance, when the interchange of ballads, folk tales, and popular stories was at its easiest": Frye, *Anatomy of Criticism*, p. 116.

the eternal. Romances may come and go, but romance plots remain, and they tie popular culture to a stable realm of literary value. Construing popular culture as romance turns critical attention away from the "bad" popularity of the topical, the faddish, the fashionable, or the commercial, and toward an unchanging essence of archetypal meaning. It "saves" popular culture by paring away its supposed excrescences.

Frye's revaluation of popular culture has multiple effects on his reading of Shakespeare. First among them is a willingness to address at least some popular elements in the plays (although Frye cannot ultimately be said to have played a decisive role in encouraging the subsequent "boom" in studies of Shakespeare and popular culture). Second is his effort to readjust the Shakespeare canon by defending the late romances. In *A Natural Perspective*, Frye dissents from "those critics who find the height of Shakespeare's achievement in the great tragedies, and feel that the romances of the final period represent an exhaustion of vitality or a subsiding into more facile and commercial formulas. My own view is that the turn to romance in Shakespeare's last phase represents a genuine culmination."[39] This defense of Shakespearean romance is taken up again in *The Secular Scripture*, which devotes particular attention to *Pericles*.

Frye's interest in popular culture and romance does not, of course, develop in a vacuum. His acknowledgment that archetypal criticism works "best" on popular culture because mythic narratives are most apparent there suggests a reversed line of influence: it is the rise of mass culture which enables Frye's brand of criticism to develop in the first place. The pressure exerted by mass culture may prompt academic criticism to reject it, as in the New Critical belief that close reading and a cult of the difficult will immunize students against advertising and popular songs. Or, as in Frye's case, it may turn critical attention toward narrative continuities between high and popular culture in an attempt to both accommodate and contain the latter.

Suggestive parallels between Frye's critical method and the practices of popular culture are especially striking in the case of Shakespeare. As I remarked earlier, Frye "pre-prepares" literary works for analysis by converting them to narratives, a process which secures the coherence of his critical system by making all literary forms commensurable. In the case of Shakespeare, this means treating plays as if they were tales or stories. Frye's critical practice thus bears a certain resemblance to the literary labors of Charles and Mary Lamb in producing their *Tales from Shakespeare* (1807). But the late nineteenth and early twentieth centuries witnessed

39. Frye, *Natural Perspective*, p. 7.

the growth of a veritable industry for producing popularized, narrative versions of Shakespeare. *Shakespere Boiled Down*, which we examined in Chapter 2, was just one of a multitude. At least twenty-one new prose redactions of the plays were published in the years between 1882 and 1917 alone, most by women and most intended for children or young readers.[40] The majority of these collections, moreover, which often bore such titles as *Shakespearian Fairy Tales*, *Typical Tales of Fancy, Romance, and History from Shakespeare's Plays*, or *Phoebe's Shakespeare*, featured the comedies and romances, since these were considered most appropriate for young readers. (Plays like *Titus Andronicus* don't fare especially well in these volumes). Thus not only Frye's narrativizing practice, but his revisionary championing of the comedies and romances, was already anticipated, the better part of a century beforehand, by the mass publishing market.

Almost all of these collections of tales present themselves as a way for children (or, in some cases, adults) to experience Shakespeare without needing to cope with the difficulties of language presented by the actual plays. That is, they pose as propaedeutic devices meant to anticipate and eventually give way to the richer and fuller experience of the plays themselves. But in the order of experience things work otherwise, and readers of such volumes almost certainly grew up to experience Shakespeare's plays as dramatic reenactments of the romantic "tales" known in youth— that is to say, as mere elaborations or echoes of a more basic ur-narrative. Similar effects are produced by comic-book versions of the plays, which began appearing in the 1950s, only a few years before the publication of *Anatomy of Criticism.*

Frye's narrativizing method thus brings him into real and uneasy proximity with the products of mass culture. As I argued in Chapter 2, literary modernism's discomfort with this culture had to do not only with the sense that it was degenerate in itself, but with the fact that it represented a division of what was once felt to be a unified cultural public sphere into mass and avant-garde audiences. Frye's reconfiguring of mass culture as the "popular" is an attempt to patch this public sphere back together through a liberal inclusion/containment of high culture's "other." For Frye, as for Eliot and Leavis before him, Shakespeare represents a particularly successful reconciliation of popular and high culture. Frye's in-

40. I derive this number from my own survey of volumes held in the Folger Shakespeare Library, the New York Public Library, and Sterling Library at Yale University. My research was hardly exhaustive; hence the number of volumes I give is almost certainly an underestimate of the actual number produced.

novation is to specify romance, a form at once popular and hieratic, as the reconciling medium.

The ultimate failure of Frye's solution—and with it, the eventual eclipse of his method—resulted not so much from its internal deficiencies as from the disruption of the liberal consensus on which it relied. This process began in earnest during the 1960s, when the feminist, civil rights, and student movements initiated a fundamental cultural realignment. All of these movements generated countercultures which contested the hegemony of the dominant liberal culture, and each did so in part by injecting into public discourse areas of cultural experience which had been bracketed or suppressed in the classical model of the public sphere (for example, the body and the domestic sphere in the case of feminism), and in part by establishing alternative public spheres to the dominant one. Modernism's fear of a culture divided in two thus gave way to the prospect of multiple fractures.

Frye's investment in cultural unity rendered him not so much opposed to the new separatist tendencies as incapable of grasping them. His notorious comparisons of the student movement of the 1960s with the Nazis suggests a fundamental misprision of the counterculture as aiming to establish a new totalitarianism, thus ignoring its tendencies to "drop out" or simply absent itself from the hegemonic culture.[41] Frye, that is, could imagine the disintegration of liberalism, but only through the imposition of a more rigid and thoroughgoing totality—not through a decentering multiplication of partial publics or counterpublics.

Within the universities, different cultural constituencies were able to establish disciplinary and institutional structures (women's studies, African American studies, popular culture studies, etc.), each with competing canons and methodologies, which would carve up the institutional base of Frye's hoped-for cultural unity. Much of the recent important work done on literary romance, for instance, has been produced by feminist scholars, arguing issues such as whether romance imposes patriarchal norms on female readers or provides them with ways of articulating women's experience.[42] *The Secular Scripture* contains a chapter entitled

41. See, e.g., *Critical Path*, p. 155.
42. See, e.g., Tania Modleski, *Loving with a Vengeance* (Hamden, Conn.: Archon, 1982); Janice Radway, *Reading the Romance: Women, Patriarchy, and Popular Literature* (Chapel Hill: University of North Carolina Press, 1984); Carol Thurston, *The Romance Revolution: Erotic Novels for Women and the Quest for a New Sexual Identity* (Urbana: University of Illinois Press, 1987); Jan Cohn, *Romance and the Erotics of Property: Mass-Market Fiction for Women* (Durham: Duke University Press, 1988); Dana Heller, *The Feminization of Quest Romances: Radical Departures* (Austin: University of Texas Press, 1990).

"Our Lady of Pain: Heroes and Heroines of Romance" in which the reader can sense that Frye is dimly trying to come to terms with issues raised by the women's movement, but is unwilling even to consider the notion that romance might be "gendered" in such a way as to divide an abstractly universal reading public. The perception of romance as feminized probably had much to do with its derogation by Eliotic modernism, and Frye's attempt to recuperate romance only as a popular and not as a women's mode simply represses this problem.[43]

Likewise, the recent burgeoning of Shakespeare criticism from multicultural and postcolonial perspectives has focused largely on plays which are strongly influenced by the genre of romance: *The Tempest*, of course, but also *Othello, Antony and Cleopatra*, and *The Merchant of Venice*.[44] While Frye viewed romance as a thesaurus of ur-narratives, and thus as the very glue of literary unity, more recent criticism treats romance rather as a privileged conduit for cultural otherness. Frye's attempt to rehabilitate romance involved making a "sub-literary" genre respectable in the eyes of the academy. Little could he have imagined a time in which multiple, competing constituencies *within* the academy would fasten on romance, including Shakespearean romance, with the purpose of dismantling his dream of literature as a unified body.

My point, however, is not to portray Frye as a hopeless laggard in some triumphalist narrative of multiculturalism. For one thing, Frye's criticism anticipates much of what has displaced it. As I have tried to show, his interest in popular literature intuits a seismic shift in the culture, even if his treatment of romance tries to recuperate popular culture for an older liberal synthesis. Another forward-looking element in Frye's criticism is its interest in the thematics of desire, which was recognized as novel at the time.[45] Frye argued that the "popular" element in romance results

43. Eliot's intense interest in Renaissance dramatists is balanced by a relative indifference to figures such as Spenser and Sir Philip Sidney, who worked in the romance mode. Eliot's sense of the gendered nature of romance is revealed not only by poems such as *Marina* but by the fact that he discusses *The Faerie Queene* and Sidney's *Arcadia* in an essay titled "Apology for the Countess of Pembroke." In that essay he opines, "The works of Sir Philip Sidney, excepting a few sonnets, are not among those to which one can return for perpetual refreshment; the *Arcadia* is a monument of dulness": Eliot, *Use of Poetry*, p. 44. (Jesse Weston's book on romance, however, is crucial to *The Waste Land*.) In her critical essays, Virginia Woolf championed figures such as Sidney and Spenser, who tended to be slighted by Eliot, and her private writings reveal explicitly feminist motives underlying her interest in Renaissance romance. See Alice Fox, *Virginia Woolf and the Literature of the English Renaissance* (Oxford: Clarendon, 1990).

44. See, e.g., Margo Hendricks and Patricia Parker, eds., *Women, "Race," and Writing in the Early Modern Period* (New York: Routledge, 1994).

45. See, e.g., Krieger, *Northrop Frye*, p. 21.

largely from its kinship to wish-fulfillment and fantasy: "The actual world, as such, keeps dreaming and waking, play and work, in a continuous antithesis . . . [but] the improbable, desiring, erotic, and violent world of romance reminds us that we are not awake when we have abolished the dream world: we are awake only when we have absorbed it again."[46] Frye's emphasis on the role of fantasy and desire in romance engaged realms of experience that the New Criticism tended to avoid, as did his overtly visionary conception of the mythic world. While Frye had, in general, little patience with the counterculture of the 1960s, one can detect a general congruence between his visionary poetics and certain themes of that culture. By the mid-1970s Frye was touting the "relevance" of romance, invoking writers such as Jack Kerouac and claiming that a "pastoral, paradisal, and radically simplified form of life obviously takes on a new kind of urgency in an age of pollution and energy crisis, and helps to explain why romance seems so contemporary a form of literary experience."[47] Frye was sympathetic to a good deal of what constituted the counterculture, wishing only that it didn't have to be a *counter*culture but could be absorbed into the dominant framework—which to some extent did occur, as a complementary tendency to the continued splintering of culture.

One way of assessing the fate of Frye's critical method is to trace the subsequent history of one of its most essential elements. The role of myth in Frye's thought was to secure the imperiled unity of culture by organizing itself into coherent mythologies, and by engaging the most primordial levels of human experience, such as fantasy and desire. Myth, in a sense, steps in to conserve the public sphere when the powers of reason, on which it originally claimed to rely, seem to have exhausted themselves. Yet when myth began to catch on, in the 1970s, its cultural function was almost directly opposite to what Frye had intended. Feminists (such as Mary Daly), Native Americans, and African Americans, among others, began to draw on mythic traditions not in order to forge a syncretic cultural unity but rather to organize the experience of counterpublics and to insist on cultural difference. At the same time, the syncretic tradition lived on in the work of Joseph Campbell and in various forms of New Age spirituality, where it began to take on the form of a "lifestyle" (as in Campbell's book *Myths to Live By*) and, in the case of New Age movements, entered into an ambiguous relationship with commodity culture. Moreover, these two tendencies, though opposed in many respects,

46. Frye, *Secular Scripture*, pp. 58, 61.
47. Ibid., p. 179.

clearly influenced and drew on one another (as in, for instance, New Age appropriation of the Native American mythologies which were revived for a very different purpose). Myth provides a vantage onto the ambiguities of multiculturalism, subject as it is to a dialectical tension between cultural identity politics and a commodified syncretism which bears less resemblance to the grand mythic systems of high modernism than to techniques of postmodern pastiche.

A key to understanding this complex situation (and Frye's role within it) may be provided by Oskar Negt and Alexander Kluge's concept of the "media public sphere," whose emergence marks a decisive stage in the evolution of capitalist culture. While the bourgeois public sphere as described by Habermas brackets all particular life-contexts in order to represent abstractly the supposed interests of society as a whole,

> the tendencies of the consciousness and programming industry, advertising, the publicity campaigns of firms and administrative apparatuses have altogether different roots. These public spheres of production are nonpublicly anchored: in contrast to the traditional form of public sphere, they work the raw material of everyday life and they derive their penetrative force directly from the capitalist production interest. By circumventing the intermediate realm of the traditional public sphere . . . they seek direct access to the private sphere of the individual.[48]

Abandoning the abstractions of the traditional public sphere for concrete appeals to personal interests and life-contexts, the mass media can target multiple, specific groups. As Miriam Hansen puts it: "By a logic that is key to Negt and Kluge's concerns, the global unification of the public sphere through electronic media and transnational networks of production and consumption goes hand in hand with a diversification of appeals and constituencies, as the media strive to get [an] ever more 'direct' grasp on the 'raw material' of people's experience."[49] Comments Hansen: "This structural diversification, however, does not automatically translate into a 'new cultural politics of difference' (Cornel West)."[50] Perhaps not, but the one simulates the other through both a multiplication of markets and a rendering public of previously "private" realms of experience. The media public sphere serves, among other things, as

48. Oskar Negt and Alexander Kluge, *Public Sphere and Experience: Toward an Analysis of the Bourgeois and Proletarian Public Sphere*, trans. Peter Labanyi, Owen Daniel, and Assenka Oksiloff (Minneapolis and London: University of Minnesota Press, 1993), p. xlvi.

49. Miriam Hansen, "Foreword" to Negt and Kluge, *Public Sphere and Experience*, p. xii.

50. Ibid., p. xii.

a mechanism for recuperating potentially divisive or subversive cultural difference into the logic of the market. (A paradigmatic example was its conversion of the counterculture of the 1960s into various forms of consumption and lifestyle.) But this recuperative movement would probably not be possible if the media public sphere did not also create an enabling if ambiguous context for the birth of such movements in the first place. In the United States and Western Europe, the multiplication of counterpublics and countercultures since the 1960s has occurred with the consumerism of the media public sphere already firmly established as a background.

By mapping the transformations of cultural space under late capitalism, Negt and Kluge can help us to understand Northrop Frye's critical system as a reaction to the rise of the media public sphere. As I remarked earlier, Frye attempts to retain the role of public critic while abjuring the functions of aesthetic judgment and doctrinal or ideological debate that had defined the role of the critic in the traditional public sphere. He thereby expels from critical discussion all those areas of concern that the public sphere had traditionally claimed for rational discussion. In effect, he wants to retain the form of the bourgeois public sphere while evacuating its content. In its place, as we have seen, he substitutes a thematics of desire which in turn reflects the consumer culture of the postwar era. Frye's system attempts to impose a unified and pseudo-public character on essentially private acts of literary consumption. Like the media public sphere, his system bypasses the traditional realm of public issues in order to work directly on the "raw material" of desire and experience. His very definition of popular literature as a mode in which wish-fulfillment takes unmediated forms suggests a conception of the popular associated less with a particular class culture than with television and other mass media. Frye's progressive (if relative) tolerance for mass culture, and his embracing of his own distinctive conception of the popular, reorganize the high literary canon so that it can be consumed in a manner more harmonious with the demands of the media public sphere.

As Hansen points out, Negt and Kluge associate the mass media's diversification of appeals and constituencies with a global unification through transnational networks of ownership, production, and consumption.[51] The unifying tendencies inherent to the traditional public sphere

51. Frye's critical theory mimics the unifying movements of late capital in constituting a mythic structure of virtually global reach, thereby situating national literatures in a transnational context. To some degree, this simply reflects a comparativist framework inherited from Frazer and others. But I think that Frye's situation as a Canadian critic in the second half of the twentieth century plays a role as well. As a neighboring country bombarded with

are thus enhanced by the media public sphere, which, Negt and Kluge argue, effects a "real" as opposed to a merely "formal" subsumption of consciousness parallel to the distinction between the real and formal subsumption of capital.[52] Commenting on Marx's description of social wealth under capital as an "immense collection of commodities," they update this concept to take into account advanced techniques of production and marketing:

> Although the total range of commodities [now available] does not have the form of a unified whole, in which the elementary forms are related to one another by structural laws, the individual purchaser of a commodity is nevertheless no longer confronted by this commodity in isolation or by an accumulation of individual commodities. Rather, he is party to a complex of services and commodities structured according to the interests of profit. The simplest of these forms, which can still be understood as "an immense collection of commodities" but in no sense follows an anarchic principle, is the department store (as a real body of commodities, which confronts a customer who believes that he is buying individual commodities). As a result, perceiving a commodity always gives rise to an association with the totality of commodities, so that the whole department store is potentially a commodity that imposes itself upon the purchaser.[53]

Modern consumers "thus respond primarily to products that provide not individual satisfactions, or individual use-values, but that offer whole cycles of them in the form of a context of living."[54] It is almost superfluous to point out the parallels between Frye's totalizing system, in which individual works evoke "whole cycles" of context, and the mode of consumption described by Negt and Kluge. The visionary ecstasy produced by confrontation with the total, anagogical body of literature as displayed in the *Anatomy of Criticism* may have more than a

---

U.S.-based mass media, Canada had an early taste of the fragility of national cultures in the face of giant media cartels. Moreover, Canada's division between French- and English-speaking cultures necessarily weakened the nation-state as a cultural unit. By focusing on poetic language as the basis of the literary, New Criticism in the United States relied on linguistic unity and continuity to define cultural tradition. Compared to this, Frye's emphasis on literary narrative is deterritorializing, freeing literary works from local or even national contexts and reorganizing them into a "global" yet strongly Eurocentric order.

52. On real versus formal subsumption of capital, see Louis Althusser and Étienne Balibar, *Reading Capital* (London: New Left Books, 1970), pp. 236–41, 302–3.

53. Negt and Kluge, *Public Sphere and Experience*, pp. 130–31.

54. Ibid., p. 157.

little in common with the commodified delirium induced by the copious displays of the department store. While Frye describes the "popular" as an archaic and timeless element in literature, in fact his mode of constructing the category corresponds to an historically specific stage in the development of late capitalism. Frye's conception of the popular as that which provokes desire and wish-fulfillment in order to universalize and organize them answers precisely to the version of the popular produced by the media and their modes of address to consumers. The new modes of popularity known as mass consumption contain their own potential for subversion and resistance, of course, but Frye's critical method reproduces the dynamic of consumer capitalism in its most pacifying aspect.

We may now be in a position to reassess Frye's failure to make the "leap" to postmodernity. As a strongly centered and totalizing system, Frye's critical theory resists the proliferation of counterpublics that marks a multicultural environment as well as the textual decentering that characterizes poststructuralism. One possible response is to charge Frye with various forms of metaphysical illusion and ideological backwardness, and consign him to the darkness that reigned before postmodern enlightenment. This response, however, feeds a dangerously self-congratulatory view of the present cultural situation. Another course is to view Frye's abstracting and totalizing tendencies as grasping—admittedly in somewhat symptomatic form—an objective movement within the dialectic of late capitalism. Frye's system embodies the reunifying or reterritorializing movement which not only counterbalances late capitalism's multiplication of cultural publics, but also provides the very condition for their possibility. The economic dynamic of "postmodern" culture, moreover, is already present in capitalism's monopoly phase, as witnessed by modernism's engagemnet with mass culture. Frye is thus not some antediluvian remnant, but in fact represents the specter of social forces still very much in play—and, moreover, entangled uncomfortably with more progressive cultural movements. He is not so much the ancestor as the bad conscience of a postmodern criticism—a judgment which might be extended to modernism more generally. By containing the popular, Frye represents the capacities for containment within an economy which not only tolerates but to some degree actively encourages the proliferation of cultural difference. As we shall see in this chapter's third and final section, a primitive version of the same process is already at work in Shakespearean romance, where commodity culture at once encourages and sublates the "local."

The Topical and the Transcendental:
Shakespeare's *Pericles*

While Frye's revision of the Eliotic canon may be one of his most enduring legacies, his championing of romance seems to have had only limited success in Shakespeare studies. It cannot be said that the late romances have received the kind of sustained critical attention they might have if Frye had pressed home his claim that these plays represent a genuine culmination of Shakespeare's career. Yet this local failure in Frye's revisionary aims may paradoxically represent the success of his argument about the nature of romance. For if romance is as strongly conventional and anti-representational as Frye argues, if it so strongly resists historical contextualization in favor of immanent literary structures, then Shakespeare's late romances will offer little purchase for the kinds of historical approaches that now predominate. In fact, myth critics and formalists have been particularly attracted to the late romances, while New Historicists have, on the whole, directed more attention to the chronicle histories and the Roman plays.[55] Despite a flurry of interest in questions of colonialism in *The Tempest*, historical critics have paid little heed to the romances *as romances*, and hence questions of literary mode or genre have ceded place to topical readings, which tend to ignore both the whole structure of individual works and the late romances as a putative grouping of plays. The recent critical fortunes of the romances have revealed a seemingly irreconcilable tension between the topical and the transcendental—between, that is, a critical school invested in localized historical contextualization and one which detaches literary works from history and organizes them into autonomous, totalizing structures. This tension, moreover, is homologous to the situation described at the end of the previous section, in which the media public sphere at once organizes commodity culture into more global structures and, at the same time, achieves a more targeted form of address aimed at delimited, localized constituencies.

Among Shakespeare's late plays, *Pericles* occupies a privileged position for Frye because it represents the purest expression of its literary mode: of all the romances it is the "romanciest." "*Pericles* . . . seems to be a

---

55. See Rajiva Verma, *Myth, Ritual, and Shakespeare* (New York: Advent Books, 1992), p. 62: "The Romances as a group have been thought to be the most amenable to the myth and ritual approach." Verma's survey shows that the romances have at least enjoyed disproportionate attention from myth critics, whereas "the history plays, with the important exception of the two parts of *Henry IV*, have, not surprisingly, elicited few commentaries in terms of the myth and ritual pattern" (p. 38).

deliberate experiment in presenting a traditional archetypal sequence as nakedly and baldly as possible."[56] By this Frye means in part that *Pericles* is the most consistently archaic or primitive of the late romances, the one that digs deepest into subterranean patterns of myth and imagination, beginning with the incestuous riddle-game posed by King Antiochus. This opening, he argues, is compelling but not realistic or believable, and "where so uncritical a participation is demanded from us, the action cannot be lifelike: it can only be archetypal."[57] What might be seen as a liability of romance (far-fetched plots) here becomes a virtue, by fore-grounding literary convention.

A similar strategy governs Frye's treatment of the narrative structure of romance. In *The Secular Scripture*, Frye distinguishes between what he calls the "hence" narratives of realistic fictions, in which at least an il-lusion of logic and causality creates a seemingly coherent sequence, and the "and then" narratives of romance, in which unrelated events simply pile up or accumulate.[58] A typical plot device of romance (and of *Pericles* in particular) is the shipwreck, which causes the narrative to veer literally and figuratively off course, introducing unanticipated locales, adventures, and characters. Here again an apparent lack or absence is turned to advantage, for "in *Pericles* the discontinuity of the action forces us to see the vertical shape of the whole story."[59] By "vertical shape" Frye means those ranked, timeless states of being, leading from the divine down to the infernal, which define the archetypal structure of romance, and which are here distinguished from a chronological ("horizontal") se-quence of narrative events. This vertical axis organizes the Apollonius-story on which *Pericles* is based:

At the beginning Apollonius encounters a king who is living in incest with his daughter, so that his daughter is also his wife: at the end Apollonius himself is a prince united with his lost wife and daughter. The story proceeds toward an end which echoes the beginning, but echoes it in a different world. The beginning is the demonic parody of the end, and the action takes place on two levels of experience. This principle of action on two levels, neither of them corresponding very closely to the ordinary world of experience, is essential to romance, and shows us that romance presents a *vertical* perspective which realism, left to itself, would find it very difficult to achieve. The realist, with his

56. Frye, *Secular Scripture*, p. 51.
57. Frye, *Natural Perspective*, p. 32.
58. Frye, *Secular Scripture*, pp. 47–48.
59. Ibid., p. 52.

sense of logical and horizontal continuity, leads us to the end of his story; the romancer, scrambling over a series of disconnected episodes, seems to be trying to get us to the top of it.[60]

The metanarrative of romance moves between these vertical poles, starting with "themes of descent" into a demonic, chaotic, absurd, or restrictive world, and ending with "themes of ascent" to a divine, free, meaningful, or satisfying world. In *Pericles*, this takes the form of a Job-like narrative of tribulations in which the hero loses his kingdom, his wife, and his daughter before regaining them all at the end. And this enclosing macro-narrative is mirrored in the multiple resurrections, salvations, and escapes from the sea that pepper the plot. *Pericles* thus inscribes a mythic "cycle" of tragic fall followed by comic redemption, yet the overarching ring-structure which binds the story together is composed of seemingly random, disconnected events; somehow, a thousand accidents produce a miraculous design. Romance thus assumes the form of a totality, yet it is not an "organic" one since, instead of arising from its components, it seems imposed from without: chaos soup poured into the shapely bowl of providence. I would like to call this form a "horizontal totality" (horizonal, not horizontal) to indicate a structure glued together only at its outermost periphery and not throughout its interior.

Frye's contention that *Pericles* is "vertically" structured implies discontinuities not only within the play's narrative but also between that narrative and its historical context. Because *Pericles* so fully adheres to literature's autonomous totality of archetypes, it supposedly abandons all representational aims and presents a smooth, unbreachable surface to historical scrutiny. Whatever the theoretical merits of this argument, it is true that *Pericles* has discouraged historical critics almost as effectively as King Antiochus's row of impaled heads does prospective suitors.[61] This fact, however, is merely symptomatic of what I take to be a larger problem: Frye's indifference to history is matched by the New Historicism's seeming indifference to literary form. Are we forced to choose between a criticism which is localizing not only in its choice of historical contexts

60. Ibid., pp. 49–50.

61. The only recent, historicizing readings of the play of which I am aware are David Bergeron, *Shakespeare's Romances and the Royal Family* (Lawrence: University Press of Kansas, 1985), pp. 117–36; Steven Mullaney, " 'All That Monarchs Do': The Obscured Stages of Authority in *Pericles*," in Mullaney, *Place of the Stage*, pp. 135–51; and Constance Jordan, " 'Eating the Mother': Property and Propriety in *Pericles*," in *Creative Imitation: New Essays on Renaissance Literature in Honor of Thomas M. Greene*, ed. David Quint, Margaret W. Ferguson, G. W. Pigman III, and Wayne A. Rebhorn (Binghamton: Medieval and Renaissance Texts and Studies, 1992), pp. 331–53.

but in its tendency to scavenge texts for parts, and one that is attentive to form, but at the cost of historical specificity? For its part, *Pericles* seems unbothered by this dilemma, for while embodying the apparently "timeless" conventions of romance, the play also engages from time to time in topical, or at least anachronistic, commentary on contemporary issues. These topical moments are not, moreover, mere excrescences or digressions but go to the heart of the play's *form* as romance. By examining them I hope to show how much of Frye's approach can be rescued for a historicizing criticism.

Before proceeding, however, I should note that my strategy of Shakespearean reading in this chapter will reverse that found in my other chapters. Elsewhere I employ allegory to dislodge the certainties of historicism; here, by contrast, I try to restore the historical dimension to an ahistorical structuralism. Yet the goal is ever the same: to reinstate the productive tensions of modernism's historical allegory.

The first of the overtly topical moments in *Pericles* occurs in act 2, scene 1 of the play, when Pericles, having just been shipwrecked, washes on shore at Pentapolis. (I am assuming that this scene is written by Shakespeare, but this assumption is not, strictly speaking, crucial to my argument.)[62] There he comes upon a group of fishermen in conversation:

62. The authorship and dating of *Pericles* have been subject to long-running dispute. Textual and stylometric analysis currently favor George Wilkins as the principal author of acts 1 and 2, but the case is by no means airtight, and there is a good deal of counterevidence, including testimony by contemporaries, to support exclusive authorship by Shakespeare. The principal stylometric support for Wilkins comes from a series of articles by M. W. A. Smith: "The Authorship of *Pericles*: New Evidence for Wilkins," *Literary and Linguistic Computing* 2 (1987): 221–30; "The Authorship of Acts I and II of *Pericles*: a New Approach Using First Words of Speeches," *Computers and the Humanities* 22, no 1 (1988): 23–41; "A Procedure to Determine Authorship Using Pairs of Consecutive Words: More Evidence for Wilkins's Participation in *Pericles*," *Computers and the Humanities* 23, no. 2 (1989): 113–30; "Function Words and the Authorship of *Pericles*," *Notes and Queries* n.s. 36, no. 3 (September 1989): 333–36; "The Problem of Acts I–II of *Pericles*," *Notes and Queries* n.s. 39, no. 3 (September 1992), 346–55. Smith's studies show that acts 1 and 2 of *Pericles* reveal a slightly higher stylistic affinity with Wilkins's play *The Miseries of Enforced Marriage* than with Shakespeare's other late plays, although they also show a much higher affinity with late Shakespeare than with all the other Renaissance playwrights tested. Moreover, as Smith himself admits, the tests are based on relatively small samples because only the one play can be attributed to Wilkins and only two of the five acts of *Pericles* are being compared to it. Moreover, the attribution of *Miseries* to Wilkins is not absolutely certain. Eric Sams, "The Painful Misadventures of *Pericles* Acts I–II," *Notes and Queries* n.s. 38, no. 1 (March 1991): 67–70, contests Smith's findings, adducing a good deal of contemporary evidence and advancing the thesis that *Pericles* is actually an early play, later reworked. Smith (1992) is a response to Sams, showing that the first two acts of *Pericles* are stylistically much closer both to Wilkins and to the late Shakespeare than to the early Shakespeare. MacD. P. Jackson, "*Pericles*, Acts I and II: New Evidence for George Wilkins," *Notes and Queries* n.s. 37, no. 2 (June 1990): 192–96, weighs in for Wilkins based on another stylometric test, but Thomas

Third Fisherman. Master, I marvel how the fishes live in the sea.

First Fisherman. Why, as men do a-land; the great ones eat up the little ones. I can compare our rich misers to nothing so fitly as to a whale: 'a plays and tumbles, driving the poor fry before him, and at last devour them all at a mouthful. Such whales have I heard on a' th' land, who never leave gaping till they swallow'd the whole parish, church, steeple, bells, and all.

Pericles. [*Aside*] A pretty moral.

Third Fisherman. But, master, if I had been the sexton, I would have been that day in the belfry.

Second Fisherman. Why, man?

Third Fisherman. Because he should have swallow'd me too, and when I had been in his belly, I would have kept such a jangling of the bells, that he should never have left till he cast bells, steeple, church, and parish up again. But if the good King Simonides were of my mind—

Pericles. [*Aside*] Simonides?

Third Fisherman. We would purge the land of these drones, that rob the bee of her honey. (2.1.26–47)

Like many of Shakespeare's lower-class characters, the fishermen violate the historical fiction of their play in order to comment directly on contemporary events. The rich misers who swallow entire villages are clearly enclosing landlords; and the composition of *Pericles* in 1607–8 makes it likely that Shakespeare alludes to the recent spate of enclosures in Warwickshire that led to the Midlands Uprising of 1607. This same event also colors the food riots at the beginning of *Coriolanus*, and just as Menenius Agrippa saves the day for the patricians with his parable of the stomach, here we get an emetic version of the same conceit when the whale's belly is forced to disgorge its contents. Yet the differences between the two plays illuminate the nature of dramatic romance. In the Roman play, the

Merriam, "*Pericles* I–II Revisited and Considerations Concerning Literary Medium as a Systematic Factor in Stylometry," *Notes and Queries* n.s. 37, no. 2 (September 1992): 341–45, applies a battery of stylometric tests and finds that both acts 1 and 2 and acts 3–5 show a greater stylistic affinity to the late Shakespeare than to Wilkins.

While Smith's tests favor Wilkins as the primary author of acts 1 and 2, they also suggest that Shakespeare contributed to this portion of the play and that Wilkins had a hand in acts 3–5. Act 2, scene 1, which I consider here, is viewed as probably Shakespearean even by some of those who favor Wilkins as the primary author of acts 1 and 2. Authorial attribution is less important to me than the assumption, confirmed by stylometric analysis, that *Pericles* is a late play, or at least one that was heavily reworked around 1607–8.

response of the plebs is insurrectional; in *Pericles*, the redress of grievances is mediated by king and church. Indeed, the discourse of politics here puts on a semi-theological or "mythic" garb centered on an unmistakable allusion to the biblical story of Jonah and the whale.

The story of Jonah, as Northrop Frye and others have noticed, resonates throughout *Pericles*.[63] (Pericles can overhear the fishermen's discussion of the whale because he had been caught in a storm at sea while leaving Tarsus. Jonah is swallowed by the great fish during a storm at sea on the way to Tarsus.) It thus ties the fishermen's local discourse to the larger contours of the play. This story, moreover, narrates the fundamental structure of romance as described by Frye: the hero's descent into a demonic or fallen world followed by a salvational reascent. In the Christian tradition, of course, Jonah serves as a typological prefiguring of Christ's death and resurrection, and thereby of the general resurrection awaiting mankind. In *An Exposition upon the Prophet Jonah* (1600), George Abbot writes: "As this hath bene deduced from the example of our Prophet, . . . Jonas was in the fishes belly, so was Christ in the grave: Jonas came forth from thence, so did Christ rise againe, his rising doth bring our rising, his resurrection, ours, because he was the first fruits of all those that do sleep."[64] *Pericles* seems to invoke this typological framework in the fishermen's image of salvation through the ringing of the church bells and through the fishermen themselves, from whose profession Jesus recruited his disciples.

The brief exchange among the fishermen invokes three different but complexly interrelated discourses or codes: a topical, political allusion to enclosing landlords; the biblical tale of Jonah and the interpretive structures of Christian typology; and finally, the literary conventions of romance. For Frye, the last of these is necessarily in tension with the first two, since romance resists not only extraliterary allusion or representation but also Christian dogma, with which it exists in a relation of metadoxy. His approach enables us to ask some pertinent questions about *Pericles*. How does dramatic romance "process" contemporary events? And what exactly is the relation between Shakespearean romance and Christian myth and doctrine, with which it constantly flirts?

We may begin to answer these questions by addressing a third relation: that between the play's religious and political codes. Biblical prophets such as Jonah were frequently invoked by early modern writers to criticize

---

63. See Frye, *Natural Perspective*, p. 149, and Norman Nathan, "*Pericles* and *Jonah*," *Notes and Queries*, n.s. 3, no. 1 (January 1956): 10–11.

64. George Abbot, *An Exposition upon the Prophet Jonah* (1600), STC 34, p. 196.

contemporary abuses, as in Thomas Lodge and Robert Greene's play *A Looking Glasse for London and England* (c. 1586). One of the leading villains of this play is a usurer of Nineveh who confiscates a gentleman's lands and a poor man's cow until frightened by Jonah's terrifying prophecies into returning both.[65] The rich misers in act 2, scene 1 of *Pericles* are similarly encouraged by the ringing of the church bells to disgorge the lands they have enclosed. This prophetic element is reinforced by the typological resonance of the Jonah-story, and particularly by its millennial foreshadowings of a general resurrection. In *Pericles* the story of Jonah assumes just such a millennial, collective resonance, for it is not merely an individual but rather an entire parish that is swallowed and vomited forth by the whale.

In *Pericles*, unlike *Coriolanus*, reference to the problem of enclosures is mediated in the first instance by the prophetic and typological codes of Christian tradition. The political body of the Roman plebs is replaced by the body of the church, and popular insurrection takes on a vaguely apocalyptic cast. By inserting contemporary events into the codes of biblical narrative and Christian typology, Shakespeare brings them into conformity with the structural principles of romance. Historical event, one might say, becomes romance narrative—a narrative of decline or decadence followed by redemption or ascent.

This narrative not only transforms the topical problem of enclosure, but provides for its inclusion in a play whose studious archaisms tend to renounce or evade contemporary issues. Enclosure merits a place in *Pericles* because it is read as a symptom of social decline, of the deterioration of an older form of agrarian community into the "fish-eat-fish" world of rapacious landlords and hapless victims. Decline or decadence pervades the various settings of *Pericles*, from King Antiochus's incestuous palace to the fallen luxury of Tharsus to the syphilis- and brothel-ridden realm of Mytilene. The Levantine culture of the play is marked by social disintegration and a vaguely "Asiatic" quality of sybaritic excess. By changing the name of his story's hero from Apollonius to Pericles, Shakespeare adverts to the ideal of Periclean Athens from which the late Hellenistic world of *Pericles* has so visibly declined. Almost everyone in the play's governing classes—Antiochus, Dionyza, Lysimachus—is somehow corrupt or tyrannical.

---

65. Compare ibid.: "The keeping backe of the poore, for the speeding of the rich to gain friends to our selves, or to be enriched with money, cometh neare within this compasse . . . If such sinnes should be among us, they may be accounted farre greater, then they could be in Ninive, because we have had many Jonasses, who have long cried out against them" (pp. 22–23).

At the same time, several of the play's locales—Antioch, Ephesus, and especially Tarsus, later to be known as the birthplace of Saint Paul—are associated with the world of the apostles and the early Christian church. The atmosphere of *Pericles* is heavy with futurity, specifically with the arrival of a messiah who will convert its decadent cities into the landscape of redemption. King Cymbeline, it has often been noted, was ruler of Britain at the time of Christ's birth, but *Pericles,* even more than *Cymbeline,* gestures toward an imminent spiritual reformation. Cynthia Marshall has argued that eschatological traditions, as embodied in sermons, medieval doomsday plays, and Corpus Christi resurrection plays, inform all of the late romances.[66] The story of Jonah, fraught with typological and apocalyptic significance, assimilates the topical issue of enclosure to a well-nigh global narrative that informs *Pericles* and Shakespeare's other late plays. To what end, we have yet to see.

Drawing on such medieval religious forms as the miracle play and the saint's life, and incorporating the millennial and typological traditions discussed above, *Pericles* may well seem a crypto-Christian play. And so it might be, were it not for the equally powerful presence of non-Christian divinity, such as the appearance of the goddess Diana at Ephesus and the distinctly pre-Christian thaumaturgy of Cerimon which revives Thaisa. Shakespeare's late plays are full of non-Christian gods—Jupiter in *Cymbeline,* Apollo (offstage) in *The Winter's Tale,* Ceres and Venus in Prospero's masque, even the semidivine figure of Prospero himself in *The Tempest*—whose presence manages to dispel any Christian "feel." If *Pericles* is not a Christian play, this is not because it fails to allude to Christianity, but because it is not defined by it. Pericles himself may recall biblical figures such as Jonah, Job, and Christ, but he resembles Oedipus and Odysseus just as strongly. The late romances are suffused with a sense of religious mystery which cannot be pinned down to a specific set of beliefs. They engage thematic elements crucial to Christian tradition— faith, resurrection, salvation—while detaching these from an exclusively Christian context. In some sense they really do embody Frye's ideal of a "metadoxy." Belief, by the time we reach *The Tempest,* is invested not in a god or a doctrine but in the power of artistic imagination itself. But it remains to be seen whether this is purely the effect of romance as a literary mode or whether more specific historical determinants play a role.

A second plotline in *Pericles* further develops the relations between

66. Cynthia Marshall, *Last Things and Last Plays: Shakespearean Eschatology* (Carbondale: Southern Illinois University Press, 1991), esp. pp. 119–29.

topicality and romance. In act 4, Marina is sold by pirates to a brothel in Mytilene, where she enrages her new employers by preaching to her customers and converting them to virtue. These scenes don't refer to events as specific as those which inspire the fishermen in act 2, scene 1, but they are strongly anachronistic, abandoning the Hellenistic world of the play for the recognizable liberties of London—those areas outside of municipal control in which markets, fairs, brothels, and public theaters flourished. At the same time, the romance mode temporarily gives way to something more like Jacobean city comedy, with its urban swindlers and moneygrubbing citizens.

Steven Mullaney has written admirably of these brothel scenes, focusing on the role of London's liberties as demarcated sites of commercial activity, prostitution, and popular theater. Mullaney argues that Marina's redemptive "performances" both evoke and repress the relation between Shakespeare's play and the emerging capitalist marketplace, and he adds considerable historical specificity to Fredric Jameson's observation that Shakespearean romance attempts to distance itself from the "bustling commercial activity at work all around it."[67] It is certainly clear that the brothel scenes bring *Pericles* uncomfortably close to home, and that they portray a commercialized world that is jarring within the otherwise aristocratic milieu of the play.

The vexed relations between *Pericles* and commerce become still clearer when we juxtapose the brothel scenes of acts 4 and 5 with the earlier discussion among the fishermen in act 2, scene 1. Both sets of scenes anachronistically engage contemporary England, and both involve encounters between lower-class characters and members of Pericles' family. Both groups of lower-class characters, moreover, hope to be enriched by their newfound arrivals. The metaphors with which the Bawd describes her diseased prostitutes at the beginning of 4.2 ("The stuff we have, a strong wind will blow it to pieces, they are so pitifully sodden" [ll.18–20]) recall the fishermen's earlier reports of watching Pericles's ship sink in the storm, while her very trade is punningly connected with that of the "fishermen."

Parallels of language and situation point to deeper thematic connections. The exploitative enterprise of the bawds, which consumes both clients and prostitutes through venereal disease, resembles the "fish-eat-fish" world described in 2.1. In addition, the commercial activities of London's liberties and the enclosure of common lands in the countryside are both manifestations of nascent capitalism, for the expulsion of peas-

67. Mullaney, *Place of the Stage*, p. 141, citing Jameson, *Political Unconscious*, p. 148.

ant tenants was a necessary prerequisite both for a market in land and for agrarian wage-labor. The two topical or semitopical references in *Pericles* thus invoke rural and urban symptoms, respectively, of a broader transition to a capitalist economy. Both, moreover, do so by focusing on demarcated social spaces—enclosed commons and the London liberties— which bear comparison with one another.

The scenes in Mytilene lack an organizing biblical narrative comparable to that of Jonah and the whale, although Marina's miraculously preserved virginity has a Christian cast. But the episode as a whole certainly embodies the romance plot as described by Frye, with Marina's descent into the hellish brothel-world leading to salvational reascent. And just as in the Jonah-story told in 2.1, this salvation takes on collective dimensions: Marina's sermons on virtue not only protect her but convert the gentlemen of Mytilene, leading to a collapse of the brothel's business. Marina's preaching voice miraculously redeems a predatory urban commerce, just as the ringing of the church bells prompts enclosing landlords to disgorge their victims. Marina's sojourn in Mytilene represents the triumph of dramatic romance over Jacobean city comedy, and with it the reformation—almost the reversal—of early capitalism.

If the codes of romance may be said, in one sense, to "repress" the realities of an early market economy, they may be said in another to connect merely topical or local instances of it into a more globalizing process. *Pericles* certainly intuits a deep relation between the births of urban and agrarian capitalism, even as it subjects both to a utopian desire for reformation or transcendence. The play's strategies of response will become clearer when the relations between enclosures and liberties are further specified.

The importance to early modern theater of London's liberties has been discussed in various books and articles.[68] According to Jean-Christophe Agnew, the unregulated commerce of the liberties marks a transition between the localized market*places* of medieval England and the generalized market *process* of a capitalist economy. He describes the liberties as "a new extraterritorial zone of production and exchange [which] sprang up outside of London's ancient marketplaces and thus out of reach of their juridical, ceremonial, and talismanic protections— and restrictions."[69] The freedom from local municipal controls enjoyed

68. See, e.g., Mullaney, *Place of the Stage*; Jean-Christophe Agnew, *Worlds Apart: The Market and the Theater in Anglo-American Thought, 1550–1750* (New York: Cambridge University Press, 1986); and Susan Wells, "Jacobean City Comedy and the Ideology of the City," *ELH* 18, no. 1 (Spring 1981): 37–60.

69. Agnew, *Worlds Apart*, p. 50.

by the liberties and their markets and fairs led the Crown to call increasingly for their incorporation.[70]

The enclosure of common lands represented a similar breakdown of the traditional, communal structures of agrarian production. It has recently been argued that enclosure, along with ascertainment and other methods of expelling tenant farmers, was not driven by a profit motive but resulted from attempts on the part of landlords to secure economic and political control of their estates against both peasants and the Crown.[71] Regardless, enclosures effectively helped to dissolve feudal relations of production and thus opened the way for capitalist agriculture. Like the liberties, enclosures withdrew limited areas from the dominant relations of production, but in so doing prepared a totalizing revolution in those economic and social relations. Just as the liberties began to substitute a market process for the spatially limited marketplace, enclosures helped to dismantle the integrity of the manor as unit of production by expelling traditional tenants and creating a national market in land. Enclosures and liberties are both demarcated places that foretell the abolition of place, local or "topical" sites that announce the arrival of a global process.

This process may be described in part as a detaching of economic activity from the integument of political, communal, and ritual practices in which it had formerly been contained. Its result is the relative autonomy of the economic which characterizes the capitalist mode of production. In the early seventeenth century, that which would eventually replace the older mode of production is far less visible than is the process of dissolution to which traditional social and economic forms are exposed. Early Jacobean culture reads this transitional state as one of decadence, disintegration, or corruption—variously depicted in the tawdry moneygrubbing of city comedy, the dissolute Italianate courts of Jacobean tragedy, and the decaying Hellenistic world of *Pericles*. But unlike other modes of Jacobean drama, romance (including, but not limited to, Shakespearean romance) counters perceived corruption with a utopian, redemptive, and transcendental movement.

Pericles, however, stages not only this utopian wish but also its effective paralysis, manifested in part as an irresolute balance of nostalgic and chiliastic impulses. In the fisherman's speech, for instance, it is unclear whether the ringing of the parish bell looks forward or backward. Does

70. Mullaney, *Place of the Stage*, pp. 136–37.
71. See Richard Lachmann, *From Manor to Market: Structural Change in England, 1536–1640* (Madison: University of Wisconsin Press, 1987).

it invoke the parish church as the center of older forms of village solidarity and dream of reconstituting a lost communal ethos, or is it instead anticipatory and apocalyptic? *Pericles* as a whole is awash in medievalisms, from Gower's role as chorus to the knightly tournament of act 2, scene 2, to the formal influence of romance and especially of older religious forms such as the saint's life and the miracle play. In a number of ways Shakespeare's play seems sympathetic to pre-Reformation Christianity, and it is probably no coincidence that *Pericles* was included in the Book-List of the Jesuit English college at St. Omer in 1619 or that it formed part of the repertory of a provincial Catholic acting troupe in 1610.[72] At the same time, the play labors under a recognizably protestant sense of impending reformation, signified in a late Hellenistic world awaiting the birth of Christ. This strain comes closer to the surface in Marina's edifying discourses at Mytilene, where beneath the garb of the romance heroine one can just glimpse the figure of the protestant preacher (the Bawd even complains of her at one point that "she would make a puritan of the devil, if he should cheapen a kiss of her" [4.6.9-10]). The liberties of London provided safe haven not only for markets, brothels and theaters, but also for Puritans; hence Marina's sermons observe a kind of local decorum.

Hesitating between desires for past and future, for a Roman and a Puritan faith, *Pericles* seems at the mercy of a transcendental urge that has reached an impasse. The play, one might say, *wants* to be religious; it reacts to the dissolution of older social structures, and the absence of any visible social agency that might stem or reverse the tide, with a turn to the divine. Yet its theological impulse is doubly blocked. The Roman faith is unavailable because for England it is an historical anachronism, while the more radical Protestant reformers tended to have little tolerance for public theaters, and Shakespeare throughout his career shows little sympathy for them in turn. The result of this impasse, for Shakespeare, is romance—a pseudoreligious mode governed by a powerful but abstract providence, an unanchored fascination with questions of faith, and a sense of the divine constructed from a pastiche of Christian and non-Christian sources, tending, in the end, toward aesthetic religion. Something like Frye's metadoxy takes form here, but it seems the product less of liberal detachment than of a syncretism born of frustration.[73]

72. Willem Schrickx, "*Pericles* in a Book-List of 1619 from the English Jesuit Mission and Some of the Play's Special Problems," *Shakespeare Survey* 29 (1976): 21–32; for more on *Pericles* and English recusant culture, see John Murphy, *Darkness and Devils: Exorcism and "King Lear"* (Athens: Ohio University Press, 1984).

73. In taking the transcendental impulse of the romances "seriously," I might well be

We are now in a position to grasp the cultural work done by the form of romance in *Pericles*. The governing social dilemma addressed by the play is, as I have said, the dissolution of older systems of cultural stability and the apparent lack of any immanent principles of order to take their place. Both Shakespeare's play and early modern England reacted to this dilemma by hoping for the reimposition of order "from above." The fisherman of 2.1, for example, looks to King Simonides to purge the land of enclosing landlords and thus restore the structures of village life that can no longer sustain themselves at a local level. In fact, the Crown did tend to side with the peasantry against enclosure during the early Tudor period, although this policy was permanently reversed when Warwick became Lord Protector during the minority of Edward VI.[74] Likewise it was the Crown which pressed for greater restrictions upon the liberties of London in the face of ineffective municipal control, and tried to regulate price-gouging by merchants and middlemen.[75] In both cases, crises generated by the parcellized sovereignty of the late feudal polity provoked an attempted re-territorialization of authority at the national level. Local instability caused by the erosion of traditional mechanisms of control led to the imposition (or attempted imposition) of order from above.

Shakespearean romance, I would argue, effects a similar displacement

accused of overlooking the skeptical elements that accompany them, embodied for instance in figures such as Autolycus and Caliban. *The Winter's Tale*, it seems to me, is the late play which most forcefully drives faith and skepticism into conflict. Nowhere is this truer than in the scene of Hermione's resurrection. There Leontes's (and presumably our) doubts are put definitively to rest, yet the scene tries hard to revive them. For instance, the choice of Julio Romano as the supposed sculptor of Hermione's "statue" is hardly random. Romano was probably best known not for his paintings but for a series of pornographic drawings depicting the gods copulating in various positions. Invoking his name thus revives precisely those obsessive imaginations of adultery that Leontes is forced to repress. We may remember here that Hermione's name associates her with Hermes, father of the trickster-figure Autolycus. The ending of the play thus refuses to dismiss the possibility that Leontes's suspicions were correct after all, and this is partly its point. Leontes's murderous, misogynistic rage is not the opposite of his earlier, unquestioning belief in Hermione's chastity but only its other side. Genuine faith, for Shakespeare, does not exclude doubt but incorporates it, and the greatest faith must therefore contain the highest degree of skepticism. (For a wonderfully skeptical reading of *The Winter's Tale* see Howard Felperin, " 'Tongue-Tied Our Queen?': The Deconstruction of Presence in *The Winter's Tale*," in Patricia Parker and Geoffrey Hartman, eds., *Shakespeare and the Question of Theory* (New York: Methuen, 1985), pp. 3–18. My feeling is that in the delicate balance between Shakespearean skepticism and the faith required by the romance mode, Shakespeare's early plays ultimately incline toward the former while the late romances incline toward the latter. That this shift marks a growing conservatism I will not contest.

74. Lachmann, *From Manor to Market*, pp. 90–91.

75. See Agnew, *Worlds Apart*, p. 51, on the Elizabethan *Book of Orders* (1587).

upward. The plot of *Pericles* is marked by a series of disasters at the local level which are somehow righted by the play's larger design. At the level of content, romance stages an opposition between accident and providence which is resolved at the level of form by what I have called the horizonal totality. *Pericles* depicts the dissolution and subsequent reimposition of local structure by means of a totalizing movement from without. It may sound at this point as if the play simply adopts the ideology of royal absolutism; but the play's transcendental movement reflects its lack of faith in any existing social institution, either political or religious. Virtually every governor or king in the play is depicted as tyrannical or corrupt, and Pericles, the one just king, essentially abdicates and flees his kingdom early on. The totality imposed on *Pericles* arises not from any immanent principle of order but comes strictly from without, or above, the horizon of the play's represented world.

Despite its explicit hostility toward contextualization, then, Northrop Frye's theory of romance can contribute to an historical analysis of *Pericles*. In particular, his conception of literature as totality is helpful in addressing a play which, first, reads "local" disorders as signs of a more global crisis and, second, designs a "total" if transcendental response to that crisis. One reason for the closeness of the fit is that Frye's theory of romance (and of literature generally) not only describes but enacts certain romance themes. His conception of literature as a defensive totality, guarding its autonomy against threats of external synthesis, may well recall Marina in the brothel, shielding her magical chastity against threats of sexual and commercial pollution. The transcendental aspect of romance, and therefore its utopian force, depend in Frye's view on the integrity of literary form. In some respects Frye's critical system is simply another romance fiction which, like *Pericles* itself, both mimics and devises a utopian response to the totalizing movement of capital.

In *A Natural Perspective*, Frye offers some intriguing connections between the formal structures of *Pericles* and those of high modernist literature:

> And just as the structure of *Pericles* anticipates opera, with its narrative *recitativo* and its dramatized arias, so it also anticipates the kind of modern poem where, as in Eliot's *The Waste Land*, the narrative connective tissue is cut out and only the essential scenes are presented. Eliot's debt to *Pericles* is partly recorded in his *Marina*, and some of Eliot's readers have felt that the ideal dramatic form he speaks of so often is better represented by *The Waste Land*, which is close to *Pericles* not only

in its fragmentation but in its symbolism of Phoenician sailors, sterile fornication, and deliberate archaizing, than it is by his more conservative stage plays.[76]

It does not vitiate the force of Frye's insight if we reverse the directions of causality here and suggest that his understanding of the structures of romance is largely mediated by the influence of literary modernism. *The Waste Land* perfectly embodies the form I have designated as horizontal totality; the poem's sense of cultural and social dissolution, which finds its formal equivalent in the literary fragment, is balanced by a re-territorializing impulse embodied in the search for an overarching *mythos* of social stability and rebirth. *The Waste Land* is a kind of tragic counterpart to *Pericles*, inspired by a comparable sense of social pessimism and by a similar inability to locate new sources of social order. Frye's reading of the structure of *Pericles* thus depends largely on Eliot's own manipulation of romance structure. Yet Eliot is surely not alone in this. Joyce's *Ulysses* also operates a conspicuous tension between its overarching mythic order and the more aleatory world of everyday life in the city. Both works exhibit double tendencies toward internal destructuration and horizontal totality.

Here I wish to invoke, and adapt, Georg Lukács's reading of high modernist form as a symptom of reification. For Lukács, the abstract, quantifying logic of the commodity-form installs itself first in the production process itself, where more traditional and organic practices of production are broken down into standardized, mechanized components and then reassembled at the more global level of the factory. This rationalizing pattern of fragmentation followed by reassembly into a more inclusive, totalizing process is reproduced in the structures of the bureaucratic state and, if we pick up hints offered by Manfredo Tafuri, in modernist city planning as well.[77] Lukács tends to grasp modernism solely under the sign of fragmentation, and to criticize it for dissolving literary realism's totality of form.[78] That is, he connects modernist form to only one half of the dynamics of reification. I would argue that modernist texts can

76. Frye, *Natural Perspective*, pp. 28–29.

77. Georg Lukács, *History and Class Consciousness: Studies in Marxist Dialectics*, trans. Rodney Livingstone (Cambridge: MIT Press, 1971), pp. 83–110; Manfredo Tafuri, *Architecture and Utopia: Design and Capitalist Development*, trans. Barbara Luiga La Penta (Cambridge: MIT Press, 1976).

78. See Georg Lukács, "Realism in the Balance," in Ernst Bloch et al., *Aesthetics and Politics* (London: New Left Books, 1979), pp. 28–59, and "The Ideology of Modernism" in Lukács, *The Meaning of Contemporary Realism*, trans. John Mander and Necke Mander (London: Merlin Press, 1963), pp. 17–46.

best be understood in relation to reification's total movement, in which forms are first broken down and then reassembled into a more inclusive if less "organic" totality. It is this aspect of modernist form which is then elevated to the level of critical system by Frye.

Frye's reading of Shakespearean romance exemplifies what I have been calling historical allegory, mapping Renaissance texts onto the forms of literary modernism and, at a deeper level, onto the structures of reification. At the same time, Shakespearean romance exerts its own counter-influence on Frye's reading of high modernism, while romance provides literary modernism with a structural paradigm for its own engagement with reified culture. It is owing to this dialectical influence that to allegorize is not necessarily to falsify; Frye's approach uncovers essential elements in the construction of *Pericles*. What seems to mediate between Shakespearean romance and Frye's critical system is the capitalist economy, which provokes a "totalizing" movement in both. Yet these two historical moments are also very different, and a closer look at the relation between *Pericles* and nascent capitalism will reveal some important differences between Shakespearean and modernist versions of romance.

As Steven Mullaney has noted, *Pericles* establishes a thoroughly ambiguous relation with the capitalist market. The play employs romance as a form of escape from the commercial realities in which public theater finds itself implicated, but also alludes at times to its own commercial status. Marina at the brothel seems to embody romance's power to redeem a debased form of commerce, yet Marina's own relation to that commerce is complex. When her virtuous admonitions reform Lysimachus, he gives her gold anyway, rather as if she had capitulated to his original request. Indeed, all of Marina's gentleman visitors arrive with keen sexual appetites and leave without them, so that her virtuous sermons may be said to perform a service at least somewhat like the prostitute's. And while she objects to selling her body, she does offer to engage in more wholesome forms of wage-labor for her employers. In doing so, the chaste Marina merely literalizes the then-current turn of phrase in which prostitutes were said to "sell their virtue."[79] Mullaney argues that Marina's performance in the bawdy house relies on an equivalence among stage, brothel, and market which Shakespeare attempts to repress.[80] While *Pericles* addresses this theme less candidly than does its

79. Susan Wells ("Jacobean City Comedy," p. 57) quotes John Marston's play *The Dutch Courtesan* on a prostitute: "Her shop has the best wares, for where these still sell but cloth, satins, and jewels, she sells divine virtues, as virginity, modesty, and such rare gems, and those not only like a petty chapman, by retail, but like a great merchant by wholesale."

80. Mullaney, *Place of the Stage*, pp. 143–45.

main literary source, Lawrence Twine's *Painful Adventures*, I see its handling of such matters as indicating, not repression, but rather an admission that the play, like Marina, is still engaged in marketing itself even though its wares are now more "virtuous." Shakespearean romance, despite its redemptive and quasi-religious aspirations, still profits from the commercial world whose corruption and debasement it decries.

The transcendental impulse in Shakespearean romance relies on the belief in a realm of values separate from, and irreducible to, those of the marketplace. In *Pericles* this largely involves a search for archaic or precapitalist forms of culture and exchange. The question for romance, in the context of Jacobean drama, is whether these forms can sustain themselves as an autonomous sphere or whether they succumb to the leveling force of commodity exchange. Does Marina descend into the brothel-world in order to redeem it with her beautiful, antiquated virtue, or does she become hopelessly entangled in it? Perspective on her mission is provided by Ben Jonson's play *The Alchemist*, in which the prostitute Doll Common disguises herself as the Faerie Queene to receive a client. By staging a phony "ascent" into the romance world, Doll Common both inverts and degrades the figure of Marina and thereby specifies the relations between city comedy and romance. In *The Alchemist*, romance fictions are nothing more than moneymaking devices to be passed off on unwary gulls. The play's mountebank-hero, Subtle, is indeed an alchemist, since he transforms the "aura" of antique systems of value into gold; but he thereby reveals the fact that money is now the only signifier of value, the sole object of seemingly mystical or divine significance in a corrupt, secular, and cynical world. Jonsonian city comedy is committed to the worldly immanence of values, while *Pericles* attempts to disrupt the logic of the marketplace by reinjecting it with authentic romance as an alien but redemptive body.

Pericles can be said to achieve its goal insofar as it maintains the high seriousness of the romance mode. There is, to be sure, a comic improbability to Marina's success in fending off so many amorous clients, yet her miraculous virtue is never exposed to the corrosive effects of Jonsonian satire. On the contrary, it is city comedy which, like the gentlemen of Mytilene, finds itself unexpectedly converted by victorious romance.[81] The price of this victory, however, seems to be the substitution of a mere romance-effect for any alternative realm of value. *Pericles* certainly conveys

81. *Pericles* was written around the same time not only as *The Alchemist* but also as Francis Beaumont's *Knight of the Burning Pestle* (written 1607). The challenge for *Pericles* is to present romance drama "straight" at a time when the mode was being satirized.

the archaic, magical atmosphere of romance, but this results from collecting together the most heterogeneous forms of aura. The dragon-guarded, Hesperian fruit of Antiochus's forbidden passions, the gorgeous decadence of Tharsus, the chivalric splendor of the medieval tourney, the hierophantic pomp of Diana at Ephesus, the Aesculapian mysteries of Cerimon, are mixed together and sprinkled liberally with assorted miracles, salvations, resurrections, and divine punishments. *Pericles* doesn't really retreat into a romance world; rather, it ransacks that world for a hodgepodge of numinous effects. Even the distinction between naïve and sentimental romance can't quite account for the calculated and commercially formulaic impression that the play can give when we step outside the circle of its enchantment and examine the means by which it casts its spell. Ironically (or not), *Pericles* does the work of the market by establishing relations of equivalence, or commensurability, among the forms of different places, times, and cultures. Its own activity—as it seems to recognize—is finally no different from Subtle's in *The Alchemist*: the marketing of aura.

This is not to suggest that *Pericles* is entirely a cynical production. The play registers what seems to be a genuine sense of social crisis, and its mode of response to that crisis is romance. Yet its own redemptive impulses are compromised by the dilemma of trying to market romantic fiction. In this sense, the transcendental movement of romance is indeed captured by the worldly immanence of commerce. But *Pericles*, a play whose idea of redemption is strictly transcendental, will necessarily find it troubling to admit this fact.

The reason, I believe, is Shakespeare's conception of the market—or rather, the lack of such a conception, whose place is only imperfectly filled by that of money. The famous set pieces on the power of money, particularly those in *Timon of Athens*, emphasize gold's ability to overturn or dissolve traditional social relations and hierarchies of value. The money-form, in other words, is grasped solely as a cultural solvent. For obvious historical reasons, the market itself cannot yet be conceived as something that contains its own principles of order—the "invisible hand" of the political economists. Only when the capitalist economy becomes relatively autonomous can the market begin to appear as an immanent (if contradictory) totality and operate as a kind of immanent providence. Even Lukács, who hardly adopts a free-market ideology, depicts reified society as an abstractly but internally organized mechanism. Likewise, the horizontal totality of Frye's critical system arises from a process of self-organization among its constituent works, or words—owing mainly to the fact that this system symptomatically re-enacts the movement of capital itself. In *Pericles*, however, "society" is unified only by the perception of generalized crisis; the horizonal totality which imposes at least a provisional order must therefore come from without.

If this makes it sound like Shakespeare aspires to the higher condition of being Northrop Frye but is historically blocked from achieving it, we may simply reverse our criteria and say, not that *Pericles* "lacks" a way of imagining an immanent totality, but that Frye lacks the ability to imagine a contradictory or crisis-ridden one. What *Pericles* shares both with Lukács and with the early modernists is a sense of impending disaster or emergency, associated with the more disruptive or volatile aspects of the capitalist market. Frye, riding the long postwar boom, seems less aware of economic and social contradiction. Sitting at the still center of modernism's turning world, he spins an allegory of his own repose.

CHAPTER

4

The Jewish Question:
Shakespeare and Anti-Semitism

Foretexts

When I dragged behind the nursemaid who held my younger brother by the hand, sometimes I heard a shout behind me, and if I turned round would see a grinning boy, making faces and shaking his fist at me. For a long time I took no particular notice, but as time went on I heard the shout oftener and asked the maid what it meant. "Oh, nothing!" she replied. But on my repeatedly asking she simply said: "It is a bad word."

But one day, when I heard the shout again, I made up my mind that I would know, and when I came home asked my mother: "What does it mean?" "Jew!" said Mother. "Jews are people." "Nasty people?" "Yes," said Mother, smiling, "sometimes very ugly people, but not always." "Could I see a Jew?" "Yes, very easily," said Mother, lifting me up quickly in front of the large oval mirror above the sofa.

I uttered a shriek, so that Mother hurriedly put me down again, and my horror was such that she regretted not having prepared me. Later on she occasionally spoke about it.

—Georg Brandes, *Reminiscences of my Childhood and Youth*[1]

What, reduced to their simplest reciprocal form, were Bloom's thoughts about Stephen's thoughts about Bloom and Bloom's thoughts about Stephen's thoughts about Bloom's thoughts about Stephen?

---

1. Georg Brandes, *Reminiscences of My Childhood and Youth* (New York: Duffield, 1906), pp. 17–18.

He thought that he thought that he was a jew whereas he knew that
he knew that he knew that he was not.

—James Joyce, *Ulysses*[2]

Which is the merchant here? and which the Jew?
—Shakespeare, *The Merchant of Venice*

The three foretexts to this chapter are bound by lineal ties as well as
figural resemblances. The Danish critic Georg Brandes's study *William
Shakespeare* (1895–96; English trans. 1898) provided James Joyce with
much of the source material for Stephen Dedalus's Hamlet-theory in the
"Scylla and Charybdis" chapter of *Ulysses*, and thus Brandes (including,
as I will argue later, his Jewishness) helped to mediate the relation between Shakespeare and Joyce. I cite this arresting episode from Brandes's
Reminiscences because in narrating the traumatic origins of the author's
Jewish identity it juxtaposes two elements that will prove crucial to my
own exploration of Judaism and modernism: the question and the mirror. The phrase "the Jewish question" or *die Judenfrage* was introduced
in the 1840s by the German philosopher Bruno Bauer in a series of left-
Hegelian pamphlets directed against Jewish demands for political enfran-
chisement. It became a kind of shorthand for the question of Jewish
emancipation, but here I wish to broaden its sense. "The Jewish question" means not merely the question of what to *do about* the Jews, or even
the question *of* Jewishness, but also, and perhaps more fundamentally,
Jewishness *as* question—an interrogatory rather than an ascription. For
Brandes, Jewishness begins as a series of questions—"What does [that
word] mean?" "Nasty people?" "Could I see a Jew?"—but the answers
only initiate new realms of uncertainty. Behind the question "am I (or,
is she or he) a Jew?" always lie further questions, including: Who or what
are the Jews? A religion? A tribe? A race? A nation? All three of my
foretexts frame Jewishness in the context of the question. The passage
from Joyce's *Ulysses* comes, of course, from the "Ithaca" chapter, where
everything is posed as a question. But even here, Stephen's position as
gentile occupies a realm of relative certainty ("He knew that he knew
that he knew that he was not") while Bloom's Jewishness is founded upon
conjecture ("he thought that he thought that he was a jew"). Portia's
famous question from *The Merchant of Venice* is ostensibly asked only in
order to identify the two parties to the trial held in act four. Yet for many

2. James Joyce, *Ulysses* (New York: Vintage, 1961), p. 682. All subsequent references are
to this edition.

readers, it opens up larger uncertainties about the possibility of distinguishing between Jews and Christians in Shakespeare's play. Even Shylock's famous "Hath not a Jew eyes?" speech is composed almost entirely of questions, as if his identity could be expressed only in this form, and thus as a nonidentity.

In Brandes's story, the Jewish question is "answered" (insofar as it receives any answer at all) when his mother holds him up in front of the mirror, a gesture which at once instigates and forever fixes his essentially alienated relation to his ethnicity. The request to *see* a Jew, imagined as the other, is unexpectedly fulfilled by a vision of the self, but a vision that is distanced, inverted, and opposed to the viewer. The young Brandes shrieks at the traumatic assumption of an identity which structures the self *as* an other, splitting it irreparably. But the story contains a residue of uncertainty. What exactly does Brandes's mother intend to show him? His own image, by means of the mirror, or the mirror itself? Perhaps the question "Could I see a Jew?" can only be answered by displaying a mirror. Not very long after Shakespeare wrote *The Merchant of Venice*, there appeared a German publication entitled *Der Calvinische Judenspiegel* (1608) or "The Calvinist Jewish-Mirror," which satirically paralleled Calvinism and Judaism.[3] Recent readings of *The Merchant of Venice* which have tried to question the play's apparent anti-Semitism (and I am thinking here particularly of René Girard's) have argued that Shylock is merely the double, or mirror image, of the play's Christian characters, who persecute him because they have projected onto him what they hate in themselves. The image of the Jew as mirror, employed as a tactic by anti-anti-Semitism, nevertheless has a long history within anti-Semitic discourse. Indeed, I would say that it constitutes an especially complex and ambiguous strain within that tradition.

Defenders of *The Merchant of Venice* often comfort themselves by noting the differences between Shakespeare's Shylock and Marlowe's demonic Jew Barabbas. Barabbas is the Jew as terrifying "other," but Shylock is more sympathetic, more "like the others" in both his virtues and his vices. Portia's question "Which is the merchant here? and which the Jew?" (4.1.174) suggests that Shylock and Antonio are basically indistinguishable, that Shylock is the *Judenspiegel* in which Christian society may view itself. Yet this relation of supposed equivalence still leaves the Jew in an exposed position. Even if one accepts the view that the play's Christians are as bad as Shylock, and hypocritical to boot, one is still left with

3. Cited in Werner Sombart, *The Jews and Modern Capitalism*, trans. M. Epstein (London: T. Fisher Unwin, 1913), pp. 250–51.

the fact that the Jew mirrors only society's vices and becomes thereby a standard of degeneration. "See, they're even worse than the Jews!" Something similar occurs in Nietzsche's *Genealogy of Morals*, where the "slave-morality" of Judaism is used as a club to beat Christian *ressentiment*, and in Marx's "On the Jewish Question," where Jewish business practices hold the mirror up to bourgeois society at large. In both cases the primary targets are not Jews but the dominant groups in German society; indeed, both works (especially Marx's) can make some claim to being anti-anti-Semitic by dissolving the differences which allow the Jew to be demonized as an "other." Yet in both cases the vices of the dominant groups are figured as further developments or elaborations of an originally tainted Jewish essence. If the Jews' enemies are even worse than they, this is because they are super-Jews, Jews to the second power, the "real" Jews in relation to which the originals are now only pale reflections. Nevertheless, the anti-Semitism of writers such as Shakespeare, Nietzsche, and Marx is so ambiguous and hotly debated that, like Jewishness itself, it can best be formulated as a question rather than an accusation.[4]

Indeed, my goal in this chapter is not to attempt some definitive answer to the question of whether *The Merchant of Venice* is an anti-Semitic play, but rather to interrogate the categories through which this question has been argued. In particular, I want to examine some of the strategies used to "rehabilitate" the play, and to put them in historical and cultural context. As its very name suggests, "anti-anti-Semitism" turns out in many ways to be the mirrored inversion of anti-Semitism, which raises the (possibly unanswerable) question of whether it is anti-Semitism's antagonist or equivalent.

In the late nineteenth and early twentieth centuries, Jews were made into mirrors not only of bourgeois or Christian society, but of modern life itself. Associated with commerce, urban life, rootlessness, journalism, psychoanalysis, liberalism and socialism, the Jew "became in the city the prototype of both the avant-garde in thought and art, and the enemy undermining society."[5] The Jew, in short, is refashioned into an allegory of modernity. Karl Kautsky described the modernist period (suggestively,

---

4. On Marx, see Julius Carlebach, *Karl Marx and the Radical Critique of Judaism* (London: Routledge and Kegan Paul, 1978). On Nietzsche, see Yirimahu Yovel, "Nietzsche, the Jews, and *Ressentiment*," in *Nietzsche, Genealogy, Morality: Essays on Nietzsche's "On the Genealogy of Morals,"* ed. Richard Schacht (Berkeley: University of California Press, 1994), pp. 214–36 and references therein.

5. Ira B. Nadel, *Joyce and the Jews: Culture and Texts* (Iowa City: University of Iowa Press, 1989), p. 184.

for my purposes) as "the renaissance of anti-Semitism,"[6] and this "re-naissance" is vividly apparent in the writings of modernists such as Ezra Pound and T. S. Eliot. Eliot's "Burbank with a Baedeker; Bleistein with Cigar" defames Jews largely on account of their cosmopolitanism and hybridity, characteristics of Eliot's own modernist poetic which he projects onto a demonized "other."[7] At the same time, the discourse of anti-anti-Semitism, with its roots in both the liberal and radical strains of nineteenth-century culture, makes its presence felt in the works of James Joyce. *Ulysses* has variously been dubbed anti-Semitic, philosemitic, and anti-anti-Semitic.[8] I would place Joyce in the line of those writers, from Shakespeare on, for whom the Jew is both question and mirror. *Ulysses* provides an especially rich field for exploring the relations between the modernist construction of Shakespeare and the modernist construction of Judaism, and it thus offers a powerful vantage onto the strategies used either to condemn or to rescue *The Merchant of Venice* in our century. By reading Shakespeare's play through the lens of modernism, it may be possible to assess the means by which we try to assimilate this play to liberal sensibilities.

Jewish Shakespeare

Although we have no real proof of its accuracy, the Droeshout engraving has ensconced itself as our accepted rendering of Shakespeare's image. In the nineteenth century things were more complicated; English women and men who wanted to behold the visage of their nation's greatest poet were confronted with a bewildering assortment of portraits and busts of varying appearance and authenticity. Among these, the Chandos portrait reigned as the popular favorite (Figure 4). But in his book *Life Portraits of Shakspeare* (1864), J. Hain Friswell found something

6. Karl Kautsky, *Are the Jews a Race?* (New York: International Publishers, 1926), p. 163.

7. On the theme of hybridism in Eliot's poem, focusing on the figure of Luther Burbank, breeder of hybrid plants, see Crawford, *Savage and the City*, pp. 64–66.

8. Suggestions of anti-Semitism can be found in Maurice Samuel, "Bloom of Bloomusalem," *Reflex* 4, no. 1 (January 1929): 11-20 and 4, no. 2 (February 1929): 10–16, and in Robert M. Adams, *Surface and Symbol: The Consistency of James Joyce's "Ulysses"* (New York: Oxford University Press, 1972). The view of Joyce as philosemitic is too widely held to require individual citations. Nadel's *Joyce and the Jews* is representative. The useful phrase "anti-anti-Semite" occurs in Edmund L. Epstein, "Joyce and Judaism," in *The Seventh of Joyce*, ed. Bernard Benstock (Bloomington: Indiana University Press, 1982), p. 224. For a nuanced treatment see Bryan Cheyette, " 'Jewgreek is greekjew': The Disturbing Ambivalence of Joyce's Semitic Discourse in *Ulysses*," *Joyce Studies Annual* 3 (1992): 32–56.

Figure 4. The Chandos portrait of William Shakespeare, by John Taylor. By permission of the National Portrait Gallery, London.

disturbing in the Chandos portrait, and his anxious remarks were echoed by later scholars:[9] "The picture, which is in oil, and on canvas, is at first glance disappointing. One cannot readily imagine our essentially English Shakespeare to have been a dark, heavy man, with a foreign expression, of a decidedly Jewish physiognomy, thin curly hair, a somewhat lubricious mouth, red-edged eyes, wanton lips, with a coarse expression, and his ears tricked out with ear-rings." Friswell goes on to note that these physical traits "have given rise to the suggestion that the portrait painter persuaded our poet-actor to sit to him when he had assumed the dress and character of his own masterly creation—Shylock."[10]

Friswell's anxious speculations strangely anticipate Georg Brandes's anecdote. A portrait is not a mirror, of course, but in "our essentially English Shakespeare," Friswell hopes to see reflected his nation's own racial and cultural character. It is with some surprise, then, that he imagines he sees a "decidedly Jewish physiognomy"; the image produces an unexpected sense of cultural self-estrangement. It is as if not only Shakespeare's face but that of England itself were transfigured by a fantasized *Verjudung* or "Judaizing."[11] Theories of *Verjudung* became commonplace in the nineteenth century; Nietzsche and the young Marx were only two of the most famous thinkers to formulate them. Friswell may seem eccentric in attaching it to Shakespeare, but he is not unique in this respect.

The signifiers of Shakespeare's Jewishness are for the most part physiognomic and therefore racial: the dark complexion, curly hair, "wanton lips," and, of course, the prominent nose—which Friswell doesn't even bother to mention, taking it as implicit in the phrase "Jewish physiognomy." But these racial characteristics are conjoined with cultural ones: a "foreign expression" (whatever that means) and those exotically Orien-

9. See, e.g., J. Parker Norris, *The Portraits of Shakespeare* (Philadelphia, 1885).

10. J. Hain Friswell, *Life Portraits of Shakespeare* (London: Samson, Low, Son, & Marston, 1864), pp. 31–37.

11. I completed this chapter before the publication of James Shapiro's important book *Shakespeare and the Jews* (New York: Columbia University Press, 1996). But I am struck, as other readers will surely be, by parallels between Shapiro's treatment of Jewishness and English national identity in the early modern period and my treatment of similar issues in the late nineteenth and early twentieth centuries. I am especially grateful to Shapiro's book for alerting me to the existence of recent books and articles which perpetuate the fantasy of a Jewish Shakespeare even beyond the period covered in this chapter. For an example from an anti-Semitic perspective, see Elliott Baker, *Bardolatry* (London: Holofernes, 1992), chap. 2: "Is Shakespeare Jewish?" From a Jewish perspective, see Neil Hirschon, "The Jewish Key to Shakespeare's Most Enigmatic Creation," *Midstream* (February/March 1989): 38–40, and David Basch, *The Hidden Shakespeare: A Rosetta Stone* (West Hartford, Conn.: Revelatory Press, 1994).

tal earrings.[12] Friswell (and others, apparently) draws on these aspects of the portrait to formulate the comforting hypothesis that Shakespeare's Jewish appearance is the product of artifice, a mere dramatic role. But this solution raises more questions than it answers. Since it cannot account for Shakespeare's basic physiognomic features, it suspends his Jewishness between race and culture instead of replacing one with the other. It thus foregrounds the difficulties of the "Jewish question"—are the Jews a racial or a religious or a national group? It also raises the problem of why Shakespeare would either choose or allow himself to be painted as Shylock, a character who had traditionally been regarded with either loathing or derision. In 1864, the actor Henry Irving had not yet presented on stage his famous interpretation of Shylock as "the type of a persecuted race; almost the only gentleman in the play, and the most ill-used."[13] It is true that by mid-century, partly through the influence of William Hazlitt, "the idea of an impressive, half-sympathetic Shylock was well established."[14] But Shylock still must have seemed a strange choice on Shakespeare's part for the only "authentic" portrait in which the playwright appeared to don the role of one of his own characters.[15] Did Shakespeare somehow see himself in the character of Shylock? Is his *Verjudung* cultural as well as racial? Such questions persist into the modernist period, along with Friswell's fantasy of a Jewish Shakespeare.

"Prove that he was a Jew." The librarian John Eglinton poses this challenge to Stephen Dedalus as the latter expounds his Hamlet-theory in the "Scylla and Charybdis" chapter of Joyce's *Ulysses* (p. 205). The "he" in this instance is Shakespeare rather than Hamlet, and *Ulysses* does in fact produce an image of Shakespeare with a "distinctly Jewish physiognomy." Joyce's cultural identification with the Jews has long been recognized, as have the "philosemitic" elements in *Ulysses*.[16] The resemblance between Leopold Bloom (whom Wyndham Lewis called Joyce's "Jewish self-portrait")[17] and Stephen Dedalus's construction of

12. In a footnote Friswell acknowledges that earrings were fashionable among young aristocratic men of the time but finds it unusual for a mature man like Shakespeare to wear them.

13. Irving quoted in John Gross, *Shylock: A Legend and Its Legacy* (New York: Simon and Schuster, 1992), p. 147.

14. Ibid., p. 133.

15. Friswell does mention a bad forgery of Shakespeare holding a pair of scales. "The scales indicated that it was the portrait of Shakespeare in the character of Shylock" (p. 112).

16. See n. 8.

17. Lewis cited in Cheyette, "Jewgreek," p. 33.

Shakespeare were also pointed out some time ago.[18] But while the informing influence of Shakespeare on Bloom is clear, the reciprocal *Verjudung* of Joyce's Shakespeare has not, I believe, been sufficiently appreciated.

In what sense, or senses, is Joyce's Shakespeare Jewish? Stephen Dedalus provides some initial clues while presenting his Hamlet-theory:

> —And the sense of property, Stephen said. He drew Shylock out of his own long pocket. The son of a maltjobber and moneylender he was himself a cornjobber and moneylender with ten tods of corn hoarded in the famine riots. His borrowers are no doubt those divers of worship mentioned by Chettle Falstaff who reported his uprightness of dealing. He sued a fellowplayer for the price of a few bags of malt and exacted his pound of flesh in interest for every money lent. How else could Aubrey's ostler and callboy get rich quick? All events brought grist to his mill. Shylock chimes with the jewbaiting that followed the hanging and quartering of the queen's leech Lopez, his jew's heart being plucked forth while the sheeny was yet alive. (*Ulysses*, p. 204).

Stephen manages to provide an indirect explanation, long after the fact, for Friswell's conjecture that the Chandos portrait might represent Shakespeare in the role of Shylock. Perhaps the moneylender is, to borrow Wyndham Lewis's phrase, Shakespeare's "Jewish self-portrait," his *Judenspiegel.* Even more significant than the content of Stephen's remarks, however, may be their origins. The connection between Shylock and the case of the Jewish physician Roderigo Lopez had first been made by the critic Sidney Lee, in *The Gentleman's Magazine* and later in his life of Shakespeare.[19] The suggestion that Shakespeare might have drawn his own image in Shylock because he was himself a moneylender and a man "at that moment preoccupied with the ideas of acquisition, property, money-making, wealth" comes from Brandes.[20] Lee was criticized for maintaining in his book that Shakespeare wrote plays only for money.[21] Brandes and Lee, both of whom were Jewish, provide matter not only

18. William Schutte, *Joyce and Shakespeare: A Study in the Meaning of "Ulysses"* (New Haven: Yale University Press, 1957).

19. S. L. Lee, "The Original of Shylock," *Gentleman's Magazine* 268 (January–June 1880): 185–200.

20. Georg Brandes, *William Shakespeare* (New York: Macmillan, 1935), p. 151. The English translation of Brandes's book first appeared in 1898.

21. Marder, *His Exits*, p. 159.

for Stephen's remarks on Shylock but for much of his lecture on *Hamlet*.[22] Yet they are not the only Jewish sources on whom Stephen Dedalus relies. Joyce antedated Karl Bleibtreu's book on Shakespeare by three years so that Stephen could refer to it.[23] And of course, Freud's interpretation of *Hamlet*, via an early version of Ernest Jones's *Hamlet and Oedipus*, influences Joyce in a more diffused and indirect way.[24] Stephen's Shakespeare is thus "Jewish," or at least partly so, because he is mediated by several Jewish sources.

But the notion of a Jewish Shakespeare also finds a more substantial embodiment in *Ulysses* via the portly figure of Leopold Bloom. The many parallels between Bloom and Shakespeare, or at least between Bloom and the Shakespeare of Stephen's Hamlet lecture, were elaborated in the 1950s by the critic William Schutte. The following is but a sample:

> As Shakespeare was overborne in a rye field by Ann Hathaway, so Leopold Bloom was overborne by Marion Tweedy on Ben Howth. Marriage for each is made necessary by the impending arrival of a girl-child. The physical intimacy of each couple is broken off after the second labor of the woman. To each is born a son; each loses his son—Shakespeare after eleven years, Bloom after eleven days. Each is thereby left without either father or son. . . . Both "Shakespeare" and Bloom are cuckolds; neither seeks legal or physical redress. Shakespeare's only method of retaliation, Stephen suggests, is the dramatizing of stories in which the names of his treacherous brothers are attached to villains. Bloom enumerates various possibilities for retribution, but as we might expect, he finally decides to do nothing.[25]

What Schutte does not note is that many of these parallels of event and temperament also touch on stereotypically Jewish traits and themes. Both Bloom and Shakespeare are "commercial traveller[s]" (*Ulysses*, p. 505), and Shakespeare's life-journey from Stratford to London and back engages not only the Odyssean circle but also Old Testament themes of exodus and exile, as well as the figure of Ahuaserius, the Wandering Jew. Shakespeare's "Jewish" obsession with wealth and property finds an echo in Bloom's impractical money-making schemes. The domestic misadven-

22. See the appendix to Schutte, *Joyce and Shakespeare*. Joyce made use of Frank Harris's biography as well as those of Brandes and Lee, but to a lesser extent, as Schutte shows.

23. Nadel, *Joyce and the Jews*, p. 45. Karl Bleibtreu argued in *Der wahre Shakespeare* (Munich: G. Müller, 1907) that Shakespeare's works were really written by the Earl of Rutland.

24. Nadel, *Joyce and the Jews*, p. 205.

25. Schutte, *Joyce and Shakespeare*, pp. 127–28.

tures of both figures are played against then-current belief in the strong investment of the Jews in family and home life. Likewise, their failure to seek either violent retribution or legal redress for wrongs done to them involve traditional views of the Jews as patient, long-suffering, even passive in the face of adversity or oppression.

The most direct confrontation of Bloom and Shakespeare occurs during the "Circe" chapter:

Lynch
(*Points.*) The mirror up to nature. (*He laughs.*) Hu hu hu hu hu hu.
(*Stephen and Bloom gaze in the mirror. The face of William Shakespeare, beardless, appears there, rigid in facial paralysis, crowned by the reflection of the reindeer antlered hatrack in the hall.*)

Shakespeare
(*In dignified ventriloquy.*) 'Tis the loud laugh bespeaks the vacant mind.
(*To Bloom.*) Thou thoughtest as how thou wastest invisible. Gaze. (*He crows with a black capon's laugh.*) Iagogo! How my Oldfellow chokit his Thursdaymomun. Iagogogo! (*Ulysses*, p. 567)

This dense moment will require some unpacking. The first, obvious point is that Shakespeare's reflected image is constituted by the combined faces (and gazes) of Stephen and Bloom. A closely related conflation of two into one occurs somewhat earlier in the "Circe" chapter, in the hallucinatory pairing of Philip Drunk and Philip Sober: "(*The Siamese Twins, Philip Drunk and Philip Sober, two Oxford dons with lawnmowers, appear in the window embrasure. Both are masked with Matthew Arnold's face.*)" (*Ulysses*, p. 518) "Philip Drunk" and "Philip Sober" represent the Hellenic and Hebraic strains which, as Matthew Arnold argues in *Culture and Anarchy*, must combine to form a balanced culture.[26] They also clearly represent the inebriated Stephen and the notoriously sober Bloom. The later conflation of Stephen and Bloom into Shakespeare also engages the theme of the Hellenic and the Hebraic, only now the immediate source is not Matthew Arnold but rather Heinrich Heine: "Shakespeare is at once Jew and Greek; or rather, both elements, spiritualism and art, prevail and are reconciled in him, and unfold in higher unity."[27] Stephen and Bloom, Jewgreek and Greekjew, mime—or rather, parody—Heine's "higher unity" of Hebrew and Hellene in forming a grotesque, paralytic reflec-

26. Cheyette, "Jewgreek," p. 47.
27. Heinrich Heine, "Ludwig Börne: A Memorial," in Heine, *The Romantic School and Other Essays*, ed. Jost Hermand and Robert C. Holub (New York: Continuum, 1985), p. 271.

The Jewish Question 169

tion of Shakespeare, just as Philip Drunk and Philip Sober both enact and critique Arnold's idealized cultural unity.

Heine's belief that Shakespeare successfully combines Greek and Jew serves as a utopian counterpart to Friswell's anxious fantasy of a half-Jewish Shakespeare. Indeed, Joyce's use of Heine strongly inverts Friswell, for now it is a Jew who looks into the mirror and is startled to find Shakespeare looking back—not a "Jewish" Shakespeare in Friswell's sense, since this beardless Bard has nothing un-English about him, but a Shakespeare who is culturally marked through the discourse of Hebrew and Hellene. Interestingly, this hybrid Shakespeare addresses himself not to Stephen, the aspiring artist and *Hamlet*-theorist, but to Bloom, to whom he mockingly (and mock-archaically) says: "Thou thoughtest as how thou wastest invisible." What Bloom thought invisible was his status as cuckold, now rendered comically apparent by Shakespeare's antlered horns.[28] But Bloom's desired invisibility also clearly extends to his religious and racial heritage. Hence this paralyzed, antlered Shakespeare may also recall *"that stony effigy in frozen music, horned and terrible, of the human form divine"* (*Ulysses*, p. 140)—that is, Michelangelo's Moses, as described in the "Aeolus" chapter. Shakespeare renders Bloom doubly vulnerable by revealing his cuckold's horns *and* his Moses's horns. Like the young Georg Brandes held up to the mirror, the Jewish Bloom finds himself suddenly caught in the ineluctable modality of the visible.

Suddenly—but not uniquely. Bloom is repeatedly reflected in or associated with mirrors in the course of *Ulysses*,[29] a fact that pertains both to his status as Jew and to his role as uncanny double of Shakespeare. One interesting example occurs in the "Ithaca" chapter, when Bloom contemplates his home library, including "Shakespeare's *Works* (dark crimson morocco, goldtooled)" (*Ulysses*, p. 708) reflected in a mirror. Here the mirror causes the "inverted volumes" (*Ulysses*, p. 709) to read from right to left, like the Hebrew which Bloom earlier imagines his dead son Rudy studying (*Ulysses*, p. 609), while the "dark crimson morocco, goldtooled" of the Shakespeare volume evokes slightly exotic, Eastern associations.[30] Bloom's mirror thus affords him another "Jewish" Shake-

28. Earlier, Blazes Boylan "hangs his hat smoothly on a peg of Bloom's antlered head" (*Ulysses*, p. 565).

29. See, for instance, *Ulysses*, pp. 307, 413, 433–34, 536, 707–8.

30. Joyce's description of the binding seems intended to evoke the Moor Othello, to whom the mirrored Shakespeare of "Circe" alludes, and possibly even the Prince of Morocco in *The Merchant of Venice*, who is also associated with gold (he picks the gold casket) and crimson (he challenges other suitors to "let us make incision for your [Portia's] love / To prove whose blood is reddest, his or mine").

speare. But it is not just that Shakespeare and the Jewish Bloom are brought together *through* mirrors; rather, they are brought together *as* mirrors. What they reflect in each other is the fact that each is a mirror.

In what sense were Jews seen as mirrors? A mirror is a surface defined precisely by its lack of qualities, which allows it to reproduce the image of anything brought within its field. So the Jews, in their assimilationist and adaptional tendencies, were claimed to become the image of their cultural environment. In *The Jews and Modern Capitalism* (1911), Werner Sombart writes:

> Perhaps the clearest illustration of the way in which Jewish traits manifest themselves is the fact that the Jew in England becomes like an Englishman, in France like a Frenchman, and so forth. And if he does not really become like an Englishman or a Frenchman, he appears to be like one. . . . That Jewish talent should so often have nothing Jewish about it, but be in accord with its environment, has curiously again and again been urged as evidence that there are no specifically Jewish characteristics, whereas in truth it proves the very opposite in a striking fashion. It proves that the Jews have the gift of adaptability in an eminently high degree.[31]

Sombart notes the Jews' "undoubted talent for journalism, for the Bar, for the stage, and all of it is traceable to their adaptability."[32] Sombart's tone is typical of a good deal of anti-Semitic discourse of his era, mixing genuine admiration with strong undercurrents of suspicion. The adaptability of the Jews enables them to assimilate to their host cultures, yet they can only *appear* to be like Englishmen or Frenchmen. As mirrors of their surroundings, the Jews lack any spiritual essence other than a mimetic one, and this places them dangerously beyond comprehension. How can we know what a mirror is thinking? If a mirror reflects indiscriminately, what loyalties can it have? At one point in the "Circe" chapter, Bloom contracts his face so as to resemble many historical personages (*Ulysses*, p. 495), thus manifesting his characteristically Jewish talent for mimicry and self-adaptation. As a Jew, Bloom can never convince the anti-Semites of the "Cyclops" chapter and elsewhere that he is anything more than the imitation of a "real" Irishman.

But it is precisely in his role as Jewish mirror that Bloom most resem-

31. Sombart, *Jews*, p. 270.
32. Ibid., p. 273.

bles Shakespeare. Lynch, it will be recalled, "summons" Shakespeare by pointing to the wall mirror in Bella Cohen's establishment and announcing "the mirror up to nature"—a line which describes not only the ideal player, as Hamlet would have it, but Shakespeare himself, the supreme embodiment of a "negative capability" who creates world upon world without ever revealing his own face in it. "Scylla and Charybdis" cites Coleridge's description of Shakespeare as "myriad-minded," a term which in *Finnegans Wake* suggestively becomes "mirror minded."[33] Shakespeare is a "Jew" because he exemplifies the Jew's supposed ability to engage in ceaseless mimetic reflection of the world.

To act as mirror or mimic requires a boundless capacity for protean self-transformation, adaptation, and assimilation. It implies, as Sombart suggests, the absence of any essence or stable core of identity other than the fact of constant mimesis. Such a conception of the Jew would clearly appeal to Joyce, since *Ulysses* is a novel obsessed with metamorphosis, metempsychosis, flux and reflux, circulation and return. Bloom's Jewishness is not what Gilles Deleuze and Félix Guattari call the "becoming-Jewish of the non-Jew"[34] but precisely a "becoming not-Jewish of the Jew." Bloom's ethnicity is intangible and unlocatable because of his many assimilationist gestures, uncertain credentials, and violations of Jewish law: he is an uncircumcised, thrice-baptized fancier of pork and organ meats with a gentile mother and a father who converted to Protestantism before his son's birth. His Jewishness is not a fact but a *question*, posed explicitly by Ned Lambert: "Is he a jew or a gentile or a holy Roman or a swaddler or what the hell is he? says Ned. Or who is he?" Shortly thereafter he is described as "one of those mixed middlings—A fellow that's neither fish nor flesh—Nor good red herring" (*Ulysses*, p. 337–38). Like the Shakespeare of the Chandos portrait, Bloom is a Jewish *question*—an admixture, insinuation, or suspicion rather than an identity or essence.

Critics have reacted variously to Bloom's protean Jewishness. Erwin R. Steinberg has argued that since Bloom fails to meet all religious and cultural standards for Judaism, he isn't a Jew at all, and the whole issue is a critical red herring.[35] Stanley Sultan sees Bloom as Joyce's ironic attack on bigotry, since he is at once not Jewish enough for the rabbis

33. James Joyce, *Finnegans Wake* (New York: Viking, 1964), p. 576.
34. Gilles Deleuze and Félix Guattari, *A Thousand Plateaus: Capitalism and Schizophrenia*, trans. Brian Massumi (Minneapolis: University of Minnesota Press, 1987), p. 292.
35. Erwin R. Steinberg, "James Joyce and the Critics Notwithstanding, Leopold Bloom is Not Jewish," *Journal of Modern Literature* 9, no. 1 (1981-82): 27–49.

and yet quite Jewish enough for the anti-Semitic Dubliners of *Ulysses*.[36] Interestingly enough, the debate over Bloom's Jewish credentials repeats similarly legalistic denials of Shylock's Jewishness earlier in the century. Maurice Packard's *Shylock Not a Jew* (1919) and Robert Friedlander's *Shakespeare and the Jew* (1921) argued that Shylock's violations of Talmudic law and Jewish ethics meant that he bore "no likeness to the Jew of any age."[37] John Eglinton's challenge to prove Shakespeare a Jew finds its ironic counterpart in such efforts to prove that both Bloom and Shylock are *not*. But as Bryan Cheyette notes, "That Bloom cannot be confined by such 'scientific' knowledge, paradoxically, defines his indeterminate Jewishness."[38] Ira B. Nadel strikes a similarly anti-essentialist note in his book *Joyce and the Jews*, where he argues that "Joyce's Judaism is textual, his Jewishness cultural."[39] Nadel demonstrates the influence on Joyce of Maurice Fishberg's work *The Jews: A Study of Race and Environment* (1911), an anthropological analysis which shows that the Jewish people share neither a pure and exclusive racial heritage nor a set of fixed cultural characteristics. The Jews, Fishberg argues, are a heterogeneous people, of mixed origins further compounded by centuries of intermarriage. Moreover, they do not present an unchanging cultural face but constantly adapt to new environments (though Fishberg denies that they show any special talent for acclimatization). This anti-essentialist conception clearly appealed to Joyce, whose protagonist Bloom announces "mixed races and mixed marriage" (*Ulysses*, p. 490) as part of his hallucinated, millennial role during the "Circe" chapter. It is also readily apparent why Joyce's understanding of Judaism would appeal to the poststructuralist, multicultural convictions of much recent criticism. A Judaism which is constitutively heterogeneous, construction rather than nature, question rather than fact, protean and transformational rather than unchanging and essential, will clearly resonate with the preoccupations of contemporary cultural theory. In particular it opposes the essentialisms that tend to cluster around the concept of race—a concern that motivates Fishberg's book, which argues against the notion that Judaism is racial, physiological, and therefore inassimilable to European culture. Leopold Bloom represents a Jewishness that, while retaining a recognizable if indefinable core, is always in the process of becoming something else, a Jewishness that is fundamentally both protean and par-

36. Stanley Sultan, " 'What the Hell is he? says Ned?': Why Joyce Answers the Question with a Question," *James Joyce Quarterly* 23, no. 2 (Winter 1986): 217–22.
37. Robert Friedlander, *Shakespeare and the Jew* (New York: E. P. Dutton, 1921), p. 12.
38. Bryan Cheyette, "Jewgreek," p. 39.
39. Nadel, *Joyce and the Jews*, p. 9.

tial. Here as elsewhere, however, a strategy designed to counter one version of anti-Semitism generates another, for horror of racial mixing, contamination and consequent degeneration were every bit as powerful as fears of an alien, eternally separate race. Bloom's status as "mixed middling" (a term applied to his sexual as well as ethnic status) generates contempt among his fellow Dubliners, just as it is the *hint* rather than the indisputable *fact* of a "Jewish" Shakespeare that spooks Friswell. Similarly, the notion of the Jew as *question*, while it may have for us a certain post-structuralist appeal, also provided grist for the mill of anti-Semitic conspiracy theorists. The building blocks of paranoid systems are not facts (even invented ones) but doubts, suspicions, insinuations. Jewishness as question can arouse as much hostility as it dissipates.

The suspicion that attaches itself to Jewish identity emerges in the "Scylla and Charybdis" chapter. Georg Brandes and Sidney Lee, Stephen Dedalus's two main Jewish sources, are explicitly invoked during a discussion of the authenticity of Shakespeare's *Pericles*, which Stephen has just used as evidence. Challenged by John Eglinton on the validity of including that play in the Shakespeare canon,

—Mr Brandes accepts it, Stephen said, as the first play of the closing period.
—Does he? [responds John Eglinton] What does Mr Sidney Lee, or Mr Simon Lazarus, as some aver his name is, say of it? (*Ulysses*, p. 195)

Lee did in fact change his name—from Solomon Lazarus Lee, or Simon Lazarus Levi, according to different sources[40]—at the suggestion of Benjamin Jowett. His first published essay, "The Original of Shylock," appeared in *Gentleman's Magazine* under the neutral initials S. L. Lee. By invoking Lee's original, Jewish name, Eglinton raises questions about Lee's identity and "authenticity" at the very moment when Stephen invokes another Jewish critic to support the canonical authenticity of *Pericles*. Eglinton thereby implicates Stephen's reliance on Jewish scholars with his taste for (as Eglinton puts it) "the bypaths of apocrypha" (*Ulysses*, p. 195). The unsoundness of Stephen's Hamlet-theory, Eglinton insinuates, is somehow connected with the untrustworthiness of Jewish critics who try to hide their own identities.[41] By arguing that Shakespeare

40. C. H. Firth, "Sir Sidney Lee, 1859–1926," *British Academy Proceedings* 15 (1929): 445; Marder, *His Exits*, p. 159.
41. Elliott Baker makes a similar slur against Lee in *Bardolatry*, p. 29.

was really the Earl of Rutland, Karl Bleibtreu's book also presents a case of muddied or questionable identity.

Shakespeare's "Jewishness," in fact, derives in large part from his mixed or uncertain status. Stephen describes the Bard at one point as "Rutlandbaconsouthamptonshakespeare or another poet of the same name" (*Ulysses*, p. 208). By merging various candidates of the so-called authorship controversy into a kind of protean conglomerate, Stephen creates a fitting counterpart to Ned Lambert's description of Bloom as "a jew or a gentile or a holy Roman or a swaddler or what the hell is he?" In his plays Shakespeare metamorphoses into a world of characters; "he is all in all" (*Ulysses*, p. 212), insists John Eglinton. But as the authorship controversy shows, Shakespeare's protean identity extends beyond the world of the plays into that of biography and history. The sheer mass of Shakespearean scholarship, criticism and speculation provides an archive vast enough to "prove" virtually anything, and thus to manufacture Shakespeares to order, "as you like it."[42] Stephen's Hamlet-theory, crafted out of equal parts scholarship and sophistry, simply effects one more protean transformation of this plastic archival matter. When John Eglinton says "Prove he was a Jew," what he means is, "if you can prove *that* you can prove anything." And Stephen, glorying in his intellectual and rhetorical skills, accommodates him. In this sense Shakespeare is Jewish only because, as a protean entity, he can be shaped into anything, including a Jew. But in another sense, it is precisely this protean character that makes him (not as one thing among others, but above all) Jewish.

I have been using the word "protean" advisedly, because it seems to me that "Scylla and Charybdis" parallels and reworks the earlier "Proteus" chapter. There, Stephen grapples with the ceaseless transformation of the material world, embodied above all in the vast flows of the ocean, in the course of composing a brief lyric poem. "Scylla and Charybdis" is another oceanic chapter. But while critics have endlessly debated the bipolar dangers represented by the mythological creatures of its title (Aristotelianism vs. Platonism, realism vs. mysticism, etc.), little has been said about the waters running between them. These, I would suggest, are the Shakespearean archive itself, that churning textual sea, which Stephen attempts to bind into a distinct form ("Shakespeare"), much as Menelaus did to Proteus in order to make him yield up his truth. Stephen does manage to produce a relatively coherent Shakespeare, but the fixity

42. Or as Haines uncharitably puts it, "Shakespeare is the happy hunting ground of all minds that have lost their balance" (*Ulysses*, p. 248).

of the image is only temporary. Stephen's Shakespeare soon disintegrates under the combined assaults of interruption, interrogation, and skepticism, until Stephen is forced to admit that even he doesn't believe in his own theory (*Ulysses*, p. 213–14).

Likewise, Bloom's many assimilationist and secularist gestures "dilute" his Judaism to the point where it seems on the verge of vanishing entirely. And yet something remains—a few scraps of half-remembered prayers, a set of vague but recognizable habits and dispositions—which manage to survive and constitute for Bloom an irreducible sense, despite evasions and denials, of his cultural identity. One can never say fully how Bloom is Jewish—the evidence is hopelessly muddled—and yet clearly, somehow, he is. His Judaism, moreover, tends to erupt in the context of remembered traumas, such as his father's suicide or his son Rudy's early death.

A similar dialectic of fixity and flux subtends the very process by which Joyce constructs his Jewish Shakespeare, who in this regard typifies the problems of reading and interpretation engendered by *Ulysses*. In most respects, Joyce's Jewish Shakespeare is only a mischievous invention, a mere phantasm or hallucination cast up by the play of the text in its ceaseless, Charybdis-like flows and eddies. Yet even when the provisional, indeed sophistical basis of this construction is revealed, it refuses to dissipate entirely, much as Friswell's analysis of the Chandos portrait causes us to "see" a somewhat Jewish Shakespeare even though we recognize the purely fantastic nature of the idea. Some stony kernel or core remains, Scylla-like, unmoved amidst the textual flow. Like Bloom's Judaism, the Jewish Shakespeare survives its Joycean deconstruction.

This curious persistence does not, moreover, end with *Ulysses*. The Jewish Shakespeare which Joyce inherits from Friswell, Brandes, and Lee passes on into the academy in critical discussion of *The Merchant of Venice*. My proof text here will be René Girard's essay " 'To Entrap the Wisest': A Reading of *The Merchant of Venice*."[43] Girard's essay exemplifies modernist strategies for recuperating *Merchant* from charges of anti-Semitism, above all in championing an ironic reading of the play but also in grappling with the themes of *ressentiment* and the scapegoat.

Girard's argument, in brief, is that *Merchant* can sustain both an anti-Semitic and an anti-anti-Semitic reading. For the unenlightened, anti-Semitic masses, Shakespeare provides the comfortably stereotyped figure

43. Girard's essay originally appeared in *Literature and Society*, ed. Edward Said (Baltimore: Johns Hopkins University Press, 1980), 100–119. I will cite from the slightly revised and expanded version that appears as a chapter in René Girard, *A Theater of Envy: William Shakespeare* (New York: Oxford University Press, 1991), pp. 243–55.

of the evil Jew in Shylock. At the same time, *Merchant* is a typically Shakespearean investigation of the themes of conflictual mimesis, undifferentiation, and scapegoating. Thus the play's opening antithesis between
Christian and Jew breaks down in an ironic demonstration that Antonio
and Shylock are really doubles of each other. Venetian society scapegoats
Shylock not because he is its "other" but because he is its unflattering
mirror, and because his demystifying directness pierces their hypocritical
self-idealization. This second, ironic reading is visible only to a sophisticated in-group that includes Shakespeare himself. Hence *Merchant* is a
"paradoxical" text that encourages both anti-Semitic prejudice *and* its
ironic critique.

Both the strengths and weaknesses of Girard's essay betray typically
modernist tendencies. The strengths include his skepticism toward the
liberal, sentimentalizing reading of Shylock as persecuted victim, while
the weaknesses include his credulous reliance on irony as an antidote to
prejudice. Girard's depiction of Shylock as a double or mirror image of
the play's Christian characters rejects liberal attempts to render him like-
able or sympathetic. This latter strategy, which relies on Shylock's indisputable moments of humanity—the "Hath not a Jew eyes?" speech, his
feelings of betrayal upon learning that Jessica had sold the ring his wife
Leah gave him, his sudden illness after being broken, humiliated, and
forcibly converted by the Christians in court—defined the liberal tradition of reading the play, from William Hazlitt though Henry Irving. But
the liberal reading of the Jew as sympathetic victim proved vulnerable to
a modernist appropriation of Nietzschean *ressentiment.* Nietzsche, of
course, had brought the notion of *ressentiment* to bear chiefly on Christian
culture, though he proclaimed its Jewish origins. But predictably, it came
to be turned back against the Jews by writers such as Werner Sombart,
Max Scheler, and, most disturbingly, Max Weber. Weber's view of Judaism as a "pariah religion" held that the Jews' sense of themselves as a
"chosen people" depended on their continued persecution; hence the
Jews' pariahdom was self-willed and did not depend on actual hostility
or prejudice for its existence. The Jews' *ressentiment*, Weber argued, made
it impossible to assimilate them to European society as long as they persisted in their devotion to Judaism.[44] Weber's theory of Jewish *ressentiment*
turned the liberal conception of the Jew-as-victim on its head. For Hazlitt
and Irving, Shylock was Shylock *because* he was persecuted; they implied
that if Jews ceased to be victimized by a Christian society and were instead

44. See Gary A. Abraham, *Max Weber and the Jewish Question: A Study of the Social Outlook of His Sociology* (Urbana: University of Illinois Press, 1992).

assimilated into it, their resentful wishes for revenge would cease. For Weber and others, Jews *desired* persecution to feed their own resentment.

A particularly odious variation on Weber's view has proven surprisingly resilient in *Merchant* criticism. First formulated by Bernard Grebanier in 1962, it has reappeared in the pages of *Shakespeare Studies* as recently as 1988.[45] According to this theory, Shylock is not in fact victimized by the Christians in the play but simply puts on the *role* of the "persecuted Jew" in order to win sympathy and pursue his own nefarious ends.[46] While Weber did not deny the wrongs done to Jews but merely held that their sense of persecution was independent of these, Grebanier's thesis denies to Shylock either real suffering *or* genuine feelings of persecution. He is rather, in this view, a Machiavellian plotter who employs Christian guilt for his own purposes.[47]

I cite such views only in order to show how theories of *ressentiment* can undermine liberal attempts at constructing a sympathetic Shylock. It is his understanding of the instability of sympathy, I believe, as well as a hard-nosed attention to the details of the play, that causes Girard to reject a "liberal" reading of Shylock. Commenting on the "Hath not a Jew eyes?" speech, Girard observes: "The text insists above all on Shylock's personal commitment to revenge. It does not support the type of 'reha-

45. Bernard Grebanier, *The Truth about Shylock* (New York: Random House, 1962); Marion D. Perret, "Shakespeare's Jew: Preconception and Performance," *Shakespeare Studies* 20 (1988): 261–68.

46. In order to maintain this view, it is necessary to believe that Shylock *lies* when he claims that Antonio spat on him, kicked him, and cursed him, even though Antonio does not deny these actions, and in fact promises to repeat them. Grebanier, who at least has the courage of his absurd convictions, holds that Antonio is far too good a man to have committed the acts of which Shylock accuses him, and that he refuses to debase himself by denying Shylock's outrageous charges. Perret merely relies on Grebanier's theory without addressing the "evidence" in support of it. It would be equally naïve, of course, to maintain that every one of Shylock's self-defenses is a spontaneous *cri de coeur* and that he is above making tactical use of past sufferings. There is probably no moment of apparent sincerity in Shakespeare which is not haunted by theatrical inauthenticity. But to deny past wrongs done to Shylock when even Antonio does not is to fly in the face of all textual evidence and to indulge in pure anti-Semitic fantasy.

47. I received an unexpected lesson in the strange economies of anti-Semitism when, in the spring of 1996, I delivered part of this chapter as a lecture at Johns Hopkins University. After the lecture, a group of faculty, including Professor Ronald Paulson, took me to dinner at a restaurant in my hotel. While riding in the hotel elevator, Professor Paulson suddenly turned to me and said: "Spell Grebanier backwards." Puzzled, I complied with his request and was suddenly seized with horror when I realized that it spelled "Reinaberg." My specimen anti-Semite turns out to be Jewish! Grebanier isn't explicitly "outed" in the few brief biographical portraits of him, but Professor Paulson assures me that it was common knowledge. *The National Cyclopaedia of American Biography*, vol. 60 (Clifton, N.J.: James T. White, 1981), notes discreetly that Grebanier "lectured at the Young Men's and Women's Hebrew Association, New York City, from 1974" (p. 213).

bilitation' naively demanded by certain revisionists. But it unequivocally defines the symmetry and the reciprocity that govern the relations between the Christians and Shylock."[48] Girard's reading will therefore insist not that Shylock is better than he appears to be, but that the Christians are as bad as he appears to be. This recourse to the *Judenspiegel* has its own ambiguities, as I have already argued. What is of interest here is Girard's recognition that a liberal reading of Shylock cannot survive the assault of a theory of *ressentiment*. Hence his own strategy, which may be the best available under the circumstances, is to deflect the concept of *ressentiment* away from its later, more overtly anti-Semitic trajectories and back to its original, Nietzschean intent: as a critique of Christian morality. Shakespeare's Venice, argues Girard, is "a world in which even the difference between revenge and charity has been abolished."[49] The only difference between Shylock and the Christians is that the former's "charitable" offer of a loan without interest paradoxically and self-consciously recognizes charity as a form of revenge, while the latter frequently experience their own revenge as charity, that is, in a mystified form. In Girard's reading it is not Shylock but the Christian Antonio who embodies the logic of Nietzschean *ressentiment*: "The quintessential Venetian, Antonio, the man who is sad without a cause, may be viewed as a figure of the modern subjectivity characterized by a strong propensity toward self-victimization or, more concretely, by a greater and greater interiorization of a scapegoat process that is too well understood to be reenacted as a real event in the real world."[50] Thus Antonio is at once the most violently resentful character in the play *and* the one most eager to play the Christian role of sacrificial lamb. Shylock understands as revenge what Antonio can only experience as *ressentiment*. The Shylockian *Judenspiegel* reflects not the appearance but the hidden essence of Christian morality.

Girard's treatment of *ressentiment* and its relation to scapegoating bears comparison with Joyce's. On the one hand, *Ulysses* clearly depicts anti-Semitism as a form of scapegoating. In the "Circe" chapter Bloom assumes the eponymous role of scapegoat in the Old Testament ritual of purification (*Ulysses*, p. 497), while J. J. O'Molloy reveals the arbitrary nature of anti-Semitic victimization by recommending "When in doubt persecute Bloom" (*Ulysses*, p. 464). On the other hand Joyce seems to endorse a variant of the Weberian or anti-Semitic theory of *ressentiment*

48. Girard, *Theater of Envy*, p. 244.
49. Ibid., p. 247.
50. Ibid., pp. 252–53.

by depicting Bloom as taking masochistic pleasure in his own persecution. Upon being chosen as ritual scapegoat and condemned to stoning, Bloom reacts as follows: "(Rubs his hands cheerfully.) Just like old times. Poor Bloom!" (*Ulysses*, p. 497). Bloom's social masochism is clearly tied to the sexual masochism he exhibits in the presence of Bella Cohen. The latter, in turn, has been traced to Joyce's use of the works of the anti-Semitic psychologist Otto Weininger. Critics have attempted to defuse Joyce's extensive borrowings from Weininger's book *Sex and Character* by arguing (plausibly, but by no means decisively) that they are ironic.[51] But even granting the premise of an ironic or parodic intent leaves unanswered questions about the effectiveness of irony as a means of neutralizing anti-Semitic discourse—as I shall argue in the case of Girard.

The case of Joyce illustrates two constraints informing Girard's reading of *Merchant*: not only does a liberal reading of the Jew as victim prove vulnerable to the discourse of *ressentiment*, but that discourse may itself turn against either anti-Semite or Jew. Similar ambiguities attach themselves to Girard's strategy of treating Shylock as Antonio's double or mirror image. The problem with this *tu quoque* argument is that it convicts the Christian characters in Shakespeare's play of acting in what can be construed as a "Jewish" fashion. A well-meaning magazine article of the late nineteenth century which attempted to show how Shylock was cheated by the Christians in the courtroom scene was entitled "Shylock the Jew-*ed*."[52] In his book *The Harmonies of "The Merchant of Venice,"* Lawrence Danson writes: "The *malice* with which Antonio has, in the past and now, publicly reproved and humiliated Shylock, convicts him of being, in this instance, himself spiritually a 'Jew.' "[53] If it seems paradoxical, to say the least, to blame Antonio's anti-Semitism on some inner "Jewishness," it is nevertheless perfectly consistent with the notion of the *Judenspiegel* which also governs Girard's essay and (it must be said) Shakespeare's play. With respect to the latter, it seems that Shylock's forced conversion from Judaism to Christianity at the end of the courtroom scene merely inverts the more diffuse conversion of Christian to "Jew" that occurs throughout the play, culminating in Portia's vengeful legal-

51. See Marilyn Reizbaum, "The Jewish Connection, Cont.," in *The Seventh of Joyce*, ed. Bernard Benstock (Bloomington: Indiana University Press, 1982), 229–37; Robert Byrnes, "Bloom's Sexual Tropes: Stigmata of the 'Degenerate Jew,' " *James Joyce Quarterly* 27, no. 2 (Winter 1990): 303–23. The Joyce-Weininger connection was first pointed out by Richard Ellmann.

52. Anon., "Shylock the Jew-*ed*," *Temple Bar* 45 (1875): 65–70.

53. Lawrence Danson, *The Harmonies of "The Merchant of Venice"* (New Haven: Yale University Press, 1978), p. 32.

istic tactics during the courtroom scene. The *tu quoque* strategies implicit in an "ironic" reading of the play can thus slide imperceptibly into the myth of *Verjudung* or "Jewification." If Shylock demystifies the Christians by reflecting their true selves, he also (and thereby) contaminates or mixes their cultural identity by revealing its unexpectedly "Jewish" component.

As applied to *Merchant*, then, Girard's concept of "undifferentiation" proves to be a blunt instrument. The doublings and ramifying similarities he traces surely do occur, but he seems excessively certain that these ironize the play's Christians, thereby ignoring potential connections between undifferentiation and the myth of *Verjudung*. Despite his insistence on the collapse of apparent antitheses *within* the dynamic of the plot, however, Girard sustains some crucial structural oppositions in order to make his reading of *Merchant* work. The first of these is his distinction between scapegoating as structure and scapegoating as theme, which in turn divides the audience. *Merchant*, argues Girard, at once enacts the scapegoating of Shylock and raises this process to thematic self-awareness by rendering it ironic. Scapegoating as structure panders to the majority of Shakespeare's original audience, whom Girard depicts as literal-minded, anti-Semitic vulgarians. By contrast, the ironies sustaining scapegoating as theme are "highly effective with the knowledgeable few" but "completely invisible to the ignorant multitude."[54] The original distinction between scapegoating as structure and scapegoating as theme thus generates, and is in turn sustained by, a set of supplementary oppositions: between exoteric and esoteric audiences, between literalism and irony, and last but not least between anti-Semitism and anti-anti-Semitism.

Although Girard insists that *Merchant* generates seemingly antithetical movements, he does not want to argue that these latter fall prey to anything like the process of undifferentiation that engulfs Antonio and Shylock. *Within* the play opposites merely collapse, but *Merchant* itself boasts a "paradoxical" structure that sustains contradictory yet distinct interpretations.[55] However muddy things may turn in Venice, differences remain well defined for Shakespeare and for his privileged auditors. "Shakespeare is fully conscious of the gap between the difference of the static structure [of his play] and the nondifference of tragic action." And as for us, "our certainty is perfect" that Shakespeare's intentions in *Merchant* are ironic.[56] Thus there is also no chance either that Shakespeare

54. Girard, *Theater of Envy*, p. 254.
55. Ibid., p. 251.
56. Ibid., pp. 254, 251.

is a vulgar anti-Semite or that we, Girard's readers, can become confused with the literal-minded multitudes who batten upon the anti-Semitic surface of the play. *They* fall prey to the lure of false appearances, while *we* penetrate to the play's truth by perceiving the ironic distance between patent and latent. In fact, Girard's essay defines *three* distinct levels of consciousness: the literal, the ironic, and a third (cynical rather than ironic) level occupied by Shakespeare and Girard, who not only can appreciate *Merchant*'s critique of anti-Semitism but who also, in a worldly-wise manner, forgive the play for succumbing to the profit motive and pandering to its less enlightened patrons. Although he borrows Shakespeare's phrase "To entrap the wisest" for the title of his essay, Girard quite plainly insists that *Merchant* does *not* entrap the wisest, at least not those who are as wise as Shakespeare and himself.

It seems clear, however, that Girard defends his own and Shakespeare's purity of intent by indulging in certain idealizations that he would never entertain when looking "inside" a play. His basic premise—that awareness of literary irony somehow inoculates the clever reader against anti-Semitism—would seem to be massively refuted by modernism itself, as represented by such figures as Eliot, Pound, Lewis, or Céline. Moreover, the seemingly distinct categories that operate "outside" the play appear, upon closer inspection, to be projections of the supposedly collapsing oppositions within its plot. Girard's twin audiences pit an elite and anti-anti-Semitic "in-group" against a mass of vulgar outsiders. But *Merchant* also deploys an elite (though this time anti-Semitic) "in-group" against the vulgar outsider Shylock. Portia, the member of this in-group who displays the most sustained and exquisite sense of irony, is also the play's most successful and vigorous persecutor of Shylock. Neither the plot of *Merchant* nor the history of the modern era supports the clear distinctions that Girard tries to draw in his essay on the play; nor, on the other hand, does it support a typical Girardian "plot" in which initial opposites collapse irreversibly into one another. It has not been my intention to argue that anti-Semitism and anti-anti-Semitism are really the "same thing," although I have attempted to show that they are not exactly opposites, either. Rather, I have portrayed them as mirror images, which situates each as both a reflection and an inversion of the other. It is one of the paradoxes of the mirror that it can sustain distance without difference. This mirroring relation renders it maddeningly difficult to "decide" whether *Merchant* is an anti-Semitic play.

It may be no more than a suggestive accident that Girard's book *A Theater of Envy* places the revised *Merchant* essay directly before the essay on Stephen Dedalus's Hamlet-theory in *Ulysses*. But since suggestive accident seems to be the main causal mechanism of *Ulysses* itself, this one may repay further thought. At first sight the conjunction doesn't count for much. Girard's analysis of the mechanisms of anti-Semitism and anti-anti-Semitism is, as I have argued, less supple and nuanced than Joyce's, although both writers employ the figure of the mirror. Then, too, Girard does not address Stephen's construction of a "Jewish" Shakespeare. And yet Girard's *Merchant* essay also fashions an implicitly Jewish Shakespeare who, in some ways, resembles Stephen's.

Girard does not offer, in the manner of Georg Brandes, any cultural or biographical evidence to suggest that Shakespeare might sympathize or identify with Shylock. "Identification" with characters is, in Girard's view, only a ruse or lure offered to the naive by the ironic text. Dim-witted anti-Semites may "identify" with the Christians in persecuting Shy-lock, but Girard insists that no one may engage in sentimental communion with Shylock himself—least of all Shakespeare, who is too fully engaged in second- and third-level gamesmanship to side with char-acters in his play. And yet there is something about Shakespearean con-sciousness as Girard portrays it—something at once playfully ironic, piercingly acute, and deeply cynical—that finds a kind of counterpart in Shylock. Certainly, Girard's depiction of *Merchant* as a violent demystifi-cation of the play's Christians places Shakespeare in a position that is structurally analogous to Shylock's. If Shakespeare is no admirer of his Jewish creation, he at least resembles him in being (as Girard would have it) an anti-anti-Semite, and a devastatingly clever one at that. But the resemblance does not end there. For if Shakespeare sees through the hypocrisies of persecution, he is nevertheless willing to indulge the prej-udices of the anti-Semitic majority in his audience—and he does so in order to fill seats in the theater. Business, in other words, comes before principle—another "Jewish" quality. And what exactly are Shakespear-ean business ethics? According to Girard, Shakespeare actually produces two versions of *Merchant*. One, a brilliantly ironic performance, is distrib-uted to the privileged members of Shakespeare's intellectual tribe. The other, an inferior product, is doled out to the ignorant multitudes. But was not this distinction between "brother" and "other" a frequent com-plaint levelled by anti-Semite against Jew? Deuteronomy, it was frequently noted, forbade lending at interest to fellow Jews but permitted it when dealing with gentiles. The charge that Jews dealt righteously with each other but cheated non-Jews was repeated for centuries. According to Gi-rard, Shakespeare engages in a similar double standard, by which he privileges not his co-religionists but his co-ironists. The "debased" *Mer-chant* is, as the phrase goes, "good enough for the goyim," while the better-quality goods are reserved (though at the same price) for Shake-speare's own "people." Girard's Shakespeare, like Friswell's (and Bran-des's and Joyce's) begins to reveal unexpectedly "Jewish" lineaments. And what of Girard himself? He does his best to keep a kosher kitchen by not mixing proscribed categories: milk with meat, vulgar with elite, literal with ironic, anti-Semite with anti-anti-Semite. But this ritual purity, which keeps *Merchant* and Girard himself above moral reproach, is dif-ficult to maintain when its founding opposition of Jew and gentile begins to dissolve. If even Shakespeare can turn Jewish, who is safe?

"I am much ashamed of my exchange": The Jew and the Money-form

Portia's notorious question, "Which is the merchant here? and which the Jew?" (4.1.174) proposes not only a mirroring of characters but a crossing of categories. In comparing Antonio and Shylock, Portia mixes religious and economic identities, for she distinguishes not between Christian and Jew or between merchant and usurer but between mer-chant and Jew. In so doing she calls attention to a more widespread infiltration of economic and religious "value" which has become widely apparent to ironizing readers of the play—including Girard. Recent work, much of it by Marxist critics, has explicated the role of economic history and economic ideology in the play, particularly as it relates to Shylock's role as moneylender. If Shylock and Antonio confront each other as representatives of usurer's and merchant's capital, respectively, they nevertheless inhabit these roles in different ways. While Antonio is, among other things, a merchant, Shylock has often seemed to be nothing but a moneylender; his economic position suffuses his social being in a way that Antonio's does not. The very word "shylock" has detached itself from its original bearer and, to a degree unique among Shakespeare's creations, gone on to live a life of its own. A "shylock" is any greedy, usurious, or extortionate person. The word retains its anti-Semitic col-oring, but can be applied to gentile as well as Jew—just like the colloquial verb "to jew," which means to cheat, swindle, or overcharge someone. In a play in which characters sometimes momentarily freeze into alle-gorical statues (Portia's "I stand for sacrifice" [3.2.57] or Shylock's "I stand for judgment" [4.1.103]), Shylock often seems to personify usu-rer's capital or, more vaguely, the power of money. And what is true of Shylock may be said of the figure of the Jew more generally. One of the forces fueling the "Jewish question," as I noted earlier, was a certain taxonomic perplexity about whether the Jews were a religious, racial, cultural, or national entity. To this we must now add the belief that they may be an economic one.

In *The Merchant of Venice*, Shylock's economic role poses certain challenges to the resources of dramatic representation. At the opening of the trial scene, the Duke says to Antonio:

> I am sorry for thee. Thou art come to answer
> A stony adversary, an inhuman wretch,
> Uncapable of pity, void and empty
> From any dram of mercy. (4.1.3–6)

Ostensibly these lines describe Shylock; but Shylock's bond is being upheld only because to abrogate it would threaten "the trade and profit of the city" (3.3.30). Antonio's real "stony adversary" is thus capital itself, whose inexorable demands are merely expressed *through* Shylock. It is capital which, like the skull in Portia's golden box, proves "uncapable of pity, void and empty / From any dram of mercy" (4.1.5–6). The doubled referent of the Duke's words thus locates a duplicity in Shylock's role, forced as he is to function as a character in his own right (and a memorably vibrant one at that) *and* as the personification or incarnation of an impersonal economic force. Shylock's own "stony" nature may reflect, in part, the allegorical mortification he must undergo in order to serve as capital's puppet or (to use Marx's term) "bearer." The case of Shylock enables us to ask: How is the image of the Jew configured so as to enable him or her (him, usually) to "represent" capital? What kinds of representational torsion are at work in order to invest the Jew with this allegorical role?

The Jew, of course, is not associated with capital in general, but rather with usurer's or (later) banking capital—that is to say, with finance and circulation rather than industry or production. Usurer's capital had been notorious since Aristotle precisely because it involved a purely monetary transaction (and profit) without ever mediating the exchange of commodities or productive labor. Shakespeare's Shylock neither imports useful goods like Antonio nor owns land like Portia: his wealth, in the form of jewels and bags of ducats, is both portable and sterile, as Jessica and Antonio (respectively) remind him. He is neither more nor less exploitative than the other Venetians, but he does suffer the misfortune of working an unusually conspicuous mode of exploitation, one lacking any social cover or indirection. Even the Duke's slaves are tucked quietly away on his estate; we learn of them only because Shylock alludes to them polemically in court. Shylock's own usurious bargains are made publicly on the Rialto, without any cultural mediation or alibi. His role as economic scapegoat is thus connected with his vulnerable and visible position within the realm of economic circulation; it is not capital as such but rather money capital that he is forced to represent. In his 1931 essay "Money and the Merchant," Max Plowman (recalling the language of *Merchant*'s Duke) writes: "Money is today what Shylock was to the world of Venice—the forbidding aspect, the dark principle, the shadow in the sun, the grim necessity. Its logic is inhuman."[57] The role of money capital plays different roles in different economic and historical formations, of course; but the association of the Jews with money capital exposes them to a remarkably consistent form of abuse. This abuse grew especially vituperative during the modernist period, when the rise of finance capital (that is to say, the union of banking and industrial capital) fueled already-existing fantasies about Jewish financiers plotting world domination.

The connection between Jews and money was elaborated rather fancifully in Werner Sombart's book *The Jews and Modern Capitalism*. In the final part of that book, Sombart attempts to explain the putatively crucial role played by the Jews in the rise of modern capitalism by arguing for a kind of spiritual affinity between money and the origins of Jewish culture:

> For in money, the two factors that go to make up the Jewish spirit are united—desert and wandering, Saharaism and Nomadism. Money is as little concrete as the land from which the Jews sprang; money is only a mass, a lump, like the flock; it is mobile; it is seldom rooted in fruitful soil like the flower or the tree. Their constant concern with money distracted the attention of the Jews from a qualitative, natural view of life to a quantitative, abstract conception. The Jews fathomed all the secrets that lay hid in money, and found out its magic powers. They became lords of money, and, through it, lords of the world.[58]

For Sombart, Jews and money share an abstract, quantitative, and deterritorialized essence. As I shall argue in this section, what Jews and money actually share is a complex relation to social visibility. Money is the form

57. Max Plowman, "Money and the Merchant," *Adelphi* (1931); rpt. in *"The Merchant of Venice": A Casebook*, ed. John Wilders (1969). Compare Grebanier, *The Truth about Shylock*: "Yes, most of the world has adopted Shylock's philosophy, which is the philosophy of banks. No one expects compassion from a bank" (p. 213).

58. Sombart, *Jews*, p. 344. Sombart is clearly inspired here by a passage in Marx's *Capital* which traces the origins of money to nomadic peoples, though not specifically to the Jews. See Marx, *Capital*, 1:183.

in which economic relations are at once manifested, occulted, and displaced; and since Jews have traditionally been forced to occupy the sphere of money or circulation, they too suffer a peculiar form of prominence which renders them the apparent but displaced locus of capitalist exploitation. This privileged yet exposed visibility, I maintain, undergirds not only the Jews' status as scapegoats but also their seemingly inevitable role as mirror for bourgeois society. In what follows, then, I shall entertain (though in a very different key) Sombart's intuition that the Jews are not only associated with money but are, in a deeper yet purely analogical sense, actually *like* money. The Jew is forced to play a representational role with respect to bourgeois cultural values very like the one that money plays with respect to economic value. In order to develop this thesis I shall follow Marx's phenomenological treatment of the "origins" of the money-form in the early chapters of *Capital* and, using this as a guiding thread, investigate Shylock's role within the representational dilemmas of *The Merchant of Venice*.[59]

Marx opens his analysis of the commodity-form by distinguishing between the commodity's use-value (those concrete, physical properties which enable it to satisfy specific needs or desires) and its exchange-value (or, more properly, just "value"), which is the socially necessary labor needed to produce it. Commodities are exchanged because as use-values they fulfill different needs, but the ratios of exchange which determine the "price" of a given commodity reflect the quantity of socially necessary labor it embodies. While a commodity's appearance and physical properties render its use-value directly visible, they do not immediately reflect or register the amount of labor required to produce it. "We may twist and turn a single commodity as we wish; it remains impossible to grasp it as a thing possessing value."[60] The commodity, like the king in medieval political theory, possess two bodies: a visible body of use and an invisible body of value. In Chapter 1 of *Capital*, Marx analyzes exchange-value as the *Erscheinungsform* ("form of appearance") of value, the visible manifestation of value's invisible content.

Marx begins his analysis with the simplest case: that of two commodities—he chooses a coat and twenty yards of linen—which require the

59. Strictly speaking, what Marx offers in his chapters on the commodity and money in Vol. 1 of *Capital* is a parody of Hegelian phenomenology. I put the word "origin" in quotation marks because these chapters undertake not an historical but a structural explication of the money-form. Yet Marx allows his analysis to appear at times like an historical account because he is parodying, among other things, the double narrative of historical and phenomenological unfolding in Hegel's *Phenomenology of Spirit*.

60. Marx, *Capital*, 1:138.

same amount of socially necessary labor time to be produced, and thus represent equivalent values. In this situation, the physical body of commodity B can serve as the visible representation of the value of A. The twenty yards of linen, we may now say, is "worth" one coat, whereas the linen's attempt to serve as its own measure of value—twenty yards of linen = twenty yards of linen—would produce only a meaningless tautology. Here the "use-value [of commodity B] becomes the form of appearance of its opposite, value." Or as Marx puts it elsewhere, "the physical body of commodity B becomes a mirror for the value of commodity A."[61] Commodity B is not yet what we would call money, but it already fulfills one of money's essential functions—it is an embodiment or measure of the value of other commodities. Money, for Marx, is the privileged mirror of value.

Marx adds at this point a witty footnote which will prove helpful in analyzing *Merchant*:

> In a certain sense, a man is in the same situation as a commodity. As he neither enters into the world in possession of a mirror, nor as a Fichtean philosopher who can say "I am I," a man first sees and recognizes himself in another man. Peter only relates to himself as a man through his relation to another man, Paul, in whom he recognizes his likeness. With this, however, Paul also becomes from head to toe, in his physical form as Paul, the form of appearance of the species man for Peter.[62]

In *Merchant*, Antonio is indeed a man who finds himself "in the same situation as a commodity" when Shylock's bond values his life at 3,000 ducats. In the realm of human, as opposed to economic, value, however, Antonio finds his mirror in the figure of Shylock. And it is no accident that the Jew, like money, finds himself converted into the universal embodiment of value.

It is important to grasp that the value relation between two commodities, as analyzed by Marx, involves equivalence but also asymmetry. "The relative form of value [commodity A, whose value is being expressed] and the equivalent form [commodity B, which expresses the value of A] are two inseparable moments, which belong to and mutually condition each other; but, at the same time, they are mutually exclusive or opposed extremes, i.e. poles of the expression of value."[63] Insofar as commodity

61. Ibid., pp. 148, 144.
62. Ibid., p. 144.
63. Ibid., pp. 139–40.

B functions as the equivalent of commodity A, it in effect gives up or sacrifices its original use-value to serve as the embodiment of A's value. As equivalent form, the coat abandons its place among the world of use-values in order to serve as mirror. It is no longer a thing that gives warmth but a thing that reflects the value of A. The equivalent form has, in a sense, become subordinated to the relative form. "In its value-relation with the linen, the coat counts only . . . as embodied value, as the body of value."[64] The physical body of commodity B has relinquished those specific qualities which made it a unique use-value in order to take on a new life as the mirror of commodity A's immaterial body, the body of value.

Marx's analysis of the value form and its phenomenological dilemmas illuminates Shylock's role in *The Merchant of Venice*, but it finds its most direct Shakespearean equivalent in the theme of the three caskets, which I shall employ here as a mediating device. Marx's "simplest case" is reflected in Portia's silver casket, whose inscription reads "Who chooseth me shall get as much as he deserves" (2.7.23). In other words, the chooser shall receive his equivalent value; therein he shall find that which manifests or represents his intrinsic worth. This is clearly how Morocco understands the inscription when, considering the silver casket, he says: "Pause there, Morocco, / And weigh thy value with an even hand" (2.7.24–25). Morocco uses the word "value" to mean his worth as a man, but the reference to weighing clearly invests it with a quantitative, economic meaning as well. (Morocco's words foreshadow Portia's demand that Shylock should "tarry a little" [4.1.305] and make certain that he weighs out exactly a just pound of Antonio's flesh).

The representational dilemmas embodied in the game of the caskets prove remarkably similar to those addressed by Marx. Like economic value, the "value" weighed by Morocco is not immediately visible in its bearer. Indeed, Morocco goes to some length to insist that his intrinsic worth *cannot* be read in his dusky appearance. What the silver casket provides is a material or symbolic object whose physical properties mirror the value of the chooser. It is the equivalent form of value to the chooser's relative form of value. This mirroring or reflective function is emphasized repeatedly when Aragon actually chooses the silver casket. The enclosed inscription refers to fools "silver'd o'er" (2.9.69), a phrase which, in addition to its primary meaning of "silver-haired," may also recall the silvered glass of mirrors; and the lines "Some there be that shadows kiss, / Such have but a shadow's bliss" (2.9.66–67) almost cer-

64. Ibid., p. 143.

tainly allude to Narcissus. The problem of narcissism is, in fact, central to the episode with Aragon (whose name roughly suggests "arrogant"). He rejects the golden casket because, as he says,

> I will not choose what many men desire,
> Because I will not jump with common spirits,
> And rank me with the barbarous multitudes. (2.9.31–33)

Unlike Morocco, Aragon has no doubts about himself, and chooses the silver casket because of his confidence in his intrinsic worth: "I will assume desert" (2.9.51). For his pains, he gets a fool's head, which is explicitly described as his double or mirror image.

This episode is crucial for several reasons. First of all, Aragon stands in for those narcissistic readers of the play who will choose between Antonio and Shylock, or gentiles and Jews, based only on which one presents a more gratifying reflection of themselves. The episode thus offers an allegory of reading for *Merchant* as a whole. Moreover, it diagnoses narcissism not only as a pathology of desire but as a cognitive delusion—for Aragon's choice is tautological as well as self-serving. When he says "I will assume desert," he reveals the circularity of his sense of worth, which is based not on comparing himself objectively with others but on narcissistic self-absorption. (Indeed, at the very moment when he is supposedly choosing a wife, his cogitations return obsessively to himself.) Aragon is, in effect, the Fichtean philosopher who can say "I am I," or the twenty yards of linen which tries to express its value in twenty yards of linen. He represents not the value-relation but its short-circuiting.

The cognitive dimensions of Aragon's failings are symbolized by the "portrait of the blinking idiot" whose "fool's head" doubles his own and thereby parodies the Socratic injunction to self-understanding: "Know thyself." For this, Aragon has substituted "love thyself," which in cognitive terms means "know *only* thyself." But his is not the play's sole collapse of Socratic self-examination; Antonio ends his very first speech by declaring that "I have much ado to know myself" (1.1.7), a phrase which could profitably be hung from the neck of all his fellow Venetians. Antonio's failure of self-knowledge is actually a collective phenomenon among the play's gentile characters, who judge themselves and their social order through the tautology of self-regard. Only Shylock contains enough social difference or otherness to serve as an "equivalent form" in which the other characters may see themselves truly reflected, thus breaking the narcissistic circle.

Shylock's association with the money-form, then, finds its counterpart in his function *as* the play's money-form—or rather, as we shall call it at this point, the equivalent form. Like Marx's exemplary coat, Shylock in his "Jewish gaberdine" is the material object in which the play's gentile characters may read their souls or invisible values. And like the commodity in its role as equivalent form, Shylock is both denied an ordinary place in the social world of the play and subjected to the others whom he reflects. As Jew, and as equivalent form, Shylock must relinquish his own nature in order to measure the natures of others. He is the play's privileged *Erscheinungsform*, a man "silver'd o'er" who serves at once as money and mirror.

Shylock not only provides *Merchant*'s gold standard for cultural and moral "value"; he also sustains a conspicuous interplay between these values and economic ones, thereby allegorizing his own function in the play. But his bond with Antonio, or such ejaculations as "my ducats, and my daughter!" (2.8.17), should not be seen as *reducing* the value of human life to money-values; rather, they show how all value is created and judged by a process which is exemplified in the economic realm. His repeated and tactless demonstrations of this fact may be the real crime for which Venice cannot finally forgive Shylock.

The danger of this view, however, is that it designates Shylock as the play's locus of truth—an implicit assumption of Girard's analysis and of virtually all ironic readings of *Merchant*. To "choose" Shylock over Antonio or Bassanio or Portia as, if not a more appealing, then at least a more honest or perspicuous or demystified character, is to play our own version of the casket game, and to imagine that some absolute or privileged measure of value can be identified beneath a differential play of appearances. Neither Marx's analysis of the value-form nor a close reading of Shakespeare's play justifies such an assumption.

The relative form of value, with which Marx begins his analysis of the commodity, has the advantage of providing an *Erscheinungsform* for what would otherwise be an invisible quantity. But it is precisely a *relative* form, which compares the amount of value contained in the two commodities without providing an absolute measure of either. Thus, as Marx points out, "if the values of all commodities rose or fell simultaneously, and in the same proportion, their relative values would remain unaltered."[65] The twenty yards of linen is "mirrored" in the coat because each contains the same amount of expended labor-power. But if, owing to advances in production techniques, the labor-time required to produce each of these were halved, they would still contain equal quantities of

65. Ibid., p. 146.

labor, and would not measure or even register the absolute reduction in expended labor. Thus exchange-value at once provides value with a mode of appearance and, at the same time, constitutively and irrevocably *occludes* it from any possibility of representation. The system of exchange-value, with its endless but merely relative expressions, effects the equivalent of a primal repression or indeed a foreclosure of value.

Something like the same problem afflicts *The Merchant of Venice*, where Shylock can provide only a relative, not an absolute, measure of value. Comparing Shylock with gentile characters does not ground the play's truth but rather sets loose a floating system of equivalences. Like exchange-value, Shylock serves as a necessary measure and manifestation of value—but also causes it to circle, tautologically, around a void. Carefully calibrating Shylock's and Antonio's relative worth ignores the fact that the absolute value of both may be dropping precipitously without affecting this moral casuistry in the least.

Once again, the game of the three caskets illuminates a larger epistemological problem in the play. Here the relevant episode is the choice made by the Prince of Morocco, who chooses the golden casket. Unlike Aragon, Morocco is provoked into at least a few moments of self-doubt by the inscription on the silver casket and hence does not fall into its immediate, narcissistic tautology. Instead of basing his decision on his own value, Morocco reads the caskets and their inscriptions as cyphers of *Portia's* worth:

> Is't like that lead contains her? 'Twere damnation
> To think so base a thought; it were too gross
> To rib her cerecloth in the obscure grave.
> Or shall I think in silver she's immur'd,
> Being ten times undervalued to tried gold?
> O sinful thought! never so rich a gem
> Was set in worse than gold. (2.7.49–55)

Portia seems to occupy a position analogous to that of value here; she is the hidden content which is at once revealed and occulted by the differential play among the caskets. Morocco tries to solve his conundrum by assuming that Portia, most valuable among women, must be set in gold, most valuable among metals. But, as the inscription on the gold casket reads, "Who chooseth me shall gain what many men desire" (2.7.5). Value is thus not intrinsic but sustained by the desire of others. And the "value" of gold is immediately debased by the death's head inside the casket, from whose *memento mori* perspective all worldly riches are dross.

For Marx, of course, exchange-value measures not the relative desirability of commodities but the relative labor-times congealed in them; yet the value of the abstract labor-power expended on a commodity depends in turn on the social desirability—the use-value—of that commodity.[66] Use-value is never measured even relatively by exchange-value, yet it is its necessary foundation. And it introduces a new, if less fetishized, circularity by suggesting that objects are valuable because they are valued. As Morocco discovers, there is no way to "break through" the play of relative values to some irreducible core beneath. Portia's very name derives from the Latin *portio,* a word related to *pars* or part, which in turn comes from an Indo-European base meaning "to sell, hand over in sale, whence L. *par,* equal, *parare,* to equate."[67] Portia's name suggests a process of portioning or proportioning, dividing, equating, or trading. Thus she is not the hidden essence lying imperturbably beneath the ephemeral and differential play of values, like some beautiful shell resting at the bottom of a troubled sea, but an interiorized reflection of that surface and its vicissitudes.

One may assume that it is not because of cowardice but because he somehow intuits the demonic circularity of the casket-game that Morocco suggests another method of choosing:

> Bring me the fairest creature northward born,
> Where Phoebus' fire scarce thaws the icicles,
> And let us make incision for your love,
> To prove whose blood is reddest, his or mine. (2.1.4–7)

Morocco prefers incision to decision, a direct cutting through to the hidden content rather than a choice among surfaces. Yet even the act of cutting only leads to further comparisons; it taps a hidden vein of interiority, but only to make of it a new surface, whose redness initiates new differential relations. Incision cannot, therefore, break through the circularity of the code and gain access to some unmediated piece of the real; but it is true that the slicing or biting of flesh is the way in which *Merchant* attempts to figure this possibility. Both incision and decision, the cutting into and the cutting between, are attempted modes of resolution, escape routes from the tautologies of exchange value. In *Merchant,*

66. To clarify the point: Marx holds that labor must be socially useful in order to produce value at all. But the value of a commodity depends on the amount of socially useful labor expended to produce it, not upon the "degree" of its usefulness or desirability.

67. *Webster's New World Dictionary of the American Language,* 2d ed. (New York: World, 1970), p. 1035.

however, they are repeatedly foiled by circumcision, literally the circular cut—at once the ritual sign of Shylock's Jewishness and the tautology of the code of exchange-value which he represents.[68] The circular movement of relative values opens up a void or hole in the real, which the fantasies of incision or decision attempt to fill. The former of these is one which I shall develop further on; the latter activates all ethical or ethico-political readings of the play, such as Girard's. But *Merchant*'s game of decision (Shylock or Antonio or Portia or . . . ?), like the game of the caskets, is evacuated by the circularity of exchange-value. Instead of allowing us to choose a "best" character and invest her or him with some special ethical or cultural or political value, the play insistently demonstrates the futility of this process. Shylock's privilege is to manifest not truth but precisely this futility.

For Marx, the circularity of exchange-value is rendered visible when he moves from the isolated or accidental form of value to the total or expanded form: "z commodity A = u commodity B or = v commodity C or = w commodity D or = x commodity E or = etc."[69] The defects of this form are readily apparent: "Firstly, the relative expression of value of the commodity is incomplete, because the series of its representations never comes to an end. The chain, of which each equation of value is a link, is liable at any moment to be lengthened by a newly created commodity, which will provide the material for a fresh expression of value. Secondly, it is a motley mosaic of disparate and unconnected expressions of value."[70] Hence the total or expanded form quickly passes over into the general form of value:

$$\left. \begin{array}{l} 1 \text{ coat} \\ 10 \text{ pounds of tea} \\ 40 \text{ pounds of coffee} \\ 1 \text{ quarter of corn} \\ 2 \text{ ounces of gold} \\ 1/2 \text{ ton of iron} \\ x \text{ commodity A, etc.} \end{array} \right\} = 20 \text{ yards of linen}$$

It is important to note that in passing from the isolated form to the total or expanded form and then to the general form of value, nothing has

68. Shapiro, *Shakespeare and the Jews*, pp. 113–30, shows that the theme of circumcision is not merely incidental to *The Merchant of Venice* but is central to the play's imaginative structure.

69. Marx, *Capital*, 1:154.

70. Ibid., p. 156.

materially altered in the value-relation; only its form of expression has changed, and these different forms reveal different aspects of value. In the general form, one commodity has separated itself out from the chain of motley value-expressions and assumed the role of general equivalent. Or, as Marx puts it, "the general relative form of value imposes the character of universal equivalent on the linen, which is the commodity excluded, as equivalent, from the whole world of commodities."[71] Though not quite yet money, the general equivalent has already taken on a "Jewish" aspect, being excluded for the purpose of serving as equivalent, that is, for the purpose of mirroring not one given commodity but the whole world of them. In addition, the general form begins to express the peculiar fetishism that will mark the money-form. Although the linen is really just one commodity among others, with no special characteristics or virtues, the general *form* of value invests it with an apparent privilege. It suddenly becomes the sun around which the other commodities revolve; and because it and it alone now mediates the exchange of commodities, it appears as if value inhabits it in a unique way. Although excluded from the world of commodities, the linen has seemingly become the master commodity, the commodity of commodities from which the logic of the entire system now appears to emanate. The only thing that separates the linen from money is that its physical being still betrays its former function as a use-value. Money is, originally, nothing but a commodity (gold) which serves as general equivalent and whose physical form reflects that function.

Marx's careful analysis of the origins of money in the simplest value-relation is intended to demystify money, to show that there is precisely nothing special about it. Like every other commodity, its value is determined by the amount of labor required to produce it, and like every other commodity it has a use-value (in this case, to serve as a general equivalent, measure of price, and medium of exchange). Only a special form of commodity fetishism makes it seem as if, in the words of the song, "money makes the world go round." As Marx puts it, "the money-form is merely the reflection thrown upon a single commodity by the relations between all other commodities."[72] Thus the secret of capitalism lies neither in the money-form nor in the sphere of circulation in general, but Marx must tear away the veils of mystification attaching themselves to money before revealing the essential mechanism of capitalist production.

71. Ibid., p. 159.
72. Ibid., p. 184.

In demystifying money, however, Marx also—if only incidentally—demystifies the position of the Jew, to whom the fetishism of money also, unfortunately, attaches. It is a curious fact that discussions of Marx and anti-Semitism focus almost exclusively on the two early articles against Bruno Bauer, published in a journal which was almost immediately confiscated by the Prussian police and was therefore read by virtually no one. It is true that in those early articles and elsewhere, Marx's arguments in favor of Jewish emancipation are mixed with anti-Semitic views. It is also true that Marx never acknowledged the existence of a Jewish working-class movement, and that he tended to depict Jews *tout court* as bourgeois. But it should be said that Marx's mature economic system provided, if only implicitly, a powerful demystification of anti-Semitic sentiment by exposing the nature of the money fetish. Anti-Semitic fantasies of Jewish bankers conspiring to achieve worldwide domination merely projected onto the Jews the same fetishism embodied in the mistaken belief that "money makes the world go round." By transferring attention from the sphere of circulation to that of production, Marx's analysis of capitalism shifted focus away from those forms of economic activity traditionally engaged in by Jews.

The specific fetishism attaching to the money-form can help explain the workings of anti-Semitism not only in *The Merchant of Venice*, but also in Joyce's *Ulysses*, whose modernist form, as I have already suggested in the previous chapter, owes something to the dynamics of reification. The encyclopedic coherence of Joyce's novel results in part from a series of symbolic correspondences between the cultures of different geographical and historical regions. Drawing on the theories of Victor Bérard and others, Joyce creates a floating system of equivalences which the novel complicates and ironizes but nevertheless sustains. One such series may be represented as follows: Jew = Greek = Phoenician = Irish. . . . This equation is meant to suggest at least a formal resemblance to Marx's "total or expanded form" of value. And in fact, what Marx identifies as the "defects" of that form—its heterogeneous, motley quality and its constitutive incompleteness—are exploited by Joyce to literary advantage. By forming an endless chain rather than a hierarchical order, Joyce's serial correspondences prevent any term from mastering or organizing the others. What *Ulysses* aims for is, rather, an endless circulation, flow, or exchange among terms rather than crystallization into a structure—a crucial fact, because globalizing theories like Bérard's contain at least the capacity for paranoid systematization.

This capacity is realized in anti-Semitic theories of Jewish-Masonic world conspiracies, which like Bérard's theories or Joyce's novel organize vast stretches of history into a web of imagined interconnection. Here, however, the structure of fantasy resembles not Marx's total or expanded form but rather that of the general equivalent or money-form:

$$
\left.\begin{array}{l}
\text{Freemason} \\
\text{Jacobin} \\
\text{Bolshevik} \\
\text{Capitalist} \\
\text{etc.} \ldots
\end{array}\right\} = \text{Jew}
$$

In this static, paranoid structure, the Jews are not part of a general flow or exchange but are the one term capable of connecting others (such as Bolsheviks and bankers) who would otherwise seem antithetical. Moreover, the equal sign works in only one direction, for the Jews are seen as the hidden reality for which the others are merely superficial masks. Here the Jews have assumed the full burden of the money-fetish, serving not only as the mirror or general equivalent of world history but as the apparent source or origin of historical relations which are in fact projected onto them. It is in their role as general equivalents within paranoid systems that the Jews become most precisely "like" money.

Ulysses engages in a complex form of play with anti-Semitic conspiracy theories. Characters such as Haines and Mr. Deasy voice anxiety about the economic power of Jews, and Bloom himself recites part of the oath of the Freemasons (*Ulysses*, p. 609), thereby "confirming" one anti-Semitic fantasy. Bloom is imagined in the "Ithaca" chapter as "an estranged avenger, . . . with financial resources (by supposition) surpassing those of Rothschild or of the silver king" (*Ulysses*, p. 728), but it is his own hallucinations in the "Circe" chapter that most fully embody anti-Semitic fears. When he is proclaimed mayor of Dublin, "*the standard of Zion is hoisted*" (*Ulysses*, p. 487), and not long thereafter he gives birth to gold and silver children who are placed in high positions of public (principally commercial) trust (*Ulysses*, p. 494). It seems safe to say that Joyce's use of anti-Semitic theories is (primarily) ironic. But it also highlights a potential danger within the novel's very form by showing how its fluid totality can suddenly congeal into paranoia, if one term in the series is precipitated out as a general equivalent. The form of *Ulysses* is stretched, one might say, between two merely virtual but irreducible poles, with paranoid hypercoherence at one end and pure dissemination at the other. Bloom, as Jew, simultaneously embodies both of these virtualities: he is both protean being without essence and focus of conspiratorial fantasy. Money, too, is both medium for the endless "metamorphosis of commodities"[73] and the merely apparent or projected source of commodity exchange as system.

While it is true that money is really just another commodity, money fetishism is not exactly the same thing as commodity fetishism: "What appears to happen is not that a particular commodity becomes money because all other commodities universally express their value in it, but, on the contrary, that all other commodities universally express their values in a particular commodity because it is money. The movement through which this process has been mediated vanishes in its own result, leaving no trace behind. . . . The riddle of the money fetish is therefore the riddle of the commodity fetish, now become visible and dazzling to our eyes."[74] As in commodity fetishism, the value which results from a social relation appears to be an intrinsic quality of the commodity as physical object; but in the case of money fetishism, this fact becomes "visible and dazzling to our eyes." Money fetishism is, in other words, the *Erscheinungsform* of commodity fetishism—commodity fetishism raised, as it were, to the second power. What begins as a concrete social relation—the exchange of products of labor—first becomes a circular code operating among the commodities themselves. Then that code appears to emanate from one master commodity, which, in merely measuring the relative values of other commodities, seems thereby to impart value to them. The money-form is the place where the code of exchange-value achieves its most circular expression,[75] where it folds over onto itself. Yet precisely as a result of this, money seems to become the magical *source* of the code, to possess a kind of solidity or intrinsic value which all other commodities lack. The emptiest term, the one which concentrates in itself the tautology adhering to the code of exchange-value, appears as the master element, the magical source of the real—a position rather like that of the Lacanian phallus.[76] This position is also the one

73. Ibid., p. 198.
74. Ibid., p. 187.
75. This has to do with money's double function as measure of value and standard of price. Prices, which are the *Erscheinungsformen* of exchange-value, are expressed not in quantities of labor time but in standard weights of precious metal—a pound sterling, for example. Prices do not even directly represent the relative exchange-values of commodities, but mediate that relation once more by equating the value of the commodity with that in a given quantity of money, and then expressing that quantity through its relative relation to a standard of price, which was originally a given weight of precious metal
76. This homology has, of course, already been elaborated by Jean-Joseph Goux, who notes "the congruence between the phallic signifier as the general equivalent of objects of drive and currency as the general equivalent of objects of labor": *Symbolic Economies: After Marx and Freud*, trans. Jennifer Curtiss Gage (Ithaca: Cornell University Press, 1990), p. 129. Without engaging in an extended critique of Goux's approach, let me say merely that I

occupied by Shylock in *The Merchant of Venice*, for it is just insofar as he embodies the emptiness of the mirror—that is, insofar as he merely reflects others around him—that he paradoxically attains his apparent status as the play's bearer of truth. His substantiality is a function of his insubstantiality, of his ability to cause reflection to close into a loop.

Once again, the casket game illuminates this paradox—with Portia, not Shylock, playing the role of money-form. Portia, it seems fair to say, is the privileged term of the casket game, at once its motivation and its prize. Portia plays the role of the hidden essence or reality lying beneath the play of differential surfaces, the "truth" which only the wise guesser will attain. Yet Portia herself is afflicted by suspicions of her own emptiness: "But the full sum of me / Is sum of nothing" (3.2.157–58),[77] she admits to Bassanio, in a phrase which is truer than her modesty intends—for the casket game perfectly bears out her intuition. More important, perhaps, than the question of whether she cheats to help Bassanio win (she surely does) is the question of what, exactly, Bassanio does win. Bassanio's first exclamation of joy upon choosing the "right" casket is telling: "Fair Portia's counterfeit!" (3.2.115). At the very moment when Bassanio thinks to have discovered the hidden truth, he is confronted with another representation, another mediation. His words, moreover, suggest a second meaning: fair Portia *is* counterfeit, empty, a sham, the sum of nothing, just as she claims. Bassanio's description of the portrait reinforces this suspicion:

> Here in her hairs
> The painter plays the spider, and hath woven
> A golden mesh t' entrap the hearts of men
> Faster than gnats in cobwebs. But her eyes—
> How could he see to do them? Having made one,
> Methinks it should have power to steal both his
> And leave itself unfurnish'd. (3.2.120–26)

---

arrive at this homology through a somewhat different reading of the opening chapters of *Capital* and with different results. Goux, for instance, articulates the three Lacanian registers of the Imaginary, the Symbolic, and the Real with money's three functions as, respectively, measure of value, medium of circulation, and means of payment. (See Goux, pp. 47–48.) I, by contrast, find a homology to the Lacanian Real in a dyad of the commodity's use-value and the worker's body, which I shall elaborate further on. Goux, it seems to me, maintains an insufficiently strict distinction between value and exchange-value and thus overlooks the crucial problematic of the *Erscheinungsform*.

77. "Sum of nothing" is the Folio reading, which I adopt here in place of the Riverside editors' choice, "sum of something."

Bassanio's reaction to the image verges on idolatry or fetishism. Moreover, his fantasy of an eyeless portrait surely recalls the skull with the "empty eye" (2.7.63) contained in the golden casket, just as the "golden mesh" of the portrait's hair evokes the golden casket itself and its false allure. Thus Portia's picture somehow doubles or reproduces the vacant death's head which symbolized the void. The opening lines of the scroll attached to the picture contain an unrecognized but sardonic (and relevant) moral: "You that choose not by the view, / Chance as fair, and choose as true" (3.2.131–32). In a play concerned with the letter of the law it will be wise to take this inscription literally: those who choose not by the view chance *as* fair and choose *as* true as those who don't. Not better, mind you—exactly the same. Choosing the lead casket produces identical results to choosing the gold or silver ones, for the chooser's reward is a counterfeit Portia, at once empty death's head and mocking fool's head. The prize is dust, and the magical term which at once gets the play of surfaces going and promises to resolve it turns out to be merely one more equivalent surface which immediately seeps away into the others. Only Bassanio's fetishizing relation to the portrait sustains its seemingly magical properties.

Whatever its intrinsic interest, I want to treat the casket game as a kind of epistemological commentary on the role of Shylock in the play. The fetishizing or idolatrous representation of Portia simply transposes into another key the more hostile fetishization of Shylock—the result of his relation to the money-form. Her empty centrality mirrors and explicates his. Yet to be more precise, it is the *Jew*—or a certain construction of the Jew—who is treated as money. Shylock cannot be entirely contained by this role; if on the one hand he represents the play's most blatant adherence to monetary value, he also most blatantly violates it. If he is the play's major fetish, he also attempts most vigorously to break through the fetishism of money's code.

One way he does so is by telling the story of Jacob and Laban, which he offers as a kind of parable defending interest. Shylock's description of Jacob's sheep, and of the homely world of agricultural labor, provides the play's only glimpse into the realm of production, both human and natural, in which none of the play's characters—usurers, merchants, landed aristocrats, and courtiers alike—engages. Antonio's reaction to the story ("Was this inserted to make interest good? / Or is your gold and silver ewes and rams?" [1.3.94–95]) insists on an unbridgeable distance between Jacob's sheep and the money-form on which the entire Venetian economy (not only Shylock's business) relies.[78] I would argue

78. This opposition is undercut somewhat by the fact that if ewes and rams are not gold

that Shylock's tale opens a window onto something corresponding roughly to what Marx calls use-value; and it is telling that the play offers only mediated access to this realm, via Shylock's narration. Even Antonio's luxury goods, his spices and silks, are represented exclusively through imaginative conjecture. In Shakespeare's Venice, a world defined by exchange-value and the money-form, use-value can be summoned up solely in the shadowy guise of narrative referent.

In his illuminating essay on *The Merchant of Venice*, Marc Shell observes that Shylock's tale of Jacob and Laban builds a subtle constellation of puns on "ewes," "use," and "Iewes."[79] The conceptual links forged by these puns may be articulated with the play's encoding of value. "Ewes," considered as a food source, inhabit the realm of "use," understood here not as "usury" but as usefulness. Ewes/use denotes the realm of use-value which falls into the hole scooped out by the circular code of exchange-value. As a result of its occlusion, use-value comes to hold a place analogous to that of the Lacanian Real, or rather to that hole in the Real denoted by castration.[80] In political economy, this void is then stopped up, or rather papered over, by the money-form, the phallic signifier whose tautological significance substitutes for the missing Real. So, too, in Shakespeare's play, where "gold and silver" occupy the vacancy left by "ewes and rams." Or rather, not gold and silver directly, but the "Iewes," money's fetishized personifications in the play, and their profession of "use" or usury, wherein money breaks all direct connection with the world of useful commodities and seems, in circular fashion, to generate itself from itself. The puns connecting "ewes," "use," and "Iewes" do not simply flow together in some semantic brew, then, but sustain a finely wrought set of relationships which define the structural position of Shylock. Ewes/use/Iewes operates a series of phonetic sub-

---

and silver, they were at one time used as a form of money. Bassanio's comparison between Portia's hair and Jason's "golden fleece" (1.1.174) also muddies what Antonio takes to be an unbridgeable distance between sheep and precious metals.

79. Marc Shell, "The Wether and the Ewe: Verbal Usury in *The Merchant of Venice*," in Shell, *Money, Language, and Thought: Literary and Philosophical Economies from the Medieval to the Modern Era* (Berkeley: University of California Press, 1982), pp. 49–51.

80. It might seem that I am falling prey to what Derrida would call an "onto-theology," with use-value occupying the place of hidden essence that my own analysis has recently denied to Portia. It is certainly true that use-value is just another code, and one which, as Baudrillard has shown, is dependent or parasitic on exchange-value. Use-value comes to occupy the place of the Real not because of something intrinsic to it but only because of its status as the occluded or foreclosed. On the Lacanian Real see Slavoj Žižek, *The Sublime Object of Ideology* (New York: Verso, 1989). For a marvelous elucidation of the Real in its relation to Shakespeare, see Julia Reinhard Lupton and Kenneth Reinhard, *After Oedipus: Shakespeare in Psychoanalysis* (Ithaca: Cornell University Press, 1993).

stitutions whereby the Jew as fetish comes to occupy, but not fill, the void left by the disappearance of use-value.

Shylock reacts to his fetishized position by attempting to cut through it and grasp the occluded real for which he is forced to substitute. Just after retelling the story of Jacob and Laban, he effectively embodies or enacts its juxtaposition of ewe and Jew through his "merry bond" with Antonio. He would never actually try to collect his pound of flesh, insists Shylock, since

> A pound of man's flesh taken from a man
> Is not so estimable, profitable neither,
> As flesh of muttons, beefs, or goats. (1.3.165–67)

But in fact Antonio's flesh is for Shylock what the sheep were to Jacob—a source of enrichment and even nutrition, since it will both eliminate an economic competitor and feed Shylock's hatred. The priority of these two motives is of some importance for the play's conception of the Jew. The anti-Semitic reading of Grebanier's insists that Shylock's motives are primarily financial, and that his apparent hatred of Antonio merely veils a cunning economic rationalism.[81] Brandes, by contrast, says of Shylock that "His vengefulness is many times greater than his rapacity. Avaricious though he be, money is nothing to him in comparison with revenge. . . . His hatred of Antonio is far more intense than his love for his jewels; and it is this passionate hatred, not avarice, that makes him the monster he becomes."[82] While both readings render Shylock repulsive, they do so in significantly different ways. Grebanier's Shylock is entirely defined by money; Brandes's is driven by more primitive, seemingly "pre-economic" passions. Both views find support in the play, but I think that the bond with Antonio is important primarily for its violations of fiscal reason. Shylock's own daughter attests she heard him swear "he would rather have Antonio's flesh / Than twenty times the value of the sum / That he did owe him" (3.2.286–88). Shylock does not want Antonio dead for the fiscal gain it will bring him. He wants Antonio's flesh; he wants to *eat* Antonio, thereby satisfying his cannibalistic desire to "feed upon" the Christians (2.5.14). Antonio is, for Shylock, an embodiment not of exchange-value but of use-value, like the tasty flesh of Jacob's sheep. True, Antonio brings the rate of usance down in Venice, but Shy-

81. This view has also been maintained—mistakenly, I believe—by other Jewish critics. See, e.g., Derek Cohen, "Shylock and the Idea of the Jew," in *Shylock*, ed. Harold Bloom (New York: Chelsea House, 1991), p. 312.

82. Brandes, *Shakespeare*, p. 167.

lock hopes to cut *beneath* the chain of exchange-value to some underlying substance, the nutritive gobbet of flesh whose fascinating power embodies the disgusting sublimity of the Lacanian Thing—an unassimilable bit of the Real drenched in abjection. It is no surprise that this gobbet, like Jacob's sheep, never appears upon the stage; it exists only as a theoretical condition of the bond, and as Shylock's constitutive fantasy, never to be realized.

Like the Prince of Morocco, Shylock wants to "make incision" and thus attain that which is foreclosed by the code of exchange-value. But the prize he hopes to win is himself, his own humanity, indeed his own body, now encased within the fetishism of the money-form. On the one hand, the bond converts Antonio's substance into embodied money (one pound of flesh equaling 3,000 ducats) and thus parodies Shylock's own fetishized role as the embodiment or personification of money. Yet in the excavated flesh of Antonio Shylock would also find the mirror or equivalent of his own occluded self which, pricked, bleeds. Shylock's seemingly primitive or cannibalistic passion is thus not, as it would seem, somehow anterior to the economic; it is, rather, a sophisticated if desperate tactic waged at once within and against the web of exchange-value and the money-form.

I should at this point note a certain slippage that results from my alignment of Lacanian and Marxist paradigms, in particular from my comparison between Marx's concept of use-value and the Lacanian Real. It is true that use-value serves as a foreclosed material support for the code of exchange-value, and thus occupies a position not unlike that of the Real. But in discussing Antonio's pound of flesh as the Lacanian Thing, I have passed somewhat beyond the Marxist conception of use-value as mere utility into a more ambivalent and sublime region. Can this bleeding chunk of flesh, product of Antonio's Christ-like passion, this dripping substance of suffering, possibly be coordinated with the axes of need and satisfaction associated with the use-value? Am I not, moreover, twisting Shakespeare's play rather unmercifully in forcing it to conform to anachronistic categories?

Let me return to my original premise, which is that Marx's conception of exchange-value as the *Erscheinungsform* of value might help elucidate Shylock's role as mirror of value in *Merchant*. As we have seen, Marx's treatment of the *Erscheinungsform* is a highly complex, even ironic one, since the mode of appearance of value also guarantees its disappearance, along with that of use-value, from the code of exchange-value. It should be noted, however, that *Capital* is not an elegy to either use-value or value, which are, respectively, the qualitative and quantitative aspects of concrete labor. *Capital* is, rather, an analysis of the capitalist mode of production as, simultaneously, a mode of economic exploitation. Marx's ultimate point of reference is therefore not the commodity itself, but the workers who produce it. And his analysis of exchange-value and the money-form is not an attempt to restore to the commodity its lost metaphysical rights or ontological transparency as use-value but rather to prepare for his examination of the key concept of surplus-value, by means of which the labor contract can both pay producers "fully" for their labor-power and, at the same time, extract unpaid labor from them. The ability of exchange-value, and particularly of the money-form, both to manifest and to occlude value takes on a new dimension when money is used not as means of payment but as capital, when among other things it purchases that special commodity known as human labor-power. Then the fetishism which makes money seem to be the source of value obscures value's real source in the worker; and the circularity of exchange-value obscures not the value of individual commodities but the unpaid transfer of value effected by the wage contract. The commodity, considered first as both use-value and value, is, in the order of Marx's analysis, essentially a preliminary stand-in for the labor (and laborer) that produces it. The occulting of the *product* of labor stands in for the occulting of the *producer*, the exploitation of human muscle, bone, and spirit which occurs behind factory doors and within the seeming transparency of the wage contract. The whole point of Marx's analysis of commodity fetishism is to show that what appears to be a set of social relations among objects is really a set of material relations among persons; hence his analysis of the commodity is a self-consciously fetishized and displaced way of exploring social relations. The foreclosure of value, and of use-value, from the code of exchange-value simply rehearses, in the language of objects, the foreclosure of the producer within capitalist production.

The opening chapters of *Capital* thus operate a highly sophisticated and self-conscious "slippage" between commodity and worker, which are doubly bound: the former is the product of the latter, but the latter's labor power is also a commodity. Marx's coat, which initially floats about of its own ghostly will, is eventually placed on the back of the living worker who made it. All commodities, Marx shows, are drenched in the sweat and blood of the producers who are exploited in creating them. Only the fetishism of the commodity-form, and of the money-form, magically wipes these away. For Marx, there is no commodity whose production has not exacted a pound of the producer's flesh.

Marx, it is interesting to note, quotes *The Merchant of Venice* to make just this point in Volume I of *Capital.* In the first of two citations, Marx notes that factory owners refused to give child laborers work breaks for rest or food when they discovered that the Factory Act of 1844 did not specifically require them to do so:

> Workers and factory inspectors protested on hygienic and moral grounds, but Capital answered:
>
> > "My deeds upon my head! I crave the law,
> > The penalty and forfeit of my bond." . . .
>
> Hence capital demanded and obtained the satisfaction not only of making children of 8 drudge without any interval from 2 to 8:30 P.M., but also of letting them go hungry.
>
> > "Ay, his breast,
> > So says the bond."[83]

Here Capital speaks in the voice of Shylock as it demands its right to extract every legal ounce of strength—or pound of flesh—from the worker's body. Later in Volume I, after showing how Capital imperils the lives of workers by depriving them of their means of production, Marx quotes Shylock's response to the Duke's pardon:

> > "You take my life
> > When you do take the means whereby I live."[84]

Now Shylock speaks on behalf of the worker, but once again the issue is material existence, the worker's bodily *substance*. In stretching Shylock between Capital and Labor, victimizer and victim, Marx not only pays heed to Shylock's complex role within the play but also focuses on that seemingly impossible bond between the fetishized abstractions of the wage contract and the horrifying concreteness of the suffering body. In *Merchant* this bond is expressed, indirectly but with almost hallucinatory vividness, by Bassanio when he gives Antonio's written plea for help to Portia:

> > Here is a letter, lady,
> > The paper as the body of my friend,

83. Marx, *Capital*, 1:399–400.
84. Ibid., p. 618.

> And every word in it a gaping wound
> Issuing life-blood. (3.2.263–66)

Bassanio's description clearly recalls another text: Shylock's bond, which also drips with Antonio's blood. For Marx, this bond would be precisely the labor contract, wherein the worker sells his own body, in the form of labor-power, to the capitalist. Shylock thus proves useful to Marx as a way of figuring one of the central theoretical conundrums addressed by Volume I of *Capital*: how is it that the code of exchange-value, whose circularity cuts it off from the concreteness of social relations, nevertheless manages to sink its teeth into the worker? How does the money-form, wherein this code achieves its tautological, fetishized perfection, get a grip on the producer's very body, producing suffering, exploitation, disease, and death? Shylock's knife, we might say, cuts the path which Marx's theoretical incisiveness will attempt to trace.

It is clear that Marxist concepts such as use-value are "unavailable" to Shakespeare both for historical reasons and because a poetic and dramatic discourse is not a theoretical one. Yet Shakespeare can be said to depict through literary means what Marx describes in analytic terms. Specifically, *Merchant* foreshadows Marx's movement from use-value to the laborer's body as the occluded Real of commodity fetishism, and it does so through a kind of poetic condensation. The implied conjunction between "ewes" and "use" provides the play's closest approach to a notion of use-value. But it is significant that this "commodity" is a living one, and that its very consumption is predicated upon slaughter. The play's privileged image of "use" is thus already imbued with suffering, which Shylock transfers to a human subject (at first only metaphorically) when he compares Antonio's flesh with that of sheep or goats. A play which quite self-consciously employs the motif of the scapegoat surely understands that the relations between humans and domestic animals are already proto-social. Antonio is no proletarian, of course, but Shylock manages to draw another, fairly direct parallel between Jacob's sheep and the laboring body. As I argued earlier, it is thematically important (even though, from a dramaturgical perspective, readily understandable) that Jacob's sheep never appear physically on stage but are narrated by Shylock as part of a self-apologizing speech. But Shylock is also the sole means of access to yet another unrepresented but highly relevant "herd." In a later speech of self-defense, given when challenged in the courtroom by the Duke to release Antonio from his bond, Shylock replies:

> You have among you many a purchas'd slave,
> Which like your asses, and your dogs and mules,
> You use in abject and in slavish parts,
> Because you bought them. Shall I say to you,
> "Let them be free! Marry them to your heirs!
> Why sweat they under burthens? Let their beds
> Be made as soft as yours, and let their palates
> Be season'd with such viands"? You will answer,
> "The slaves are ours." So do I answer you:
> The pound of flesh which I demand of him
> Is dearly bought as mine, and I will have it. (4.1.90–100)

This speech is a nodal point in which several of the play's strands converge. In comparing the Duke's treatment of his slaves to his treatment of asses, dogs, and mules, Shylock recalls the domesticated animals of the Jacob and Laban story. These narrated but otherwise invisible slaves stand in for the sheep of the earlier speech; and the violence implicitly required for the "use" of the ewes echoes in the Duke's covertly violent "use" of his slaves. Moreover, in comparing his bond with Antonio to the Duke's purchase of those laboring bodies, Shylock anticipates the very sense in which Marx will later quote his words. As in *Capital*, then, it is the suffering, laboring body which serves as the occluded Real of *The Merchant of Venice*, and as in *Capital* this fact is first anticipated through the occlusion of *use* (ewes). Significantly, Shylock's cunning intelligence offers our only glimpse of these otherwise hidden realms. In a sense, then, Shylock stands in neither for Marx's capitalist nor for his worker but, in a weird way, for Marx himself. It is Shylock, after all, who insistently "cuts through" the fetishism of Venetian society to uncover its covert suffering and exploitation, and who is reviled for his efforts by the ruling groups. Precisely because he is forced to live the part of the money-fetish, Shylock the Jew penetrates its secrets most incisively. Perhaps this is part of his inheritance to a later, fellow Jew who will accomplish the same task in a different discursive mode.

It is interesting to note, if only as a coda, that the relation between the Jew and money-fetishism played a role within economic theory, or at least within the sociology of economics, during the modernist period. By associating the birth of a capitalist economy with the inner-worldly asceticism of English Puritans, Max Weber's *The Puritan Ethic and the Rise of Capitalism* (1905) countered widely held beliefs that "Jewish rationalism" was at the core of capitalist business practices.[85]

Werner Sombart's *The Jews and Modern Capitalism* (1911), written in direct response to Weber's book, attempted to shift both the credit and the blame for capitalism back onto the Jews. Weber answered Sombart in turn with his theory of the Jews and "pariah capitalism" in *Economy and Society* (1922). The Weber-Sombart debate is notable both for the ways in which it adapts certain aspects of the Marxist tradition and for the light it throws on the position of the Jews in the early twentieth century.

Although Weber differs from Marx in seeking a cultural and ethical explanation for the rise of capitalism rather than a material one, he retains certain of Marx's assumptions. One is that any historical treatment of the problem must focus on England as the birthplace of a specifically industrial (as opposed to mercantile) capitalism. A second, related assumption is that capitalism must be grasped mainly through the category of production and not through trade or commerce. Simply by choosing the English test case, Weber automatically dissociates modern capitalism from the Jews, since the latter had no economically appreciable presence in seventeenth-century England. And Weber's thesis of a protestant work ethic shifts attention to productive labor, rather than traditional forms of Jewish economic activity such as commerce and moneylending, as the engine of modern capitalism.

In attempting to refocus attention on the Jews, Sombart's book necessarily moves back from the sphere of production to that of circulation. For Sombart, capitalism arises not from productive work but from a spirit of rationalism, abstraction, and calculation which he associates both with the Jews and with money. Sombart does not specifically attempt to refute Weber's thesis—in fact he praises *The Puritan Ethic* for providing an indispensable basis for his own study—but he insists that the characteristics which Weber associates with Puritanism were really Jewish in origin, and that they infiltrated English Protestantism by way of its devotion to Old Testament ideals. "It might well be suggested," writes Sombart, "that that which is called Puritanism is in reality Judaism."[86] Sombart's depiction of Puritanism as a mere epiphenomenon, a superficial expression of a Jewish essence, evokes the paranoid structures of anti-Semitic conspiracy theorists and suggests that the form as well as the content of his argument is an expression of the money-fetish.[87]

85. Abraham, *Max Weber*, p. 205.
86. Sombart, *Jews*, p. 192.
87. Sombart's thesis also neatly inverts an oft-repeated reading of Shakespeare's Shylock,

Sombart's book clearly represents a theoretical regression from Marx's and Weber's position that modern capitalism results from a bourgeois organization of labor. But this regression is not random; certain historical developments encourage it. One of the primary characteristics of what Marxists regarded as a new, "imperialist" phase of capitalism in the early twentieth century was the rise of so-called finance capital. According to the economist Rudolf Hilferding, Marx's division of capital into industrial, financial, and commercial fractions was valid for the industrial phase of capitalism. But when banks and joint-stock companies encouraged the formation of monopolistic cartels, industrial and financial capital were fusing into the historically unprecedented form that Hilferding identified as finance capital.[88] This fusion only reinforces the seeming dominance of financial over industrial capital, or of circulation over production, and thereby encourages the diabolical connection between anti-Semitism and the money-fetish. Sombart employs the theory of finance capital to predictable ends: "The commercialization of industry was the gap in the hedge through which the Jews could penetrate into the field of the production and transportation of commodities, as they had done earlier in commerce and finance."[89] (Weber, by contrast, emphasized the continuing absence of Jewish factory owners.)[90] Others were content to maintain that the Jews controlled production indirectly, through the banks. One of these was Ezra Pound, whose 1944 pamphlet *Gold and Work* quotes Antonio's line, "Or is your gold and silver ewes and rams?"[91] In the modernist period, Shylock continued to provide fodder for those

of whom it is frequently suggested "that that which is called Judaism is in reality Puritanism"—i.e., that everything from Shylock's economic practices to his supposedly laconic way of speaking derives not from Italian Jewry, an exotic tribe of whom Shakespeare would have known little, but from the behavior of English Puritans whom he observed every day. Without delving into the merits of this argument we may note, first, that it makes of Shylock precisely a *Calvinische Judenspiegel*, and second, that once again modernist anti-Semitism complicates strategies for rehabilitating the play (it does no good to claim that Shylock is "really" a Puritan if Puritans are, in their turn, "really" Jews). Similar charges of "Judaizing" were, of course, leveled at protestant sects in England during the early modern period as well. See Shapiro, *Shakespeare and the Jews*, pp. 22–23.

88. Hilferding's book *Finance Capital* was published in Germany in 1910. For a useful discussion and critique of Hilferding's theories, see Anthony Brewer, *Marxist Theories of Imperialism: A Critical Survey* (Boston: Routledge & Kegan Paul, 1980), pp. 79–100.

89. Sombart, *Jews*, p. 110.

90. Abraham, *Max Weber*, p. 231. Weber's theory that Jews remained entrenched in a speculative "pariah capitalism" had its own anti-Semitic elements, however. Weber felt that Jewish economic organization lacked creativity and reflected the Jews' stubborn determination to remain social outsiders. See Abraham, pp. 22, 231.

91. Ezra Pound, *Selected Prose, 1909–1965*, ed. William Cookson (New York: New Directions, 1973), p. 347. I was alerted to this citation by Gross, *Shylock*, p. 231.

for whom, as Adorno and Horkheimer put it, "the responsibility of the circulation center for exploitation is a socially necessary pretense."[92] One example is Harold Sherwood Spencer's *Democracy or Shylocracy: A brief for men and women who labour to make the world safe for Democracy, only to find themselves enslaved by Capitalism and their earnings controlled by the Monopolists* (London, 1918).[93] Because its imperialist phase concentrates ever more attention onto the sphere of circulation, the capitalist economy reinforces the Jew's status as a substitute object of scrutiny and suspicion. Shylock's daughter Jessica may be, as she says, "ashamed of my exchange," but Shylock is shamed by exchange as such and by its fetishizing logic, which singles him out for abuse.

Which Is the Critic and Which the Jew?

It might well be objected that my analysis of *The Merchant of Venice* bypasses its aesthetic dimension, and that my theoretical apparatus hangs heavy chains about Shakespeare's comedy. Do I not treat as a demystifying tract what is, after all, a *play*? Does not all this mucking about in the economic obscure the poetic beauty of speeches such as the one by Lorenzo at the opening of act 5?

> How sweet the moonlight sleeps upon this bank!
> Here will we sit, and let the sounds of music
> Creep in our ears. Soft stillness and the night
> Become the touches of sweet harmony.

92. Horkheimer and Adorno, *Dialectic of Enlightenment*, p. 174.
93. See also Harold Begbie and F. Carruthers Gould, *Great Men* (London: Grant Richards, 1901), which includes in its gallery of caricatures a representation of Sir Michael Hicks-Beach, the (non-Jewish) Chancellor of the Exchequer, as Shylock. Accompanying the illustration is a poem titled "Greed and Labour" (p. 34). Here are some representative lines:

> When we are all tucked in bed,
> Weary of our strife for bread,
> Shylock though his chamber paces,
> (Making hideous grimaces)
> Thinking, scheming, in his turnings,
> How to rob us of our earnings, . . .
> Ay! the crafty Jew once stole
> Lumps of sugar! knobs of coal!
> Such a man deserves to be
> Cast into the deepest sea.

> Sit, Jessica. Look how the floor of heaven
> Is thick inlaid with patens of bright gold.
> There's not the smallest orb which thou behold'st
> But in his motion like an angel sings,
> Still quiring to the young-ey'd cherubins;
> Such harmony is in immortal souls,
> But whilst this muddy vesture of decay
> Doth grossly close it in, we cannot hear it. (5.1.54–65)

While our "muddy vesture" renders us deaf to heaven's music, a demystifying intention may force the critic to *resist* the anodyne harmonies of Shakespeare's play, as if they were a siren's song threatening to lull us into moral complacency. René Girard is explicit on this point: "The elegance of the decor and the harmony of the music must not lead us to think that everything is right with the Venetian world."[94] As Girard correctly grasps, *Merchant* sustains an extended analogy between musical and social harmony; hence the play's aesthetic dimension works on behalf of its beautiful gentile characters and of Venice's superficially harmonious social order. Girard's ironic resistance to the aesthetic typifies the artistic and critical practices of modernism. Yet it is also written into Shakespeare's play itself, in the theme of the three caskets. Bassanio, pondering his choice of gold, silver, and lead caskets, delivers a veritable sermon against the dangerous allure of beautiful surfaces (3.2.73–107). His speech, ranged against Lorenzo's in act 5, embodies the play's unusually prominent and difficult opposition between analytical and aesthetic modes.

Critics of *Merchant* have tended to divide themselves between those who, like Girard, react primarily to the hypocrisies and contradictions of Venetian society and those who, like C. L. Barber and Lawrence Danson, respond instead to the play's harmonies. Danson's book, entitled *The Harmonies of "The Merchant of Venice"*, explicitly adopts the concept of harmony as an antidote to what the author regards as excessively or polemically ironic readings of the play. (A third grouping, represented by Marxist critics such as Walter Cohen and Michael Ferber, acknowledges both the ideological and the utopian elements in the play's representation of a socially unified Venice.)[95] "Harmonious" or aestheticizing commentators defend the play's gentile characters while their ironizing

---

94. Girard, *Theater of Envy*, pp. 245–46.

95. Walter Cohen, *Drama of a Nation: Public Theater in Renaissance England and Spain* (Ithaca: Cornell University Press, 1985), p. 206; Michael Ferber, "The Ideology of *The Merchant of Venice*," *English Literary Renaissance* 20, no. 3 (Autumn 1990): 458–63.

counterparts want to expose or demystify them. Criticism of *The Merchant of Venice* thus reproduces conflicts within the play, and often on the same terms.

Shakespeare's play and its commentators throw into especially stark relief a problem which haunts contemporary criticism more generally: the seemingly irreconcilable tension between literary experience and literary theory. As Paul de Man puts it: "There is something bleakly abstract and ugly about literary theory that cannot be entirely blamed on the perversity of its practitioners. Most of us feel internally divided between the compulsion to theorize about literature and a much more attractive, spontaneous encounter with literary works."[96] To his credit, de Man does not attempt to evade the severity of this choice, even though he is not averse to harvesting the pathos of his sacrifice in the service of a subtly self-heroizing rhetoric. The dilemma he addresses here is not only exemplified in criticism on *The Merchant of Venice* but thematized in the play itself.

If Lorenzo serves as the play's emblem for an aestheticizing criticism, then Shylock is the play's representative of the ironizing critic. Shylock's often devastating ability to expose the hypocrisies of his gentile tormentors is clearly linked to his lack of aesthetic responsiveness. Expressing disgust for "the vile squealing of the wry-neck'd fife" (2.5.30), Shylock is notoriously hostile to music; and it is his resistance to the allure of harmony, as well as his own mistreatment at the hands of the Christians, which enables Shylock to see through the mystifications of Venetian society. Yet he also pays a price for his anaesthetic incisiveness; for as Lorenzo observes, in language which clearly if indirectly points to Shylock:

> The man that hath no music in himself,
> Nor is not moved with concord of sweet sounds,
> Is fit for treasons, stratagems, and spoils;
> The motions of his spirit are dull as night,
> And his affections dark as Erebus. (5.1.83–87)

Shylock does not really resist harmony; he is, rather, deaf to it, having no music in himself. In this sense he is not so much an ironizing critic as he is the aesthete's disparaging vision of that critic as someone who, instead of interrogating the allure of beauty, simply cannot respond to it at all.

---

96. Paul de Man, "Sign and Symbol in Hegel's *Aesthetics,*" *Critical Inquiry* 8 (Summer 1982), 761.

In place of musical sensibilities Shylock possesses a devotion to the written word. Danson describes him as a "diabolical literalist" who obeys "a law of death, the killing law of the letter."[97] Shylock's literal-mindedness is clearly of a piece with his indifference to beauty; he prefers the abstractions of the text to the harmonies of music. In choosing the letter over the spirit, Shylock both defines himself as a Jew and becomes the anachronistic signifier for a kind of reading which I have hitherto called "ironic" but now wish to identify more broadly as "theory." Literalist, ironist, and materialist, Shylock both preempts and allegorizes any theoretical reading of *Merchant*, including my own. His stature as master theoretician is, moreover, of a piece with his status as Jew—if not inherently, then at least as the Jews are constructed by a discourse which comes to imagine them in a complex relation to the concept of "theory."

In *Merchant*, gentile discrimination against Shylock spends some time floundering about before it discovers its appropriate medium. In act three, scene one, Salerio errs in attempting to distinguish Shylock from his daughter Jessica on bodily grounds: "There is more difference between thy flesh and hers than between jet and ivory, more between your bloods than there is between red wine and Rhenish" (3.1.39–42). Salerio's language of racial difference implicitly invokes the play's one black character: the Duke of Morocco, who hopes to win Portia by comparing the redness of his blood with that of her other suitors. Salerio thereby awakens the ever-present suspicion that the Jews are not a religion but a race. Shylock immediately counters with his "Hath not a Jew eyes?" speech, in which he insists—definitively and effectively—that the body is a source of continuity, not of difference, between gentile and Jew. After this, Salerio's insinuations of racial difference are never repeated. But the logic of difference, exiled from the flesh, proceeds to root itself in even more fertile ground: the realm of spirit. As he releases Shylock from the death penalty in act four, the Duke of Venice announces: "That thou shalt see *the difference of our spirit*, / I pardon thee thy life before thou ask it" (4.1.368–69, my emphasis).[98] The Duke's sentiments here hark back to Romans 2:28–29: "For he is not a Iewe, which is one outwarde: nether is that circumcision, which is outwarde in the flesh: / But he is a Iewe which is one within, & circumcision is of the heart, in the spirit, not in the letter."[99] The circumcising line of difference, which isolates Shylock

97. Danson, *Harmonies,* pp. 90, 81.

98. Compare Jessica earlier: "But though I am a daughter to his blood, / I am not to his manners" (2.3.18–19).

99. Quoted in Danson, *Harmonies,* p. 32. This biblical theme is adapted by the Jewish anthropologist Maurice Fishberg in his monumental study *The Jews: A Study of Race and*

in *Merchant,* inscribes itself in the spirit, not in the flesh. The realm of spirit is not, however, a purely ethical or theological one; already it begins to take on aesthetic qualities. Lorenzo observes of the man "who hath no music in him" that "the motions of his *spirit* are dull as night." Shylock suffers from a deficiency of spirit which alienates him both from Christian grace and from the joys of beauty.[100]

An imputation of spiritual and aesthetic difference would powerfully shape the image of the Jew in modern times as well. The tone for much of nineteenth-century cultural discourse on the Jews was set by Hegel, as Lionel Gossman has recently shown.[101] Hegel argued that the sublimity of the Jewish religion depended on God's separateness from and nega-tion of the created world. Unlike the Greeks, for whom divinity was ex-pressed in the beauty of artistic images, the Jews adopted a more abstract, spiritual form of worship. As Hegel's thought developed, it came to re-spect Jewish sublimity as both a religious and an artistic principle.[102] The

---

Environment (1911), where, as with Shylock, it serves to fend off racial distinctions: "It is not the body which marks the Jew; it is his soul. In other words, the type is not anthropo-logical or physical; it is social or psychic. It is not the complexion, the nose, the lips, the head which is characteristic; it is his soul which betrays his faith. Centuries of confinement in the Ghetto, social ostracism, ceaseless suffering under the ban of abuse and persecution have been instrumental in producing a characteristic psychic type which manifests itself in his cast of countenance which is considered as peculiarly 'Jewish' " (p. 165).

In *Ulysses,* Joyce plays with the notion of a bodily and hence racial Judaism when the gynecologist who examines Bloom in the "Circe" chapter announces that "the *fetor judaicus* is most perceptible" (*Ulysses,* p. 493). As Joyce knew well from his reading of Fishberg, the myth of the *fetor judaicus* ("Jewish stink"), which dates back to Fortunatus, is "chiefly due to either a blunder or a malicious trick of the copyist of the Middle Ages, of the passage from Ammianus Marcellinus (xxi, 5) of Marcus Aurelius, who substituted '*Judaeorum feten-tium*' for '*Judaeorum petentium*'—i.e., ill-smelling, for turbulent" (Fishberg, p. 314). Like Moses's "horns," the *fetor judaicus* results from textual misprision—a fact that would appeal to Joyce for obvious reasons. The Jews are truly a "people of the book" when even their ascribed bodily characteristics are the result of textual effects.

100. The depiction of Shylock as unmusical is ironic, since among the relatively few Jews living in Tudor England was a group of musicians invited by Henry VIII to improve the level of performance at court. "They and their families stayed on, and the most successful of them established important dynasties of performers and instrument makers" (Gross, *Shylock,* p. 34). In the nineteenth century, Richard Wagner helped sustain the image of the unmusical Jew with his viciously anti-Semitic screed "Das Judentum in der Musik" (1850; trans. as "Judaism in Music" in *Richard Wagner: Stories and Essays* [London: Peter Owen, 1973], pp. 23–39).

101. Lionel Gossman, "Philhellenism and Anti-Semitism: Matthew Arnold and His German Models," *Comparative Literature* 46, no. 1 (Winter 1994): 1–39.

102. In the 1827 edition of *Lectures on the Philosophy of Religion,* Hegel even ranks Jewish worship above the Greek as approaching more nearly the conception of Spirit. The *Aesthetics* is also quite respectful in its treatment of Jewish sublimity. It should be said here that Gossman's essay, while generally informative, is quite tendentious in its treatment of Hegel,

young Hegel, however, tended to depict this difference as a sign of the Jews' aesthetic and spiritual poverty: "An image of God was just stone or wood to them; . . . they despise the image because it does not manage them, and they have no inkling of its deification in the enjoyment of beauty or in a lover's intuition."[103] The Jews' alienation from both natural and created beauty is, according to the young Hegel, compounded by their alienation from social ties: "The first act which made Abraham the progenitor of a nation is a disseverance which snaps the bonds of communal life and love. The entirety of the relationships in which he had hitherto lived with men and nature, these beautiful relationships of his youth (Joshua 24:2), he spurned."[104] Deprived of feelings of beauty and human brotherhood, *Geist* or Spirit dwindles into mere abstract intellect: "The alienation which is the condition of theoretical erudition does not require . . . moral pain, or the sufferings of the heart, but only the easier pain and strain of the imagination which is occupied with something not given in immediate experience, something foreign, something pertaining to recollection, to memory and the thinking mind."[105]

Although Hegel's depiction of the Jews improved over time, this portrait of the abstract, soulless, intellectualizing mind caught on among German anti-Semites who resented the disproportionate presence of Jews in higher education. Werner Sombart asked rhetorically: "Are we not continually struck by the Jew's love for the inconcrete, his tendency away from the sensuous, his constant abiding in a world of abstractions? And is it only accidental that there are far fewer Jewish painters than literary men or professors? . . . It comes to this, that they behold the world not with their 'soul' but with their intellect."[106] In this caricature of the Jew we first hear the kinds of complaint that will later be directed against literary theory and its practitioners. Whether or not theory is, in part, a "Jewish" invention, anti-Semitic discourse conceives of it that way. The

largely because it represents Hegel's early views almost exclusively and ignores the subsequent development of his thought.

103. "The Spirit of Christianity," in Hegel, *On Christianity: Early Theological Writings*, trans. T. M. Knox (New York: Harper & Row, 1961), p. 192, cited in Gossman, "Philhellenism," p. 7.

104. Hegel, "Spirit of Christianity, " p. 185, quoted in Gossman, "Panhellenism," pp. 6–7.

105. "On Classical Studies," in Hegel, *On Christianity*, pp. 327–28, quoted in Gossman, "Panhellenism," p. 6. It should be noted that this passage is not addressed explicitly to the Jews; but it conforms unmistakably to the spiritual portrait that Hegel paints of them in his early works.

106. Sombart, *Jews*, pp. 262, 264.

resistance to theory first takes the historical form of a resistance to the Jews.

In recent times, Jean-Joseph Goux has treated Jewish culture more favorably as a formative influence on the birth of theory.[107] In his book *The Iconoclasts*, Goux maintains that the Mosaic proscription against images (and, in a larger sense, against the aesthetic) becomes an enabling condition for the theoretical revolutions inaugurated by Marx and Freud. Both thinkers, Goux argues, resist the imaginary lure of the image (be it the manifest content of the dream and the artwork or the false glow of the fetishized commodity) in order to discover the symbolic Law that subtends it. While analyzing Freud's interpretation of Michelangelo's *Moses*, Goux observes—in terms nicely suited to an appreciation of Shylock—that "the Judaic theoretician's quintessential gesture is the denunciation of illusion—even more, for example, than it is the ethical temptation to formulate new values. . . . The image is a disguise, a trap. Likewise, Freud confronts the work of art—whether painting or sculpture—only to dissolve and reduce its iconic dimension though analytic verbalization."[108] Freud, like Shylock, prefers the letter of the law to the beauty of the image, and like Shylock too he is an iconoclast who comes to destroy cherished social illusions.

Goux's remarks on Marx are also pertinent to *The Merchant of Venice*. As a critique of money which is also a critique of Jews, *On The Jewish Question* undeniably contains anti-Semitic elements. Yet it is, Goux observes, "nevertheless a perfectly Judaic gesture" in that it embodies "Moses' iconoclastic furor" against worshipping the work of one's hands.[109] Money is, in effect, the golden calf that bourgeois society has adopted as its fetish. Marx's resistance to the ideological-aesthetic illusions of the money-form finds a literary correlate in *Merchant*'s anti-aesthetic discourse, which urges renunciation of golden caskets (and golden characters) rather than golden calves, and does so in ways which are clearly associated with Shylock's role as moral iconoclast.

Goux's approach does not negate but simply revalues the identification of Jews and theory already present in the post-Hegelian tradition—yet another instance of the labile opposition between anti-Semitic and philo-Semitic discourse. An adherence to the textual abstract is now conceived

107. For a different way of arguing the same relation, see Susan A. Handelman, *The Slayers of Moses: The Emergence of Rabbinic Interpretation in Modern Literary Theory* (Albany: State University of New York Press, 1982).

108. Goux, *Symbolic Economies*, p. 140. This volume contains translations of several chapters of *Les Iconoclastes*.

109. Goux, *Symbolic Economies*, pp. 159–60.

not as a pathology of *Geist* but as a means of penetrating the lures of the imaginary (a position which, it should be pointed out, is also implicit in Hegel's more mature writings on the Jews). Shakespeare's *Merchant* perfectly anticipates neither Goux's nor Sombart's depiction of the Jew. Rather, the play's ambivalence toward Shylock finds a later historical echo in these contrasting assessments of Jewish intellect.

Yet in this context it is important to specify exactly which *Merchant of Venice* is being adduced as evidence, for the conflict between ironizing and idealizing, or between theoretical and aesthetic, approaches to Shakespeare's play also involves some disagreement about the very object of analysis. In short, when we speak of *Merchant*, do we mean a written text or the play as embodied on the stage? This ambiguity has become endemic to Shakespeare studies, institutionalized in journals such as *Shakespeare Quarterly* which lead double lives as organs of literary and dramatic criticism. Normally one prefers to view these two approaches as mutually complementary, but here their potential conflicts come to the fore. Thomas Moisan has recently argued that "the *Merchant* as a piece of *theater* distances itself from the subversive resources it yields as a *text*. . . . Indeed, nothing better attests to the will and power of dramatic art to divert attention from the ideological contradictions it reflects to its own playful alterity than the sense that has permeated a good deal of criticism on the *Merchant* that 'somehow,' through some combination of conventions comic, festive, and carnivalesque, the play manages to transcend the issues its text problematizes to render a dramatically, theatrically, satisfying experience."[110] Part of the theatrical satisfaction offered by *Merchant* is sensual: the playgoer can take pleasure in listening to the melody of Portia's song as Bassanio ponders the caskets and in viewing the richly beautiful costumes worn by Venice's leading citizens. In the theater, beauty takes not only poetic but also sensible form. Hence, the resistance to decor and harmony enjoined by Girard becomes even more difficult to sustain. The theatrical imaginary, which anti-theatrical writers of the early modern period depict as a subversive force, here works in the service of orthodoxy, cementing solidarity with the gentile characters and overpowering Shylock's dissonant tones with the (now actual) harmonies of *The Merchant of Venice*.

The play's double status opposes the aesthetic (and implicitly gentile) playgoer to the anaesthetic (and implicitly Jewish) reader, thus splitting

110. Thomas Moisan, "Which is the merchant here? And which the Jew? Subversion and Recuperation in *The Merchant of Venice*," in *Shakespeare Reproduced: The Text in History and Ideology*, ed. Jean E. Howard and Marion F. O'Conner (New York: Methuen, 1987), pp. 200–202.

readers into two camps as well. One camp attends to the harmonious "spirit" of the play by dwelling on its pleasures and assimilating the text to performance. For this camp, Shylock's demystifications are an irritating noise. The other insists on the letter of the text as against its spirit. By resisting harmonious surfaces and exercising a virtually talmudic discipline of reading, it uncovers the skull hidden within the golden casket. While this camp may not side with Shylock, it discovers that it is nevertheless *like* Shylock. Literary critics are, like the Jews, a people of the book who understand that the spirit inheres only within the letter.

The Jews, then, are associated not only with the text as opposed to the image but also with a distinctive *style* of reading, construed as literalizing or legalistic. In post-Hegelian discourse this difference is reworked as the opposition between allegory and symbol. Gossman argues that for Hegel, "Judaism represents the dead world of allegory in contrast to the living world of symbol."[111] As given, this statement is seriously misleading; but it contains an element of truth. Hegel associates the Jews not with allegory but with the sublime; yet in the *Aesthetics*, allegory is treated as a debased cousin of the sublime, with which it shares a disjunction between signifying image and signified content. Hegel in no way depicts allegory as "Jewish" (his only examples are taken from classical and Christian literature) but allegory and the sublime both negate that organic unity of form and content, image and spirit, which is represented by symbol. In the 1827 *Lectures on the Philosophy of Religion*, Hegel writes: "In the religion of beauty we have a reconciliation of the meaning with the material, with the sensible mode, with being for another; the spiritual reveals itself wholly in this outward manner. The outward mode is a sign of the inner, and this inner is completely recognized in the shape of its externality. Sublimity, by contrast, simultaneously annihilates the matter of the material in which the sublime appears."[112] In the *Aesthetics*, allegory is described as a degeneration of the sublime in which the content is finite rather than infinite, and in which signified concepts are represented by personified figures whose connection is secured by conscious design rather than by a more organic or substantive unity.[113] But if Hegel does not directly connect Judaism and allegory, he does suggest a mediated alliance in their shared opposition to the realm of symbol. The traits of

111. Gossman, "Philhellenism," pp. 8–9.

112. Georg Wilhelm Friedrich Hegel, *Lectures on the Philosophy of Religion*, vol. 2, *Determinate Religion*, trans. R. F. Brown et al. (Berkeley: University of California Press, 1987), p. 678.

113. G. W. F. Hegel, *Aesthetics: Lectures on Fine Art* (1835), trans. T. M. Knox (Oxford: Clarendon, 1975) pp. 398–402.

abstraction and lack of aesthetic sensitivity that anti-Semitic discourse attributed to Jewish intellect would certainly reinforce this association. In the modern period, then, not only is *The Merchant of Venice* appropriated for anti-Semitic (and anti-anti-Semitic) allegory, but allegory itself is drawn into the field of anti-Semitic discourse.

The bond between allegory and Judaism in post-Hegelian thought is suggestive for the development of literary theory in general and rich in ironic implications for the critical career of Paul de Man in particular.[114] Here, however, I want to concentrate on its relevance to *The Merchant of Venice*. It is, of course, Christian readers who have tended to interpret *Merchant* allegorically. But as Lawrence Danson notes, "the first report of the play's specifically Christian allegorical element" appears to have been delivered "in 1916 to the Jewish Historical Society (as with a nice irony it so happens) by Sir Israel Gollancz."[115] Irony adheres to the Christian content of Gollancz's lecture but not necessarily to its allegorical form, which may even find a model in Shylock. Commenting on Shylock's characteristic mode of expression, Brandes writes: "Oriental, rather than specifically Jewish, are the images in which he gives his passion utterance, approaching, as they so often do, to the parable form. . . . Specifically Jewish, on the other hand, is the way in which this ardent passion throughout employs its images and parables in the service of a curiously sober rationalism, so that a sharp and biting logic, which retorts every accusation with interest, is always the controlling force."[116] With the word "curiously" Brandes suggests a disproportion or disjunction between passion and intellect; even when in the grip of emotion, he insinuates, Shylock employs his images in the service of a surprisingly rational design. Shylock is, in this regard, an allegorist.

Brandes's view of Shylock, moreover, finds seeming confirmation within the play. Following Shylock's parable of Jacob and Laban, Antonio responds:

> *Ant.* Was this inserted to make interest good?
> Or is your gold and silver ewes and rams?

114. In a late essay, de Man finally addresses the role of the Jewish sublime in Hegel's *Aesthetics* ("Hegel on the Sublime," in *Displacements: Derrida and After*, ed. Mark Krupnick [Bloomington: Indiana University Press, 1983], pp. 139–53). But de Man never fully confronts his own dependence on Jewish practices of reading, derived in large part from Walter Benjamin.

115. Danson, *Harmonies*, p. 14. For more on Gollancz, see Shapiro, *Shakespeare and the Jews*, pp. 78–79.

116. Brandes, *Shakespeare*, p. 167.

Shyl. I cannot tell, I make it breed as fast.
But note me, signior.

Ant. Mark you this, Bassanio,
The devil can cite Scripture for his purpose.
An evil soul producing holy witness
Is like a villain with a smiling cheek,
A goodly apple rotten at the heart.
O, what a goodly outside falsehood hath! (1.3.94–102)

Presenting a scission between surface and interior, form and content, Shylock embodies the disjunctions of allegory which also color his parable. When Antonio asks "Or is your gold and silver ewes and rams?", he highlights the seemingly arbitrary connection between the figures of Shylock's story and their signified content. In Christian symbolism, the image of the lamb appears to embody the Savior's sacrificial meekness; in Shylock's allegory (to Antonio's ears, anyway), these living creatures contrast with the barrenness of metal, despite Shylock's witty retort. Shylock has forged a catachresis or abusive metaphor which twists the parable away from its inherent "spirit," and into a foreign meaning. *Merchant*, however, tends to ironize rather than endorse Antonio's proto-Hegelian critique: first because Antonio himself is a "goodly apple rotten at the heart" and second because the casket game teaches the necessity of disjunctive reading. The golden surface of the first casket acts not as symbolic embodiment but as allegorical negation of its hidden content. The caskets thus invert yet sustain Shylock's Jewish mode of reading. In the parable of Jacob and Laban, "gold and silver" serve as unnatural signifieds while in the casket game they become misleading signifiers; both cases, however, sustain an allegorical rather than a symbolic structure, and they mark *Merchant* itself as a deceptive, "Jewish" text.

The repeated links between allegory and gold in *The Merchant of Venice* produce yet further ironies that undercut Antonio's position. When he asks "Or is your gold and silver ewes and rams?" Antonio suggests that the two classes of things are incommensurable or incomparable, and that Shylock's parable violates this difference. But as a merchant, Antonio constantly exchanges commodities for money, and so equates the two. He is thus a practical allegorist—and Shylock merely a theoretical one. In lending money for money, Shylock observes the decorum of exchanging like for like, while Antonio makes his fortune through the very abolition of differences he criticizes in Shylock's tale. If *The Merchant of Venice* associates allegory with the figure of the Jew, then, it also associates it with merchandizing or commodity exchange. Allegory occupies both the spritual realm of religious difference and the practical, moneymaking realm.

A similar split can also be found in post-Hegelian thinking. There, as we have seen, allegory and theory both point to a presumed deficiency in *Geist* or spirit which results in the elevation of abstract intellect over contemplation of nature and art. Another strain of this tradition, however, this one represented by Ludwig Feuerbach and the early Marx, depicted the Jews as defiling spirit not by rising "above" it into pure abstraction but by falling "below" it into the realm of egotism and practical need. In *The Essence of Christianity*, Feuerbach claims that "utilism is the essential theory of Judaism" and that Jehovah "is nothing but the personified selfishness of the Jewish people."[117] The Jew "makes Nature the abject vessel of his selfish interest, of his practical egoism," and therefore cannot rise to the disinterested, theoretical and aesthetic contemplation of nature practiced by the Greeks. Feuerbach's contrast between Hebrew and Hellene is cast in language richly suggestive for a reading of *Merchant*: "The Greeks looked at Nature with the theoretic sense; they heard heavenly music in the harmonious course of the stars; they saw Nature rise from the foam of the all-producing ocean as Venus Anadyomene. The Israelites, on the contrary, opened to Nature only the gastric sense; their taste for Nature lay only in the palate; their consciousness of God in eating manna."[118] Shylock is indifferent to nature's beauty but he does express a cannibalistic desire to "feed upon / The prodigal Christian" (2.5.14–15); by contrast, Lorenzo's speech on the music of the spheres embodies Feuerbach's conception of a theoretical attitude toward nature. When in that same speech Lorenzo exhorts "Look how the floor of heaven / Is thick inlaid with patens of bright gold" (5.1.58–59), his disinterested allusion to gold for purely aesthetic ends contrasts with Shylock's more practical and egotistical concern with money.

Money, in fact, provides the link through which Marx's "On the Jewish Question" adapts Feuerbach's views: "What is present in an abstract form in the Jewish religion—contempt for theory, for art, for history, for man as an end in himself—is the *actual* and *conscious* standpoint, the virtue, of the man of money."[119] Marx's essay seeks to find the secret of the

---

117. Ludwig Feuerbach, *The Essence of Christianity*, trans. George Eliot (1854; New York: Harper & Row, 1957), pp. 113–14.

118. Ibid., p. 114.

119. Karl Marx, "On the Jewish Question," in *Early Writings*, trans. Rodney Livingstone and Gregor Benton (New York: Vintage, 1975), p. 236.

Jewish religion in the economy, conceived as a practical sphere of moneymaking; Jewish philistinism, egotism, and practicality are merely the religious expression of bourgeois philistinism, egotism, and practicality.

Marx's own theoretical project in "On the Jewish Question" places him in an ambiguous relation to Feuerbach's construction of Judaism. On the one hand, Marx still shares Feuerbach's belief in the superiority of theory to practice, and therefore echoes the latter's criticism of the Jews: "*Judaism* could not develop further as a *religion*, could not develop further theoretically, because the world-view of practical need is by nature narrow-minded and rapidly exhausted. The religion of practical need could not, by its very nature, find its completion in theory but only in *practice*, precisely because its truth is practice."[120] At the same time, however, by tracing the religious essence of Judaism to moneymaking activity, "On the Jewish Question" itself adopts practice as an explanatory agency. Unlike Feuerbach, Marx is not content to posit the Jewish character as a mysterious given but describes it as the ideological reflux of *praxis*. And this seed, of course, will develop into the very essence of his method, which may be described as a theory of social practice.

"On the Jewish Question" thus finds itself in the grip of a paradox or conundrum. It criticizes the Jews for embodying the spirit of practice and thus failing to ascend to the realm of theory. Yet at the same time it moves the whole notion of theoretical critique in the direction of practice—and hence of the Jews. Jean-Joseph Goux's observation that "On the Jewish Question" is both anti-Semitic and yet a "perfectly Judaic gesture" holds true not only for the question of the fetish but for the question of practice as well;[121] for what Marx now offers as a criticism of the Jewish religion—that "its truth is practice"—he will soon advance as the very essence of his method.

Rather than advertise his theory of practice as a form of "Jewish" thinking, however, Marx will proceed by purging from the concept of practice all formerly Jewish associations. In the first of the "Theses on Feuerbach" he criticizes *The Essence of Christianity* because Feuerbach "regards the theoretical attitude as the only genuinely human attitude, while practice is conceived and fixed only in its dirty-judaical manifestation. Hence he does not grasp the significance of "revolutionary," of "prac-

---

120. Ibid., p. 240.
121. See Goux's extremely suggestive analysis of Feuerbach's and Marx's theoretical projects as attempting to reappropriate the Imaginary and the Symbolic, respectively: *Symbolic Economies*, p. 156.

tical-critical" activity."[122] Here the phrase "dirty-judaical manifestation" (*schmutzig-jüdischen Erscheinungsform*) is an intriguingly overdetermined one. The word *schmutzig* (dirty) is meant to invoke the notion of money as dirt or shit, and hence to reject Feuerbach's restricted conception of practice as capitalist (i.e., Jewish) activity. Yet it also identifies Judaism itself as a kind of *Schmutz* or dirt clinging to the concept of practice, which must be cleansed before being handled. Judaism, moreover, is once again cast as the *Erscheinungsform* of practice, its privileged mode of visibility to the social world. The Jews are like money both because they are associated with money as dirt or shit and because they are the *Erscheinungsform* which Marx's theoretical insight must penetrate or pass through. If the "Theses on Feuerbach" begin, as Louis Althusser claims, Marx's epistemological "break" with Feuerbachian humanism, they also represent a continuing break with any explicit Jewishness even as they found an implicitly "Jewish" theory of practice.[123]

The image of the Jew as practical, materialist, and therefore in some sense sub-theoretical, was transferred from Germany to Victorian England largely by Matthew Arnold's famous chapter on Hebrew and Hellene in *Culture and Anarchy*. "To get rid of one's ignorance, to see things as they are, and by seeing them as they are to see them in their beauty, is the simple and attractive ideal which Hellenism holds out before human nature." Hellenism encourages a disinterested, playful cast of mind that makes both theoretical speculation and aesthetic appreciation possible. The Hellenes are "full of what we would call sweetness and light."[124] Hebraism, by contrast, is defined as "this energy driving at practice, this permanent sense of the obligation of duty, self-control, and work, this earnestness in going manfully with the best light we have."[125] Though a source of moral seriousness, Hebraism tends to be narrow-minded and mechanical; in the end, it contributes to the philistine's "concern with making money and the concern for saving one's soul."[126] It should be no surprise, given the resemblances between Arnold's depiction of the Jews and those of Heine, the young Marx, and Feuerbach, that Arnold explicitly borrows the German concept of *Geist* to lambaste England's philistines—or, as he will call them elsewhere, "the Hebraising Philistines."[127]

122. Karl Marx and Frederick Engels, *The German Ideology*, ed. J. C. Arthur (New York: International Publishers, 1978), p. 121.
123. Louis Althusser, *For Marx*, trans. Ben Brewster (London: Verso, 1979), pp. 41–86.
124. Arnold, *Culture and Anarchy*, p. 167.
125. Ibid., p. 163.
126. Ibid., p. 186.
127. In *Friendship's Garland*, the imaginary Prussian "Arminius" introduces the concept

The two images of Jewish character presented here—as excessively abstract and theoretical or excessively practical and materialist—would seem to be irreconcilable. Yet they coexisted and sometimes mixed freely during the nineteenth and twentieth centuries. Werner Sombart, for instance, identifies "four elements, intellectuality [i.e., abstraction], teleology [i.e., practical means-end rationality], energy, and mobility" as "the corner-stones of Jewish character" which imbue the Jews with the spirit of money.[128] The same contradictory elements converge in *The Merchant of Venice*, where Shylock is both an abstractly allegorical *and* a self-interestedly practical reader of the Bible. Let us return to Antonio as he reacts to Shylock's parable of Jacob and Laban:

> This was a venture, sir, that Jacob serv'd for,
> A thing not in his power to bring to pass,
> But sway'd and fashion'd by the hand of heaven.
> Was this inserted to make interest good?
> Or is your gold and silver ewes and rams? (1.3.91–95)

Antonio counters Shylock's parable with what Michael Ferber aptly calls "the ideology of risk."[129] By calling Jacob's pact with Laban a "venture," Antonio invokes a doctrine that justifies the profits of "merchant adventurers" like himself who risk losing their investments on the high seas. Because his enterprise entails the possibility of loss, Jacob's prosperity must, in Antonio's view, be attributed to the hand of heaven rather than to his own activity. By contrast, usurers such as Shylock who demand security for their principal and hence risk nothing make unjustifiable profits. This economic distinction, moreover, fits nicely with the Protestant doctrine of salvation through divine grace versus the Jewish doctrine of justification through works (fulfillment of the Law). Both associate the Jews with "practical egoism" and Christian merchants with a divinely sanctioned passivity. Antonio then extends this critique to Shylock's use of the biblical story. "Was this inserted to make interest good?"—in other words, are you twisting this story for your own profit? Shylock is, in Antonio's view, too "interested" a reader, one who pillages Scripture for his personal advantage instead of attending disinterestedly to its true

---

of *Geist* to Arnold's English readers. While Arminius often seems to be treated at least half mockingly, the cultural ideals he expounds correspond closely with Arnold's. (See *Culture and Anarchy*, pp. 36–37, 40–42, 44–46, 48–49, 332–33.) The phrase "Hebraising Philistines" occurs in *Culture and Anarchy*, p. 254.

128. Sombart, *Jews*, p. 268.

129. Ferber, "Ideology," pp. 446–47.

meaning. He cannot ascend from the letter to the spirit because he is grounded in a mode of reading excessively devoted to practice—indeed, to "dirty-Judaical" practice.

Shylock's practical habits of reading, as it happens, find a literary descendent in Joyce's Leopold Bloom. In the "Ithaca" chapter, Bloom

> reflected on the pleasures derived from literature of instruction rather than of amusement as he himself had applied to the works of William Shakespeare more than once for the solution of difficult problems in imaginary or real life.

> Had he found their solution?
> In spite of careful and repeated reading of certain classical passages, aided by a glossary, he had derived imperfect conviction from the text, the answers not bearing on all points. (*Ulysses*, p. 677)

Bloom's method of reading, at once philistine and rabbinical, vainly attempts to convert Shakespeare's works into a practical guide to conduct. Bloom, the Jewish mirror of Shakespeare, is thus revealed to be at best only one half of a whole that requires the aesthetic, playful, and disinterested qualities of the Greek sensibility for its completion. His "practical egoism" is critiqued not by a carping Antonio but by the text of Shakespeare's works, which yield up only "imperfect conviction" in response to his enquiries. Yet even this failure is the sign of a certain textual rigor, since Bloom's methodical, practical approach leads him to the correct discovery that literary texts do not, in fact, ever lead to perfect conviction. Although he remains unresponsive to the aesthetic dimension of the text, Bloom displays an interpretive tenacity which fends off the delusive comfort of sought-for answers. Disappointment, one might say, is built into his mode of reading. And in this, at least, it begins to anticipate some of what we have come to know as theory.

So, too, does Shylock's relation to the text—at once literalist and abstract, practical and allegorizing, ironic and partial. What Shakespeare's and Joyce's portrayals of a "Jewish" brand of reading share most deeply, perhaps, is less a set of common characteristics (although these are also striking) than a sense of balanced achievement and sacrifice, in which incisiveness is purchased at the cost of beauty. "Jewish" and "Greek" modes of reading thus emerge as choices—not as free choices but as alternatives defined by a logic of mutual exclusion: Shylock or Lorenzo, irony or beauty. And even if, in Shakespeare and Joyce, we seem to have found writers whose immensity encompasses both modes, what *Ulysses* and *The Merchant of Venice* insist on, each in its own way, is that "jewgreek" or "greekjew" are not syntheses but violent yokings together of opposites, in perpetual contradiction. For those of lesser capacity, like myself, theory is an unchosen choice, productive at once of certain insights and of certain doubts and imperfect convictions. Shylock or Lorenzo. In my own case, I find my interpretive strategies toward *The Merchant of Venice* already present there, wielded by a bearded figure in a gaberdine. Peering into the play, I discover that it has become a mirror, and that a reader much like myself looks out at me. His face is the face of Shylock.

CHAPTER

Hamletmachines

W. S. Gilbert

Pietro, the proprietor of a troupe of mountebanks, arrives at an inn on a picturesque Sicilian pass. He learns, to his delight, of an impending visit by the Duke and Duchess of Pallavicini. The Duke, it appears, is "a mad enthusiast in the matter of automata."[1] As part of his show, Pietro plans to exhibit (and, with any luck, sell to the Duke) "the two world-renowned lifesize clockwork automata, representing Hamlet and Ophelia . . . as they appeared in the bosom of their families before they disgraced their friends by taking to the stage for a livelihood" (p. 371). As it happens, Pietro's automata are *so* realistic that they have been detained by the police at Palermo for lack of passports. Fortunately, an alchemist has been staying at the inn. His experiments have resulted in a series of increasingly violent explosions, the last of which finally blew the poor fellow to smithereens. Among his remains is found a vial of liquid which, if diluted, has the effect of making whoever drinks it become whatever he pretends to be. Pietro needs only convince Bartolo and Nita, his clown and dancing girl, to dress up like the automata and drink this potion. Bartolo (himself a failed Shakespearean actor whose Hamlet was met with laughter) objects: "What! I become a doll—a dandled doll? A mere conglomerate of whizzing wheels, salad of springs and hotch-potch of escapements? Exchange all the beautiful things I've got inside here for a

---

1. W. S. Gilbert, *Original Plays*, 3rd ser. (London: Chatto & Windus, 1924), p. 372. Subsequent page references are given in the text.

handful of common clockwork?'' (p. 374). Pietro, however, prevails, and Bartolo and Nita are duly transformed into waxwork dummies (Figure 5).

While charming and often hilarious, *The Mountebanks* (1892) was not one of W. S. Gilbert's more successful plays. (The songs were composed not by Arthur Sullivan but by Alfred Cellier, who died before the production even opened.)[2] Still, the conceit of a mechanized Hamlet was both brilliantly executed and culturally prescient. Gilbert's play inaugurated an eccentric, disjointed, but nevertheless coherent ''tradition'' of viewing Hamlet (and, less often, Ophelia) as a machine, a tradition which has persisted throughout the modernist period and into postmodern culture. Although always a minority perspective, the mechanical Hamlet presents a suggestive counterpoint to the prevailing view of this character as a uniquely rich if tortured subjectivity. Hamlet has long served as an emblem for the vicissitudes of modern consciousness. What does it mean to imagine him as a robot?

Gilbert's mechanical Hamlet, though farcical, would seem to derive in part from some hints and details in Shakespeare's play. Hamlet signs his letter to Ophelia ''Thine evermore, most dear lady, / whilst this machine is to him, Hamlet'' (2.2.123–24). The letter begins by objectifying Ophelia as well, whom it describes as ''my soul's idol'' (2.2.109). An even more suggestive moment occurs during the performance of ''The Mousetrap,'' when, in the course of one of his bawdy exchanges with Ophelia, Hamlet remarks: ''I could interpret between you and your love, if I could see the puppets dallying'' (3.2.246–47). Hamlet plays a double role in this conceit. He is the interpreter who traditionally explained the action of puppet plays.[3] But since he is also Ophelia's love, he is presumably one of the puppets as well—as, of course, is she. Moreover, since the conceit is prompted by the ongoing performance of ''The Mousetrap,'' which is in turn an interiorized reflection of *Hamlet* as a whole, Hamlet's remark implicates the entire play in the traditions of puppet theater.

In building his Hamletmachine, then, Gilbert relies in part on Hamlet's own self-designation. Oscar Wilde (who may have been an additional inspiration for Gilbert in this respect) seems likewise to have recognized

2. Max Keith Sutton, *W. S. Gilbert*, Twayne's English Author Series 178 (Boston: G. K. Hall, 1975), p. 111. Sutton refuses to blame Cellier for the play's unpopularity, insisting (rightly) that ''some numbers, like the clicking clockwork trio in Act II, rival Sullivan at his most ingenious'' (p. 112).

3. See George Speaight, *The History of the English Puppet Theatre*, 2d ed. (Carbondale: Southern Illinois University Press, 1990), p. 66.

Figure 5. Lyric Theatre, *The Mountebanks.* By permission of the Folger Shakespeare Library.

the puppet in Hamlet.[4] But he also combines *Hamlet*'s play-within-the-play with another: the puppet show in act five of Ben Jonson's *Bartholomew Fair*. (*The Mountebanks* is full of allusions to Jonson's comedies, including *The Alchemist* and *Volpone*). Leatherhead's puppet show may be another of Jonson's jibes at Inigo Jones, but it also reflects on his own comedy of humors. As Martin Butler remarks in his edition of the play, Leatherhead's performance offers a "reductive restatement . . . of the puppet-like automatism that infects most of the inhabitants of Jonson's dramatic world."[5] Gilbert's conflation of Shakespeare and Jonson thus indicates a canny and precise grasp of the role of the automaton in Renaissance drama, welding the Elizabethan melancholic, the Jacobean "humorous" character, and the puppet into one figure.

Like his Renaissance predecessors, Gilbert employs the automaton to comment on aspects of his own dramaturgy. In a perceptive study of the Savoy Operas, Alan Fischler shows that Gilbert revised the plot of comedy so that it emphasized not rebellion but submission to human law: "If traditional comic heroes are aggressive rebels against law while its enforcers are hypocrites and impostors, Gilbert's heroes either are or become passive slaves to external compulsion."[6] While law may be ridiculed in Gilbert's plays as absurd, inflexible, or self-contradictory, nevertheless its results are portrayed as satisfactory and characters are rewarded for the "mechanical applications of legal facts."[7] This thematic endorsement of legal mechanism finds its formal correlative in Gilbert's "syllogistic" plots and especially in the prosody of the songs: "His lyrics for the Savoy librettos are just as rigidly regular in fulfilling the requirements of rhyme scheme and meter as his characters are in obeying the law."[8]

The clockwork Hamlet and Ophelia of *The Mountebanks* thus incorporate and literalize the mechanicity of Gilbert's formal and thematic method. Both elements converge in a trio sung by Pietro, Bartolo, and Nita, the final stanza of which is Pietro's:

4. In Wilde's *The Decay of Lying* (1889), Vivian remarks of Hamlet, "The world has become sad because a puppet was once melancholy." Oscar Wilde, *De Profundis and Other Writings* (New York: Penguin, 1982), p. 75. When Hamlet compares himself to a pipe that can be fingered and played (3.2.358–80) he once again describes himself as a mechanical device. Hydraulic automata were popular in baroque courts of the Continent. See Joseph Roach, *The Player's Passion: Studies in the Science of Acting* (Ann Arbor: University of Michigan Press, 1985), pp. 61–63.

5. *The Selected Plays of Ben Jonson*, ed. Martin Butler (Cambridge: Cambridge University Press, 1989), 2:530–31.

6. Alan Fischler, *Modified Rapture: Comedy in W. S. Gilbert's Savoy Operas* (Charlottesville: University Press of Virginia, 1991), pp. 40–41.

7. Ibid., p. 48.

8. Ibid., p. 49.

> When a lady is disposed to be tyrannical,
> She's equal to unlimited iniquity:
> And flirting may be flirting, though mechanical—
> A fact that has the sanction of antiquity—
>
> Antic-tic, tic-tic, tic-tic, tic-tic—
> Antic-tic, tic-tic, tiquity! (pp. 389–90)

Here the clockwork mechanism thematizes both the formal precision of the song's metrical and rhyme schemes and the cultural law identified as "the sanction of antiquity," which is at once dislocated and fulfilled through exact repetition. Gilbert himself "sanctions" his theater of automata by invoking and repeating the "antique" models offered by Shakespeare and Jonson.

Gilbert's literary satire in *The Mountebanks* is complicated but not blunted by self-reference. While the mechanical Hamlet implicates *The Mountebanks* and Gilbert's whole *oeuvre* in its parody, Shakespeare's play and its cultural reception are still direct targets. In particular, the theme of mechanicity is employed both to mock and to evacuate Hamlet's famously anguished subjectivity, as in the following exchange between the transformed Bartolo and Nita:

Ni. What's wrong now?

Bar. I—c'ck—c'ck—I am not conversant with clockwork; but do you feel, from time to time, a kind of jerkiness that catches you just *here?*

Ni. No; I work as smooth as butter. The continued ticking is tiresome; but it's only for an hour.

Bar. The ticking is simply maddening. C'ck! 'ck! There it is again!

Ni. Something wrong with your works, I'm afraid. Stop a bit—I'll see. (*Opens door in chest, revealing a quantity of clockwork.*) No; all right there. Turn round. (*He does so; she opens door in the back of his head.*) No; the head appears to be empty. (*Opens door in his side.*) I see what it is; a halfpenny has got into your escapement. Stop a bit! (*Takes out halfpenny.*) (p. 388)

Like many critics, Nita/Ophelia is provoked into an analytical or investigative mode by the fact that Hamlet seems to be somehow broken. (For this ticking Hamlet, the time really *is* out of joint.) Hamlet's long-notorious "hesitations" are, in this case, readily explained by a halfpenny which is literally stuck in his escapement. Yet this answer resides in an unexpected corner, since his clockwork heart proves sound and his head is reassuringly vacant. By evacuating Hamlet himself, Gilbert's farce also empties out the long Romantic tradition which viewed Hamlet as an exquisite, fragile interiority. In doing so, it simultaneously anticipates the role of the puppet in modernist aesthetics and theory: Walter Benjamin's discussion of the puppet play and *Trauerspiel,* for instance, or Rilke's wax puppets in the *Duino Elegies.* Of the latter Rainer Nägele observes: "Puppets are 'full,' although it is not the fulness of the bourgeois heart and its metaphysical interiority but the literal interiority of a stuffed body. This interiority is pure exteriority to the core of its being."[9] Despite cultural and temperamental differences, Gilbert deserves to be included among Nägele's line of modernists who exteriorize subjectivity.

The clockwork automaton differs from the waxwork puppet, however, in introducing the additional element of mechanical repetition, which will prove central to the entire line of Hamletmachines. Gilbert's Hamlet both anticipates and displaces the classic Freudian reading by locating Hamlet's "problem" not in the field of Oedipal desire but rather in the compulsion to repeat. The issue of mechanical repetition has been raised by critics in discussion of *The Mountebanks* and of Gilbert's work generally, but in reference to Henri Bergson's essay *Laughter* rather than to psychoanalytic theory.[10] *The Mountebanks* would seem to support Bergson's view that "the attitudes, gestures, and movements of the human body are laughable in exact proportion as that body reminds us of a mere machine."[11] Yet in fact, Gilbert's play refutes Bergson's vitalism in a way that will prove suggestive for my argument.

Bergson portrays laughter as a defensive and corrective reaction to mechanical inelasticity on the part of living beings whose own nature is pliable, flexible, and hence "the complete negation of repetition."[12] He illustrates his theory with copious examples from French comic drama; but he also invokes Hamlet as a wholly unique, "living" creation who is therefore the very antithesis of the comic.[13] One of the oddities of Bergson's essay is that while he adduces innumerable instances of the laugh-

9. Rainer Nägele, *Theater, Theory, Speculation: Walter Benjamin and the Scenes of Modernity* (Baltimore: Johns Hopkins University Press, 1991), p. 28. Nägele's whole first chapter, on *Trauerspiel* and puppet-play, is relevant here. See also Benjamin, *Origins of German Tragic Drama,* pp. 124–25.

10. Fischler, *Modified Rapture,* pp. 47-49; Sutton, *W. S. Gilbert,* pp. 22–24.

11. Henri Bergson, "Laughter," in *Comedy,* ed. Wylie Sypher (New York: Doubleday, 1956), p. 79.

12. Ibid., p. 81.

13. Ibid., p. 165.

able, he has almost nothing to say about the act of laughter itself, except to observe toward the end of his essay that "there is in laughter a movement of *relaxation* which has often been noticed."[14] While it is true that laughter may produce relaxation as its aftermath, laughter itself is something very different—a repeated convulsion of the muscles and diaphragm. Laughter is indeed, as Bergson claims, a reaction to the mechanical, but as its mimetic incorporation rather than its expulsion or chastisement. Laughter is not the reaction of the living to the mechanical, but the *capture* of the living by the mechanical. All laughter is, therefore, "canned" laughter.[15]

The Mountebanks, as well as many other nineteenth-century parodies of *Hamlet*, recognizes what Bergson does not: that there is something potentially comic, because potentially mechanical, in Hamlet. A duet between Bartolo and Nita directly refutes Bergson's theory of laughter even before the fact:

> *Bar.* If our action's stiff and crude,
> Do not laugh because it's rude.
>
> *Ni.* If our gestures promise larks,
> Do not make unkind remarks.
>
> *Bar.* Clockwork figures may be found
> Everywhere and all around.
>
> *Ni.* Ten to one, if we but knew,
> You are clockwork figures too. (p. 387)

Hamlet retains his position as a privileged emblem of the modern subject, only he now redefines that subjectivity so that it is no longer beautiful, creative, or anguished, but mechanical and repetitive.

This dialectic of the "living" and the mechanized pertains not only to Hamlet as a character but also—and even more importantly—to the cultural reception of *Hamlet* itself. Gilbert's clockwork Hamlet is probably inspired by the repetitive, mannered stagings of the play that had come to dominate the Victorian stage. Max Beerbohm expressed a widely felt weariness when he wrote in 1901: "I am too much at home in Elsinore. I seem to have stayed there so often, I have written so many letters on

14. Ibid., p. 186.
15. I thank Julia Reinhard Lupton for this last phrase. On canned laughter, see Žižek, *Sublime Object of Ideology*, p. 35.

its notepaper."[16] Even more suggestive, in this context, is the language in a review of Charles Fechter's *Hamlet* in 1861: "No character has been so thoroughly *stereotyped* on our stage as *Hamlet*, and the performance is, from the outset of the scene, a complete *novelty.*" The word "stereotyping," with its suggestions of industrial process and mechanical repetition, would, of course, have been fresher and more vivid in 1861 than it is today. The reviewer strikes a similar note when he writes, "Every actor who plays with Mr. Fechter learns to place less reliance than heretofore on the pegs and wires by which he has been governed, and speaks more naturally."[17] By the latter decades of the nineteenth century, the traditional methods of presenting Hamlet had come to seem artifical, even puppet-like. A "living" Hamlet could be produced only by injecting doses of novelty into a stage tradition that now struck audiences as stale and repetitive. Russell Jackson describes a "Shakespeare Revolution" in which interpretive freedom was not only allowed to actors and directors but *demanded* of them.[18] This revolution was not limited to *Hamlet*, of course, but the weight of cultural tradition that had attached itself to this play probably made it an especially sensitive instrument for registering shifts in taste.

Gilbert was certainly aware of the problems of difference and repetition that had attached themselves to the part of Hamlet. In the 1891 farce *Rosencrantz and Guildenstern* he mocks the bewildering variety of actors who had recently portrayed the character:

> *Guildenstern*:   And what's he like?
> *Ophelia.* Alike for no two seasons at a time.
> Sometimes he's tall—sometimes he's very short—
> Now with black hair—now with a flaxen wig—
> Sometimes an English accent—then a French—
> Then English with a strong provincial "burr"
> Once an American, and once a Jew—
> But Danish never, take him how you will!
> And strange to say, whate'er his tongue may be,
> Whether he's dark or flaxen—English—French—

16. Max Beerbohm, *More Theatres*, ed. Rupert Hart-Davis (St. Albans, Herts.: Hart-Davis, 1969), pp. 359–60, quoted in Russell Jackson, "Another Part of the Castle: Some Victorian Hamlets," in *Images of Shakespeare: Proceedings of the Third Congress of the International Shakespeare Association, 1986*, ed. Werner Habicht, D. J. Palmer, and Roger Pringle (Newark: Delaware University Press, 1988), p. 111.

17. "*Hamlet* at the Princess's Theatre," *St. James' Magazine*, October 1861, 371–76, quoted in Jackson, "Another Part of the Castle," p. 112.

18. Jackson, "Another Part of the Castle," p. 112.

Though we're in Denmark, A.D., ten—six—two—
He always dresses as King James the First! (pp. 80–81)

A superficial obsession with novelty could not, in Gilbert's opinion, conquer the dreary sameness that had become inextricably tied to the stage Hamlet. (Gilbert regarded Hamlet, in any case, as a deeply ludicrous character in an ill-composed play by a writer whose works should all "be kept off the boards.")[19] The clockwork Hamlet of *The Mountebanks* satirically literalizes the problem of cultural repetition that afflicted Victorian productions of the play. But Gilbert proposes a radically new, if merely farcical, solution to the antagonism between novelty and mechanicity: he produces a "fresh" Hamlet not by making him more lifelike or "human," but by deepening the cultural petrification that has already settled over him. He fends off the deadening force of tradition not by resisting it but by making it the very substance of Hamlet's being. Paradoxically, the machine represents both tradition as repetitive propagation ("Antictic, tic-tic, tiquity") and the ceaseless innovating drives that followed in the wake of industrial modernization. This paradox, moreover, does not just happen to attach itself to Hamlet. Rather, machinery is drawn to Hamlet, and also emanates from him, because he represents in a particularly oppressive form the burden of tradition for modernist culture. This is why so many mechanical Hamlets are born, even though none of their creators seems aware of any predecessors. The "tradition" of the Hamletmachine is thus not really a tradition at all, since it is not a continuous process of allusion and development but rather a series of unconnected events, at once novel and completely repetitive. In line with this, my own chapter will leap from event to event in the history of the Hamletmachine without attempting to establish false continuities.

The conceit of the Hamletmachine is the last and, in a sense, the most daring allegorization of Shakespeare that we will explore in this study. It is the most daring because the industrial technology of the nineteenth and twentieth centuries creates such a strong sense of anachronism when

19. Letter to Mrs. Bram Stoker, 16 September 1904, quoted in Reginald Allen, *W. S. Gilbert: An Anniversary Survey and Exhibition Checklist* (Charlottesville: Bibliographical Society of the University of Virginia, 1963), pp. 76–77, and cited in Fischler, *Modified Rapture*, p. 37.

Rosencrantz and Guildenstern portrays Hamlet as a man afflicted with an uncontrollable mania for soliloquy. The plot of the piece revolves around a lost play by Claudius, recently discovered by Hamlet, which enables Gilbert to comment indirectly on Shakespeare's play: "a thing of shreds and patches welded into a form that hath mass without consistency, like an ill-built villa" and rendered comic by the "absurdity of its tragical catastrophes" (p. 85). Gilbert's criticisms foreshadow some of the views expressed in T. S. Eliot's early essay on the play.

superimposed on Shakespeare's play; it is daring, too, because it so radically revises—even makes vulgar or crude—the Romantic conception of
Hamlet's character. The machine is not only a reductive allegory, however; it also manifests the reductiveness *of* allegory, which always contains
a mechanical element. Writes Hegel:

> An allegorical being, however much it may be given a human shape,
> does not attain the concrete individuality of a Greek god or of a saint
> or of some other actual person, because, in order that there may be
> congruity between subjectivity and the abstract meaning which it has,
> the allegorical being must make subjectivity so hollow that all specific
> individuality vanishes from it. It is therefore rightly said of allegory that
> it is frosty and cold and that, owing to the intellectual abstractness of
> its meanings, it is even in its invention rather an affair of the intellect
> than of concrete intuition and the heartfelt depth of imagination.[20]

The "hollowing out" of allegorical subjectivity recalls that of the puppet,
as described by Nägele, and for a similar reason: the subjection of self to
a radical exteriority (in this case, of abstract meaning). For Hegel, this
exteriority is "catching"; although it manifests itself in the allegorical
persona, it also afflicts the allegorist, whose creative drives are reduced
to the abstraction of intellect. Allegory itself is both product and bearer
of the mechanical, and the Hamletmachine may thus be viewed as,
among other things, an allegory of allegory.

Hegel's remarks on personification allegory are of more than aesthetic
interest, however, for the "hollowing out" of subjectivity which he describes marks not only certain kinds of art but the condition of modernity
as such. T. S. Eliot's poem "The Hollow Men" is perhaps the best-known
lament for this condition in English poetry. *The Mountebanks* says much
the same thing in a more satirical vein, but Gilbert is quite explicit in
naming the "exterior" force that scoops out, and thus renders mechanical or allegorical, the modern subject. Not only is Bartolo turned into a
mechanical Hamlet for purposes of financial gain but (just in case we
didn't get the point) he bears a placard inscribed "Put a penny in the
slot." Money is the abstract force to which our now merely allegorical
personae are subjected. I will quote further from Bartolo's duet with Nita:

> Clockwork figures may be found
> Everywhere and all around.

20. Hegel, *Aesthetics*, p. 399.

Ten to one, if we but knew,
You are clockwork figures too.
And the motto of the lot,
"Put a penny in the slot!"

Usurer, for money lent,
Making out his cent. per cent.—
Widow plump or maiden rare,
Deaf and dumb to suitor's prayer—
Tax collectors, whom in vain
You implore to "call again"—
Cautious voter, whom you find
Slow in making up his mind.
If you'd move them on the spot,
Put a penny in the slot! (p. 387)

As a simple satire on greed, this is somewhat obvious and even uninter-
esting. But the image of the machine at once expresses and negates the
idea of greed as a *desire* for money. Subjects desire; machines merely
perform. The figures satirized in Gilbert's song do not so much want
money as react to its external compulsion. Their greed is not properly
internalized as desire; it is a mere tic or automatic reaction. Likewise, the
mechanical Hamlet's hesitations are caused by a halfpenny that has become jammed in his works—that is to say, a coin that has not been
properly assimilated or internalized but remains a piece of stuck exteriority. Money is figured here not as an object of desire but as a bit of the
unmetabolized Real lodged within the subject.

The compulsion figured by Gilbert as money may be more broadly
reinterpreted as the way in which the capitalist economy imprints itself
on the individual subject. In their book *The Dominant Ideology Thesis*, Nicholas Abercrombie, Stephen Hill, and Bryan S. Turner reject the concept
of a "dominant ideology" as it has been developed in Marxist theory.
Workers under capitalism are not, they argue, ideologically incorporated
or interpellated by the system; they are not burdened with a "false consciousness" that brings about a normative acceptance of exploitation.
Rather, they accept their lot on purely pragmatic grounds, as a result of
what Marx calls the "dull compulsion of economic relations."[21] Nothing
but the quotidian tug of economic reality is needed to set workers in
motion—just put a penny in the slot.

21. Nicholas Abercrombie, Stephen Hill, Bryan S. Turner, *The Dominant Ideology Thesis*
(London: George Allen & Unwin, 1980), p. 166.

Capitalism does not require belief on the part of its workers but just a habitual, automatic acceptance of their lot. In other words, it makes its workers into something *like* machines. Marx has a good deal to say in *Capital* on the subject of industrial machinery and its effects on the worker. Comparing the artisanal production of the early modern period with the industrialized production of the nineteenth century, he writes:

> In handicrafts and manufacture, the worker makes use of a tool; in the factory, the machine makes use of him. There the movements of the instrument of labour proceed from him, here it is the movement of the machine that he must follow. In manufacture the workers are the parts of a living mechanism. In the factory we have a lifeless mechanism which is independent of the workers, who are incorporated into it as living appendages.

Here Marx offers a materialist explanation for the allegorical "hollowing out" of subjectivity described by Hegel. For Marx, however, the machine merely renders concrete the subjection of the worker which accompanies capitalist relations as such. Factory production is the "real" subsumption of labor by capital which completes the formal subsumption effected by private ownership of the means of production.[22] "Hence the character of independence from and estrangement towards the worker, which the capitalist mode of production gives to the conditions of labour and the product of labour, develops into a complete and total antagonism with the advent of machinery."[23] The factory-machine physically instantiates and perpetuates an *economic* relation. If it reduces workers to puppets, it does so as the conduit of economic compulsion. Thus the machine is, besides a force of production, also an "allegorical" signifier of the way in which the capitalist economic mechanism takes hold of its subjects. This hold is exerted in an especially direct, intense, and exploitative fashion on workers but the "dull compulsion of economic reality" throbs through everyone in capitalist society. The machine is thus, for Marx, an emblem of capitalist modernity as such; and so it shall serve in this chapter as well. While I shall often employ psychoanalytical models to describe the mechanicity of the subject, I reinterpret the Freudian *Zwang* or compulsion in part as economic compulsion.

22. On formal vs. real subsumption, see Marx, *Capital*, 1:1024–38.
23. Ibid., p. 558.

Edward Gordon Craig

In his 1908 manifesto "The Actor and the Über-marionette," the director, stage designer, and drama theorist Edward Gordon Craig bewailed the unreliability of the human body as artistic medium: "Art arrives only by design. Therefore in order to make any work of art it is clear we may only work in those materials with which we can calculate. Man is not one of these materials. The whole nature of man tends towards freedom; he therefore carries the proof in his own person, that as *material* for the theatre he is useless."[24] The body is prey to passions that can unexpectedly overwhelm even the most strenuous efforts at control; hence, Craig argues, modern theater will simply have to dispense with human beings altogether: "The actor must go, and in his place comes the inanimate figure—the über-marionette we may cal [sic] him, until he has won for himself a better name. . . . The über-marionette will not compete with Life—but will rather go beyond it. Its ideal will not be the flesh and blood but rather the body in Trance—it will aim to clothe itself with a death-like Beauty while exhaling a living spirit."[25]

Craig's essay reflects a longstanding fascination on the part of dramatic theorists with the puppet or machine. The pseudo-Germanic title is probably a nod to Heinrich von Kleist's essay "Über das Marionetten Theater" (1860) as well as to Nietzsche's *Übermensch*. But Craig's thinking also resembles that of contemporary figures such as Vsevolod Meyerhold, whose system of "biomechanical" training for actors was influenced by Pavlov's psychology and by Frederick Winslow Taylor's *Principles of Scientific Management*.[26] Craig himself expresses some sympathy for the body's irrepressible demands for freedom, but insists that such demands have no place in the realm of art, where the single will of the artist must reign unopposed. The actor's body is, or should be, nothing more than a photographic instrument whose function is to reproduce an image or carry out an instruction—not to create. Craig showed little patience for popular personalities of the stage who succeeded in spite of or in violation of the rules of art.[27]

In describing the body's helpless subjection to desire, Craig observes: "It is useless for him [the actor] to attempt to reason with himself. . . . Hamlet's calm directions (the dreamer's not the logician's directions, by

24. Edward Gordon Craig, "The Actor and the Über-marionette," *Mask* 2 (April 1908): 3.
25. Ibid., pp. 11, 12.
26. See Roach, *Player's Passion*, pp. 199–203.
27. Craig, "Actor and the Über-marionette," pp. 5, 3.

the way) are thrown to the winds. His limbs refuse, and refuse again, to obey his mind the instant emotion warms, while the mind is all the time creating the heat which shall set these emotions afire."[28] Craig's allusion to Hamlet (and it is not the only one in the essay) is by no means accidental, for Hamlet proves crucial to Craig's whole conception of a marionette theater. First and foremost, portraying Hamlet as a failed exhorter to dramatic restraint makes him into a projected image of Craig himself. Both men struggle to whip unpromising human material into shape for theatrical performance. Craig's identification with Hamlet would deepen in the period following "The Actor and the Übermarionette," and it would shape his 1912 production of *Hamlet* for the Moscow Art Theater, in collaboration with Constantin Stanislavski.[29]

When he urges the visiting players to "hold the mirror up to nature," Hamlet does indeed promulgate a view of acting as reproduction rather than creation, and he thereby helps inspire Craig's later description of the actor as a "photo-machine." Craig refers to Hamlet in a similar context when he writes: "Authors found it an excellent thing to use handsome and buoyant men *as instruments*. It mattered nothing to them that the instrument was a human creature. Although they knew not the stops of the instrument, they could play rudely upon him and they found him useful."[30] The allusion, of course, is to Hamlet's famous description of himself as a musical pipe:

> Why, look you now, how unworthy a thing you make of me! You would play upon me, you would seem to know my stops, you would pluck out the heart of my mystery, you would sound me from my lowest note to the top of my compass; and there is much music, excellent voice, in this little organ, yet cannot you make it speak. 'Sblood, do you think I am easier to be play'd on than a pipe? Call me what instrument you will, though you fret me, yet you cannot play upon me. (3.2.363–72)

This speech bears comparison with the others, quoted in the previous section of this essay, in which Hamlet compares his body to a puppet or a (Cartesian) machine, a mere instrument in the hands of an animating spirit. Craig seems to want to be that animating spirit, and to "play" on

28. Ibid., pp. 3–4.
29. Craig wrote of this period: "Hamlet almost seemed to be myself... *Hamlet* was not only a play for me nor a role to be played—I somehow or other lived Hamlet day by day"; quoted in Lawrence Senelick, *Gordon Craig's Moscow Hamlet: A Reconstruction* (Westport, Conn.: Greenwood, 1982), p. 25.
30. Craig, "Actor and the Über-marionette," pp. 4–5.

Hamlet his own allegorical tune. Yet in the very passage cited here, Hamlet insists that he *cannot* so easily be played upon. In fact, Hamlet provides a thoroughly recalcitrant alter ego for Craig, and his character is in some respects as intractable to attempts at theoretical appropriation as is the actor's body, in Craig's opinion, to theatrical appropriation.

The advice to the players, in which Hamlet outlines a practice of dramatic temperance or restraint, seems to react against the earlier scene in which the traveling player recites a speech about the death of Priam, prompting one of Hamlet's notorious soliloquies:

> O, what a rogue and peasant slave am I!
> Is it not monstrous that this player here,
> But in a fiction, in a dream of passion,
> Could force his soul so to his own conceit
> That from her working all the visage wann'd,
> Tears in his eyes, distraction in his aspect,
> A broken voice, an' his whole function suiting
> With forms to his conceit? And all for nothing,
> For Hecuba!
> What's Hecuba to him, or he to Hecuba,
> That he should weep for her? What would he do
> Had he the motive and the cue for passion
> That I have? He would drown the stage with tears,
> And cleave the general ear with horrid speech,
> Make mad the guilty, and appall the free,
> Confound the ignorant, and amaze indeed
> The very faculties of eyes and ears. Yet I,
> A dull and muddy-mettled rascal, peak
> Like John-a-dreams, unpregnant of my cause,
> And can say nothing. (2.2.550–69)

Hamlet admires the player for making his body into a perfectly responsive mechanism which can produce passions on cue. He thus grants the actor a perfection which Craig will not: the perfection of the automaton. Hamlet himself is afflicted, by contrast, with the unreliable body of which Craig complains—the body that cannot answer to the demands of artistic discipline. In this respect Hamlet is perfectly consistent with his later self-description as a pipe that cannot be played upon. He conceives of himself as a machine but not as an instrument; he is a mechanism, but one that is unresponsive or broken.

Hamlet's self-analysis leads in a very different direction from Craig's, for his problem is not an excess of passion that seizes his limbs and frees them from restraint but rather an absence of passion that leaves him listless and apathetic when he ought to act. Hamlet is a pipe without breath, a machine without its ghost. As a result, he dreams not of the restrained playing he advocates in act 3, scene 2 but of a form of acting whose passionate intensity would be almost lethal to its audience: "He would drown the stage with tears, / And cleave the general ear with horrid speech" (562-63). Hamlet's language here recalls that used by his father's ghost in act 1, scene 5 to describe his own fatal message (on which we will hear more in the following section). It is the father's script which Hamlet fails to act, the father's ghost which fails to animate the son's machine, the father's "cause" of which Hamlet is yet "unpregnant." But Hamlet also offers equally unreliable material for Craig's attempts at control. As director, Hamlet demands a formal discipline which he himself cannot embody when submitted to the "direction" of the ghost. Craig invokes Hamlet to articulate an ideal of perfect responsiveness which Hamlet himself famously violates—and violates, moreover, because he is *too* dead, too mechanical, not too passionate.

Many of the concerns of "The Actor and the Über-marionette" persisted into Craig's 1912 production of *Hamlet*, in which Craig even hoped to include marionettes of Hamlet and of Rosencrantz and Guildenstern.[31] Although this plan was never realized, Craig's conception of Hamlet reworked themes found in his earlier essay. Craig envisioned Hamlet as a man transformed by the meeting with his father's ghost, a man who had been allowed a terrifying glimpse into the world of death, of the spirit, of the future, and who therefore could no longer continue living in the realm of the mundane. Hamlet's death drive was to be personified by "the silvery figure of a woman who tempted Hamlet to come to her. This was what Hamlet called 'Not to be,' that is, not to exist in this unworthy little world, to go out of it, to die."[32]

Death is, for Craig's Hamlet, an imperative that is directed outward as well as inward. His failure to avenge his father's death results not from moral scruples or Oedipal conflicts but from a purifying mission that cannot possibly be completed by any single act. Stanislavski described Craig's Hamlet as "the great cleanser of the earth who had at last found the secrets of life on earth in the arms of death."[33] Having seen the disembodied world, Hamlet takes it upon himself to purge the earth of

31. Craig, quoted in Senelick, *Moscow Hamlet*, pp. 84-85.
32. Constantin Stanislavski, *My Life in Art*, trans. J. J. Robbins (Boston: Little, Brown, 1935), p. 520.
33. Ibid., p. 517.

organic, fleshly existence, embodied in his parents. Craig imagines Gertrude as "a fat woman who flops on sofas all day and night," but even the ghost is "not yet sufficiently purged." King Hamlet appears not in armor but as a rotting skeleton swathed in a winding sheet. "This material is a tattered shroud, putrescent or ripped to shreds—fabric decaying on the rotting, once comely body." The ghost himself "is bolt upright, because of rigor mortis. He is a skeleton gnawed away by worms. Only fragments of flesh hang from the bones in places, as in certain illustrations of Death."[34]

Hamlet, by contrast with both of his parents, is the disembodied. "Can we not make the actors realize," asks Craig, "that Hamlet himself *is* the spirit, buried in matter, that is to say, not [that] Hamlet himself is buried in material, but that Hamlet is spirit, and all that surrounds him is material."[35] While this conception of Hamlet as pure spirit may seem to contradict the earlier one of Hamlet as puppet or machine, both aim to purge the organic body, the body of passions. (For Craig, moreover, this organic body seems also to be a maternal one, represented by his fat, flopping Gertrude.) Craig's Über-marionette was designed to "go beyond" life; "its ideal will not be the flesh and blood . . . it will aim to clothe itself with a death-like Beauty."[36] This is why, in Craig's early plans for the Moscow production, a marionette Hamlet could alternate with the human actor: the spirit and the mechanical body are one.

The most innovative and controversial part of Craig's production, however, was the stage sets, which consisted mostly of painted rectangular screens giving the effect of cubist compositions or, at times, of cityscapes. In the essay on the Über-marionette, Craig had attacked the use of "gorgeous decoration" and elaborate scenery for plays.[37] The painted screens of *Hamlet* were designed not only to convey this minimalist aesthetic but also to abstract the play from any concrete historical setting. Most important, perhaps, was that these pure geometric forms redoubled, on a formal level, the play's thematic rejection of organic existence. If even King Hamlet's ghost was insufficiently purged, the ideal of pure spirit would have to be removed from the realm of character altogether and relocated in the space of modernist design. Craig's screens (dis)embodied the flat, inorganic condition toward which Hamlet aspired. They represented an aesthetics of the death drive, the pure instantiation of the Über-marionette.

34. Craig, quoted in Senelick, *Moscow Hamlet*, pp. 63, 81, 47.
35. Ibid., p. 67.
36. Craig, "Actor and the Über-marionette," p. 12.
37. Ibid., p. 10.

The question of design in *Hamlet* took on an intriguingly Oedipal dimension for Craig himself. His son revealed that Craig "saw in the Ghost [of King Hamlet] his own father," the scene designer E. W. Gordon.[38] Craig portrayed the Ghost as still afflicted with the maternal flesh; his father's "essence" was therefore projected onto the abstraction of design itself, safe from the vicissitudes of organic existence.

Craig's production of *Hamlet* is less an interpretation of the play than a symptomatic repetition of Hamlet's own governing fantasy: that of escape from maternal demand into the abstraction of paternal law. But if Craig's set design, like the imagined figure of the Über-marionette, offered a hoped-for release from the contingency of bodily existence and its passions, this theatrical fantasy provoked results almost as catastrophic, in their own way, as did Hamlet's in the fictional world of the play. For one thing, conservative critics of Craig's production reacted badly to its cubist design. One described an "impression of stylization which would more accurately be termed sterilization"; another claimed to be stifled and sickened by "Screens, screens, and more screens. Screens without end"; a third complained of "the sharp corners of the desolate cardboard constructions, the endless space, the nauseating gold paper, the right-angled intersections of lines, worthy sketches for some elevator or other technical structure, modernist cubes for some ultra-modern smoking room."[39] More telling, perhaps, were the difficulties in realizing Craig's plans. Once having designed the sets, Craig departed for Italy, leaving Stanislavski and his co-director, Leopold Sulerjtsky, in charge. They, however, found it impossible to realize Craig's vision with the available materials. "May a time come," lamented Stanislavski, "when newly discovered rays will paint in the air the shadows of color tones and the combinations of lines. May other rays light the body of man and give it that indefiniteness of outline, that disembodiment, that ghostliness which we know in our waking and sleeping dreams. Then, with a hardly seen ghost in the image of a woman we will be able to realize Craig's conception of Hamlet's 'To be or not to be.' But with the use of ordinary theatrical means the interpretation suggested by Craig looked like a piece of hokum." [40] Forced to work with "disgusting glue, paint, papier mâché and properties," Stanislavski found himself entrenched in the very material, organic world that Craig's sets were designed to transcend.[41] This

38. Edward Craig, *Gordon Craig: The Story of His Life* (New York: Knopf, 1968), p. 259, quoted in Senelick, *Moscow Hamlet*, p. 25.

39. Quoted in Senelick, *Moscow Hamlet*, p. 175.

40. Stanislavski, *My Life in Art*, p. 520.

41. Ibid., pp. 519–20.

paradox reached its ludicrous climax an hour before the first night's performance. Stanislavski recalls:

> I was sitting in the auditorium and rehearsing the maneuvers of shifting the screens for the last time. The rehearsal ended. The scenery was put up for the first scene of the play and the stage hands were allowed to rest and drink tea before the beginning of the performance. The stage grew empty, the auditorium was as quiet as a grave. But suddenly one of the screens began to lean sideways more and more, then fell on the screen next to it, and the entire scenery fell to the floor like a house of cards. There was the crack of breaking wooden frames, the sound of ripping canvas, and then the formless mass of broken and torn screens all over the stage.[42]

In an insensible parody of tragic "fate," the falling screens knock one another over into a torn heap, eerily reminiscent of the pile of bodies with which *Hamlet* itself ends. Having sought to escape the contingency of the organic in the regularity of the mechanical, Craig finds that the body's vicissitudes are not so easily evaded. The catastrophe of the first night's performance, however, does not represent a breakdown in the smooth running of the Hamletmachine. Rather, the Hamletmachine works *by* breaking down, as we also saw in the case of Gilbert's Bartolo: the clockwork always catches, the screens always fall. Craig's fundamental misconception was not to imagine Hamlet as an automaton, but rather to imagine the automaton itself as efficient, reliable, obedient, predictable. The Hamletmachine fascinates because it is a machine that does *not* work.

Jean Cocteau

The Infernal Machine, by Jean Cocteau, turns on a riddle: how can the story of Oedipus be replayed in a post-Freudian world, one in which everyone already "knows about" Oedipal desire? Unlike Sophocles' guileless and afflicted city, Cocteau's Thebes is fully enlightened, cynical, and decadent. Its citizens suspect that the story of Oedipus and the Sphynx is just some political ploy. Its queen, Jocasta, is a jaded cosmopolite with a pronounced sexual taste for young soldiers. She is already in the habit of bringing her conspicuously "Freudian" dreams to Tiresias

---

42. Ibid., p. 521.

for interpretation. In such a knowing world, what place remains for tragic *anagnoresis*? How can Oedipus's crime achieve its original, traumatic effect? Or, to pose the problem at a different level: can Sophoclean drama still signify for a modern audience? Or has Freud brought about the (nontragic) death of tragedy?

The first act of *The Infernal Machine* takes place on the ramparts of Thebes, where the ghost of Laius has been appearing nightly in a vain attempt to warn Oedipus and Jocasta of their fate. *Hamlet*, then, makes its own ghostly appearance in Cocteau's play; it becomes part of the infernal machine. By fusing Thebes's palace and Elsinore, Cocteau clearly invokes Freud's Oedipal reading of *Hamlet*, and thereby installs *The Interpretation of Dreams* as a crucial subtext for his own play. The ghost that hovers over Thebes' ramparts, cursing and afflicting them, is not only Laius, then, and King Hamlet, but Freud himself. As such, it is not the traditional *revenant*, the ghost returned from the past, but rather a ghost who returns from the future—the future of a cultural line generated from Sophocles's play which will include Shakespeare, Freud, and ultimately Cocteau himself. This ghost, we might say, is the ghost of Oedipal tradition.

Freud's reading of *Hamlet* in *The Interpretation of Dreams* is very much concerned with such a tradition, and hence with literary or cultural history itself:

> Another of the great creations of tragic poetry, Shakespeare's *Hamlet*, has its roots in the same soil as *Oedipus Rex*. But the changed treatment of the same material reveals the whole difference in the mental life of these two widely separated epochs of civilization: the secular advance of repression in the emotional life of mankind. In the *Oedipus* the child's wishful phantasy that underlies it is brought into the open and realized as it would be in a dream. In *Hamlet* it remains repressed; and—just as in the case of a neurosis—we only learn of its existence from its inhibiting consequences.[43]

Freud's narrative condenses the histories of the subject and of civilization. Not only does *Oedipus* express "the child's wishful phantasy," but it can do so overtly because Greek culture itself is in a childlike, immature state. *Hamlet* represents a later stage in the life of the subject and of literary history in which Oedipal wishes must be repressed. This narrative

43. Sigmund Freud, *The Interpretation of Dreams*, trans. James Strachey (New York: Avon, 1965), p. 298.

has been elaborated with great brilliance by Julia Reinhard Lupton and Kenneth Reinhard, who regard *Hamlet* as Oedipal *Trauerspiel*, a mournful and decadent repetition of its Sophoclean original.[44] Freud's narrative, of course, is comprised of three terms, not two; he positions *The Interpretation of Dreams* as the third great Oedipal "classic." In Freud's book, however, the Oedipal secret is neither innocently enacted nor neurotically repressed but scientifically analyzed and laid bare. Freud, to be sure, repeats Oedipus's role as heroic riddle-solver. Yet he does so with a difference. In Sophocles, the Sphynx's riddle dies with the Sphynx; Oedipus does not *publish* the answer, at least to our knowledge. This is in keeping with his heroic stature; it is not for everyone to know the secret of the Sphynx, just as it is not for everyone to be a tragic hero. In Sophocles, the Oedipal condition is not yet universal; it is reserved for royalty. The same is true for Hamlet, though here the question arises of whether he is *adequate* to his Oedipal destiny (Oedipus is saddled with an unavoidable curse, while Hamlet is given a *commandment* in relation to which he may fall short). Freud, however, introduces a new era of the Oedipal in which it is rendered at once scientific and democratic. Now not only can everyone "know" about the Oedipus complex, but everyone can "have" one. Thus Oedipal desire has truly entered its late phase. After its Greek morning and Elizabethan afternoon it settles into its Germanic/modernist evening, when it hobbles about on a walking stick. This is not to deny the initially scandalous nature of the Freudian discovery. But after a first burst of excitement, the Oedipal dilemma suffers the fate of any solved puzzle: it simply passes into the realm of common wisdom. When its riddle is solved, there is nothing left for the Sphynx but suicide. When his riddle (and Hamlet's) is solved, Oedipus dissolves into a ghost. This is the condition with which *The Infernal Machine* begins. At stake is not only psychoanalysis but the tradition of tragic drama whose fate it now bears in its hands. In an essay appropriately entitled "Le scandale de la verité," Shoshana Felman reverses this relation: for her, it is Cocteau's retelling of Oedipus that has assumed responsibility for the cultural status of psychoanalysis: "At an initial level, the scandal [of *The Infernal Machine*] resides in *the loss of scandal*, in the fact that the analytic shock has itself become a cliché, that the tragedy has become a farce."[45] For Felman, the banalization of Freud's scandalous knowledge is represented in Oedipus's encounter with the Sphynx, when he "solves" her riddle (she ac-

---

44. Lupton and Reinhard, *After Oedipus.*

45. Shoshana Felman, "Le Scandale de la verité," in *Discours et pouvoir*, ed. Ross Chambers, *Michigan Romance Studies* 2 (1982): 20. The translation is my own.

tually gives him the answer, out of weariness at killing) without having understood a thing. Reducing the "analytic enigma" to a "password," Oedipus's answer stands for the sociocultural discourse of "Freudianism" which implants a superficial cleverness and an even deeper incomprehension. Thus it is that the cynical knowingness of Cocteau's Thebans cannot ward off the repetition of Oedipal tragedy. In fact, this knowingness is the very medium of tragic *nemesis*: it is the *méconnaissance* that secures Oedipus's doom. *The Infernal Machine*, then, ultimately preserves the scandal of psychoanalytic knowledge, which it does by enacting the Lacanian maxim that "les non-dupes errent."

For Felman, the "infernal machine" is Oedipal desire, whose scandalous, enigmatic, and ultimately tragic nature tears through the comforting veils thrown over it by "Freudian" ideology. This reading is compelling on its own terms, and perhaps even more so as a symptom of the desire that animates Lacanian theory: a desire to resuscitate and sustain the shock of psychoanalysis, which always threatens to dissipate into the password of received wisdom. Faced with becoming banal, merely thematic, and predictable (an interpretive machine), psychoanalysis is constantly challenged to regenerate the monstrosity of its truth. This dilemma, however, is not peculiar to psychoanalysis. It is, rather, endemic to the whole project of modernism, and particularly to the avant-garde, which must continually revive the scandal of the new against the threat of its assimilation into what Hans Robert Jauss has called the "horizon of expectations."[46] Here we arrive at what is, in Felman's reading, the unposed question: What are the conditions under which scandal tends to evaporate? For Sophocles, the story of Oedipus was at once shocking and completely traditional; its status as a received narrative of the culture did not compromise its power. For Cocteau, however, the Oedipus legend is threatened by a culture so acclimated to shock that it is largely buffered against it. In this sense, Cocteau's "infernal machine" is nothing other than modernity itself in its capacity to extinguish the traumatic.

Enter *Hamlet*, which for Cocteau represents above all the "fading" of Oedipus. On the ramparts of Thebes, the ghost of Laius makes his nightly appearance, vainly trying to warn Oedipus and Jocasta of their tragic state. Unlike King Hamlet, however, this ghost cannot impart his fearful secret. As a young soldier reports to Jocasta, "it was a strain for him to materialize, and every time he came close to saying what he meant, he

---

46. Hans Robert Jauss, *Toward an Aesthetic of Reception*, trans. Timothy Bahti (Minneapolis: University of Minnesota Press, 1982), esp. chap. 1, "Literary History as Challenge," pp. 3–45.

disappeared" (p. 25). Laius's difficulties are ambiguous. On the one hand, Laius suggests that infernal forces are preventing him from delivering his fatal knowledge. On the other hand, his fading seems actually to result from excessive familiarity. A more senior soldier remarks to a younger one: "He doesn't frighten us. Not our old ghost, Laius. He doesn't still make your guts quiver, does he? Perhaps the first time . . . But not afterward. He's not a bad ghost, he's a friend" (p. 9). Repetition has rendered this apparition predictable, banal, even comforting: the soldiers now look forward to his appearance for entertainment (p. 12). If Laius's presence begins to flicker out, this is because he is now expected. The alien has been absorbed into the mundane.

For Cocteau, King Hamlet's ghost represents something that is no longer attainable: a fatal knowledge, an announcement so traumatic, so unexpected that its advent grips the body in a deathly *jouissance*:

> I could a tale unfold whose lightest word
> Would harrow up thy soul, freeze thy young blood,
> Make thy two eyes like stars start from their spheres,
> Thy knotted and combined locks to part,
> And each particular hair to stand an end,
> Like quills upon the fearful porpentine.
> But this eternal blazon must not be
> To ears of flesh and blood. (1.5.15–22)

King Hamlet's secret holds a utopian promise for modernism: that of an unassimilable newness. Ranged against this, however, is the deadening power of repetition: the ghost has already appeared on three successive nights, "jump at this dead hour" (1.1.65). The very occasion to deliver his deadly word, then, depends on an incipient predictability.

Cocteau's play invokes King Hamlet in an amused but mournful way, since all that can now be retrieved is the *fading* of his traumatic message. But in isolating and foregrounding this element of trauma, Cocteau lights upon a fundamental—perhaps *the* fundamental—mechanism of *Hamlet* itself. Hamlet's famous delay is the symptom of his inability to assume a symbolic mandate. Slavoj Žižek describes the play as "a drama of *failed interpellation*" in which the Father's commandment is never fully internalized by the son.[47] If the Father's Law finally has its effect (Hamlet does, in the end, carry out the prescribed revenge), it does so not through conscious reason but as unconscious, traumatic cause. To put it

47. Žižek, *Sublime Object of Ideology*, p. 120.

differently, Hamlet never *fulfills* the Father's commandment; rather, he blindly and automatically *repeats* it. Hamlet's revenge is not an "act" in the ethical sense but a kind of spasmodic reflex: he blindly strikes out, first at Polonius, and later at Claudius, under the pressure of unanticipated situations that interrupt rather than resolve his delay. King Hamlet's commandment is effective, therefore, not because of any "reasons" it contains but because of a stupid, traumatic excess that attends its enunciation. It works as a shock that precipitates a (delayed) repetition—as pure, exteriorized compulsion (*Zwang*) that acts automatically rather than through interiorized obedience or assent. The ethical, inner dimensions of Hamlet's being—as exemplified in the famous soliloquies—are merely retroactive attempts at symbolization, at attaching meaning after the fact to a traumatic "cause." The template for Hamlet's being is provided by the genre of revenge tragedy which this play so exquisitely distends. In revenge tragedy, one murder "demands" another, which is retroactively granted a symbolic meaning as justice or revenge, but which in fact operates as blind repetition that responds to, without ever encountering, a traumatic cause. It is as this unleashed repetition-compulsion that Hamlet is, ultimately, a machine.

Hamlet serves Cocteau as a way of positioning his own play's relation to modernity—positioning it, that is to say, as a commentary *on* modernity. This position is defined, in the first instance, through the fading of King Hamlet's traumatic word. Yet the play soon regresses from its own enlightened beginning to a fully archaic, mythic mode. *The Infernal Machine* opens as post-Freudian parody, staging Oedipus in a world that can no longer take his problems seriously. Yet by the end, Cocteau attempts to reinstate Oedipal tragedy in its original form (with what success or coherence, it is difficult to say). Felman reads in this atavism of the tragic a psychoanalytic moral; yet it is also, clearly, a statement about the experience of the early twentieth century more generally, in which enlightenment has no power to stave off disaster. Tragedy rips through the veneer of cynical consciousness, asserting its blind, brutal mechanisms in spite of all apparent "progress."

The play's tragic structure begins to crystallize when the Sphynx, angered at Oedipus's hubristic misunderstanding of her riddle, throws off her earthly form and becomes Nemesis or Vengeance. As such she is the pure embodiment of tragic repetition. Just before he reveals to the Sphynx her true identity as Nemesis, Anubis describes for her a construction of time that negates the linear, progressivist conception of history embraced by enlightenment:

ANUBIS, taking the side of her dress. Look at the folds in this fabric. Press them together. Now, if you run a pin through them, then withdraw the pin and smooth out the material so that the folds are gone, do you think a simpleton would believe that those spaced-out holes were all made at the same time by the one pin?

SPHYNX. Of course he wouldn't.

ANUBIS. Man's time is folded and hidden in eternity. But I, the God of the Dead, see the whole life of Oedipus unfolded, stretched out before me like a picture in one dimension. All the episodes, from his birth to his death, are pinpricks in the fabric of time. (p. 54)

Here is Cocteau's most vivid illustration of the "infernal machine": time as a series of unintelligible repetitions, strung together into a nonlinear, discontinuous pattern. Each "event" in the series is traumatic, a puncturing which figures the real as a hole in the web of the symbolic, around which meaning strives in vain to organize itself. This conception of time, as I have argued, is also at work in *Hamlet* and in the entire "tradition" of the Hamletmachine, which propagates itself through blind repetition. *The Infernal Machine* is, itself, one pinprick in this constellated pattern.

What lends *The Infernal Machine* its paradoxical structure (and compromises the monitory reading offered by Felman) is the fact that mythic time is at once the vengeful negation of modernity and its structural equivalent. Repetition is both the sign of a tragic, traumatic, and hence timeless condition *and* the means through which trauma "fades" over time. Tragic repetition is not so much the means of punishing a cynical, enlightened consciousness as it is the reverse side of this consciousness— the other surface of the pierced cloth. Such is the nature of mechanical repetition that it is at once jarring and dulling, producing a subject who is traumatized but (or rather, therefore) catatonic, anaesthetized.

In *Beyond the Pleasure Principle*, Freud locates his discussion of trauma and the repetition compulsion within the field of industrialized modernity: "severe mechanical concussions, railway disasters, and other accidents involving risk to life," including so-called shell shock, produced by the mechanized warfare of World War I.[48] In his writings on Baudelaire, Wal-

---

48. Sigmund Freud, *Beyond the Pleasure Principle*, trans. James Strachey (New York: Norton, 1959), p. 10. Even little Ernst of the fort-da game interiorizes this modernity, venting his anger on his toys by urging them to "Go to the fwont!" like his father (p. 15). The problematic of loss as addressed in *Beyond the Pleasure Principle* clearly develops themes broached in the earlier "Mourning and Melancholia" (written 1915; pub. 1917), an essay inspired in part by the problem of "mass mourning" during World War I. (Compare two of Freud's

ter Benjamin converts Freud's book into a full-fledged theory of aesthetic modernity. Baudelaire's poetry, Benjamin argues, responds to an urban world in which "the shock experience has become the norm."[49] Drawing on Freud's argument that "consciousness arises instead of a memory trace," and that the former functions primarily to bind potentially traumatic stimuli, Benjamin reads Baudelaire's verse as inscribing a split between *Erlebnis* (consciousness of a lived event) and *Erfahrung* (experience associated with the richness of involuntary memory). Paradoxically, Baudelaire both cushions or defends against the experience of shock and perpetuates it—and in doing each of these he feeds a certain desire in his readers. For if modern urban life assaults the consciousness of its inhabitants, it also produces "traumatophile types" who develop a taste, indeed a need, for shock experience.[50] "Thus technology has subjected the human sensorium to a complex kind of training. There came a day when a new and *urgent need for stimuli* was met by the film. In a film, perception in the form of shocks was established as a formal principle" (my emphasis).[51] In film, as in urban experience, mechanical repetition imprints itself upon consciousness as both trauma and template. Aesthetic modernity arises when the repetition of shock begins to replace the recurrence of tradition as the fundamental paradigm of cultural and sensory experience.

Once having installed a need for stimuli, however, aesthetic modernity has trouble fulfilling it. In the "Baudelaire" section of the *Passagenarbeit*, Benjamin writes: "The dialectic of commodity-production in high capitalism: the novelty of products receives—as a stimulus for demand—a previously unknown significance. At the same time there appears a conspicuous ever-the-sameness in mass production."[52] Modernization is an imperative to innovate which nevertheless faces a cultural law of entropy: shock, repeated, dulls. Benjamin clearly formulates this law in his discussion of baroque allegory: "If it is to hold its own against the tendency to absorption, the allegorical must constantly unfold in new and surprising

other essays of 1915, "Thoughts for the Times on War and Death," *Standard Edition* 14: 275–300, and "On Transience," *Standard Edition* 14:303–7.) Little Ernst's "modernity" appears above all in his surprising lack of affect after his mother's death ("the little boy showed no signs of grief" [p. 16, n. 7]). His consciousness is so "cushioned" by repetitive play that real trauma no longer moves him. Is this anaesthetized state really so different from shell shock?

49. Walter Benjamin, *Illuminations*, trans. Harry Zohn (New York: Schocken, 1969), p. 162.

50. Ibid., p. 163.

51. Ibid., p. 175.

52. Benjamin, *Passagen-Werk*, 1:417.

ways. . . . Allegories become dated, because it is part of their nature to shock."[53] This dialectic of innovation and reabsorption can be traced throughout modernist aesthetics, from Viktor Shklovsky's concept of "defamiliarization" to Hans Robert Jauss's aesthetics of reception, in which the new is always reassimilated to the horizon of expectations which it initially violates. For the various avant-garde movements of the early twentieth century, shock does not merely exceed the horizon of expectations; rather, it *constitutes* that horizon—it becomes precisely what is expected, or demanded. The avant-garde is a machine for the production of shock, but one that increasingly succumbs to its own entropy.

This cultural paradox is at once a reflection and a product of the economic process that subtends it. As Benjamin (for instance) recognized, the demand for shock or novelty in the realm of art simply mimics the dynamic of capitalist modernization, which is itself driven by insistent innovation. And, as described by Marx, capitalist production is subject to dialectical reversals similar to those that afflict avant-gardist production. In both cases, individual efforts at innovation produce a kind of "rebound effect" which thwarts them at a more general level. For Marx, the driving force behind industrial innovation is so-called "relative surplus value," which grants extra profits to individual firms which are able, through technological advances, to produce the same product for less labor-time.[54] But ultimately, labor-power is the only commodity that can create new value (and new profit); hence, while reducing labor (or "variable capital") as a proportion of total capital expenditures grants individual firms marginal and temporary advantages over their competitors, collectively and overall it produces a "tendency for the rate of profit to fall."[55] The correlate to this, in the field of cultural production, would be something like a general tendency for the rate of *surprise* to fall.

This is the dilemma into which *The Infernal Machine* inserts both itself and *Hamlet*. As Cocteau's Tiresias puts it, enunciating a law to which his creator is also subject, "Only originality surprises—and rules" (p. 65). For Cocteau, and indeed for all other modern readers, *Hamlet* is not just a classic of the stage but a work that has become particularly entangled in its own status as a classic, with the result that it is at once the most original of plays and, precisely because of this, the most expected of plays. *Hamlet* embodies modernity's infernal machine because it carries within itself the whole trajectory of repetition which leads from shock to cliché.

53. Benjamin, *Origin of German Tragic Drama*, p. 103.
54. Marx, *Capital*, 1:643–72.
55. Marx, *Capital*, vol. 3, trans. David Fernbach (New York: Vintage, 1981), pp. 317–75.

The Hamletmachine is a contrivance of repetition that produces . . . precisely its own fading away.

Jacques Lacan

Jacques Lacan's lectures on *Hamlet* comprise part of his unpublished sixth seminar, devoted to "Desire and Its Interpretation."[56] It is in the course of this seminar, and largely apropos of his reading of *Hamlet*, that Lacan introduces the three graphs of desire, culminating in the notorious "che vuoi?" diagram.[57] By way of form, perhaps, as much as content, these enigmatic figures register Lacan's distinctive and radically exteriorized conception of desire as an apparatus or structure. Lacan similarly describes *Hamlet* as "a kind of mechanism [*une espèce d'appareil*] . . . in which human desire is articulated."[58] Lacan's graphs of desire, as well as his reading of *Hamlet*, have been treated to incisive and sensitive commentary.[59] In examining his construction of a Hamletmachine I am interested less in explicating Lacan's theory of desire than in tracing his *own* desire as it both propagates and distends the Freudian legacy. In addition, I hope to show that Lacan's reading of *Hamlet* registers a certain anxiety about the problem of tradition (Freudian and otherwise) in the modern age. For Lacan, modernity is a Cocteau-ian "infernal machine" which threatens to consume the legacy of the past.

Lacan's *Hamlet* lectures appeared in the journal *Ornicar?* under the intriguing but possibly misleading title "Hamlet, par Lacan"—misleading because, while Lacan appropriates and thus to some degree re-authors *Hamlet*, he distinctly does *not* place himself in the Shakespearean position. His role is, rather, defined by the punning, albeit strained, subtext of the

56. All my quotations of the Sixth Seminar come from the excerpts reprinted as "Hamlet, par Lacan" in *Orincar?* 24 (1981): 7–31; 25 (1982): 13–36; 26–27 (1983): 7–44. The three installments are cited here by roman numerals I–III followed by page numbers. An abridged version of III, under the title "Desire and the Interpretation of Desire in *Hamlet*," trans. James Hulbert, appeared in *Literature and Psychoanalysis: The Question of Reading, Otherwise*, ed. Shoshana Felman (Baltimore: Johns Hopkins University Press, 1982), pp. 11–52. When I cite from the parts of III translated by Hulbert I have used his translation, except where I note a modification. Otherwise all translations are mine.

57. The three graphs also appear in "The Subversion of the Subject and the Dialectic of Desire in the Freudian Unconscious" in Lacan, *Écrits: A Selection*, pp. 292–325. For a helpful explication, see Žižek, *Sublime Object of Ideology*, pp. 87–129.

58. I, 24. In II, 16, Lacan avows that what interests him about *Hamlet* is not this or that theme but "the whole of the work, its articulation, its machinery" (*l'ensemble de l'oeuvre, son articulation, sa machinerie*).

59. See Lupton and Reinhard, *After Oedipus*.

Ornicar? title: "Hamlet par(le) Lacan," Hamlet *speaks* Lacan. In the identification that organizes his treatment of the play, Lacan does not play the part of Hamlet; rather, he is played *by* Hamlet, who knows all his stops. Lacan occupies the position of puppet, or ventriloquist's dummy, animated by the voice of the Other.

Lacan's play, like Shakespeare's, is directed by a ghost—the ghost of the Father whose law is inscribed on the son. "To be sure, [Hamlet] has received the express command of his father, admired above all. Certainly, everything works together to prompt him to act. And he does not act" (I, 14). The problem, for Lacan, is not just that Hamlet fails to obey the father, but that he fails to obey him despite admiring him "above all." "We have to do here with a play that opens shortly after the death of a father who was, *so his son Hamlet tells us,* a very admirable king, the ideal king and father" (I, 11; emphasis in original). It is the son upon whom it falls to maintain the father's ideal status—indeed, to create it, as Lacan's skeptical italics suggest. Surely Hamlet protests too much, and therefore fails to execute the beloved father's commandment despite every stated intention of doing so.

Of course, Hamlet is not the only one laboring under the ghostly injunctions of an ideal father. "You will see . . . that we will always vigilantly maintain [*nous veillerons à toujours maintenir*] Hamlet there where Freud has placed him" (I, 10). The verb *veiller,* to keep night watch, clearly evokes the scenes on the battlemants of Elsinore where Hamlet encounters the ghost—and Lacan, like Hamlet, promises to remain vigilant, to sustain the paternal text. For who would not carry out the commands of such an ideal father? Freud's brief remarks on *Hamlet* are so clear and just, Lacan informs us, that all further attempts at elaboration are mere "excursions and embellishments" (I, 10). Freud "leaves long after him those matters with which authors have been engaged ever since" (I, 11). Yet despite the perfection of this testament, the others have failed to respect it: "Authors have drifted [*dérivé*] since Freud according to the whims of analytical exploration" (I, 10). But Lacan, the good son, will oppose this drift, *maintaining* Hamlet in the exact spot where Freud has placed him [*à la place où Freud l'a mis*]. Of course, this situation already attributes a certain debility to the Father, who requires the (good) son to sustain him. As a ghost, the father is there but not there; he can give orders, but depends on the son to carry them out. This ontological problem occupies Lacan at the very opening of his meditations on *Hamlet,* where he interprets "To be or not to be" in reference to the son's desire "to maintain [*maintenir*] the maternal phallus" (I, 7). "In the exact spot where he has placed it," one is tempted to add. The phallus, like Cocteau's Laius, is in the habit of fading: it establishes an epistemological as well as an ontological paradox in attempting to ground speculation on the void. Lacan, as Hamlet, finds himself in the circular position of sustaining a paternal injunction that may have been issued by a phantasm.

Epistemological questions of this sort are central to Lacan's reading of *Hamlet*. What distinguishes Hamlet from Oedipus in Lacan's view is that Oedipus acts blindly to fulfill his fate while Hamlet *knows* (III, 15) after his interview with the ghost. Lacan, moreover, introduces his analysis of *Hamlet* in the context of the following specimen dream from *The Interpretation of Dreams*: "*His* [the patient's] *father was alive once more and was talking to him in the usual way, but* (the remarkable thing was that) *he had really died, only he did not know it.*"[60] Lacan employs the phrase "he was dead, only he did not know it" to introduce the concept of the "not-knowing of the Other" [*l'ignorance de l'Autre*], which will prove crucial to his reading of Shakespeare. The dream of the dead father's return, of course, evokes the ghost's appearance in *Hamlet*, and Lacan will later make the connection explicit by insisting that, by contrast with this dream, in *Hamlet* "the father knew" (II, 30). Initially, however, he elaborates on the "not-knowing" of the Other by considering the crucial moment at which the child discovers that his parents don't know all his thoughts. By means of this recognition, the child now knows something he did not know before, and what he knows is that his parents do not know what he knows. As a result, his thoughts now become *his* thoughts, yet only provisionally, since his "possession" of them is still knotted up in his relation to the Other. Moreover, "There is a correlation between this *not knowing* on the part of the Other and the constitution of the unconscious. The one is in a way the inverse of the other" (I, 12). In knowing that the Other does not know, the child creates the space of that not-knowing which is the unconscious.

This complex relation between knowledge and ignorance will, Lacan assures us, play itself out in *Hamlet*; but since Hamlet also "speaks" Lacan, it doubles back into the latter's discourse. What Lacan is describing here is nothing less than the origin of originality, the possibility of having thoughts that are, at least provisionally, one's own. Insofar as Lacan himself plays Hamlet to Freud's ghost, he is condemned to repeating the thoughts of the Father: "And thy commandment all alone shall live/ Within the book and volume of my brain, / Unmix'd with baser matter" (1.5.102-4). The very project of a "return to Freud" circumscribes Lacan's thoughts within the knowledge of the Other. In order to have his

60. Freud, *Interpretation of Dreams*, p. 466.

own thoughts, he must find the Father's blind spot. However, if we are now to ask what it is that Freud does not know, we will not get very far simply by repeating the formula of the dream—he did not know *that he was dead*—because the death of the Father is the result, not the content, of what he does not know. (As Lacan points out in Seminar XI, the true formula for atheism is not "God is dead" but "God is unconscious.")[61] In any case, the "not-knowing" of the Other is simply *supposed* on the part of the subject. The attribution of ignorance to the Other is an enabling fiction for the intellectual autobiography that Lacan is (unconsciously?) writing here.

Such issues prove central to Lacan's reading of *Hamlet*, where the Father's knowledge paralyzes the son:

> The father and the son, the one and the other, know. This community of demystification is precisely the motive that makes it difficult for Hamlet to take up action. What are the paths by which he will be able to meet up with his act, to accomplish what must be accomplished? What detours will make that act possible, which is in itself impossible precisely to the degree that the Other knows? It is this detour, it is these paths which must be the object of our attention, it is these which will instruct us. (I, 16)

Insofar as he is barred both from acting and from not acting by the knowledge of the Other, Hamlet must accomplish his goal by means of a detour or byway. After much delay, dilation, and indirection, he will in the end "fulfill" the Father's commandment, but in such a way that, as Lacan points out, the fatal thrust passes through him rather than comes from him. Not surprisingly, Lacan declares that it is the detour resulting from Hamlet's impasse that must interest us. Like the psychoanalytic reader, Hamlet must "by indirections find directions out."

But here again, Hamlet's necessities animate Lacan, for whom Freud's legacy is at once enabling and potentially constraining. If the father and the son *both* know, then the son can act only by following the father's directions indirectly. Hence the *retour à Freud* necessitates a *détour*, a certain dilatory movement which sustains the dialectically inverted ignorance both of the self and of the Other. Here we arrive at the very method of the Lacanian seminar, with its thousand intellectual excursions carried out under the alibi of commentary on the master's texts.

61. See Jacques Lacan, *The Four Fundamental Concepts of Psychoanalysis*, trans. Alan Sheridan (New York: Norton, 1978), p. 59.

Not only is Lacan's discourse on *Hamlet* itself a necessary detour through which his own intellectual self-production may be allegorized, then, but it is a detour which revalues and redefines the very idea of the detour so that it is no longer a mere means to an end but, in some sense, the end itself. Yet precisely by remaining a *détour* (and hence bound by the promise of the *retour*, no matter how long deferred), it also distinguishes itself from the *dérive* or "drifting" practiced by the revisionists (the psycho-analytic establishment, in Lacan's view). Hamlet-Lacan neither fulfills the Father's commandment "with wings as swift/ As meditation, or the thoughts of love" (1.5.29–30) nor abandons it. Rather, he throws himself into the art of "excursion and embellishment," which is all that remains to the *Hamlet* commentator after Freud.

The figure of the detour not only establishes a complex interplay between knowledge and ignorance but immerses it in a distinctive temporality, founded on deferral and repetition (i.e., return) and bearing the marks of Lacan's notion of "logical time."[62] The temporal themes broached at the beginning of Lacan's analysis of *Hamlet* prepare the way for his later meditations on Hamlet and "the hour of the Other" (*l'heure de l'Autre*). But they also engage with models of cultural temporality which will animate Lacan's project of reading, and will produce an image of modernity very like Cocteau's "infernal machine." The most important of these models emerges in a discussion of Ernest Jones's treatment of the play:

> Jones has thrown this point [the secret of King Hamlet's death] into relief in his article *The death of Hamlet's father*. In the primitive saga, the king is indeed massacred by his brother, under a pretext having to do with his relations with his wife, but everyone knows about it, the massacre takes place in front of all. In *Hamlet*, by contrast, the thing is hidden, but—and this is the important point—the father knows about it and comes to unveil it. *There needs no ghost, my lord.* Freud cites several times this reply of Horatio's, which has become a proverb—*There needs no ghost, my lord*, there's no need of a ghost to tell us that. And in fact, as far as the Oedipal theme is concerned, we ourselves have known about it for a long time. But in the construction of *Hamlet*'s tale, we don't know it yet, and it is highly significant that it's the father who knows and who comes to tell us. (I, 13)

62. See Jacques Lacan, "Logical Time and the Assertion of Anticipated Certainty: A New Sophism," *Newsletter of the Freudian Field* 2, no. 2 (Fall 1988): 4–22.

In this particular revision of the original story, Lacan informs us, themes of knowledge and secrecy are closely intertwined. The murder of King Hamlet, originally a public fact, now becomes a secret that only the dead father can deliver. Unlike the father of Freud's dream, King Hamlet not only knows that he is dead but knows how he has died—a puzzling fact, since, as he himself relates, he was asleep in his garden when the poisoning occurred. King Hamlet is thus both the Other and the barred Other, at once omniscient and unconscious, an impossible or paradoxical overlapping of complete awareness and complete ignorance.

As before, moreover, questions of knowledge are embedded in a temporal framework. The phrase "There needs no ghost, my lord . . . To tell us this" points to an expired secret, to a piece of information that may once have been news but now has degenerated into common knowledge, so that it is unworthy of a spectral messenger. The ghost can guarantee its own authenticity only by revealing forbidden truths; the dead Father must share a secret in order to sustain his status as the Father. Thus Hamlet devotes much of the play to verifying the news that the ghost has delivered to him. But to Horatio, who asks what the ghost said, he gives only a false secret or tautology, that "There's never a villain dwelling in all Denmark / But he's an arrant knave." To which Horatio responds, "There needs no ghost, my lord, come from the grave / To tell us this" (1.5.123–26). Hamlet's false secret, designed to produce ignorance, is the inverse of the ghost's true secret, which produces a deadly knowledge.

Lacan's meditations focus on the rate of decay of secrets, their entropic dispersal into common lore. In mapping *Hamlet* onto his own situation, Lacan transforms this lapsed secret into the Oedipal theme: "We, ourselves, have known about it for a long time." There needs no Freudian ghost come from the grave to tell us this. As in *The Infernal Machine*, the dead Father's secret has lost its power to shock, and hence he himself threatens to fade away. Perhaps this is what it means when the father in the dream doesn't know that he is dead: he doesn't know that his *secret* has died, that he bears only the ghost of what was once a living knowledge. Lacan seems to construe *Hamlet*'s cultural work in relation to this dilemma. Although it is true that we have all known the Oedipal secret for a long time, in the way *Hamlet*'s story is constructed we once again don't know it, and we need the father to come and reveal it. Shakespeare's play produces a contrived state of innocence in order to revivify the father's knowledge.

Just as King Hamlet's story encodes a thinly veiled reference to the Garden of Eden and the Fall of man, so *Hamlet* itself returns us to a childlike ignorance so that the Father may again pour the poison of knowledge into our ears. The task of *Hamlet* in modernity is to restore the enigma to Oedipal knowledge, to make us feel our ignorance in relation to it once more, and thereby to revive the fading ghost of Freud. The parallels between Lacan's project and Cocteau's now seem striking indeed. In *The Infernal Machine*, the Oedipal secret has degenerated into the password which is circulated but not understood, and must once again be rendered traumatic. Likewise, the phrase "There needs no ghost . . . to tell us this" refers not to the actual secret of the ghost but to the banality that Hamlet has substituted for public consumption. Hamlet (and Lacan) knows the father's true secret, the enigma which still has the power to signify. Like Nemesis in Cocteau, Lacan must enforce a traumatic return of this enigma to counter its dissipative or vulgarizing repetitions. This is what Lacan means when he vows to *maintain* Hamlet exactly where Freud has placed him. It is not just that Hamlet threatens to drift, in the hands of the revisionists, but that he threatens to fade or disappear, in the manner of the maternal phallus. To maintain Hamlet where the father has placed him means to defamiliarize that placement, to reinstate a knowledge in such a way that what we thought we knew can now be seen as ignorance. Shakespeare's revision of the "primitive saga" reverses cultural entropy in that it turns a fact "that everyone knows about" back into a secret. This is Lacan's task as well: to vindicate the father by retranslating his degraded, public knowledge back into an enigmatic discourse, to trace a detour such that the "return" to Freud encounters a new and unanticipated object.

Saving Freud, however, means in part saving him from himself. In the *Hamlet* lectures, Lacan allows a rare note of criticism to creep into his discussion of Freud. This note (like the cock's crow in *Hamlet*) is sounded three times, and always with regard to the same point: Freud's narrative of modernity as a process of degeneracy, implicit in his treatment of *Hamlet* as a more repressed, "neurotic" treatment of the same themes treated more openly in *Oedipus Rex*. Lacan asks:

> What is it that distinguishes Hamlet's position in relation to the fundamental plot of Oedipus? Why is this variant of Oedipus so striking? For in the end Oedipus didn't put on so many airs, as Freud remarked in an explanatory note to which one has recourse when one has nothing to say. My God, everything's going downhill, we are in the period of decadence, we other moderns, we twist ourselves about six hundred times before doing what the others, the good, the brave, the ancients, did right off—that's no explanation. We ought to be suspicious of every reference to the idea of decadence.

If it's true that we moderns are in that position, we cannot content ourselves, at least if we are psychoanalysts, with the reason—our nerves aren't as solid as those of our fathers. (II, 29)

Although Lacan seems to be mocking the use to which Freud's explanation has been put by others, elsewhere (I, 12) he criticizes the explanation itself and speculates that the corrosive influence of Nietzsche may be to blame for this lapse in Freud's thinking.

Before hazarding a guess as to why the idea of modernity as decadence elicits such a forceful reaction from Lacan, we ought to look more closely at the idea itself. First of all, it is far from certain that a narrative of decadence can legitimately be extracted from Freud's discussion of Hamlet and Oedipus. *Hamlet* and decadence is, however, a topic addressed in Max Nordau's book *Degeneration* (1892–93), a rambling attack on the decay of fin-de-siècle culture. Although it focuses on the late nineteenth century, Nordau's book finds symptoms of degeneration even in some of Shakespeare's tragic characters. For instance, Nordau attributes Hamlet's weakness of will to "nervous exhaustion" or, more technically, "neuraesthenic aboulia."[63] Conversely, Nordau's generalized portrait of "the degenerate" (in a chapter titled "Fin-de-Siècle") bears a striking resemblence to Hamlet:

> With this characteristic dejectedness of the degenerate, there is combined, as a rule, a disinclination to action of any kind, attaining possibly to abhorrence of activity and powerlessness to will (*aboulia*). . . . With the incapacity for action there is connected the predilection for inane reverie. The degenerate is not in a condition to fix his attention long, or indeed at all, on any subject, . . . It is easier and more convenient for him to allow his brain-centres to produce semi-lucid, nebulously blurred ideas and inchoate embryonic thoughts, and to surrender himself to the perpetual obfuscation of a boundless, aimless, and shoreless stream of fugitive ideas; . . . He is tormented by doubts, seeks for the basis of all phenomena, especially those whose first causes are completely inacessible to us, and is unhappy when his inquiries and ruminations lead, as is natural, to no result. . . . The degenerate is incapable of adapting himself to existing circumstances.[64]

As a late-Elizabethan melancholic, Hamlet does indeed partake of a certain fin-de-siècle quality, providing Nordau with a useful instance of cul-

63. Max Nordau, *Degeneration* (New York: D. Appleton, 1895), p. 355.
64. Ibid., pp. 20–22.

tural and nervous degeneration. There is no evidence, however, that Nordau's views influenced Freud's treatment of *Hamlet*. Lacan's unusual criticism of Freud is made even stranger by the fact that Lacan seems to be projecting the theme of degeneration onto Freud's text.

In any case, with his third mention of degeneration theory Lacan seems to soften his earlier stance: "Of that which Freud himself has indicated to us, in a fashion perhaps a bit fin de siècle—that something might have doomed us no longer to live the Oedipus except in a distorted form—of that there is surely an echo in *Hamlet*" (III, 35). And as if to strengthen this notion, Lacan points out that in the title of Freud's essay "Die Untergang des Oedipus Complex," *Untergang* may indicate either "dissolution" or "decline, decadence." Ought we then to read *Hamlet* as a late, decadent form of the Oedipus legend, a kind of Oedipal *Trauerspiel?* Lacan implants the idea in a way that would seem hard to revoke, and yet he does then try to revoke it. As to the suggestions of a decadent phase of Oedipus in Freud's ambiguous title, "he meant in each individual life" (III, 36). Every one of us lives through a decadence of the Oedipus complex, and *Hamlet* does indeed illustrate the complex in its phase of decay, but this decay is staged in our individual histories, not in history as such. Thus Lacan carefully undoes the knotting together of individual and historical time that organizes Freud's discussion of *Oedipus* and *Hamlet*. Oedipus is a mythic character, not an historical one; if he "declines," he does so in a mythic way—that is, in a way that can be repeated without change. The stakes in Lacan's reading of *Hamlet* are thus very high indeed, being no less than the status of history itself within the field of psychoanalytic thought.

Lacan's lectures on *Hamlet* are organized by two competing temporalities: one based on decadence and the other based on repetition. The first of these results in an historical (entropic) loss of the past, while the second attempts to negate the first through a circular, mythic (and hence nonhistorical) return. At one level, repetition is inscribed in Lacan's very project of the "return to Freud."[65] At another, it emerges in the graphs of desire, which map out a complex circuit of (alienating) detours and (dislocating) retroversions. But within this larger machinery of repetition, how is Hamlet himself situated?

Lacan's fundamental departure from the classical Freudian reading of the play involves a shifting of attention from Hamlet's desire *for* the mother to the desire *of* the mother, or the (m)Other, on which Hamlet's

---

65. See Jacques Derrida, *The Post Card: From Socrates to Freud and Beyond*, trans. Alan Bass (Chicago: University of Chicago Press, 1987), pp. 303–4.

being depends. Hamlet is, in effect, caught within the demands of an inconsistent Other, doubly articulated as the ghost's implacable insistence on revenge and as Gertrude's seemingly voracious sexual appetite. The absolute dependence of the neurotic on the demands of the Other is manifested, moreover, though the medium of *time*. Hamlet is, as Lacan insists, "always suspended at the hour of the Other" (III, 14). For the neurotic, the time is always out of joint because it is never his hour, always the Other's:

> I have said that hysteria is characterized by the function of a desire that is unsatisfied and obsession by that of one which is impossible. But there is, beyond these two terms, an inverse relation between the one case and the other with respect to time—the obsessive procrastinates, because he always anticipates too late, while the hysteric always repeats that which is initial in his trauma, a certain too-soon, a fundamental immaturity. (III, 13)[66]

In the case of the hysteric, a premature and hence unassimilable encounter with sexuality provokes the compulsion to repeat—the Symbolic "automaton" (as Lacan calls it in the eleventh seminar) which attempts to avoid the "tuché'" of the traumatic Real. The obsessive "inverts" this repetition of the too-soon by anticipating too late: his elaborate, apotropaic ceremonies are designed to ward off a traumatic encounter which has already occurred. As Freud insists, however, obsessional neuroses always involve a "substratum of hysterical symptoms."[67] Hamlet's anguished temporality is clearly both obsessional *and* hysterical, repetitive *and* procrastinating. Moreover, as Lacan insists, these two temporal dislocations simply invert each other. Obsession is also, and equally, a structure of repetition. As Freud notes, obsessive patients "become the victims of distressing and apparently senseless ceremonials which take the form of the rhythmical repetition of the most trivial acts (such as washing or dressing) or of carrying out meaningless injunctions or of obeying mysterious prohibitions."[68] Hamlet both labors under a mysterious prohibition and carries out a meaningless injunction—meaningless not because it lacks all sense but because its ultimate effectiveness results from the

66. A line seems to be missing from the English translation of this passage ("Desire and the Interpretation of Desire in *Hamlet*"), resulting in the the attribution of the hysteric's temporality to the obsessive.

67. Sigmund Freud, "The Neuro-Psychoses of Defense," *Standard Edition*, 3:168.

68. Sigmund Freud, "The Claims of Psycho-Analysis to Scientific Interest," *Standard Edition*, 13:173.

senseless, traumatic excess that attaches to it. The absence of meaning marks a repeated act as operating under the sign of *Zwang* or compulsion, which is always a repetition-compulsion (*Wiederholungszwang*). Hamlet's subjection to this automaton, and its paradoxical temporalities, is summed up in his agonized complaint: "I do not know / Why yet I live to say, 'This thing's to do.'" (4.4.43–44). Hamlet's famous, obsessive procrastination betrays his attachment, in Lacan's reading, to an "impossible object." But since Hamlet also "speaks" Lacan, it is worth noting that the Lacanian seminar operates under an identical temporality, stretched between the poles of endless procrastination (*détour*) and insistent repetition (*retour*).

The competing Lacanian temporalities of repetition and decadence engage most directly, for Hamlet and *Hamlet*, in the problem of mourning. Lacan writes that "the Oedipus enters its decline to the degree that the subject is obliged to do his mourning for the phallus" (III, 37). The decadence or dissolution of the Oedipus complex is nothing other than this process of mourning for a loss that will never fully be made good: "Whatever sacrifice is made to the Other, the subject is never rendered his life back by the Other" (III, 37). Although the lost phallus never returns, the process of mourning is itself based in repetition: as Freud describes it, the mourned object is invoked again and again so that each of its various aspects and qualities may be de-cathected. Mourning always, therefore, has something ceremonial about it; its structure resembles that of the obsessional neurotic's repeated rituals.

The opening crisis of *Hamlet*, as Lacan construes it, is precisely a failure of mourning, marked by an insufficiency of ritual. Hamlet first encounters this problem as an external one: it is the *others*, and particularly his mother, who do not mourn. Lacan goes so far as to construct a kind of "soliloquy" for the insatiable Gertrude: "I am what I am, with me there's nothing to be done, I'm a real cunt . . . me, I don't know about mourning" (II, 23). Fully satisfied with the "real" phallus of Claudius, Gertrude does not register symbolic lack. Missing nothing, she is what she is; hence she neither obeys the law of prescribed forms nor incorporates a lost object. It is the (m)Other's insatiable demand, Lacan argues, that renders the law of the Other inconsistent for Hamlet. Put more simply, Gertrude "teaches" Hamlet how not to mourn. Despite his initial promise to "remember" the ghost (1.5.92-112), Hamlet also falls prey to procrastination; he, too, does not mourn properly. Here we must attend to Lacan's precise formulation: "The Oedipus enters its decline to the degree that the subject is obliged to do his mourning for the phallus" [*avoir à faire son deuil du phallus*] (III, 37). "Avoir à faire" means "to have to do" in the sense of being obligated to do something, but it also implies that this thing is still to be done, that it has not yet *been* done. Hence the "decline" of the Oedipus seems to turn (if we read Lacan's phrasing exactly) not on the actual act of "mourning the phallus" but on being under an injunction to mourn which has not been fulfilled. "I do not know/ Why yet I live to say, 'This thing's to do.'" (4.4.43–44).

Although Lacan insists that the "decline" of the Oedipus has only an individual and not an historical meaning, his meditations on the mourning process do imply an historical direction. In seeking to explain the problem of mourning, Lacan has recourse to Freud's myth, elaborated in *Totem and Taboo*, of the murder of the primordial father. Lacan notes that this Freudian fable is "perhaps the only example of an invented myth that comes from our historical age" (III, 34). The Freudian myth is a remnant or survival of mythic circularity in the confines of history's "one-way street":

> The relation between law and crime is one thing. Something else is that which develops from it when the tragic hero—who is Oedipus and also each one of us virtually at whatever point in our being we reproduce the Oedipal drama—renovates the law on the tragic plane and, in a sort of lustral bath, reassures its rebirth. (III, 34)

Not only does the content of myth depict the "rebirth" or "renovation" of tragic law through the hero's suffering, but we too "reproduce" the Oedipal drama by enacting it today. Repetition becomes the medium for an essentially unhistorical transmission of the Oedipus complex through time. This medium is not merely an ideal or immaterial one, however. "The tragedy of Oedipus responds strictly to a definition . . . of tragedy as ritual reproduction" (III, 34). The theater of classical Athens is a social institution in which repetition takes on an institutional, material form: *ritual* reproduction, which is in a sense the collective equivalent of the obsessional's ceremonies. If *Oedipus* represents a relatively pure (because mythic) form of repetition, this is because it is the product of a culture in which ritual, tradition, and custom still predominate. *Hamlet*, by contrast, opens with the decay of ritual—specifically, rituals of mourning.

Mourning, as Lacan describes it in the sixth seminar, is a mobilization of the entire system of signifiers in an (impossible) attempt to fill the "hole in the real" produced by the absence of the mourned individual. In place of the missing signifier that could fill this hole there come those imaginary projections of mourning, especially *ghosts*, whose appearance signifies the failure of an adequate funerary ritual. For Lacan, the ghost is less an individual than a collective delusion, and one that points to a crisis in the very structure of the Other, insofar as the latter is supported by collective social institutions:

> And in effect there is nothing of the signifier that can fill the hole in the real if it is not the totality of the signifier. The work of mourning accomplishes itself at the level of the *logos*—I say *logos* rather than *group* or *community*, although the group and the community insofar as they are culturally organized are its supports. The work of mourning is from the start a satisfaction given to the disorder produced because of the insufficiency of the signifying elements in the face of the hole created in existence. For it is the signifying system in its entirety that is placed in question by the least mourning. (III, 30–31)

Lacan is careful to avoid a sociological reduction here: it is not an insufficiency in a given cultural system of mourning but rather a lack inherent to the signifier as such, and even to the whole system of signifiers, that renders it incapable of filling the hole in the real. In this sense funerary rites are always, by definition, insufficient. Even under the best of cultural circumstances, mourning can do no more than manifest the place of a "missing" signifier whose lack renders the Other inconsistent, and hence incapable of supporting our being. Yet mourning as such is still a social activity—it pertains to a *logos* which is sustained by a set of group rituals. Mourning involves an activation, however futile, of the *system* of signifiers, which in turn assumes a certain cultural organization (and mobilization) of this system by means of ritualized institutions. *Hamlet* is marked as a "modern" play precisely because these traditional rituals of mourning are in decay, because the institutional supports of cultural repetition have ceased to work.[69] Hamlet's unceremonious stowing away of Polonius's corpse symbolizes what is for Lacan the essence of the play—"unsatisfied mourning" (III, 31). Hamlet's "modern" interiority, which distinguishes him from Oedipus, results from the breakdown of an exteriorized, collective apparatus of mourning. Oedipus simply enacts his tragic fate without thinking about it, but Hamlet falters because the institutions of the Symbolic have fallen into decay. Hamlet's dilemma arises from a modernity in which innovation has replaced the traditional machinery of ritual:

69. As Julia Reinhard Lupton points out to me, the same "modern" moment occurs in earlier works, such as *Antigone*.

The rabble call him lord,
And as the world were now but to begin,
Antiquity forgot, custom not known,
The ratifiers and props of every word,
They cry, "Choose we, Laertes shall be king!" (4.5.103–7)

In such a world, remembrance of the dead cannot be sustained—even by Hamlet himself, despite his promise to do so. All ghosts must fade.

Hamlet's modernity is, of course, Lacan's as well. For the latter it is not only Freud who threatens to disappear but Shakespeare. Near the very beginning of the *Hamlet* lectures, apropos of Hamlet's famous phrase "To be or not to be," Lacan remarks: "This formula, which gives us the style of Hamlet's position, has practically become a joke [*un canular*]. Nevertheless it remains enigmatic" (I, 7). Like the ghost itself, Hamlet's phrase has been repeated so often that it has become an empty formula, a throwaway line. The sign of modernity, as noted in the earlier discussion of Cocteau, is that repetition, divorced from ritual and custom, exhausts rather than renews.[70] The recitation of Hamlet's words in modern culture reduces them to empty signifiers, to voice without meaning, in an irreversible process of cultural entropy. To anticipate a bit, we may quote here the opening lines of Heiner Müller's *Hamletmachine*: "I was Hamlet. I stood at the shore and talked with the surf BLABLA, the ruins of Europe in back of me." Hamlet's surf is the bringer of *cultural* erosion, reducing Europe to ruins and Hamlet's once-meaningful soliloquies to insignificant babble.

And yet, for Lacan as for Cocteau, there is an enigma that survives this erosion, a secret hidden beneath the merely formulaic surface of the "password." To extract it, however, requires some care—a proper work of mourning for the culture's ghosts. It is not enough to say that Lacan, as Hamlet, will play the role of the good son, for *Hamlet* is the play defined precisely by the fact that mourning remains unsatisfied. No son, alone, is good enough or loyal enough to carry out the task properly. What is needed lies anterior to *Hamlet*, in the mythic world of *Oedipus*—a

70. Lacan's word choice is telling here. *Canular* is originally a bit of argot from the École Normale Supérieure denoting a hazing ritual imposed on new students (*Le Robert* 2:325). It is thus associated with the ritual reproduction of a venerable French institution.

Lacan alludes, once again somewhat obliquely, to a debasing repetition of Shakespeare in a footnote to "The Agency of the Letter in the Unconscious." Referring jokingly to some unkind remarks made by a "highbrow" English journalist about Racine's heroines, he claims that these remarks "incited" him "to renounce reference to the savage dramas of Shakespeare, which have become compulsional in analytical circles where they play the role of status symbol for the Philistines" (*Écrits: A Selection*, p. 176, n. 17).

ritualized, collective act of mourning, a cultural *institution* that can mobilize the entire army of signifiers. What is this institution if not the Lacanian seminar itself, with its formalized structure, its periodic rhythms, its band of sons (and daughters) gathered together, like Freud's primal horde, in memory of the father? Lacan's Shakespearean allegory is thus finally institutional, somewhat in the manner of Northrop Frye.

Also like Frye (and Cocteau), Lacan seeks to escape the direr consequences of modernity through a reversion to the archaic: in this case, the reconstitution of an organic "group" or "community" that stands against the anonymity and amnesia of a modernized, mass culture. Lacan warns that "the Oedipus complex cannot run indefinitely in forms of society that are more and more losing the sense of tragedy."[71] The Lacanian seminar is an elaborate apparatus of cultural repetition and remembrance ("Antic-tic, tic-tic, tiquity") that attempts to sustain modernity's sense of the tragic. It is a machinery for mourning and a mournful machinery—a Hamletmachine.

Heiner Müller

The Germans have a penchant for mechanizing *Hamlet.* The year 1977 witnessed the publication of *Hamletmachine* by the East German playwright Heiner Müller, while in West Germany, Peter Zadek produced Shakespeare's play in an abandoned factory.[72] The year 1979 saw the first production of *Hamletmachine* as well as Hansgünther Heyme's "electronic" *Hamlet.* Heyme's production included "a strip of eighteen television monitors and a video camera that actors occasionally turned on each other or themselves and whose pictures then appeared eighteen times in a row on the monitors. Electronic gadgets (transistors, pocket computers, walkie-talkies, microphones, cassette recorders) were handled by the actors during most of the scenes. . . . The actors divided their attention between the action itself and the recording and transmitting of it by one of these mediums."[73] This somewhat heavy-handed invocation of Walter Benjamin on mechanical reproducibility does at least render visible the problems of repetition and tradition that afflict *Hamlet* production. It also gives an intriguingly simulacral turn to the problem of split consciousness in Shakespeare's play:

71. Lacan, *Écrits: A Selection,* p. 310.
72. See Wilhelm Hortmann, "Changing Modes in *Hamlet* Production: Rediscovering Shakespeare after the Iconoclasts," in Habicht et al., *Images of Shakespeare,* p. 224.
73. Ibid., p. 226.

The most extreme form of this schizoidism occurred in the figure of Hamlet, who was played by two actors. The Hamlet onstage was almost beyond speech and incapable of contact, lost in the crude sexual fantasies of his subconscious and reduced largely to gestures and to a wondering preoccupation with his own body, which he studied in poses and grimaces in front of the video camera. Meanwhile, his alter ego in the auditorium (the director) spoke the monologues and part of the dialogues over the theater's amplifier system.[74]

Here Jacques Lacan meets German engineering. Heyme's Hamlet is parceled rather precisely among the Imaginary and the Symbolic registers. But the result does not simply instantiate the Lacanian subject through electronic media; rather, it effects a simulacral reinterpretation or restaging of Lacanian theory itself. To what degree, it seems to ask, is the orthopaedic dimension of the Imaginary bound up with the invention of film (and later video) technologies whose images seem "more real" than life itself? To what degree is the Lacanian Other dependent for its theoretical conceptualization on the advent of devices such as the radio and the loudspeaker, which abstract the order-word from any bodily incarnation and thus finally produce the disembodied voice of God?[75] Heyme's production can be read most valuably as giving a technological turn to the Lacanian reading of *Hamlet*. It does not cancel or even critique that reading but simply embodies the latter's own exteriorizing movement in an actual, material apparatus.

Something similar occurs in *Hamletmachine*, but Müller's interests are more political than technological. The play was, in fact, composed under the direct pressure of political events. Although published twenty years later, the first scenes were written shortly after the Hungarian revolt of

74. Ibid., pp. 226–27.
75. I use the phrase "the order-word" advisedly in order to invoke the chapter of that name in Deleuze and Guattari's *A Thousand Plateaus*. Of particular interest is the still from Fritz Lang's film *The Cabinet of Dr. Mabuse* which prefaces that chapter.

Lacan relates Hamlet's mysterious refusal to assassinate Claudius to the shadowy status of the phallus, which can never really be incarnated as an actual object. Interestingly, in the course of this discussion Lacan revives the old question of why Hitler wasn't assassinated, and he answers by identifying Hitler as the mysterious "object x" that homogenizes the crowd through identification (III, 42). He then returns to Hamlet and notes that Hamlet doesn't kill Claudius because "he knows that he has to strike something else than that which is there"—i.e., he has to strike the shadowy phallus itself. Here the rather abrupt and surprising excursus on Hitler casts a valuable political light on Lacan's conception of the phallus. One does not assassinate Hitler because what one must strike is not the body but a charisma which is both constituted and dispersed through electronic media: the loudspeaker, the radio, film. Hitler-as-phallus is the effect of mechanical disembodiment and thus can be found nowhere.

1956 and bear its imprint.[76] Rewriting Shakespeare's play in the context of Stalinist bureaucracy, *Hamletmachine* explores the role of the intellectual and the shape of history in the context of modern class and gender struggles.

As in the Freudian and Lacanian readings of the play, Hamlet's hesitation is attributed to his status as "split subject." For Müller, however, Hamlet's self-divisions are socially, not psychoanalytically, defined. In an interview, Müller described *Hamletmachine* as, in part, an exploration of the conflicted class position of the intellectuals, who are at once members of the middle class yet critical of the system that grants them their comforts: "You get into the establishment by fighting it. . . . But then you're 'in' and live in the dilemma that you belong, yet don't like to."[77] For Müller's Hamlet, the intellectual-as-functionary, this internalized class division becomes an actual mitosis or self-splitting during the section of the play describing the Budapest uprising of 1956:

> My place, if my drama would still happen, would be on both sides of the front, between the frontlines, over and above them. I stand in the stench of the crowd and hurl stones at policemen soldiers tanks bullet-proof glass. I look through the double doors of bullet-proof glass at the crowd pressing forward and smell the sweat of my fear. Choking with nausea, I shake my fist at myself who stands behind the bullet-proof glass. Shaking with fear and contempt, I see myself in the crowd pressing forward, foaming at the mouth, shaking my fist at myself. I string up my uniformed flesh by my own heels. I am the soldier in the gun turret, my head is empty under the helmet, the stifled scream under the tracks. I am the typewriter [*Ich bin die Schreibmaschine*]. I tie the noose when the ringleaders are strung up, I pull the stool from under their feet, I break my own neck. I am my own prisoner. I feed my own data into the computers. . . . I am the data bank. (p. 56)

76. Heiner Müller, *Hamletmachine and Other Texts for the Stage*, ed. and trans. Carl Weber (New York: Performing Arts Journal Publications, 1984), editor's introduction, p. 23. For a sustained political reading of *Hamletmachine* see Arlene Akiko Teraoka, *The Silence of Entropy or Universal Discourse: The Postmodern Politics of Heiner Müller* (New York: Peter Lang, 1985), pp. 87–121. See also Johannes Birringer, *Theatre, Theory, Postmodernism* (Bloomington: Indiana University Press, 1991), pp. 86–90.

77. Müller, quoted in Carl Weber's introduction to *Hamletmachine*, p. 15. Conceiving of Hamlet as an intellectual allows for an autobiographical reading of the character, as in the case of Lacan. Müller both plays with the formula "Hamletmachine=H.M.=Heiner Müller" (interview with Müller, quoted in *Hamletmachine*, p. 51) and has a photograph of himself displayed and torn in half as part of the play, mirroring Hamlet's own self-division.

Here the Freudian postulate of Hamlet's conflicting desires becomes two conflicting Hamlets; the character who meditates on suicide in Shakespeare's play actually strings himself up; the Lacanian "bar" turns into barricades. Yet if *Hamletmachine* attaches the phenomenon of self-splitting to social antagonism, it does not do so in a way that would reduce the former to a mere function of the latter. Or at least, it does not proffer utopian hopes that either can be healed, nor does it dream of that unified or harmonious subject which, as thinkers from Adorno to Žižek have insisted, is among the most dangerous of political mirages.[78] Rather, Müller's technique of the "synthetic fragment" enables the psychic and the political to be patched together without dissolving either term, and without losing sight of the collective dimensions of antagonism.

Müller, for instance, retains the Freudian reading of Hamlet but coarsens and externalizes it. *Hamletmachine* opens with the state funeral of Hamlet's father, a Stalinist tyrant:

> The bells tolled the state-funeral, murderer and widow a couple, the councillors goose-stepping behind the highranking carcass' coffin,. . . . I stopped the funeral procession, I pried open the coffin with my sword, the blade broke, yet with the blunt remainder I succeeded, and I dispensed my dead procreator FLESH LIKES TO KEEP THE COMPANY OF FLESH among the bums around me. The mourning turned into rejoicing, the rejoicing into lipsmacking, on top of the empty coffin the murderer humped the widow LET ME HELP YOU UP, UNCLE, OPEN YOUR LEGS, MAMA. I laid down on the ground and listened to the world doing its turns in step with the putrefaction. (p. 53)

Subjecting the Oedipal theme to the techniques of baroque *Trauerspiel* and its modernist avatar, expressionism, Müller's play invests it with a quality at once disgusting and parodic. The Oedipal father is refigured and distended into a collective, political entity: "paternalism, the disease of all Communist parties." "Socialist cultural policy," notes Müller, "posthumously cemented the father-figure."[79] In *Hamletmachine*, the ghost is the frozen paternalism of the Party, society's Other, literally "cemented" into a gigantic monument whose nostrils and ear canals are inhabited by impoverished citizens. Although this monument disinte-

78. See Slavoj Žižek, *The Metastases of Enjoyment: Six Essays on Women and Causality* (London: Verso, 1994), pp. 7–28.

79. Müller, quoted in Carl Weber's introduction to *Hamletmachine*, p. 18.

grates, it is never cleared away but persists as a rubble pile or Benjaminian ruin through which the play's characters stumble.

Hamletmachine is, in fact, suffused with references to Benjamin, from Hamlet's announcement that "A MOTHER'S WOMB IS NOT A ONE-WAY STREET" to Horatio's appearance in scene three as an angel with its head turned backwards, an allusion to the "Angelus Novus" of Benjamin's "Theses on the Philosophy of History."[80] In particular, Müller draws on Benjamin's critique of a linear, progressive conception of history which by Müller's day has passed from bourgeois (and social democratic) theory into Stalinist rhetoric. History has now become a ruin, a growing pile of debris, a gray succession of bureaucratic rulers: "The set is a monument. It presents a man who made history, enlarged a hundred times. The petrification of a hope. The name is interchangeable, the hope has not been fulfilled. The monument is toppled into the dust, three years after the state funeral of the hated and most honored leader" (p. 56). Even revolution itself has been absorbed into this performance of state: "After an appropriate period, the uprising follows the toppling of the monument" (p. 56). Müller's critical vision, however, extends beyond the "real socialist" states of the Eastern bloc to include the pacifying, mediatized cultures of the West: "Television The daily nausea Nausea / Of prefabricated babble Of decreed cheerfulness / How do you spell GEMÜTLICHKEIT" (pp. 56–57). The Stalinist state machine is merely one incarnation of the instrumental reason endemic to industrial societies. Writes Müller: "If one starts with the assumption that capitalist societies, indeed every industrial society, the GDR included, tends to repress and instrumentalize imagination—to throttle it—then for me the political task of art today is precisely the mobilization of imagination."[81] In *Hamletmachine,* Hamlet's split consciousness involves not just conflicting political affiliations but a contradictory response to just such a totalized, industrialized milieu. His monologues oscillate between agonized protest against the state and industrial apparatuses in which he is suspended and a desire to abdicate struggle and even consciousness itself: "My thoughts are lesions in my brain. My brain is a scar. I want to be a machine" (p. 57). In Hamlet's traumatized brain, the Benjaminian "shock experience" of modern life crystallizes as physical scar tissue. The desire to be a machine registers the agony of "mobilizing the imagination" against society's instrumental reason, the temptation simply to cease to strive and thus to become an unthinking cog. When Hamlet says

80. See Teraoka, *Silence of Entropy,* p. 96.
81. Müller, quoted in *Hamletmachine,* p. 138.

"I am the typewriter. . . . I am the data banks" he imagines the sublimely neutral state of being a mechanical device which submits itself without protest to the instrumental purposes of whatever hand seizes it. In industrialized society, the death drive—and with it Hamlet's notoriously suicidal urge—takes as its goal not actual death but mechanized obedience, the willingness to fulfil whatever task the system demands and to accept whatever pleasures or rewards the system offers.

What is most terrifying about Müller's play, perhaps, is that the industrialized condition not only occurs within history—which might then offer a path beyond it—but captures and defines the rhythms of history itself. *Hamletmachine* takes place in the interstitial space between Stalinist rulers, each of whom is merely a repetition of his predecessor. This transitional moment offers a seeming opportunity to throw the state machine off kilter, but the uprising itself has already been absorbed into the script of the official pageantry. In scene 4, "PEST IN BUDA / BATTLE FOR GREENLAND," Hamlet removes his makeup and costume, and the actor playing him announces: "I'm not Hamlet. I don't take part any more. My words have nothing to tell me anymore. My thoughts suck the blood out of the images. My drama doesn't happen anymore. Behind me the set is put up. By people who aren't interested in my drama, for people to whom it means nothing. I'm not interested in it anymore either. I won't play along anymore" (p. 56). He then goes on to describe the giant stone monument of the defunct leader and the uprising that tears him (Hamlet) in two. What is interesting about this moment is that it welds the numbing, repetitive succession of Stalinist tyrants to the numbing, repetitive enactment of *Hamlet*. Not only does Shakespeare's play empty out its own meaning through constant performance, but in doing so it symbolizes the performance of history, which has become unendurably routinized, and thus caught in the toils of the Hamletmachine.

Müller's Hamlet is no revolutionary, but an intellectual whose political vacillations only reinforce the logic of repetition. A peculiar sequence in scene 4 illustrates his equivocal role in the historical process:

TV screens go black. Blood oozes from the refrigerator. Three naked women: Marx, Lenin, Mao. They speak simultaneously, each one in his own language, the text:
THE MAIN POINT IS TO OVERTHROW ALL EXISTING CONDITIONS . . .
The actor of Hamlet puts on make-up and costume.
HAMLET THE DANE PRINCE AND MAGGOT'S FODDER
STUMBLING FROM HOLE TO HOLE TOWARDS THE FINAL
HOLE LISTLESS IN HIS BACK THE GHOST THAT ONCE

MADE HIM GREEN LIKE OPHELIA'S FLESH IN CHILDBED
AND SHORTLY ERE THE THIRD COCK'S CROW A CLOWN
WILL TEAR THE FOOL'S CAP OFF THE PHILOSOPHER
A BLOATED BLOODHOUND'LL CRAWL INTO THE ARMOR
He steps into the armor, splits with the ax the heads of Marx, Lenin, Mao. Snow.
Ice Age. (pp. 57–58)

Arlene Akiko Teraoka interprets Hamlet's role in this scene as that of "the bourgeois hero become counterrevolutionary."[82] Splitting the heads that call for revolutionary change, Hamlet ushers in the ice age that Teraoka identifies with capitalism. This passage is clearly about the petrification of revolutionary hope, as Teraoka correctly argues, but the threat to this hope is more complex than she suggests. For one thing, Hamlet assumes his counterrevolutionary role by donning the armor of his father, the "highranking carcass" (p. 53) whose state funeral provides the setting for *Hamletmachine*. Hamlet brings on the ice age, then, by reincarnating the paternal legacy and thus perpetuating the endless series of Stalinist rulers. Müller's grotesque portrayals of Marx, Lenin, and Mao do enunciate a revolutionary slogan, but Müller's skepticism toward linear, progressive models of history would prevent him from viewing this genealogical series in an entirely favorable light. One might best read it as a continuation of Valéry's formula, "Kant, qui genuit Hegel, qui genuit Marx . . ."[83] Müller's "Holy Family" extends this patrilineal series and moreover renders visible its status as an impossible bachelor machine by perching gigantic male heads on top of female bodies.

"Official" Marxism, Müller seems to be saying, simply redoubles bourgeois models of history instead of breaking with them. The call to revolution has been co-opted by the state, producing only "revolution" in the etymological sense—a circular movement that returns to its starting point, generating new "leaders" in much the same way that the mythic cycles of classical tragedy, as described by Lacan and Benjamin, renovate the Law. *Hamletmachine*, a play seemingly devoid of utopian content, offers no "genuine" revolutionary solution to this dilemma; instead, it depicts two unsatisfactory alternatives. The first of these might be called dilapidated repetition—a continuation of the circular or mythic model, but one that increasingly succumbs to its own entropy. Dilapidated rep-

---

82. Teraoka, *Silence of Entropy*, p. 109.

83. Paul Valéry, "La Crise de l'esprit," in his *Oeuvres* (Paris: Gallimard, Bibliothèque de la Pléiade, 1957), 1:993, cited in Jacques Derrida, *Spectres of Marx: The State of the Debt, the Work of Mourning, and the New International*, trans. Peggy Kamuf (New York: Routledge, 1994), p. 5.

etition bears a strong resemblance to the fading I described in Cocteau, but it replaces images of disappearance or ghostly attenuation with those of crumbling or falling into ruin. This is Hamlet's model of history, and it represents the fate of the ruling system if left to pursue its own course.

A second, more contestatory model is offered by Ophelia, the only other Shakespearean character actually to appear in *Hamletmachine*. Müller's Ophelia is modeled not only on the Shakespearean original but also on the Marxist revolutionary Rosa Luxemburg, the terrorist Ulrike Meinhoff (of the "Baader-Meinhoff gang" of the 1960s), and the Charles Manson follower Susan Atkins.[84] Unlike Hamlet, who only *wants* to be a machine, this Ophelia has a clock for a heart. She shares Hamlet's weariness with his role, however:

> I am Ophelia. The one the river didn't keep. The woman dangling from the rope. The woman with her arteries cut open. . . . Yesterday I stopped killing myself. . . . I smash the tools of my captivity, the chair the table the bed. . . . With my bleeding hands I tear the photos of the men I loved and who used me on the bed on the table on the chair on the ground. I set fire to my prison. I throw my clothes into the fire. I wrench the clock that was my heart out of my breast. I walk into the street clothed in my blood. (pp. 54–55)

Hamlet splits in two and occupies both sides of the barricade, but Ophelia smashes the machinery of her repression, thereby freeing herself from indefinite repetition of her role. Yet her triumph does not ring in utopia. Instead, it ends the world:

> I eject all the sperm I have received. I turn the milk of my breasts into lethal poison. I take back the world I gave birth to. I choke between my thighs the world I gave birth to. I bury it in my womb. Down with the happiness of submission. Long live hate and contempt, rebellion and death. When she walks through your bedrooms carrying butcher knives you'll know the truth. (p. 58)

The clock that Ophelia carried in her breast represents both the bad circularity of history and the reproductive cycle in which she was held captive. She liberates herself from both of these by reclaiming her womanly capacity to propagate the world. Adopting the politics of the death drive, Ophelia rejects Hamlet's model of dilapidated repetition, opting

---

84. Teraoka, *Silence of Entropy*, pp. 110–11.

instead for one immense "revolution" in which everything is reabsorbed into its maternal source and smothered there, in a kind of implosive sequel to the original Big Bang. The rest is silence.

Arnold Schwarzenegger

Arnold Schwarzenegger's film career went into brief spasm when the megahit *Terminator 2: Judgment Day* (1991) was followed by the megaflop *The Last Action Hero* (1993). Combining an action film with a wry, self-consciously postmodern spoof of such films, *The Last Action Hero* wanted to be by turns exciting, ironic, magical, and heartwarming, and it collapsed under the weight of its incoherent intentions. The story centers on Danny Mattigan, a young, fatherless boy who spends his days watching action films in a dilapidated theater on Times Square. Danny's favorite hero is Jack Slater, a shoot-'em-up LAPD detective played by Schwarzenegger. A magical ticket (originally Houdini's, and provided by the kindly old duffer who runs the theater) allows Danny to enter Jack Slater's film world. It also enables Slater and several screen villains to enter *Danny's* world, where, among other nefarious doings, they attempt to assassinate the actor Schwarzenegger at the premiere of his newest "Jack Slater" film.

While undeniably a failure, *The Last Action Hero* contains some redeeming moments, among them a brief, funny send-up of *Hamlet.* The scene begins in Danny's English class, where the predictably frumpy, middle-aged teacher tries in vain to interest her students in Shakespeare's play. "Treachery, conspiracy, sex, swords, . . . madness, ghosts," she promises. "And in the end, everybody dies."[85] She continues: "Shakespeare's *Hamlet* couldn't be more exciting. Now though it may seem that he is incapable of taking any action, he is in fact one of the first action heroes. What you are about to see is a scene from the film by Laurence Olivier. Some of you might have seen him in the Polaroid commercial (she sniffs), or as Zeus in 'Clash of the Titans.' " On the screen appears act 3, scene 3 of Olivier's production: Claudius kneels at the altar, Hamlet raises his knife to strike but then, catching sight of a saint's image, backs off. Danny's face is lit with anticipation of the blow; his hand grips an invisible knife. Disappointed with Hamlet's failure, he urges, "Don't talk, just *do* it!" Danny then fantasizes a movie trailer for his ideal remake of

---

85. *The Last Action Hero*, dir. John McTiernan (Columbia Pictures, 1993). I have placed ellipses in the quotation in place of an unintelligible word.

Hamlet, with Schwarzenegger in the title role. In a simulation of Olivier's black-and-white Elsinore, the muscled Arnold/Hamlet intones: "Hey Claudius, you killed my father. *Big* mistake!" He lifts Claudius up by the collar and flings him, backwards, through a stained-glass window, from which he plummets to his death. Cheesy, movie-ad voiceover: "Something's rotten in the state of Denmark. And Hamlet is takin' out the trash!" Cut to Arnold/Hamlet, seated outside in the graveyard, contemplating the skull of Yorick. He suddenly turns and flings the skull with precision, braining an approaching soldier. Arnold/Hamlet rampages through Elsinore, dispatching Polonius and various soldiers with an Uzi. Cheesy voiceover: "No one's going to tell *this* sweet prince good night!" Final cut to Arnold/Hamlet outdoors, Elsinore visible over his shoulder. "To be or not to be—*not to be*." (Arnold's distinctive Teutonic drawl.) He clicks open his lighter, lights the cigar. The black-and-white Elsinore detonates in Technicolor explosions and flame.

The Last Action Hero shares with almost all the other works considered in this chapter a presumption that *Hamlet* is, in some sense, obsolete. Shakespeare's Hamlet, the last *inaction* hero, clearly has no future with the Nintendo generation. Both his metaphysical ramblings and his military technology are hopelessly outdated. Refashioning *Hamlet* for our times requires pruning for the attention-deficient (Danny's *Hamlet* lasts about two minutes). It also demands a new kind of hero, a Terminator-Hamlet who kills automatically, remorselessly. The film's rendition/reduction of Hamlet's famous "To be or not to be" drains it of all Oedipal ambivalence and existential anguish. As mouthed by Schwarzenegger, the line simply operates a binary gate or switching mechanism—1 or 0, 2B or not 2B.[86] It no longer designates a frozen dilemma but simply bifurcates a flow chart of instantaneous options. Hamlet is no longer a "character" in the traditional sense, certainly not a hesitant or indecisive one, but a Turing machine into which input is fed and from which output—mostly violent—can be retrieved in microseconds. Terminator-Hamlet embodies the suspicion of some theorists of artificial intelligence that consciousness is, strictly speaking, a kind of unnecessary appendage to the workings of our brains. If Olivier's *Hamlet* exemplifies the classical Freudian reading of the play, *The Last Action Hero* effects a paradigm shift in which the subject of psychoanalysis gives way to the algorithms of cognitive science.[87]

86. A hacker T-shirt presents the "2B or not 2B" in the form of a gate diagram.

87. Lupton and Reinhard argue convincingly that the Zeffirelli *Hamlet* is to the Olivier *Hamlet* as Lacan is to Freud. See *After Oedipus*, pp. 82–88.

Ironically, in projecting the play into the future, the film version also drives it into the past, since Shakespeare's Hamlet is defined in part by his "lateness" and inadequacy with respect to an ideal of epic heroism which Schwarzenegger revives.[88] Terminator-Hamlet reveals his original to be, by contrast, an *Interminator*, meaning both that he cannot bring himself to kill (himself or others) and that he cannot, more generally, bring anything to a conclusion. Hamlet's role as the patron saint of psychoanalysis, the "analysis interminable," arises not only from his Oedipal posture but from a style and rhythm of dilation which might prove attractive to Freud, but not to Danny Mattigan. "Don't talk, just *do* it!" Danny's motto enunciates a general cultural imperative which embraces everything from Nike ads to the neo-pragmatist and New Historicist impatience with literary theory. A culture of technical performativity which defines progress largely as a function of speed will (perhaps rightly) find that it lacks the time for Hamlet or Freud. Hence Schwarzenegger doesn't flail about helplessly trying to speak Shakespearean English; rather, he seeks out those elements of Terminator-speech already embedded in *Hamlet*. The famous line "To be or not to be" is, as it happens, composed entirely of monosyllables, as are the Terminator's most memorable quips, such as "I'll be back" and "Get out!" By paring away Hamlet's loquaciousness, Schwarzenegger arrives at a deadly efficiency of speech.

The satire of this sequence, of course, is not all directed against *Hamlet*. It also includes some good-humored self-mockery of Schwarzenegger's own rather limited acting skills. But while his performance may be contrasted unfavorably with Olivier's, it perfectly embodies the deep logic of the Hamletmachine, and thus, in a certain sense, ascends from the ludicrous to the inevitable. The bodybuilder's physique, Schwarzenegger's initial and (to some degree) continuing claim to cinematic attention, is of course constructed through the most intimate relation with the machine. But this physique is not a machine—or rather, it embodies the *paradox* of the machine, since it can actually do less and less as it develops. What the powerlifter gains in bulk he loses in agility, thus becoming largely useless for actual work. Instead, he himself becomes a "work" of art as instrumentality inverts itself and produces the aesthetic. Of course, this fact is suppressed in the typical Schwarzenegger film, which represents his lumbering torso as swift and efficient. It reemerges, however, in his speech. Nothing could be more wrong than regarding Schwarzenegger's labored manner of speaking as a drawback—for his mouth, in tan-

88. On *Hamlet*'s revision of the heroic ideal, see ibid., 43 and 111, n. 21.

dem with his body, may well be the key to his success. Words do not so much emerge from his mouth as become entangled in it. Saying them is always an effort, like a power lift; a single sentence often seems to exhaust him. This is why his acting consists mostly of short phrases, which are powerful because, at some level, even these misfire. Schwarzenegger's speech, at once clumsy and tinged with a strange voluptuousness, projects the failure of instrumentality which his persona otherwise elides.[89] It is not the disappointing correlate or consequence of his body's visual presence; it is, rather, that body's most intimate testimony, the admission of a mechanical failure lurking at the heart of perfection. In describing Schwarzenegger's acting style one must above all avoid the clichéd adjective "wooden." It is not wooden but metallic—mineral acting. Schwarzenegger's Hamlet is thus not a degenerate or inferior counterpart to Olivier's; rather, it unleashes the machine that has always ticked, and ticked badly, inside of Hamlet.

William Shakespeare/Sigmund Freud

Precisely because they do not form a tradition, the works I have examined in this chapter are all the more striking in their insistence on depicting Hamlet as a machine, and moreover as a machine whose manner of operation seems to be generally agreed upon. Of the Hamletmachine, two general principles may be stated. It repeats; and something is lodged within it that encumbers, delays, or prevents repetition. But what is it about Hamlet that causes modern readers to glimpse in him, more than in any of Shakespeare's other characters, a metallic shimmer? While it would be absurd to claim that Hamlet "is" an automaton, surely *something* in the play triggers this shared intuition. Hamlet does, as we have seen, describe his body as a machine and indirectly compare himself to a puppet. But does the play nurture these brief intimations of the mechanical? And if so, what is a Hamletmachine, and how does it (not) work?

89. Schwarzenegger's original, "hard" persona has of course been progressively softened, beginning with *Kindergarten Cop*. In *Terminator 2* and *The Last Action Hero* he becomes the nurturing (if still murderous) father; in *True Lies* he is the henpecked (if still murderous) husband; while in *Junior* he actually becomes pregnant and gives birth. Another way of putting what I have been arguing here is that Schwarzenegger's original persona elided the *maternal*, and that the pleasure of his films has become increasingly organized around observing the emergence of this maternal/real.

In act 2, scene 2, Polonius insists to the Queen that Hamlet's antic disposition is a sign of madness:

> Mad let us grant him then, and now remains
> That we find out the cause of this effect,
> Or rather say, the cause of this defect,
> For this effect defective comes by cause:
> Thus it remains, and the remainder thus. (2.2.100–104)

A good Aristotelian, Polonius knows that there are no effects without causes. If Hamlet is mad, his madness occupies the linear chain of causality that governs the natural world and thereby grants it a predictable, mechanical regularity. It is because his body inhabits this chain of causes that Hamlet himself can describe it as a "machine." But Polonius, irrepressible rhetorician, then gives "effect" a turn, making it "*defect*"; whereupon it not only indicates Hamlet's mental debility but at least partly dislocates or disables the causal chain itself. This new principle of cause-and-defect jams the machinery of the world, making it stutter or catch—as exemplified by Polonius's own speech, which begins to seize up in repetitive spasms.

The law of cause-and-defect describes not only Hamlet's feigned madness but, in a larger sense, the structure of *Hamlet* itself. Impatient to learn the whole truth of his father's death, Hamlet urges the ghost:

> Haste me to know't, that I with wings as swift
> As meditation, or the thoughts of love,
> May sweep to my revenge. (1.5.29–31)

Vengeance, promises Hamlet, will be immediate and automatic—almost a reflex response to what he will hear. But despite this vow, his father's "cause" engenders no immediate effect in the son. Instead, the gears of revenge tragedy slowly grind to a halt. The machinery of *Hamlet* operates a new motive principle, enunciated by Polonius, in which effects become detached from causes. But Polonius's "effect defective" also, I would argue, defines the play's response to Oedipal tradition, for *Hamlet* "repeats" its Oedipal model in a broken or dilapidated fashion. The play, moreover, represents its own mode of repetition in the form of a writing machine which turns out, in fact, to be an erasing machine.

When Heiner Müller's Hamlet announces "Ich bin die Schreibmaschine," we should take this term to mean not only "typewriter" but also, more literally, "writing machine." Shakespeare's Hamlet is, or at least aspires to be, such a machine. To the ghost's admonition, "Remember me," Hamlet responds:

> Remember thee!
> Yea, from the table of my memory
> I'll wipe away all trivial fond records,
> All saws of books, all forms, all pressures past
> That youth and observation copied there,
> And thy commandment all alone shall live
> Within the book and volume of my brain,
> Unmix'd with baser matter. (1.5.97–104)

Hamlet describes his memory as a copybook recording the Father's will. It is as if the living brain were too unreliable a medium and had to be replaced with a more permanent, because inorganic, surface. Hamlet has seen how quickly his father's memory disappeared from the Danish court, so it is not surprising that he seeks a more durable model for inscription. In fact, his language seems to gesture even beyond the image of the copybook. "Thy commandment all alone shall live" summons up—oddly—the figure of Moses carving the Ten Commandments into the stone tables. While Joyce's Stephen Dedalus construes Hamlet as Christ figure sacrificed to the will of the ghostly Father, Hamlet himself evokes the still more obdurate, Hebraic letter of the law. He is the perfect writing machine, flawlessly reproducing a message that can never fade.

In fantasizing the immaculate reproduction of paternal law, Hamlet's writing machine provides an image for tradition or cultural propagation in general. It also, therefore, reflects on *Hamlet*'s place in tradition, by which I mean both the play's putatively filial relation to its dramatic models and its ability to project an ideal future reception. The Mosaic paradigm promises an unchanging reinsciption that will come to define the *Hamlet*-machine as well as the Hamletmachine.

But of course, Hamlet's writing machine does not live up to its ideal portrait. Precisely because the Father's commandment is a reinscription rather than an originary inscription, a prior writing must be erased to make room for it ("I'll wipe away all trivial fond records"). But the fact that this recording surface is erasable means that it cannot be relied upon to sustain the new message. If it can be erased once, it can be erased again. The Father's commandment may fade, and it does precisely that over the course of the play. As the Player King observes:

Purpose is but the slave to memory,
Of violent birth, but poor validity, . . .
What to ourselves in passion we propose,
The passion ending, doth the purpose lose. (3.2.188–89, 194–95)

Hamlet's writing machine thus instantiates the "effect defective" of Polonian physics.

This discussion of memory, permanent inscriptions and erasable surfaces must inevitably summon up Freud's famous essay of 1925, "A Note upon the 'Mystic Writing Pad.' " In that essay Freud uses the child's toy known in German as the *Wunderblock* to represent the psychic mechanisms of consciousness and memory. In particular, Freud addresses something he had been pondering since the time of the *Project for a Scientific Psychology*: the fact that consciousness and memory seem to be mutually exclusive functions.[90] Memory, Freud observes, requires the laying down of permanent traces of an event whereas consciousness requires a constant receptivity to new stimuli and thus must erase experiences as soon as they are registered. Freud therefore assigns memory and consciousness to different psychic systems, Ucs. (unconscious) and Pcpt.-Cs. (perception-consciousness) respectively. In "A Note upon the 'Mystic Writing Pad,' " Freud examines different writing technologies as metaphors for these psychic systems. Pen and paper produce permanent traces, but once the paper is filled with marks it has exhausted its capacity. Slate and chalk can be used again and again, but the marks produced are not permanent. In the child's toy known as the *Wunderblock*, these two models are combined. The *Wunderblock* is a slab of dark wax to which is attached a double layer consisting of a piece of waxed paper and, on top of that, transparent celluloid. When a stylus is pressed down on the celluloid surface, it causes the waxed paper immediately beneath to adhere to the wax, producing a darker color than the surrounding paper. One can thus write on the pad and later erase the message by lifting the waxed paper and celluloid covering. Freud compares the erasable upper layers to the system Pcpt.-Cs. and the wax slab beneath, in which all inscriptions are permanently retained, to the system Ucs. The technology of the *Wunderblock* solves, by distributing between two different components, the double requirements of retaining and erasing inscriptions. It also provides Freud with something he had long sought: an adequate metaphor for his

90. Jacques Derrida traces this problem in his essay "Freud and the Scene of Writing" in *Writing and Difference*, trans. Alan Bass (Chicago: University of Chicago Press, 1978), pp. 196–231.

theorization of psychic systems. But *Hamlet*, as well as Hamlet, "lacks" this solution—by which I mean that the play's action (or lack of action) depends on a contradictory, overlapping bond between writing and erasure. The Hamletmachine is a writing machine that does not work.

What is a writing machine, and how is it figured in *Hamlet*? A writing machine consists, at the most basic level, of an inscribing instrument (pen, pencil, stylus, etc.) and a recording surface (paper, wax, clay, etc.) In *Hamlet*, as in Shakespeare's plays generally, these elements are gendered: men are inscribing instruments, women are recording surfaces. Hermione in *The Winter's Tale* produces a child who is "the very print of the father" while Hermia in *A Midsummer Night's Dream* is compared to wax bearing her father's seal.[91] When Hamlet says "And thy commandment all alone shall live / Within the book and volume of my brain, / Unmix'd with baser matter," he apportions these two roles between his parents. "Baser matter" seems to refer not only to unimportant messages that will be erased to make room for the father's law but also to the recording surface on which that law will be inscribed. "Matter," moreover, is etymologically related to *mater* (mother), a fact that *Hamlet* repeatedly emphasizes.[92] In *Hamlet*'s figural register, King Hamlet becomes the author of an ideal, dematerialized writing (doubling his status as ghost) while Gertrude serves as the "base" recording surface whose materiality threatens to contaminate or eradicate the paternal script. At the level of character, King Hamlet issues the command to remember while Gertrude, as Lacan points out, just as insistently forgets. Gertrude, like the celluloid of the *Wunderblock*, does not retain traces of the past. Her desiring flesh offers only a spongy recording surface on which the imperatives of cultural law soon fade, like a message written in wet sand. Hamlet's ideal writing machine would include a block of unchanging, Mosaic stone. The writing machine he actually possesses, however, consists of a paternal stylus and a maternal recording surface that obliterates whatever is stored on it.

Hamlet's writing machine governs the play's Oedipal plot by interfering with the father's commandment. The Oedipus can never fully "take" on Hamlet because the maternal flesh on which it is written keeps deleting it. Hence, despite Hamlet's promises to his father, his resolution is always fading. Hamlet's "problem" is not that he is *too* Oedipal but

91. In *The Taming of the Shrew*, the licensing phrase *cum privilegio ad impremendum solum* ("with right of sole printing") is applied to Lucentio's exclusive sexual rights to Bianca (4.4.93).

92. "Now, mother, what's the matter?" asks Hamlet at 3.4.8. Compare 3.2.324–25: "Therefore no more, but to the matter: my mother, you say—"

that he isn't Oedipal enough: the guilt that should drive him to avenge his father's death disappears just when he most needs it. While the classic Freudian reading of the play sees Hamlet as trapped between two insistent but contradictory desires (kill Claudius because he killed your father and took your mother; don't kill Claudius because you, too, wanted to kill your father and take your mother), I would argue that the play depicts a failing or petering out of desire. Or if this seems too strong a claim, I would at least suggest that Hamlet's Oedipal posture is further complicated by a kind of internal entropy. Yes, his tragedy is an Oedipal one, but if Hamlet is the "modern" Oedipus, he becomes so by virtue of a tendency to lose interest in his own dilemma. Hamlet is bored with Oedipus.

It is in response to his waning of desire that Hamlet must repeatedly invent external supplements to whip himself up to the required level of interest. Chief among these is "The Murder of Gonzago," which restages the original crime less for Claudius's benefit than for Hamlet's. "The play's the thing / Wherein I'll catch the conscience of the King" (2.2.604-5). These lines suggest not only Hamlet's plan to catch Claudius but also his desire to "catch" a conscience, much in the way that one might catch a cold. Staging "The Murder of Gonzago" will reinscribe onto Hamlet the Oedipal guilt and longing which he already feels slipping away from him. Only by means of an external apparatus, a constructed machinery of desire, can Hamlet maintain focus on his mission.[93]

To identify an anoedipal Hamlet is not to reject a psychoanalytic reading, but simply to insert Oedipus into the mystic writing pad, where he is subject to erasure as well as reinscription. I want to pursue the workings of Freud's writing machine further, because it contains still more lessons about *Hamlet*. One of the most important of these concerns the metaphor of the machine itself. "A Note upon the 'Mystic Writing Pad' " not only employs a mechanical model to represent psychic systems but engages the problems of literary figuration that it entails. Freud's essay, that is, comments indirectly on what it means to represent the psyche as a machine. The essay begins by positing the relation between the mind and the writing apparatus in a relatively unproblematic fashion. The written note, Freud observes, is a way to "supplement and guarantee" the working of memory.[94] Writing and memory resemble each other, but the for-

93. Compare René Girard's fine essay "Hamlet's Dull Revenge," which similarly focuses on Hamlet's listlessness. Lupton and Reinhard explore the same phenomenon from a psychoanalytic viewpoint when they describe Hamlet's melancholic identification as "at once mortifying and idealizing" (*After Oedipus*, p. 36; see also pp. 30, 77).

94. Freud, *Standard Edition*, p. 19:227.

mer remains strictly exterior to the latter, in a way that would seem to define their metaphorical as well as practical relations. As the essay develops, however, these relations become less stable, and not only because the *Wunderblock* so successfully reproduces the workings of the psychic trace-structure that it often becomes difficult to distinguish between them.

The metaphor has its limits, as Freud admits. The *Wunderblock* fails at a certain point to imitate psychic systems, specifically because the mind does automatically what the writing machine requires external manipulation to achieve. "It is true . . . that once the 'writing' has been erased, the Mystic Pad cannot 'reproduce' it from within; it would be a mystic pad indeed if, like our memory, it could accomplish that."[95] The "human" emerges as a mystical excess of self-organization which the inanimate mechanism of the writing pad cannot emulate. If the failings of human memory sometimes call for the supplement of the written note, it is equally true that the *Wunderblock* requires human assistance in order to work at all. At the end of his essay Freud therefore introduces a human operator in order to make his metaphor "work": "If we imagine one hand writing upon the surface of the Mystic Writing-Pad while another periodically raises its covering-sheet from the wax slab, we shall have a concrete representation of the way in which I tried to picture the functioning of the perceptual apparatus of our mind."[96] Freud's *Wunderblock* resembles the chess-playing automaton with which Benjamin opens his *Theses on the Philosophy of History*: the latter wins every game, but only because a human dwarf who is a chess master is concealed within.[97] The mechanical now seems once more to be thoroughly subordinated to the human, but the matter is not so simple. Although the human makes up for what is lacking in the machine, it does so by subordinating itself to the machine: the hands now appear to "serve" the *Wunderblock*, rather than the reverse. Indeed, all we see here *are* hands, seemingly detached from their bodies and operating on their own. Freud's slightly uncanny image thus both subordinates the mechanical to the human and refigures the human as machine. The *Wunderblock* is nothing less than a device for the inscription and self-erasure of the human, which becomes entangled in a mutually supplementary relation with the mechanical. The Hamletmachine, I would argue, works along similar lines. The point is not that Hamlet "really is" a machine—that his apparent humanity is an empty

95. Ibid., p. 19: 230.
96. Ibid., p. 19: 232.
97. Benjamin, *Illuminations*, p. 253.

sheath concealing the apparatus within. It is rather that Hamlet's human qualities are at once constituted and compromised by their supplemental relation with the machine.

The *Wunderblock* holds one other lesson, which will allow us to conclude. It concerns the productivity of Freud's—and Shakespeare's—writing machines. When Derrida observes, toward the end of "Freud and the Scene of Writing," that Freud has "performed for us the scene of writing," he means in part that the essay on the *Wunderblock* engages in the very process of inscription and erasure that it describes. Derrida tracks a genealogical series of metaphors that Freud employs in the course of his career—the neuronal system, the hieroglyph, the optical apparatus, the *Wunderblock*—to write the concept of the trace, the path, or the breach. In one sense, this approach posits the insistence of an unchanging conceptual problematic which simply produces successive metaphorical "expressions" as so many symptoms. In this regard Freud's work exhibits something like a compulsion to repeat. Yet if we were to ask, "Repeat *what?*" it would be impossible to produce an originary instance, since the writing of the trace is nothing other than these metaphors and the relations of difference among them. There is no "proper" concept of the trace which can be extracted from the genealogical series of metaphors. Hence, from another perspective, Freud's writing isn't repetitive at all, or at least the effect of repetition is founded on a movement of pure production, invention, or "pathbreaking" (to borrow Freud's own neurological metaphor). The productivity of writing exceeds the boundary of the concept.

Freud's essay on the *Wunderblock* "performs" this very fact. On the one hand, Freud treats the invention of the *Wunderblock* as providing him, finally, with the long sought-for model for the apparatus of memory. From this perspective, the previous metaphors constitute a set of imperfect approximations to a longstanding conceptual problem which has at last found its "proper" representation (even though, as Freud admits, this one too contains flaws and imprecisions). Now the earlier metaphors can be jettisoned in favor of this putatively final, because appropriate, one. And yet the very apparatus described in the essay rejects this teleological movement in favor of one that juxtaposes erasure and palimpsestic superinscription, neither of which admits of progress or the "proper." James Strachey's English translation of Freud's title, "A Note upon the 'Mystic Writing Pad,'" reveals this performative dimension by suggesting that the writing of this new metaphor is itself just one more message inscribed on the *Wunderblock*, and is thus destined for erasure.

If this new metaphor is superior to the others, it is not because it more fully resembles the (proper) concept it is taken to represent, but because it registers its own self-cancellation as metaphor.

The *Wunderblock* as writing machine "performs" Freud's own writing by elevating the productivity of metaphor over the repetitive insistence of the concept. More generally, Freud's texts ought to be seen not only as imposing certain relentless Oedipal motifs, but as desiring-machines engaged in a constant activity of creativity and pathbreaking. If they have been used to constrain desire, this is because they have first been rendered captive. Or, to be more precise, the productivity of Freudian writing has been abducted into the Oedipal triangle, beyond whose boundaries it nevertheless continues to seep. The erasable surface of the *Wunderblock* represents the self-cancellation of metaphor which clears a space for new creation.

So with the Hamletmachine, which at once registers the oppressive burden of tradition and improvises a new way of imagining an old play. Hamlet's forgetfulness, his dilatory tactics, represent a failure only from the perspective of Oedipal law. From another perspective, this erasure of the paternal text opens up the possibility for a new writing, a new vision. Alongside Hamlet's feelings of filial guilt there begins to appear a countervision in which the relentless demands of the Father's spirit give way to the productive transformation of the Father's body. In Hamlet's imaginative tracing of Alexander the Great's metamorphosis from conqueror to dust to loam to cork for a beer barrel (5.1.207–12), or in his demonstration of "how a king may go a progress through the guts of a beggar" (4.3.30-31), he pictures both the erosion of paternal authority and the transformations wrought by nature's ceaseless productivity. In place of repetition comes creation; in place of the law's frozen dictates come images of material flow and ebb. Unlike Oedipal struggle, in which paternal authority is "overthrown" only to be restored by the son, here such authority begins to *drift*, and thus to become something genuinely other—indeed, to become a *process* of becoming rather than a reified entity. This is not to deny that Hamlet's dilemma is largely Oedipal; it is rather to show that the play's Oedipal triangle is built on top of, falls back on, but nevertheless fails to contain without residue, the machinic labor of desiring-production. This fact holds good not only for Hamlet but for *Hamlet*, since the Hamletmachine and the *Hamlet* machine are one. Hamlet's freedom, however circumscribed and provisional, is also that of the play. If *Hamlet* is saddled in a unique way with the burden of (its own) tradition, if it is fated to repeat itself mechanically, it also contains another kind of machine, a Deleuzian, Rube Goldberg machine that works by breaking down, by forgetting its own past and its responsibilities, by transmuting itself into something other—a broken clockwork, for instance. *Hamlet works*, like the guts of a beggar digesting a king, or like a beer barrel dispensing its festive contents. It is a machine that produces flow as well as law, creation as well as tradition or repetition. This is its essential modernity—which is to say, modernity as such.

In my end is my beginning—for the dynamic of the Hamletmachine returns us, rather precisely, to that of historical allegory, described in the Introduction to this book. As practiced by both Eliot and Benjamin, historical allegory operates a temporal logic of pure repetition. In Benjamin's case, it anticipates the "mechanical reproducibility" of his later, famous essay. At the same time, however, the *content* of modernism's historical allegory insists on (to quote Eliot again) "anarchism, . . . dissolution, . . . decay." Thus the law of exact reproduction finds its counterprinciple in the theme of dissolution, just as Hamlet's Oedipal repetitions allow for the productive decay of the father's body. Benjaminian allegory, in particular, tends to fade; it is self-canceling or self-erasing, like the Freudian *Wunderblock*, and thus clears a space for new creation. Modernism's historical allegory is thus not merely applied to Shakespeare but finds its own mechanism already, in some sense, present there. Perhaps this is part of modernism's fascination with Shakespeare, that ablest of storytellers.

Index

289

Capital and capitalism (*Cont.*)
253, 272; late, 14, 46, 137–39. *See also*
Imperialism and colonialism; Merchants
and merchant's capital; Money and
money capital; Usury and usurer's
capital
Carlyle, Thomas, 19–21, 56, 61
Carnival and festival, 77–78, 85–89, 98–
103, 108, 112
Cavell, Stanley, 107–9
Cellier, Alfred, 228
Césaire, Aimé, 46
Chandos portrait, 163–67, 172, 176
Cheyette, Bryan, 163n, 173
Christianity, 125, 145–47, 149–51, 177,
179, 180, 219, 220
Circumcision, 172, 194, 213–14
City comedy, 148, 149, 150, 156
Cocteau, Jean, 245–51, 253, 255–56, 258,
260, 267–68, 275
Cohen, Walter, 211
Coleridge, Samuel Taylor, 74, 172
Colonialism. *See* Imperialism and
colonialism
Comic books, 67, 68, 132
Commodity and commodification, 11–14,
57, 70–72, 94, 117–19, 135, 136, 138,
156, 157, 187–95, 198–204, 206, 209,
220–21, 252, 253
Commodity fetishism, 193, 195–210, 216
Consumerism and consumption, 14, 57,
66, 70–72, 77, 83, 85, 90, 91, 94–95, 98,
100, 106, 137–39
Conti, Antonio, 73, 80
Cornford, J. M., 22
Craig, Edward Gordon, 239–45
Craik, G. L., 75
Crawford, Robert, 22n, 43; 163n
Crowd psychology, 55, 59–61, 78, 82–83,
85, 87–88
Cynicism, 92, 103–7, 109–13, 127, 156–57,
182, 183, 248, 250–51

Dafora, Asadata, 35
Daly, Mary, 135
Dalzel, Archibald, 22
Danson, Lawrence, 180, 211, 213, 219
Decadence, 9, 247, 260–62, 264–68, 274–
75
Dekker, Thomas, 53
Deleuze, Gilles, 172, 269n, 288
De Man, Paul, 212, 219
DeMille, Cecil B., 64
Democracy, 56–57, 76, 97, 210

Denham, Robert, 126
Derrida, Jacques, 262n, 274n, 282n, 286
Dewey, John, 54, 76
Dissociation of sensibilities, 9, 26
Donne, John, 9
Droeshout engraving, 163

Edward VI, king of England, 152
Eliot, T. S., 1–4, 7, 9–10, 16–17, 21–28, 30–
33, 37–38, 39n, 41–46, 50–52, 61–63,
65, 69, 92–95, 98, 101, 115–20, 122,
125, 132, 134, 140, 153–54, 163, 182,
235n, 236, 288; "The Beating of a
Drum," 16, 22, 30; *Coriolan*, 38, 51; *The
Criterion*, 51; *Elizabethan Essays*, 3, 4, 7, 9,
26, 30, 31, 44, 118; "Tradition and the
Individual Talent," 2, 43; *The Use of
Poetry and the Use of Criticism*, 62, 63; *The
Waste Land*, 28, 39, 41, 43–44, 53, 92–
93, 95, 101, 153–54
Ellis, A. B., 22
Emerson, Ralph Waldo, 20
Empire Review, 20,
Enclosure, 144, 146, 147, 149–50, 152
Enfield, William, 72
Enlightenment, 69–70, 78, 80, 82, 85, 89,
90, 105–6, 112, 250–51
Expressionism, 7, 271

Fanon, Frantz, 46
Fascism and Naziism, 24, 51, 52, 55, 61–
62, 77, 133
Faverty, Frederic E., 20n, 21
Fechter, Charles, 234
Felman, Shoshana, 247–48, 250–51, 254n
Ferber, Michael, 211, 224
Feudalism, 69, 90, 150, 152
Feuerbach, Ludwig, 221–23
Films, 17, 37, 64–67, 276–79
Finance capital, 11, 186, 209–10
Finlay, John, 86–87
Fischler, Alan, 230
Fishberg, Maurice, 173, 213n
Frazer, J. G., 22, 28, 41–42
Freud, Sigmund, 41, 81n, 99, 119, 216,
238, 245–48, 250–52, 254–65, 268, 270–
71, 277n, 278, 282, 284–87
Friedlander, Robert, 173
Friswell, J. Hain, 163, 165–67, 170, 176,
184
Fry, Roger, 28, 40
Frye, Northrop, 1, 10–11, 14, 16, 41–42,
96–98, 100–101, 103, 114–43, 145, 147,
149, 151, 153–55, 157–58, 268

Lewis, Wyndham, 22–25, 27, 33, 35, 37, 42, 44, 50, 52, 55–57, 59–61, 166–67, 182

Liberalism, 52, 54, 62, 97, 122, 127, 132, 133, 162, 163, 177–80

Liberties of London, 148–50, 152

Lippmann, Walter, 54, 76, 81

Lodge, Thomas, 146

Lopez, Roderigo, 167

Lowie, Robert H., 22

Lukács, Georg, 11, 111, 154, 157–58

Lunacharsky, Anatoli, 52

Lupton, Julia Reinhard, 9n, 201n, 247, 254n, 266n, 277n, 278n, 284n

Luxemburg, Rosa, 275

Lyceum Movement, 74

Malinowski, Bronislaw, 28, 42

Manganaro, Marc, 22n, 28n, 40

Mannoni, O., 46

Manson, Charles, 275

Marcus, Leah, 45n

Marcuse, Herbert, 99

Marlowe, Christopher, 161

Marshall, Cynthia, 147

Marston, John, 155n

Marx, Karl, 11–12, 117n, 138, 162, 165, 185, 186n, 187–89, 191, 193–98, 201, 203–9, 216, 221–23, 237–38, 253, 274

Mass culture, 10, 11, 23, 51–72, 75–80, 85, 89, 92–98, 105–7, 112, 117, 118, 130–32, 137, 268

Mazer, Cary, 6

Mechanics' Institutes, 74

Meinhoff, Ulrike, 275

Merchant, Ismail, 37

Merchants and merchant's capital, 184, 220–21, 224

Meyerhold, Vsevolod, 239

Michelangelo Buonarroti, 170, 216

Middle class, 54, 63–65, 70, 72–73

Midlands Uprising, 77, 144

Mill, John Stuart, 56

Mills, C. Wright, 71

Milton, John, 21, 117, 123; *Paradise Lost*, 53

Mnoutchkine, Ariane, 17

Modernity, 26, 41, 45, 46, 94, 102, 108, 109, 120, 162, 236, 248, 250, 251–54, 258, 260–61, 267–68, 288

Modernization, 11, 26, 41, 46, 122, 235, 252, 253

Money and money capital, 157, 184–87,

190–91, 195–204, 207–9, 216, 220–23, 236–37

Moses, 170, 216, 281, 283

Mourning, 264–68, 271

Mullaney, Steven, 109, 112, 142n, 148, 155,

Müller, Heiner, 267–75, 280

Multiculturalism, 66, 128, 134–37, 139, 173

Murray, Gilbert, 22

Myth and myth criticism, 10, 41–42, 118–21, 124, 125, 127, 129–31, 135–36, 141, 250, 262, 265, 274

Nadel, Ira B., 162n, 163n, 173

Nägele, Rainer, 232, 236

Narcissus, 93, 190

Narrative, 44, 57, 118–20, 124, 130–33, 141, 146

Negt, Oskar, 11, 69n, 136–38

New Criticism, 16, 38–42, 43n, 49, 98, 102–5, 109–10, 114–15, 118, 119, 121, 125, 130, 131, 135

New Historicism, 16, 39–40, 42–50, 109–13, 140, 142–43, 278

Nietzsche, Friedrich, 61, 162, 165, 177, 179, 239, 261

Nordau, Max, 261–62

Objective correlative, 22, 31

Oedipus and Oedipus complex, 147, 232, 242, 244–51, 256, 258–68, 271, 278, 280, 283–84, 287, 288

Olivier, Laurence, 276–79

O'Neill, Eugene, 35

Other, the, 255–60, 262–64, 269, 271

Packard, Maurice, 173

Paranoia, 174, 196–97, 208

Pavlov, Ivan Petrovich, 239

Pearson, Roberta E., 64

Pease, Donald, 45, 47

Phallus, 198, 201, 255–56, 260, 264–65, 269n

Philistinism, 63

Plowman, Max, 186

Plutarch, 81

Poel, William, 65

Popular culture, 44n, 54–55, 65–67, 77–78, 109, 117, 124, 128–35, 137, 139. *See also* Mass culture

Postmodernism and postmodernity, 2, 12–13, 16, 42, 46, 109, 114, 115, 125, 136, 139, 228, 276